FOR MY PARENTS

# ACKNOWLEDGEMENTS

THIS study grew from a suggestion by Professor H. R. Trevor-Roper, to whose constant encouragement and vigilant assistance I owe my greatest debt. The many contributions made by others I have tried to acknowledge, when possible, at appropriate points in the text. However, I should like to include here the names of Dr. W. A. Pantin, Keeper of the Archives, Oxford University, and the Rev. Dr. T. M. Parker of University College, Oxford, whose continual help has contributed substantially to this book.

I am also indebted to Miss H. E. Peek, Keeper of the Archives, Cambridge University, and Mr. N. R. Ker, Librarian of Magdalen College, Oxford, for generous assistance with archival and bibliographical problems. Mr. H. O. Evennett of Trinity College, Cambridge, and Dr. Elizabeth Armstrong of Somerville College, Oxford, supplied valuable corrections and criticism. Mr. James Devereux, who is preparing a volume on the English translations of Erasmus for the Oxford Bibliographical Society, has kindly provided corrections on dating and other bibliographical problems from the materials he has gathered for that work. These and many other people in Oxford and Cambridge, and in the British Museum and Public Record Office, were laid under frequent contribution and never failed to respond with kindness and generosity. To them is due much of the pleasure which this study has afforded the author.

Finally, this book would not have been possible without the material support of the University of Saskatchewan, the Canada Council, and the Nuffield Foundation. To the Rector and Fellows of Exeter College, Oxford, for their hospitality during visits over more than a decade, I owe more than I can say.                                                                   J. K. M.

*Oxford, 1963*

# CONTENTS

# ABBREVIATIONS

UNLESS otherwise specified, the imprint of all English books cited is London, of all French books, Paris. With early printed books, the first citation (taking the text and note together) is intended to include the name of the author, the short title, publisher and date, with the *Short Title Catalogue* number. For a fuller description of the works following, see the concluding list of manuscripts and books cited. Books in the *Short Title Catalogue* are given in the List of Authors.

| | |
|---|---|
| Allen | *Opus Epistolarum Des. Erasmi*, ed. P. S. Allen |
| Dibdin | *Typographical Antiquities* (of Ames, Herbert, and T. F. Dibdin) |
| *DNB* | *The Dictionary of National Biography* |
| E.E.T.S. | Early English Text Society |
| *EHR* | *The English Historical Review* |
| Ellis | *Original Letters*, ed. Sir Henry Ellis |
| Emden | *A Biographical Register of the University of Oxford*, A. B. Emden |
| Foxe | *The Acts and Monuments of John Foxe*, ed. S. R. Cattley |
| Giles | *The Whole Works of Roger Ascham*, ed. the Revd. Dr. Giles |
| Hain | *Repertorium Bibliographicum*, with supplement and appendixes of W. A. Copinger and D. Reichling |
| Hall | Hall's Chronicle, ed. H. Ellis |
| Harpsfield | *The Life and Death of Sir Thomas Moore*, Early English Text Society |
| *LP* | *Letters and Papers, Foreign and Domestic . . . Henry VIII*, ed. J. S. Brewer and J. Gairdner |
| Maitland | *A List of Early Printed Books . . . at Lambeth*, S. R. Maitland |
| *NB* | *Nederlandsche Bibliographie van 1500 tot 1540*, Nijhoff en Kronenberg |
| O.H.S. | Oxford Historical Society |

OO          *Opera Omnia Des. Erasmi,* Leiden (1703–6)

*PMLA*      *Publications of the Modern Language Association of America*

Proctor     *An Index to the Early Printed Books in the British Museum,*
            R. Proctor

Rogers      *The Correspondence of Sir Thomas More,* ed. E. F. Rogers

*RSTC*      Revised *Short Title Catalogue,* ed. W. A. Jackson,
            Houghton Library, Harvard University

SP          State Papers, Public Record Office, London

*Span. Cal.*  *Calendar of State Papers, Spanish*

*STC*       *A Short Title Catalogue of Books, 1475–1640,* A. W.
            Pollard and G. R. Redgrave

Strype, *Cheke—The Life of . . . Sir John Cheke,* J. Strype (1821)

Strype, *Memorials—Ecclesiastical Memorials,* J. Strype (1822)

Wood, *Annals—The History and Antiquities of the University of
            Oxford,* Anthony Wood, ed. J. Gutch

Wood, *Athenae—Athenae Oxonienses,* Anthony Wood, ed. Philip
            Bliss

# 1

## THE HISTORICAL PROBLEM

IT is now over thirty years since the appearance of Lucien Febvre's 'Une question mal posée: Les origines de la réforme française', an essay which may be taken to mark a significant change of emphasis in Reformation studies, at least on the Continent. Febvre repudiated the study of Reformation history seen as a problem in 'spécificité, priorité, nationalité', terms which he would like to have purged from the vocabulary of historians. His concern, which was shared increasingly by his contemporaries, was rather with the manifold complexities of political, social, and economic life in which the religious controversy was embedded. 'C'est à cela, à tout cela que l'historien doit regarder — non aux petites règles particulières, aux petites convenances des Églises rivales.'[1]

It is some twenty years since the appearance of Marcel Bataillon's *Érasme et l'Espagne*,[2] which was, in part at least, a brilliant vindication of the approach for which Febvre had called. In the work of Bataillon, Renaudet, and others, the study of the Reformation in northern Europe found fresh inspiration through exploring the work of the humanist reformers before the period of active sectarian controversy— especially the work and influence of Erasmus. In the Spain of Bataillon all western Europe could be seen, restless in change, and, 'in her educated classes, seeking a religion which would be clear, humane and fraternal, a source of enlightenment as well as of support'. In this study, as in so many others of continental reform, it became evident that to a truly remarkable

[1] L. Febvre, 'Une question mal posée: Les origines de la réforme française', *Revue historique*, t. clxi (1929, pp. 1–73), p. 72.
[2] *Bibliothèque de l'École des Hautes Études Hispaniques*, fasc. xxi (1937).

B

degree these movements were dominated by one man, Desiderius Erasmus.

The professional study of the English Reformation has been
almost untouched by these developments, despite the work of
scholars in showing the European ramifications of the 'pre-
reform' movement. Yet it is clear that this movement did much
to prepare the intellectual milieu of Reformation controversy,
and that the disciples of this creed of humanism and reform
could be found everywhere. The sponsors of the movement
were the northern humanists themselves, along with aristocratic
patrons of scholarship, bishops and cathedral clergy, professional servants of kings, and lawyers. The common tenets were
generous and undogmatic, covering a wide range of temperament and inclination, from the practicality of a careerist
administrator to the illuminism of a Valdés. Without leaving
the broad tradition of medieval Christendom, these people
dreamed of a simplification of doctrine and reform of practice,
especially through the infusion of humanist values into the
aridities of late-fifteenth-century controversy. Among the
sponsors of the movement were Colet, More, and Fisher in
England, Lefèvre d'Étaples and Marguerite of Navarre in
France, the Cardinal reformer Ximénez de Cisneros in Spain,
Sadoleto and Contarini in Italy, Wimpfeling, Gropper, and
Pflug in Germany. In matters of Church reform their manifesto was the *Libellus ad Leonem X* presented to the Fifth
Lateran Council by Tomasso Giustiniani and Vincenzo Quirini,
and in private counsels the handbook was the *Enchiridion
militis Christiani* of Erasmus. Cosmopolitan, aristocratic, and
humane, the adherents of this party pursued a middle way
which became untenable for most of them in the tensions after
Luther's revolt; but in their time they exercised great influence,
especially where, as in the Imperial court, they were specially
protected and encouraged. Their enthusiasms and sympathies
are an important key to a period of intellectual excitement
when the shibboleths of Protestantism and Tridentine Catholicism were still unknown.

The part which England played in all this has often been touched upon but never directly explored. The early 'fellow-work' of Erasmus, More, and Colet is famous since the work of Seebohm, and since his day nothing has appreciably altered the picture Seebohm gave. The enthusiasm of these men for classical learning, their part in the preparation of Erasmus's New Testament, the historical method of Scripture interpretation they shared, their satire of inertia and religious decay, all these were the familiar tenets of the common Erasmian creed. Yet Seebohm brought his study to an end with the death of Colet in 1519, with the 'fellow-work' largely accomplished, as he thought. 'Now for three hundred years it was to stop and, as it were, to be submerged under a new wave of the great tide of human progress.'[1]

By thus extinguishing the reform party on the very eve of the great national controversy, Seebohm was partly responsible for the fragmentary treatment the movement has received since. Continental studies tend to lose interest in English humanism at the death of its greatest exponent, Thomas More, and much English work is reminiscent of Febvre's 'spécificité, priorité, nationalité'. More recent studies of Machiavellians and Henricians, of curialists and canonists, have provided distinct themes; the influence of the Cambridge reformers, among whom the 'new learning' became virtually identified with Protestantism, has provided another. But the study of English developments in isolation leaves many questions unanswered.

What can be discovered of the intellectual atmosphere of Henry VIII's court in the period before reform opinion began to adopt the colouring of sectarian partisanship? Where were the lively currents of humanistic thought, and in what channels, under what sponsorship, did they run? How widespread was the early Erasmian influence at the universities from which Henry recruited his servants? And was this Erasmian influence merely linguistic and literary, as is usually assumed, or can we

[1] F. Seebohm, *The Oxford Reformers* (3rd edit., 1887), p. 505.

find evidence that the *philosophia Christi* was fully present in educated circles from 1516, the date of Erasmus's last visit, to the period of crisis in the early 1530's?

On another level, study of the recruiting of humanist writers, especially of those with continental connexions, has raised questions about the origins of the *via media* itself. W. G. Zeeveld's *Foundations of Tudor Policy* made a signal contribution by reopening the question of humanist influence, at least in the realm of political theory. It was his conclusion that the *via media* was discovered by Thomas Starkey in Melanchthon's doctrine of *adiaphora*, concerning the realm of permissive but non-essential belief.[1] But Melanchthon was not entirely original in this. Like Starkey himself, he held allegiance to the views of the whole Erasmian party, where opinions about the need for concentration on the essentials of the faith were common property. Erasmus's own correspondence contains pleas without number for simplification of the faith along lines of the essential points of doctrine, and his English followers were as well prepared as the rest to accept the view that on many matters a wide difference of opinion threatened neither Catholic orthodoxy nor Christian unity.

Certainly the energetic translation of Erasmus's works in the third and fourth decades of the century suggests that his views were thought by some to be strongly relevant to English problems, yet no attempt has been made to study this activity as a whole, or to see it outside a purely literary context.[2] In fact, the conviction, born in Tudor controversy, that Erasmus was the real sponsor of the English religious settlement, is a hardy favourite. It is suggested as much by the

[1] W. G. Zeeveld, *Foundations of Tudor Policy* (Cambridge, Mass., 1948), pp. 137 f. Cf. Erasmus to J. Schlecta (Allen, iv. 1039), ll. 219–24.

[2] e.g., H. Exner, *Der Einfluß des Erasmus auf die englische Bildungsidee* (Berlin, 1939). Studies like that of F. Caspari, *Humanism and the Social Order in Tudor England* (Chicago, 1954), and Helen C. White, *The Tudor Books of Private Devotion* (Madison, Wisconsin, 1951), reinforce the impression of a pervasive Erasmian influence in the educational and devotional thought of the time, and make clear the need for a synthetic approach.

staunchly anti-Tridentine flavour of the Elizabethan Church as by the repeated failure of dogmatic Protestantism to take deep root. Moreover, much that has been regarded with sadness by controversialist historians of both parties as the regrettable opportunism and indifference to principle of the sixteenth-century Englishman, may come from a false understanding of the background to the religious controversy.

The career of George Day, Fellow of St. John's College, Cambridge, is typical and instructive. At one time chaplain to the martyred John Fisher, he agreed to succeed the prudent and conservative Dr. Nicholas Wilson, Fisher's friend, when Wilson declined his 1537 election to the Mastership to save the college from unfavourable royal attentions. In a year Day was transferred by court influence to King's College as Provost, and he later became a member of the Windsor Commission on the Prayer Book, Bishop of Chichester, and an able courtier. He died a Catholic under Mary, and left St. John's College a copy of the Complutensian Polyglot Bible. It is easy to cry 'opportunism' and condemn the faint-heartedness of such a man, but to do so is to prejudge the conscience of the time. His bequest alone should arouse our attention for its echo of the great design of Ximénez at Alcalá and the reforming, humanistic court of Charles V. Its possession by St. John's College commemorates a bond between the intellectual ferment in early sixteenth-century Spain and the first great English foundation to further reform through humanistic study. It is a bond provided, significantly, by a typical moderate of the English Reformation.

The library of St. John's College contained another book, since removed to the University Library, which is even more suggestive of the peculiarities of the time. It is a manuscript version of the famous treatise *Il trattato utilissimo del beneficio di Gieso Christo crocifisso*,[1] which epitomizes the whole contest between the moderate party and an awakened and aggressive conservative party. When it first appeared in 1543 it promptly

[1] Cambridge University Library, MS. Nn. iv. 43. See below, Chapter 8.

became one of the most popular devotional works of the decade, until the Roman Inquisition detected its heretical flavour and undertook its extermination. This process, combined with the usual deterioration suffered by such small and popular works, was at one time thought to have destroyed every copy. The present English manuscript version, 'The Benefit of Christ Crucified', taken from the Italian original in 1548, was translated by Edward Courtenay, himself cousin to Reginald Pole, who in turn was closely associated with that Catholic reform group which produced the original version, and whose struggles with the conservative interest haunted the closing years of his life. Edward VI's own signature and pious notations at the beginning and end of the tiny vellum volume are another link binding the English reform movement with the complexities of continental reform currents.

Indeed, the closer the examination, the more apparent is the difficulty of separating English developments from those on the Continent. It is clear that the Crown itself was the initial point of contact, and that from its first appearance English humanism is linked with Italian influence through royal patronage.[1] Andrew Ammonius, Mountjoy's discovery and Erasmus's friend at court, is in many ways a figure from the fifteenth century, infusing Italian literary influences through Church and court. Royal foundations, Regius professorships, and the provision of an Historiographer Royal all show Henry VII and his son carrying on the functions of patronage inherited from their Yorkist predecessors. In our period after 1500, however, the emergence of Grocyn, Linacre, More, and Colet, and the contact with Paris and Erasmus seem to mark a distinctively new phase. The domestic tradition is by now producing its own scholars, and with them are the patrons of a new generation. William Blount, Lord Mountjoy, is a key figure of the first decade of the century. The pupil and patron of Erasmus in Paris, he was the first Englishman to assist the Dutch scholar.

[1] Thus R. Weiss, *Humanism in England during the Fifteenth Century* (2nd edit., Oxford, 1957).

He became a close associate in England of Henry Montague, son of the Countess of Salisbury, and his daughter was the mother of Edward Courtenay. And along with these Courtenay ties, he was closely linked with the More circle throughout his lifetime. It is not surprising, therefore, to find him in the party which remained openly loyal to the displaced Queen after Henry's divorce, yet he remained happily in the royal service until his death in 1534.

The question of patronage itself requires further exploration. The More circle is of course of central importance. The family links that embraced the Rastells, the Clementses, the Heywoods, and the Mores united an exceptionally talented and productive group of reforming professional people and writers. Heywood's 'More' plays have the urbane, satirical quality which is completely fulfilled in the *Utopia* and *Praise of Folly*, and in the other activities of the circle we shall find the familiar Erasmian studies and preoccupations. Yet in the later period, to the confusion of sectarian analysis, members of this group adopted loyalties in every part of the religious spectrum, from old John Rastell, who died imprisoned by Cranmer for radical Protestantism, to Jasper Heywood, the Elizabethan Jesuit.

Henry's queens also provide important humanist and reform patronage. The first important sponsor is Catherine of Aragon, Erasmus's *egregia docta*, the patroness of Vives. Her associations with the circle of More and the religious foundations of Shene and Syon are the earlier counterpart of Catherine Parr's association with Coverdale, Cheke, and Ascham around a scholarly royal nursery. In both periods the group associated with the Queen produces significant pietistic and learned productions, remarkable for their complete and continuous loyalty to the name and programme of Erasmus. These range from Vives's *Instruction of a Christian Woman*, written for the Princess Mary, to this same royal Princess's translation, under the guidance of Catherine Parr, of Erasmus's *Paraphrase on the Gospel of St. John*. Catherine Parr herself produced, in her *Lamentacion of a Sinner*, a work which in spirit and doctrine bears a remarkable resemblance to the 'Benefit of Christ Crucified', and Princess Mary's translation of Erasmus's *Paraphrase on St. John* was included in the official version of the Paraphrases placed in all English churches by the Edwardian Government. Finally, it is revealing to find Princess Mary's half-sister Elizabeth, in the same period, presenting Catherine Parr with an autograph English version of Marguerite of Navarre's poem *Miroir de l'âme pécheresse*, condemned as heretical by the Sorbonne in 1533. It is interesting to speculate on the history of Elizabeth's master copy, possibly acquired by her own mother, Anne Boleyn, when she was in the service of the future Queen Margaret, then Duchesse d'Alençon. Through her later association with the group of Meaux and Lefèvre d'Étaples, Marguerite of Navarre became the most influential royal patron of Erasmianism in France.[1] As a patroness of humanistic evangelism, there is no other contemporary figure who so much resembles Catherine Parr herself.

These royal ladies, then, performed in England the function of Vittoria Colonna in Rome, or the Duchess Renée of Ferrara, in presiding over a powerful coterie of learned, moderate reformers and scholars. The existence of Catherine Parr's group is sufficient in itself to raise questions about Zeeveld's conclusion, that with the death of Cromwell the direct avenue from study to court was closed.[2] To see the patronage question simply in terms of Wolsey, Cromwell, and Cranmer is to miss a vital part of the story. Moreover, the companions of Prince Edward's youth in Catherine Parr's nursery school again suggest by their later careers the problems of seeing the issues of the day in terms simply of Catholic and Protestant opinion. They included, on the one hand, Henry Sidney and Edward Seymour, and, on the other, Sidney's cousin Jane Dormer, the future Duchess of Feria and indefatigable promoter of English

[1] See Margaret Mann, *Érasme et les débuts de la réforme française, 1517–1536* (1933).
[2] Zeeveld, op. cit., p. 234.

recusant interest in Spain, to whom the Antwerp edition of More's *Dialogue of Comfort*, published in 1573, was dedicated.

Even such a cursory survey of the problem shows reason to suppose that an attempt to probe the unexplored interests and activities of the English humanist community in the early sixteenth century may be quite rewarding. Attention must be given not so much to those vernacular writers who have long been known as to the humanists more narrowly defined, that group interested in the revival of classical letters. Here we shall find a number of scholars long overlooked, who contributed little or nothing to the main stream of English literature, but who in their own day made indispensable contributions in the service of Church and State to the course of the English Reformation, and to the growth of the domestic humanist tradition.

The scholarly attention which has been given to this group has been almost entirely confined to their political thought, and there will be no attempt here to rehearse the work of Gordon Zeeveld, Pierre Janelle, or Franklin Le Van Baumer. However, a wider examination of the humanist work of the period will reveal the intellectual context of this political writing, which was merely one phase, if perhaps the most conspicuous, of the Government's enlisting of humanist support. It will also help to correct the impression left by so many studies of this period, that there was no obvious intellectual or popular basis for the English Reformation under Henry: that it was achieved by an arbitrary 'act of State', plainly not inspired by Protestantism yet somehow supported by proto-Protestants and careerists, and imposed on an apathetic population with the help of some rather unremarkable political apologetic.

Initially, then, we must attempt to establish the prevailing concerns of the English learned community in the period before religious controversy became intense, and to make clear the extent to which this community was involved, not simply in literary humanism, but in the active reforming enthusiasms of the *philosophia Christi*. Once this programme itself is made more explicit, we can turn to the channels through which Erasmian opinion was circulated, and to the closely organized network of patronage. The universities must be the subject of special study, since both as public corporations and through the private activities of their members they provided such invaluable support to the King's proceedings.

It will then be necessary to examine the sudden appearance of Erasmian translation in England at a moment when the Erasmian programme seems to offer a solution to the Government's problems. This moment comes, not surprisingly, at the death of More and Fisher and the defection of Reginald Pole from the royal interest. At this critical juncture the humanist community, active since the fall of Wolsey, is called successfully to the Government's support, especially through the skilled intervention of Thomas Cromwell.

The royal marriage with Catherine Parr in 1543 marks another turning-point, this time in the direction of reconciliation, with the reunion of the royal children under one roof as a visible seal of success. Marcel Bataillon, speaking of the Imperial court at the time of the sack of Rome, remarked, 'Il y a quelques années pendant lesquelles l'érasmisme, pour l'élite intellectuelle de la cour, est une atmosphère idéologique permettant de concilier le zèle antiromain avec la volonté d'orthodoxie et la ferveur évangélique.'[1] It would be difficult to state more clearly the situation of the humanists and ecclesiastics who have been called Henrician, and for whom the closing years of Henry's reign marked a pinnacle of achievement. The Erasmian character of their ecclesiastical policies need scarcely be defined at this point, but we may refer to general outlines. Beginning with an evangelical doctrine based upon historical study of Scripture and on anti-Ciceronian classicism, they declined the general heterodoxy of the Protestant reformers. Erasmus himself, although scarcely given to a sacramental conception of religion, was sufficiently devoted to moderation and unity to stay within the central tradition that included the

[1] Bataillon, op. cit., p. 249.

Mass, pilgrimages (properly regulated and devoutly performed), and prayer for the intercession of the Blessed Virgin, with a greatly enlarged role for sermons and instruction, confession and penance, even tolerating 'le service discret de quelques religieuses'.[1] This religion of the spirit also attached the greatest importance to simplified private prayer and the use of the vernacular in all things. It is the very formula of the Henrician Church.

The circle of Catherine Parr, then, provides an essential link with the first years of Edward VI, when the first religious settlement includes the final application of the Erasmian doctrine. The further development of the English Church under Protestant influences, and the impact of all this on the humanist tradition, will conclude the present study.

The most important problem in seeking evidence for this inquiry is precisely one derived from the generally *politique* attitude of English Governments throughout this period. On the one hand English moderate opinion is protected from the pressures of Roman reaction, and on the other, an experimental attitude to Protestant influence is rarely regarded with favour. In England, therefore, there was no Sorbonne to define heresy, and, except for the work of the Council and the ecclesiastical commissioners, no systematic search for hidden books and secret opinion. In the same way the perennial prospect of change from above prevented the moderate and radical reform parties from coming to grips on a clearly defined line of doctrine.

Nevertheless, private correspondence and published works provide a wealth of information about opinion and policy. In the earlier period, moreover, university registers and private book inventories give a hitherto unused guide to the interests of the educated classes. Patronage can be detected both from correspondence and, more usefully, from dedications, and the State Papers provide the necessary links with government policy. That same source provides the best information about the rare official inquiries into opinion, since it is a general

[1] Augustin Renaudet, *Études érasmiennes, 1521–1529* (1939), p. 43.

feature of the period that the educated community seldom fell foul of official restrictions on reading. The one essential point of conformity was the Royal Supremacy, and its victims are already well known.

It is hoped that in approaching the English scene from the perspective of a pan-European movement of humanist reform, the contentions of the Henrician period will be seen as a story of substantial continuity. The complaisance of educated circles in the King's policies seems less remarkable, and the blow to the domestic tradition of learning in 1535 seems less cataclysmic. The characteristic concerns of that tradition—education, State service, and religious pietism—survive, despite the loss of More's lonely genius, to become the distinguishing features of the English scene in the reign of Elizabeth. Whereas on the Continent the humanistic and evangelical reform movement was characteristically driven underground by the warring factions of a militant Protestantism and Tridentine Catholicism, in England it found circumstances peculiarly suited to its preservation. So the Erasmian gospel, undogmatic yet definite and discoverable, provides the continuous thread, turned and twisted in the course of controversy, yet always retaining its essential identity as the link between the 'fellow-work' of the Oxford reformers and the peculiar climate of the Elizabethan settlement.

# 2

## ERASMIANISM

THE personal device of Erasmus was a puzzling symbol, the *Aenigma Termini*. It was acquired in 1506 from a ring given to him in Italy by his royal pupil, Alexander Stewart. It was on his seal and was well known to his friends as his emblem, and it was the subject of a large design by Holbein. The essential elements were always the torso of a youth with flying hair surmounting a boundary-stone, *Terminus*—thus combining youth and eternity—and the motto *concedo nulli*.

In 1528 Erasmus himself felt bound to publish an explanation of *Terminus*, and did so in a letter to Alfonso Valdés, the humanist councillor of Charles V.[1] His enemies had attacked the device as a symbol of intolerable arrogance, supposing that the motto spoke for Erasmus in his own person. This he denied to Valdés in familiar tones of mock bewilderment. How could his critics (who regarded themselves as pillars of the Church) suppose anyone of his known caution and humility to be capable of such aggressive boasting? The symbol, he insisted, came purely as the accident of a gift, and as he received it in his fortieth year he took it as an omen of approaching death and a challenge to put his life in order: 'Mors enim vere terminus est . . . .'

Yet in the course of this explanation, Erasmus repeated the Roman legend of the refusal of the gods Juventas and Terminus to remove themselves from the Capitoline to make way for the temple of Jupiter, and at the end admitted that it was partly

[1] See P. S. Allen, *Opus Epistolarum Des. Erasmi Roterodami* (Oxonii, 1906–58, 12 vols.), vii, facing p. 430; and *Opera Omnia Desiderii Erasmi Roterodami* (Leyden, P. Vander Aa, 1703–6, 10 vols.), i, facing (24). The *Epistolae* will be cited hereafter as 'Allen', followed by volume and epistle numbers; the *Opera* as *OO*. For the letter to Valdés, see Allen, vii. 2018.

because of this allusion that the device had charm for him.[1] For *Terminus* was not simply a symbol of the limitation of human endeavour, of the ineluctable dominion of Death. It represented to Erasmus, and to his friends in the circle of the Venetian publisher Aldus, the spirit of defiance. In fact, it was the Terminus-Juventas who alone among the gods dared to defy Jupiter who was adopted by Erasmus as his symbol. The speaker of the brazen motto *concedo nulli* was the deft and cautious humanist himself.

Seebohm's study of the Oxford reformers made clear their association in humanism and religious reform. It did not reveal the involvement of this group with like-minded reformers and humanists on the Continent, nor did it explain that aspect of the Erasmian spirit which the *Terminus* suggests, and which made it such a powerful threat to vested interests in the conservative order of Church and State. The Erasmus whose lucid, sinuous, epistolary style bound together an international group of reformers was more than the timorous hypochondriac scholar that he is often represented to be, and no amount of pure scholarship, however astonishing in scope, could have made him the inspiration of these reform circles. If the *Terminus* symbol suggests anything about his work, it is his satirical assault on established ideas and institutions, on those elements in contemporary life that offended his conception of a Christian society. At the heart of this conception, of course, lay the *philosophia Christi*, which provided the measure for all human activity, be it monasticism, education, the rule of princes, the devotion of the layman, or the government of the Church.

Erasmus commanded the allegiance of the best minds of his day for a reason. It was his genius to fuse into a single stream of thought the converging currents of the late fifteenth century: humanistic textual scholarship, Florentine neo-Platonism, Netherlands piety of the *devotio moderna* and the Windisheim reform movement, and the manifold discontents of a middle

---

[1] Allen, vii. 2018, ll. 41–52. E. Wind, 'Aenigma Termini: the Emblem of Erasmus', *Journal of the Warburg Institute*, vol. i (1937–8), pp. 66–69.

class suddenly aware of its power and its needs. It was this blend
which received the alluring label of *philosophia Christi*—a phrase
rich with patristic overtones, signifying a life of wisdom
entirely consecrated to God. Of scholastic dogma he was at all
times suspicious; it was on the person and life of Christ that his
attention was fixed. So an alternative designation for his conception was the *evangelica philosophia, coelestis illa philosophia*;
if the Christian life were good, the divine mysteries would be
sufficiently apprehended. Erasmus's love for the early Fathers
had many facets, and this was an important one; he was
always very close in spirit to the lasting Greek mistrust of the
Latin zeal for definition.[1]

It was this same element in the Greek mind which attracted
him under another form: the gift of satire. In the early Erasmus,
and especially the Erasmus who is the companion of More,
the vein of Lucianic satire cannot be dissociated from the
reforming motive. The greatest fruits of their collaboration,
including those which have achieved immortality, are essentially Lucianic: *Moriae encomium*, the *Utopia*, the *Colloquia*, and
their own translations of Lucian's dialogues. It was here that
*Terminus* came fully into his own.

As a starting-point for a general exposition of that protean
gospel which was the *philosophia Christi*, nothing could be
more appropriate than the prefaces to these translations which
More and Erasmus published in 1506.[2] It is not possible to

[1] Studies of Erasmian doctrine are many. The present discussion is indebted
especially to: J. B. Pineau, *Érasme: sa pensée religieuse* (1924); and Augustin
Renaudet, *Érasme, sa pensée religieuse et son action d'après sa correspondance,
1518–21* (1926), and *Études érasmiennes, 1521–29* (1939). There is also much
relevant discussion in Renaudet's *Préréforme et humanisme à Paris pendant les
premières guerres d'Italie (1494–1517)* (1916), and in *Érasme et l'Italie* (Genève,
1954). On the origins of Erasmus's thought, R. Pfeiffer, *Humanitas Erasmiana*
(Studien der Bibliothek Warburg xxii) (Leipzig / Berlin, 1931); P. Mestwerdt,
*Die Anfänge des Erasmus, Humanismus und 'Devotio Moderna'* (Leipzig, 1917);
A. Hyma, *The 'Devotio Moderna'* . . . *(1380–1520)* (Grand Rapids, Mich.
[1925]).

[2] Lucianism in Erasmus and More has been described by C. R. Thompson,
*The Translations of Lucian by Erasmus and St. Thomas More* (Ithaca, N.Y., 1940).
Cf. also Renaudet, *Préréforme et humanisme*, pp. 490–4. The present text is

read them and mistake the work for a purely literary exercise. The application to contemporary religious decay is quite explicit, and the targets are identified as falsehood and pretence, both learned and popular. The vulgar pieties of the preaching friars, like the pretentious vacuity of over-subtle scholastic theologians, are decried as a corruption of that central deposit of Christian truth which needs no human assistance to prevail. To prevent this dangerous mingling of human and divine, of the fallible with the true, we should return to the original fount of all truth and piety, Scripture, lest truth itself be discredited.

In the whole body of Erasmus's writing this conviction was the constant theme: a return to Scripture and the early sources of Christianity would provide a sovereign remedy for contemporary decay. By the time the Lucian appeared he had already proclaimed this view in his introduction to Valla's *Annotationes*, published in the previous year, and in the *Enchiridion militis Christiani*. Its impact lay in the wide appeal to educated men who hoped to bring about the restoration of integrity in religion and public life. For above all else, the call for a return *ad fontes* formed the creed of an aroused and educated laity, and the laicism of Erasmus's thought is its most important characteristic as an incitement to reform. In the *Enchiridion* it received its definitive expression, and the amazing popularity of this work in the two decades after 1515 is sufficient justification for turning to it as the centre-piece of our analysis of Erasmianism.[1]

---

*Luciani . . . opuscula . . . ab Erasmo Roterodamo et Thoma Moro . . . traducta*, Ex officina Ascensiana ad Idus Septemb. MCVI, sig. AAa, More's prefatory letter to Thomas Ruthall. It is also printed by E. Rogers, *The Correspondence of Sir Thomas More* (Princeton, 1947), letter 5; note ll. 27–33, 71–78. More's correspondence in this edition will be cited hereafter as 'Rogers'. Cf. Allen, i. 187, ll. 22 f., in Erasmus's dedication of the *Toxaris* to Richard Foxe.

[1] The *Enchiridion* was first printed in 1503, again in 1509, and in 1515, when its great reputation began. In the next six years there were twenty-three editions, according to the *Bibliotheca Erasmiana* of F. Vander Haeghen (Gand, 1893), i; cf. Allen, i. 373. It was translated into Czech in 1519, German in 1520, English about 1522, Dutch in 1523, Castilian in 1526, French in 1529, Italian and Portuguese in the next decade, and Polish in 1585.

To read this once-famous work is perhaps initially to be disappointed. It would be difficult to regard it as a treatise of profound spirituality, and it is impossible to overlook its loose and repetitious construction. Yet its once phenomenal popularity throughout Europe challenges the imagination of the modern reader. The secret is to be found in what one commentator has called its quality of exhortation.[1] Erasmus described its purpose best himself, in a letter to Colet. He said it was not intended to display virtuosity or eloquence, but to combat the common error of those who make religion consist in ceremonies, to the neglect of true piety. It is simply a manual of lay piety.[2]

His views about the *Enchiridion* were further developed by the time he prepared a fresh edition for the Froben press in 1518. This time he added a prefatory epistle to Paul Volz, Abbot of Hugshofen near Schlettstadt and a sponsor of the Bursfeld monastic reform.[3] Here Erasmus explained the role of the *Enchiridion* in terms which give its doctrine even more radical implications than did the text of the work itself.

At the outset he contrasts it with the writings of scholastics, whose speculations do nothing for the moral life of the ordinary man. In the intricate labyrinths of scholastic controversy, conducted, incidentally, in barbarous Latin, he feels the simple truths of Christ are hopelessly obscured. As a result, for the ignorant masses Christ is now dead.[4] It is possible to see here the Erasmian objection to scholasticism at its most authentic, founded not so much (if at all) on philosophical or theological grounds, but rather on resentment of a mode of

[1] J. Étienne, *Spiritualisme érasmien et théologiens louvanistes* (Louvain/Gembloux, 1956), p. 13, n. 1, and p. 14. Many, like the group of Meaux, found his devotion too cool. On this and his relations with this circle, M. Mann, op. cit.

[2] Allen, i. 181, l. 51, where Erasmus says he intends 'artificium quoddam pietatis tradere'.

[3] On the Bursfeld congregation, H. Herbst, *Das Benediktinerkloster Klus bei Gandersheim und die Bursfelder Reform* (Leipzig/Berlin, 1932). The letter to Volzius is Allen, iii. 858.

[4] Allen, iii. 858, ll. 28 f.

discourse restricted to the initiated specialists. The violent animus of humanists and reformers in this epoch against scholastic writing, about which they commonly had little real information, must be seen, at least in part, as objection to a theology which had become the exclusive monopoly of a clerical *élite*. Thus emphasis on good Latin was itself an expression of laicism, since it automatically repudiated the specialized theological language of the schools and emphasized clarity of discourse between educated laymen sharing the cultural heritage of the classics.

As the letter to Abbot Volz continues, Erasmus stresses the need for a simple yet learned exposition of the 'philosophy of Christ', the phrase which expresses both his humanistic approach and the deliberate rejection of a specialized theological science. He acknowledges the language difficulties of the ordinary man and the confusion likely to ensue from obscurities, especially in metaphors and parables, and he concludes that what is needed is a commission of pious and learned men to make a simple and accurate résumé of the essentials of the faith from the purest biblical texts and according to the best interpreters.[1]

Whatever the difficulties of such a scheme, the provision of a layman's guide to Scripture was a revolutionary proposal, which explains Erasmus's own persistent work at the Paraphrases. In the later stages of the present letter his attitude to the lay vocation to sanctity became quite explicit. He introduced the figure of human society arranged in three concentric circles about the Lamb, the inner circle containing the clergy, the second the princes and political leaders, and the third the common people. Although the responsibilities and dignity of the ranks of society vary, all are called to sanctity without regard to means and endowments, for the flame at the centre draws all else to it, and changes all to its own substance. It is conceded also that the positions of the various circles do not

---

[1] Allen, iii. 858, ll. 134–44. Also J. Lecler, *Toleration and the Reformation* (trans. T. L. Westow, New York, 1960), vol. i, pp. 125–6.

necessarily reflect the true merits of the members with respect to Christ.[1]

The special position of the laity in Erasmus's mind is quite clear in the rest of the letter. The clergy are warned not to tyrannize over their charges, as in preferring merely superstitious to truly religious men simply because the latter will not obey unthinkingly. The clergy like to be called fathers, but what natural father wishes his children to remain perpetually in infancy?[2]

Another significant metaphor is introduced, the resemblance between a city and a large monastery. Erasmus sees a properly conducted Christian city fulfilling the same spiritual purpose as a monastery, with the additional merit of being more useful to society as a whole. Since he feels that monasticism was originally an attempt simply to lead the true Christian life in a hopelessly confused and corrupt world, he sees no real reason to continue it, and his gloomy picture of the decline from monastic purity and evangelical ardour tacitly points the way to suppression. Erasmus on corrupt monasticism is no new topic; what is interesting is the evidence that he saw the daily life of the laity as a preferred and no less authentic religious vocation. Thus he refuses to distinguish a life lived with a vow of chastity from a chaste marriage.[3]

This letter to Abbot Volz, then, appearing as a preface to his new edition of the *Enchiridion*, was Erasmus's manifesto of a reformed Christianity centred on lay piety. The most complete exposition of the gospel is the *Enchiridion* itself. Examination is necessary if the implications of its wide popularity are to be realized. It also provides a framework into which his other major writings in the period can be fitted, especially those on politics and education.

[1] Allen, iii. 858, ll. 231 f. and 330-4: 'In affectibus est Christi perfectio, non in vitae genere; in animis est, non in palliis aut cibis. Sunt inter monachos quos vix recipit extremus circulus: et tamen de bonis loquor, sed infirmis. Sunt inter digamos quos Christus primo dignatur circulo.'
[2] Ibid., ll. 478-81.
[3] Ibid., ll. 507-40. On the city as a monastery, ll. 560 f. On chastity, ll. 567-9. The vow of baptism is the supreme vow for all Christians (ll. 569-72).

The opening of the *Enchiridion* expressly states its purpose, not as a treatise on spirituality, but as a handbook of daily piety. And in the same introductory section another Erasmian emphasis appears: the Pauline preoccupation. In the perpetual war against evil, Christ is the captain, but the standard-bearer is St. Paul, and the scriptural references of the work are almost exclusively to this apostle.[1]

In the second chapter the Christian knight receives his two weapons against the world, prayer and knowledge. The manna of the Israelites signifies to Erasmus not the Eucharist, but knowledge, especially of Scripture, and incessant study of Scripture is the basic defence against all evils. Mastery of Scripture, moreover, implies informed study, and a preliminary journey through the pagan philosophers is recommended both for mastery of the background and for the ethical wisdom which can be found there.[2]

In keeping with this approach, Scripture commentary is to be drawn not from medieval writers but only from the early doctors, since they were closest in time to the source of doctrine. After Paul, the four specifically named are Origen, Ambrose, Jerome, and Augustine. In addition, Erasmus insists on the 'spiritual' sense of Scripture, by which he seems to mean its inward apprehension, contrasted with the literal sense, which by itself leads merely to formalism and coldness of spirit.[3]

The next five chapters deal primarily with the nature of man, conceived primarily along lines derived from Origen, and in essentials fundamentally Pauline. The first recommendation is to attain wisdom, not of the world, but of Christ and oneself. Self-knowledge is chiefly awareness of the conflict between inward and outward man—the conflict, baldly stated, of body and soul. A vaguely Platonic analogy between human

---

[1] The Paulinism of Erasmus has been treated by Bataillon, Renaudet, and Étienne in the works cited. See also E. V. Telle, *Érasme de Rotterdam et le septième sacrement* (Genève, 1954), bk. 3, ch. 1.

[2] *Enchiridion militis Christiani*, *OO* v. 5E–F and 6F on manna; 25F on pagan authors.

[3] Ibid. 9A–B.

nature and the commonweal is not carried out very rigorously, and Erasmus's Platonism here seems to be more literary than philosophical.[1] His emphasis on the contest between man's rational (or spiritual) nature (the two seem to be equated) and his diverse appetites and affections reflects his reading of St. Paul. In the seventh chapter the most detailed analysis is given, with man's nature divided, after Origen, into spirit, soul, and flesh, where the last provokes man to sin, the first knits him to God, and the soul acts as mediator, torn between the warring natures set at variance by the Fall.

In the eighth chapter the practical side of Erasmus's evangelism is displayed in advice for true Christian living. With a knowledge of virtue and hatred of evil gained from Scripture, his Christian layman proceeds to twenty-one 'rules of combat', or canons. The first is fundamental: an assault on ignorance through faith in Christ and wholehearted dedication to the knowledge gained in the New Testament. Christ is the ever-present example and object of thought and deed. Hypocritical religious practice, a disguise for selfish ends, is vigorously attacked. The aim of life is perfect piety, seen as a spurning of the visible and transient in favour of the invisible and perfect. With this vision of two worlds parallel to the earlier view of man's dual nature, the betrayal of religion through external religious practice is vigorously attacked. External, corporal ceremonies are held not to be bad in themselves, since they are signs of piety and are an assistance to the faith of the young and ignorant, but they must be kept in place, otherwise man finds himself ensnared in a new Judaism of legalistic observances. Here the Pauline note of Christian liberty is strongly sounded, with liberty defined as unity in Christ through charity towards one's neighbours. Negatively, it is contrasted with obsessive observance of ceremonial and solitary religious practices.[2]

---

[1] On Platonism in Erasmus, Renaudet, *Études*, pp. 129–30, and Telle, op. cit., pp. 28 f.

[2] *OO* v. 26D and following.

The 'inner religion' is a main theme throughout, and the religious view which results is emphatically un-sacramental. Indeed, the sacraments are conspicuously absent. A rare direct reference occurs in canon five, where confession is mentioned in terms which make little of its sacramental character. The Christian knight is warned against accusing himself of sin merely to a man who is a priest, and is reminded that the true accusation is directed to God, in whose sight such action means inward hatred of the fault.[1]

The remaining canons elaborate the responsibilities of the Christian in the world, with extended discussion of common vices and their remedies. At all times, the reading of Scripture, meaning the New Testament, is put forward as a sovereign remedy. At the end of chapter thirteen occurs the famous dictum that monasticism is not itself piety, although it is often so represented to men who are thus ensnared against their true vocation. Here the failure of the medieval Church to provide a lay spirituality met with a classic accusation in the spirit of the new age. Erasmus will not see the religious life as the highest form of Christian vocation. It is rather a personal calling which may or may not be profitable. He will advise neither for nor against it. The real lesson is that piety has no external form or specific vocational apparatus; it is an inward state.[2] And it is amply clear that Erasmus expects his reader to be living in the world.

[1] *OO* v. 38B: 'Accusas apud Sacerdotem hominem tua peccata, vide quomodo accuses apud Deum. Nam apud illum accusare, intus odisse est.' J. P. Dolan, 'Witzel et Érasme à propos des sacrements', *Revue d'histoire ecclésiastique*, vol. liv, no. 1 (1959), pp. 129–42, in comparing the attitudes of a Lutheran moderate, George Witzel, with Erasmus's own comments on the sacraments, concludes that the common emphasis is on an increased role for the laity, on the use of the vernacular, on simplification of dogma, and on the inner purity of spirit of the recipient.

[2] *OO* v. 65C–66A: 'Monachatus non est pietas, sed vitae genus pro suo cuique corporis ingeniique habitu, vel utile, vel inutile. Ad quod equidem ut te non adhortor, ita ne dehortur quidem. Hoc modo commoneo, ut pietatem neque in cibo, neque in cultu, neque in ulla re visibile constituas, sed in iis quae tradidimus.'

This then is the handbook of Christian living which swept the educated circles of western Europe in the early decades of the sixteenth century. Here is no method of meditation, no treatise on the mystical knowledge of God, but a stern and practical guide to pious living in the world. Simplicity is the keynote, the deceptive simplicity of Scripture. The Christianity of the *Enchiridion* is both un-sacramental and un-theological, and its strength lies in its elevation of the layman's vocation, seen as the potential source of new life in a Church and society fallen into decay.

This conception had revolutionary implications. Not even the pietism of the Low Countries had produced anything so radical. Even the *devotio moderna* had recruited followers into separate communities and something approaching a regular life. The novelty of the religious view which the *Enchiridion* proclaimed was in its complete acceptance of the layman's given vocation in the world and the tacit deposing of clerical authority. With this went the warm attitude to classical writers and humanism in general, partly as preparation for the intelligent study of Scripture, partly as a separate source of practical moral wisdom. In the blending of these two themes, laicism and humanism, Erasmus captured in his writing and his own person the strongest impulses moving the educated classes of his day. He was not, of course, the only one to do so. He was one among many. And when the names of this evangelical humanist apostolate are seen to include those of Lefèvre d'Étaples and Thomas More (to name only two), one might well conclude that Erasmus's was by no means the most creative mind among them. But he was pre-eminently the movement's propagandist, by far its most prolific proponent. It is for this reason that his name is chosen to describe the common cause in which they were engaged.

The revolutionary implications of the Erasmian reform gospel were most conspicuous in his attitude to Scripture and his insistence that it should be made freely available to the ordinary layman. Here evangelism, laicism, and humanism converged in this return *ad fontes* of Christian doctrine. As a professed disciple of Valla, he expounded his views in his introduction to Valla's *Annotationes*, in the *Ratio verae theologiae* (*Methodus*), and especially in his own edition of the New Testament, with its introductory *Paraclesis* and the accompanying Paraphrases.[1]

We are here at the heart of his personal doctrine. The decisive turn in his life and studies was associated with John Colet, whatever the remoter origins of it may have been, and it hinged on a conviction that Colet had found the method for restoring true 'theology'. It is important to understand what Erasmus meant by this term, which exposes the peculiar nature of his thought. It seems clear that for Erasmus 'theology' was, quite simply, the study of Scripture according to his own critical canons. This, he felt, was the method and 'theology' of the early Fathers of the Church, and to this ancient and true system he would return, reacting against the contradictions of the scholastics. The medieval application of philosophy to Christian doctrine had been a catastrophe, burying the essential unity and simplicity of the apostolic tradition beneath mandarin constructions of highly speculative and mutually contradictory doctrine.

The true method, as Erasmus expounded it, began with a profound immersion in the classics. Here the student would acquire critical techniques, some of the necessary languages, and an indispensable familiarity with the thought and customs of the world in which Christ lived and taught. At the same time, his spirit must be prepared to approach the sacred

[1] All this writing preceded the Lutheran controversy. The *Ratio verae theologiae*, or *Methodus*, was first published at Louvain by Th. Martens, 1519; Valla's *Annotationes* appeared in 1505 from the press of Badius (Paris), edited by Erasmus from a manuscript version he discovered in the Premonstratensian abbey of Parc, near Louvain. The *Paraclesis* was published with the *Novum Instrumentum* by Froben, 1516. The Paraphrases were issued in this period as follows: Romans (1517), Corinthians (1519), Galatians (1519), Ephesians (1520? Allen, iv, p. 180), Timothy and the shorter Pauline epistles (1520; Allen, iv, p. 123); Hebrews, James, Peter and Jude, Matthew, Mark, Luke, John (epistles and gospel), and Acts all appeared between 1520 and 1524.

subject with piety and humility; the intellect alone would be insufficient. As for Scripture itself, it is the New Testament which interests Erasmus, and within it the epistles and gospels. If commentary is needed, it should be taken from the early Fathers, and at all times the best available texts should be used. Aristotle and his scholastic followers are alike to be shunned.[1]

From this approach is to be extracted a living devotion to Christ. The emphasis is on popular instruction, and on emulation of the Divine Life. It is the old Franciscan theme of Christ the sole master. It had been the common property of Deventer and the Netherlands mystics, of the adherents of the *Imitation of Christ*, and it was now emerging in Italy in neo-Platonist circles. It had, of course, an instant appeal for the devout layman, especially if it were associated with a personal discovery of the New Testament. This discovery Erasmus attempted to ensure through his Annotations on the New Testament and through his Paraphrases.

Some of the special characteristics—and special difficulties— of the Erasmian system by now become apparent. Its powerful appeal to the educated laity of the day needs no explanation, but the simplicity of his doctrine was deceptive. The insistence on applying the new techniques of humanism to the sources of Christianity was as exciting as it was embarrassing to traditionalists. With this insistence went a theological simplicity which was fully exposed by later events. The Erasmian appeal to learning and higher education was founded on special presuppositions. This 'learning' meant the classical and scriptural tongues and literatures. It was innocent of philosophical depth, and for the most part simply ignored traditional theology. The ease with which Erasmus moved from insistence on high scholarly standards to the interpretation of Christianity as a creed easily accessible to the common layman is partly explained by this.

Most striking, however, was Erasmus's calm adherence to

[1] Erasmus's correspondence with Colet is valuable here, especially Allen, i. 108 and 181, as background to the *Ratio*.

a view that metaphysical speculation in religious matters was useless. This theological positivism, as it has been called, was itself a metaphysical position which required precisely the kind of examination that he disliked. As a result, his positive scriptural bent was highly successful as long as it moved within the traditional doctrinal framework of Latin Christendom. Once this was challenged by Luther the foundations of a tacit unanimity on Catholic orthodoxy melted away, and the battle was joined on issues which Erasmus himself found as bewildering as they were uncongenial. To the end of his life he retained his deep scepticism toward scholastic dogma, side by side with an almost instinctive adherence to Catholic doctrine, worship, and authority. His refuge was unremitting editorial labour on behalf of the sources of Christian doctrine, and in this atmosphere he moved with freedom and assurance.

In the years before 1520, however, these were problems unforeseen. With impressive regularity the Paraphrases issued from the Froben press, fulfilling his ambitious scheme for bridging the gap between Scripture and a public unacquainted with the instruments of a scholarly exegesis. In these successive volumes he developed the philosophy of the *Enchiridion*, expounding to an ever-growing public the religion of inner commitment and of freedom from the formalism of a decayed 'Judaism'. In the *Paraclesis*,[1] a work with great post-Reformation circulation in Protestant circles, his views on Scripture propagation were definitively set forth. Arguing that the lost *philosophia Christi* could be restored only by return to the sources, where Christ alone is the teacher, he expressed his faith that doctrine could be understood without great critical labour by a pious and resolute spirit brought in humility to the task. The Holy Spirit would be the needed guide and interpreter, and its efficacy would in fact be greatest with simple souls. The true theologian therefore is one who leads a truly Christian life and preaches it to his neighbour. On the principle

---

[1] *Paraclesis, id est, adhortatio ad Christianae philosophiae studium, OO* vi, sig. *3–*4ᵛ.

that minds easily penetrate what is most conformable to nature, he insisted that the ordinary man might be an adequate theologian. The *philosophia Christi* thus really restores a nature created good, and human intelligence has a natural affinity for doctrines which have been understood by many, although never so well demonstrated as by Christ himself. Above all, Christianity is to be comprehended by the inner spirit of man; it is an affair of commitment (*affectibus*) rather than of syllogisms, of life itself rather than disputation, of inspiration rather than learning, of conversion rather than reason.[1]

Closely linked with this scriptural doctrine was the need to reduce the complexities of the faith to essentials. In November 1519 Erasmus confided to John Slechta his exasperation with the Roman habit of definition. The great danger was that the few truths embodied in Scripture which were essential for salvation were obscured by inessentials which confused the convictions of the multitude.[2] In his own view the essential beliefs were the hope offered by grace freely forthcoming from God through the mediation of His Son; the redemptive power of the death of Jesus; the union with his Body in baptism; and the promise of reward for a life lived in accordance with His teachings. Although we must increase in virtue, all merit must be acknowledged to come from God: this all must know and believe. Further elaborations of doctrine may be undertaken at the desire of those who enjoy them, but the masses are free to regard such matters with interest or unconcern, as they choose.

Clearly, these views served better as foundation for attack

---

[1] Ibid. *4: 'Hoc Philosophiae genus in affectibus situm verius quam in syllogismis, vita est magis quam disputatio, afflatus potius quam eruditio, transformatio magis quam ratio. Doctos esse, vix paucis contingit . . .', and the following. On the conditions needed for fruitful study of Scripture, see J. C. L. Coppens, *Les Idées réformistes d'Érasme dans les préfaces aux Paraphrases du Nouveau Testament* (Analecta Lovaniensia Biblica et Orientalia, ser. iii, fasc. 27, Louvain, 1961).

[2] Erasmus to Slechta, November 1519, Allen, iv. 1039, e.g. ll. 219 f.; also to John Carondelet, v. 1334, e.g. ll. 217–19: 'Summa nostrae religionis pax est et unanimitas. Ea vix constare poterit, nisi de quam potest paucissimis definiamus, et in multis liberum relinquamus suum cuique judicium. . . .'

against existing orthodoxies than as groundwork for a new
one. From this position Erasmus directed his campaign against
the abuses which were perhaps his true preoccupation—against
formalistic practice of pilgrimages and superstitious devotion
to relics, against degenerate monasticism and the barbarism of
opponents of the new humanism (usually a combined attack),
and against a papacy powerless to lead the reform movement,
given over by unworthy successors of St. Peter to corrupt
practice and secular politics.[1] On the positive side he filled out
his lay gospel with writings of the sort destined to have long
life in English translation—on the exalted vocation of marriage,
on prayer, and on world peace. Finally, the vast editorial
enterprise which was designed to re-establish the early Fathers
as the authentic spokesmen of pure doctrine, combined with
his Greek New Testament, provided his campaign with a
prestige and authority which changed what might have been
a pamphlet war into a major assault on the old order.

If we leave the lay gospel behind and turn to that part
of Erasmus's work which might be considered more purely
'humanistic', we discover that the two are inextricably blended,
and that the *philosophia Christi* included both. In the *Adages*,
for example, which established his reputation as a classicist of
phenomenal resources, Erasmus in a prefatory letter to Mountjoy recommended the classical authors for their moral teaching.[2]
This attitude came naturally to one whose humanist master
was Valla, whom Erasmus admired as much for the *Elegantiae*
(which in time he paraphrased) as he did for the *Annotationes*.[3]

---

[1] The most virulent contemporary expression of anger with an unworthy
Pope is the *Julius exclusus*, probably written by Erasmus at Cambridge (W. K.
Ferguson, *Erasmi Opuscula*, The Hague, 1933, p. 41) and directed against
Julius II, whose warlike pontificate epitomized all that was wrong with the
contemporary papacy in the eyes of the pre-reform party. See also J. B.
Pineau, *Érasme et la papauté, étude critique du 'Julius Exclusus'* (1924), which
includes a general discussion of Erasmus's attitude to the papacy.

[2] Allen, i. 126.

[3] R. Pfeiffer, op. cit., p. 11, 'Erasmus ... in Lorenzo Valla den Vorkämpfer
auf diesem Wege erkannt und verehrt hat.' His paraphrase was *Elegantiae L.
Vallae*, Freiburg, 1531.

From Valla he learned not only the sort of revived classicism
which he thought worthy, but the creed that Christianity should
be restored to purity through critical canons gleaned from the
classics. In fact it was Valla who had called for re-establishing
the biblical texts, and who began the enterprise of which
Erasmus's New Testament and the Complutensian Polyglot
Bible of Alcalá were distinct but related products.

Similarly in the *Colloquies*, a treasury of anecdote and
moralizing which was as popular in England as the *Adages*,
we find the same mixture of humanism and Christian piety.
In these pages Erasmus launched some of his most famous
satires of contemporary society, and it was here that his sharp
distinction between the essentials of Christian practice and the
apparatus of discipline with which the Church had surrounded
its doctrine was made most clear. In this early period the *Colloquies* were still in embryonic form,[1] and the classic production
of this kind was the *Moriae Encomium*—the *Praise of Folly*.
Without attempting an exposition of that famous work here,
it is worth while to notice that Erasmus himself claimed that
the teaching of the *Enchiridion* was elaborated in the *Praise
of Folly*.[2]

One final aspect of his secular policy requires attention here,
his attitude to government and (a problem with which it
was closely related) education. Characteristically, his view is
informed by a practical moralism and a general doctrine
inherited from his classical instructors. And, as always, it
avoids principles and theoretical formularies in favour of a
persuasive eloquence abounding in examples and appeals to
Christian conscience.

The classic source of his political thought is the *Institutio
principis Christiani*, first issued by Froben in 1516. It was written
for the Archduke Charles and, significantly, took the form of

---

[1] See P. Smith, *A Key to the Colloquies of Erasmus* (Harvard Theological
Studies, Cambridge, Mass., 1927); Pineau, *Pensée religieuse*, ch. 9.

[2] Allen, ii. 337, ll. 90–94: 'Nec aliud agitur in Moria sub specie lusus quam
actum est in Enchiridio. Admonere voluimus, non mordere; prodesse, non
laedere; consulere moribus hominum, non officere.'

an educational treatise. It is the formation of the prince's mind and spirit which concerns him, and the pronouncements on government as such come really as *obiter dicta*. The heart of his doctrine is that government must be based on liberty, and the Pauline note returns here. The prince must rule as a father to his State, with the assent of his subjects, for it is his character as a Christian which creates his greatest obligation and his distinctive responsibilities.[1] Pagans may rule as tyrants, but Christian princes must realize that their subjects have only one Master and perfect exemplar. Thus they are not entitled to dominion over their subjects, but must rule by good administration instead of imperial power and by service rather than tyranny.[2]

The prince who discharges his office well will rule with the free co-operation of his subjects in the full commitment of a Christian life. He must in fact try to emulate the prime qualities of God—power, wisdom, and goodness—for he is the visible image of God set among mortal men. While there are many types of State, the consensus of all wise men is that monarchy is best, and when properly conducted it is unquestionably so. When it is bad it is the worst form, however, and for most ordinary princes the check of aristocratic and democratic institutions is desirable. A mixed polity, in fact, seems to be his aim.[3]

Clearly this treatise was neither original in content nor systematic in form. Like the *Enchiridion*, the *Institutio* is in many respects primarily a work of exhortation. It is moralistic and fundamentally conservative, pervaded by love of an ordered society in which each member plays a recognized and respected part. Liberty is conceived primarily as freedom from arbitrary interference, and it is closely associated with belief in a united

[1] OO iv. 567A–C.
[2] After Matthew xx. 25–26. OO iv. 574B, 578C, 577D: 'Cogitato semper, dominium, imperium, regnum, majestatem, potentiam, Ethnicorum esse vocabula, non Christianorum. Christianum imperium nihil aliud esse quam administrationem, quam beneficentiam, quam custodiam.'
[3] Ibid. 576D–E.

Christendom in which peace and charity are the bonds of brotherhood. Given these sympathies, the classical ideals of education, political harmony, and the responsibility of the good ruler for the common good all fit readily into his evangelical imperatives.

Erasmus's writings on education really complete this picture, and their enormous influence in England warrants some attention to them here. The *Colloquia* and *Adagia* were both directed to an educational end, to provide students with models and examples which would also introduce them to the original sources of classical learning. The foundation of the whole system was the *De ratione studii*, a programme of studies including a basic introduction to grammar, but the most interesting complement to this in the period before the outbreak of active religious controversy was the *De duplici copia verborum ac rerum* of 1512.[1]

The *De copia* became the standard English school manual on literary style, but like the *Colloquia* and *Adagia* it was infused throughout with the Erasmian doctrine of Christian humanism. As a 'study in indirection',[2] it taught the inseparability of good classical learning from the formation of sound character, a convergence matched by that of classical culture and Christianity itself. With this in mind, we are not surprised to find that in the *De ratione studii*, the next year, it is Lucian and Lorenzo Valla who head the lists of recommended masters of Greek and Latin style respectively.[3]

---

[1] In the *Institutio*, for example, he insists that the main hope of the State is the correct education of youth (*OO* iv. 592E), and gives detailed attention to the curriculum of the Prince's education in chapter 2. This last may be compared with the general course of studies proposed in the *De ratione studii* (*OO* i. 522–30). In addition to those mentioned, the *De conscribendis epistolis* (1522) might be included among his educational works. His *Concio de puero Jesu* was written for delivery by a scholar of Colet's school and soon published in England by Redman. See Chapter 3, below.

[2] J. K. Sowards, 'Erasmus and the Apologetic Textbook: a Study of the *De duplici copia verborum ac rerum*', *Studies in Philology*, vol. lv (1958), pp. 122–35.

[3] W. H. Woodward, *Desiderius Erasmus Concerning the Aim and Method of Education* (1904), pp. 164–5.

For a systematic exposition of Erasmus's educational principles it is necessary to turn to the *De pueris statim ac liberaliter
instituendis*, published by Froben in 1529. In this work, addressed (significantly for the future history of England) to
Duke William of Cleves, he proclaims the benefits of a liberal
education for the lay public. The argument for education is
primarily a moral one, and the education of a gentleman a
matter which affects society as a whole. Good morality, like
intellectual distinction, is the product of sound training, and
human reason, man's peculiar excellence, is the faculty upon
which all sound instruction is built. Erasmus recognizes, however, the need for satisfying other aspects of human nature,
especially adapting instruction to the unformed temper of a
child. In all this, as in his insistence on good example and on
surroundings conducive to harmony and moral balance, the
classical inspiration is obvious. Clearly he aims at the education
of a governing class, and the provision of good schooling
is made ultimately the responsibility of officers of State and
Church.[1]

This then is the Erasmian message, gleaned from his principal writings in the period before the Lutheran controversy
changed the whole atmosphere of debate. To present it in this
way is to distort the impression gained especially from the
correspondence, where the aggressive side of his undertaking,
the unrelenting war on corruption, pretence, and bad faith,
justified his *Terminus* emblem. But in both its aspects, con-
structive and critical, it is clear that his creed was primarily a
pragmatic one, based on a very exportable blend of personal
religion, laicism, and humanism.

The result was his *philosophia Christi*, and we have seen that
whatever the topic, from religious reform to politics and
education, it is always that which is the real subject of

---

[1] *OO* i. 508D and 503B–C, where he discusses the charge that a child im-
mersed too much in study would lack manly qualities, a pertinent argument
for the humanists attempting to persuade the nobility to adopt a learned
education. More's example with his own family is cited with warm approval,
503A.

discussion. For Erasmus himself, the 'return to the sources' was his imperative personal contribution, inspiring his gigantic editorial activity. Despite these studies, ranging from the New Testament through the early Fathers and pagan classicists, his own creed remained uncomplex.[1] As we have tried to show, it is, above all, a lay religion which exalts the vocation in the world to an unprecedented degree. It is strongly Pauline in tone, with an emphatic antagonism between spirit (usually virtually identified with reason) and flesh. The remedies for this disharmony in man's nature are not sacramental, however, but 'inward'—a renewal of life through full commitment to the teaching of Christ. Thus, despite the emphasis on fallen nature, it is less the redemptive than the ethical Christ who prevails in the Erasmian gospel. The continuous references to the 'example', the 'wisdom', and the 'teaching' of Christ, create a cumulative impression which cannot be explained simply as the substitution of a classical for a scholastic vocabulary.[2]

[1] His work of editing and translating in this period included the following in addition to the *Novum Instrumentum* and Paraphrases: translations: Libanius, *Aliquot declamatiunculae* (1519), Euripides, *Hecuba et Iphigenia* (1506), Lucian (above, p. 15, n. 2), Plutarch (various works); editions: Cicero, *De officiis* (1501, 1520), Seneca, *Lucubrationes* (1515), Suetonius (in *Historiae augustae scriptores*, 1518), Quintus Curtius (1518), Jerome (1516), Cyprian (1519), and Arnobius (1522).

[2] The disagreement of modern scholars on the essence of Erasmus's Christianity is a further commentary on his protean qualities. This verdict of Pineau, *Pensée religieuse*, p. 187, would find fairly general acceptance: 'Il crée un état d'esprit, défavorable aux prétentions de la théologie romaine. Il incline l'intelligence de ses lecteurs au doute discret, à une sorte de scepticisme de bonne compagnie, et qui se trahit par le sourire ou par les silences respectueux. Ne disons pas, comme on le lui a tant reproché, qu'il annonce et prépare Luther: Luther pouvait trouver ailleurs les formules tranchantes et les modèles de son opposition à l'Église romaine.' Thus partial condemnation of his writings by conservative theologians did little to meet the basic problem posed by the Erasmian gospel in a period of warring orthodoxies. The Sorbonne in 1526 condemned the *Colloquia* and the following year censured thirty-two propositions from the Paraphrases. In July 1528 there was a general reiteration of the Sorbonne censures. In the same period, when England, Spain, and Protestant Germany all produced attacks on Erasmus, Italy alone

This aspect of his creed made possible the easy bridging of the gap between Christianity and pagan classicism, admitting the generalized classical view which informs his approach to educational and social problems. For Erasmus, the European Christian community is less part of the Mystical Body than a vast polity in which all members are called to play an orderly part under the providence of God. There is little interest even in well-conducted prelacy, sacramentalism, monasticism, or conventional religious observances. There is high suspicion of dogma, based on a feeling that the ultimate mysteries, as inscrutable, are best left alone. The practical creed is what matters, and here he looks to an educated laity for a renewal of Christian life. The foundations are to be international peace, education, and lay reform based on the restored sources of early (and therefore pure) Christian doctrine. It is the work less of a philosopher or theologian than a prophet: one perhaps whose coat of hair was a doctoral gown and whose wilderness a salon, but a prophet none the less.

He was a prophet with a following. The disciples were primarily aristocratic and middle-class, but they included a popular fringe which rounds out the portrait of Erasmianism as a social movement. The range of his immediate influence can be assessed in the calendar of his correspondence, in itself one of his greatest achievements. Princes, cardinals, popes, and scholars are included—Charles V and Francis I, Wolsey and John Fisher, Leo X and Reuchlin, Melanchthon, Zwingli, and Oecolampadius—in a list where these are only among the more obvious names there is a portrait of influence as such in early sixteenth-century Europe. And so the movement grew, patronized by popes, by reforming bishops and abbots, by cathedral clergy and the administrators of the new monarchies, by kings, queens, and princesses, and by aristocratic patrons from Rome to Greenwich. For in addition to scholars and

was silent and neutral, obedient to the injunctions of the papacy. It was not until 1559 that Erasmus's works were condemned by Rome, a general condemnation which was shortly relaxed in part.

statesmen, in every country there were groups of laymen of prestige and influence who proclaimed the gospel of reform. In France the most notable was the group of Meaux, of which Marguerite of Navarre was the moving spirit. In Italy there were the salons of Vittoria Colonna in Rome, Femora Gonzaga at Urbino, and of Renée, Duchess of Ferrara, while in Spain there were the numerous local societies which took heart under the protection of the Erasmian court of Charles V.[1]

It was in Spain that the reception of Erasmianism was most wholehearted, and it is there that the channels in which this thought circulated were most clearly exposed. In his masterful study of Spanish Erasmianism, Marcel Bataillon demonstrated its close association with feminine devotion, with the traditions of the Spanish *illuminati*, and with the reformed and observant religious orders. Given the official protection of court and Inquisition, the gospel of Erasmus formed a central point around which a variety of religious forces could gather. Thus the essentially uncomplicated *philosophia Christi* soon attracted a network of associated interests, from Imperial administrators who found in it support for internal reform against Roman interference, to enthusiastic *beatas* for whom the *Enchiridion* was an approved handbook of piety.[2]

If the Spain of Ximénez and Charles V was the first country to surrender completely to the Erasmian gospel, England also had a special claim to pre-eminence in the history of the movement. It was here, in all likelihood, that Erasmus received inspiration for the more laborious tasks of the *philosophia Christi*: the great editions restoring knowledge of the Greek

---

[1] Margaret Mann, op. cit.; Bataillon, op. cit., p. 536; Delio Cantimori, *Eretici italiani del Cinquecento* (Firenze, 1939).

[2] The decisive reception of Erasmianism in Spain occurred after the return of Charles V in 1525. After that time, when other pietistic works had fallen under disapproval, the *Enchiridion* remained a safe source of appeal and a ready handbook of Pauline references. This may account for its great popularity among devotees, who far surpassed its doctrine in the mystical intensity of their own devotion. See Bataillon, op. cit., ch. 4, and especially pp. 199 f.

Fathers, and the revised New Testament. In Colet, as we have seen, he encountered a new mode of historical exegesis of Scripture, and from him he may also have acquired the Paulinism we have noticed. In Richard Foxe, Bishop of Winchester, and John Fisher, Bishop of Rochester, he encountered enlightened, energetic promotion of educational foundations which would simultaneously revive the classics and the scholarly study of Scripture in England. And in England, above all, he met Thomas More.

They met on his first visit to England in 1499, and so complete was their friendship that by the time of Erasmus's second visit, in 1505, they were able to embark on the delicate task of their joint translations of Lucian. Then Erasmus found the long-awaited opportunity of study in Italy extended by Henry VII's Italian physician, and after the summer of 1506 the two men were separated once more. But by the spring of 1509 Erasmus had made his fateful decision to leave the enticements of Rome, and set out on his horseback journey through the Alps and back to his native north, and England. He was soon to be the most influential man in Europe. Behind him in the Duchy of Milan, before him in the Rhinelands, and far to his left beyond the Pyrenees there lay the inheritance of the greatest prince in the history of Europe, who in the next decade would be crowned Holy Roman Emperor as Charles, the fifth of that name. And to the north and west were the dominions of those boisterous young princes, Francis I and Henry VIII, whose youth and devotion to the new learning offered great promise to the hopes of the humanist. In his saddle-bags Erasmus carried the growing manuscript of the one work which has survived as a piece of living literature, the *Moriae Encomium* or *Praise of Folly*, dedicated, as its punning title indicated, to his closest friend, the Englishman Thomas More.

In this work Erasmus's relationship with More found its appropriate memorial. It was a satirical attack on the failings of the world they lived in, and a challenge to the new generation of rulers to correct them. Decadent religion, prelatic pride, kingly vanity, and private greed, ignorance, imposture, credulity, and deceit, all were haled into the light of Lucianic wit and reason to be drenched with the acid of mocking laughter and melted—it was hoped—into oblivion.

For behind the numerous works of satire there was deadly purpose. The claims of the Christian life, disguised by paradox, were advanced relentlessly. The targets were many. Decayed monasticism, unintellectual and unspiritual, a dead weight on the consciences (to say nothing of the lands) of Christians in every country, was assailed along with clerical failure of every kind: pluralism and simony, living both high and loose, and monopolies of power grown hateful with abuse. Vulgar piety, too, was ridiculed, for nothing aroused Erasmus so much as the superstition of the herd: shallow and automatic religiosity expressed in pointless pilgrimages, idolatrous relic-worship, calculated penances performed, preferably, by proxy and devised to circumscribe the soul's salvation within the drawstrings of a pardoner's purse. Kings also were there, including popes, who postponed the duties of their exalted calling to pursue the empty glory of conquest and temporal power, while many mourned, and Christendom moaned at the strife and neglect of souls.

Finally in their programme there was education, the universal remedy for Europe's ills: popular education in inward devotion and Scripture study, and professional humanist education for the gentle-born and prosperous, to permit them to serve their princes at home and abroad. To this was added the education of kings, so that under royal sponsorship the magic blend of classical humanism, informed lay pietism, and temporal power would bring about a second spring in Europe's affairs, with international peace and a reformed Church in which the layman's role would be vastly enlarged.

The place of More in all this is perfectly clear. In no other man did Erasmus find such a kindred spirit or such congenial learning. More's four years in the London Charterhouse, debating whether or not to become a monk, may have helped to create a depth of spirituality which was missing in Erasmus, but it certainly won the Dutch scholar's approval. The Carthusians among all other religious orders were exempt from the strictures with which Erasmus flayed his monkish opponents. And More's ultimate decision to enter a lay career made him an ideal figure of the new age. He himself translated the Life of Pico della Mirandola, who was emerging as a model for the Christian humanist layman. He lectured publicly on St. Augustine in the church of St. Lawrence Jewry in London, he defended Erasmus's New Testament before the learned world, and he enlisted the King's support to help the advocates of Greek studies in the University of Oxford.[1]

Finally, in the education of his own family he surpassed all his contemporaries in realizing the ideals of Christian humanism, infusing his own home with a spontaneity, vitality, and warmth which commanded universal admiration. Perhaps most striking of all was his insistence that the educational opportunity and attainment of his daughters should in no way fall behind those of the male pupils. The aims of education as More saw them were outlined in a letter to a tutor recommended by Erasmus himself, William Gonell, in terms which provided classic formulation of the new ideal.

All this is familiar. With it went More's work as a satirist, less commonly discussed. The joint task of translating Lucian was, it seems, his own suggestion,[2] and his enthusiasm for Lucian was known throughout the Erasmian community. In 1522 Conrad Wackers (Goclenius), successor to Adrian Barland as Latin professor at Louvain's Collegium Trilingue, dedicated his translation of Lucian's *Hermotimus* to More, and received a handsome reward.[3] More's own translations were

---

[1] Rogers, 60: To the University of Oxford, 29 Mar. 1518.

[2] Allen, i. 191: Erasmus to Richard Whitford, 1 May 1506. On the Lucianism of More and Erasmus, see also A. Hyma, 'Erasmus and the Oxford Reformers (1501–1519)', *Nederlands archief voor kerkgeschiedenis*, vol. xxxviii (1951), and an important recent discussion from the standpoint of literary criticism, H. A. Mason, *Humanism and Poetry in the Early Tudor Period* (1959), pt. i.                                                    [3] Rogers, 112.

more often published in the sixteenth century than any other
of his works, and they presented to continental scholars an
aspect of his personality which was markedly different from
that which became known in England, especially after his
martyrdom. In the work with Erasmus, the dialogues which
More himself chose were sharply pointed against greed and
pretence, vulgar superstition and credulity, and against the
indulgent, luxury-loving life.[1]

In the following decade, More added to this satiric achievement most of the Latin epigrams which were published in
1519, the year of Luther's fateful debate with Eck, when More
himself was forty-one years old. Some came from the Greek,
others were of his own composition, and assembled together
they form a timely résumé both of his classical learning and
of his satiric bent.

It would be misleading to cite examples from the Epigrams
without acknowledging the impossibility of capturing the
whole spirit of the collection in this way. They are as wide-
ranging in sympathy and interest as was More's own mind.
Nevertheless, it is fair to cite those which conveyed the common
message against the evils of the day, especially in the Church.
Greedy bishops and incompetent priests pass by, along with
misers, unfaithful wives, widowers, poets, the simple, and the
fortunate. Three were written in praise of Erasmus's New
Testament, and the opening poems praised the accession of
Henry VIII.[2] On the reformer's concern with the clergy
perhaps one alone will do:

*To an Illiterate Bishop . . .*

You, mighty father, exclaim, 'The letter kills'. This single phrase
'The letter kills' you have always in your mouth. You have taken
good care so that no letter may kill you; you do not know any letter.

---

[1] The *Menippus, Philopseudes,* and *Cynicus* respectively. For another statement of More's reform position, see the letter to Dorp, 21 Oct. 1515 (Rogers,
letter 15).

[2] *The Latin Epigrams of Thomas More,* edited with translations and notes by
L. Bradner and C. A. Lynch (Chicago, 1953), pp. 16 f.

And not idle is your fear that the letter may kill; you know that you do not have the spirit which will give you life.

Lest it should be thought that this represented only youthful exuberance, repented through caution induced by the Lutheran threat, in the second edition of 1520 this was among the epigrams added:

*To a Certain Fat Priest . . .*

You say, 'Learning puffs up a man—any man—as St. Paul himself teaches'. But you yourself avoid learning. How, then, does it happen that you, substantial father, are so inflated? You can hardly move about with your belly swollen to a fat paunch. And your mind is distended with silly nonsense.[1]

When it is considered that More's epigrams number some two hundred and fifty, ranging over a vast panorama of human merit and frailty, they can scarcely be overlooked in an appraisal of his mind. The examples cited, moreover, are a corrective to the image of More as a clerically minded layman. His devout laicism, of course, was evident through his whole career, and occasionally, as to Budé in 1518, its grounds become explicit. Writing to the famous author of the *De Asse*, who was later influential in urging the foundation of the Collegium Trilingue at Louvain, More made a special point of the fact that as a married man Budé had succeeded in acquiring a

---

[1] These two epigrams are taken from the translations of Bradner and Lynch, pp. 206 and 227. The original versions are as follows:

> Magne pater, clamas: occidit littera. In ore
> Hoc unum, occidit littera, semper habes.
> Cauisti bene tu ne te ulla occidere possit
> Littera, non ulla est littera nota tibi.
> Nec frustra metuis ne occidat littera. Scis non
> Viuificet qui te spiritus esse tibi.
>                    (No. 186, p. 85)

> Quemlibet inflat, ais, uel teste scientia Paulo,
> Hanc fugis. Vnde igitur tu, pater ample, tumes?
> Vix gestas crasso turgentem abdomine uentrem
> Inflaturque leui mens tibi stulticia.
>                    (No. 244, p. 105)

degree of learning which had once been the exclusive possession of the clergy.[1] Similarly, although More was less critical
of the scholastics than were some of his fellow humanists, he
was clearly convinced that scholastic approaches unrelieved by
humanistic learning and sympathy made barren theology.[2]

The greatest achievement of More's spirit, perhaps the most
original creative achievement of the whole European Renaissance, was the *Utopia*. In a comparison of this with the *Praise
of Folly* the contrast between the minds of More and Erasmus is already clear by 1516. For here, in addition to the
satire and common critique of contemporary society, there is
a gravity, an intellectual depth and suggestiveness through
paradox, which has recalled More's work to every generation
for fresh study. No attempt can be made here to add to the
enormous literature on the *Utopia*, but a few aspects may properly be noticed as confirming More's place in the Erasmian
circle.

An approach to the *Utopia* as a model of society erected on
a Natural Law foundation seems now to be generally accepted.[3]
As such, it was the most extended attempt made by any of the
Erasmian community to set forth one of their favourite themes,
the contrast of Christian failure and pagan virtue. As a portrait
of an ideal society, it also enabled More to explore every issue
of importance from government and property to religion
and education. The whole vision of an ordered lay society, in
which extravagance and display are shunned, in which the
community of goods is commemorated daily at the common
board, and where all dress in garments of undyed woollen
cloth, recalls unmistakably the *Enchiridion*'s comparison of a
Christian city and a large monastery. Throughout the work,
alongside a wealth of positive doctrine, the familiar criticisms

[1] Rogers, 65, ll. 19–20.
[2] e.g. Rogers, 15, ll. 886–916.
[3] Emanating from the group of More scholars around Professor A. W.
Reed, including R. W. Chambers and H. W. Donner, it is a basic principle in
the more recent studies by Edward L. Surtz, S.J., *The Praise of Wisdom*
(Chicago, 1957) and *The Praise of Pleasure* (Cambridge, Mass., 1957).

are there. Monks are to be devout and observant of their rules, yet asceticism is to be restrained and humbly undertaken, not perverse. Lucian is highly commended for his wit and humour, and the Utopians treasure a predictable catalogue of other Greek writers. Similarly, Aristotelian logic, not the scholastic version, is the recommended discipline of reason. A recent commentator has said, in fact, that 'More's silent opponent often is the unregenerate and reactionary Schoolman of his time . . .'.[1] At all times the essential harmony of reason and grace is the tacit or explicit major premiss of the work, a conviction tenaciously held by the humanist community which in itself made the full Lutheran doctrine unacceptable to most. In short, the *Utopia* viewed in this light seems a fuller exposition of the Erasmian programme than any set forth in a single work by Erasmus himself.

A glance into the future from the moment of the *Utopia*'s publication suggests at least one other commonly held principle of these reformers. Implicit in More's *Utopia*, as in all Erasmus's writing to this date, is the vision of a united Christendom. It was an essential precondition of their greatest hopes for free criticism and radical reconstruction of European faith and society. Both More and Erasmus adhered to this view to the end, each with his own integrity. That of More led him to the scaffold; that of Erasmus, to his death in the Catholic Church in the refuge of a Protestant town.[2] It was the paradox of their diverging destinies that haunted the humanist community, and the scanning of conscience was nowhere of greater moment than it was in England.

It is with this English development that we are concerned. Our first problem will be to show that this Erasmianism—this blend of humanism and reform which was the joint manufacture of More and Erasmus, swayed undoubtedly by the fervent genius of John Colet—that this creed was the characteristic

[1] Surtz, *Praise of Pleasure*, p. 103.
[2] For references to Erasmus's 'resolute loyalty' to the Roman Church, see Allen, ix. 15, n. 58, and viii. 87, note on 2123, l. 14.

allegiance of the whole English humanist community in the years before the crisis of the royal divorce, and that its influence, although based on an *élite*, extended far beyond the small coterie which Seebohm described as the Oxford reformers. When the character and concerns of this community have been described, it will then be possible to see how the humanist group fared in the great religious controversies of the day; to see how they re-formed their basic notions within the framework of their capacious creed, to take an active role in shaping a religious settlement unique in the annals of the Reformation.

# 3

## PATTERNS OF PATRONAGE

BY the turn of the sixteenth century, humanism had been domesticated in England. The earlier dependence of the new scholarship on resident foreigners and on a few adventurous and isolated patrons like Duke Humphrey had at last produced a group of men capable of original creative achievement. This change became apparent in the generations which are bridged by the association of Grocyn, Linacre, Colet, and More. Previously, the cultural reception of influences emanating from Italy occurred in Yorkist times. Although there were earlier ventures, it was then that the foundations of the domestic tradition were laid. The change is marked by the introduction of Greek learning to the universities, by the circulation of Valla's *Elegantiae* and Perotti's *Rudimenta gramaticae*, and by the appearance of John Anwykyll's *Compendium totius gramaticae*, published in Oxford in the penultimate decade of the century. William Grocyn, who entered New College from Winchester in 1465, is justly seen as the first great native product of the new traditions of learning. And in 1499, with the publication of Linacre's Latin version of Proclus's treatise, *De Sphaera*, by the Aldine press, the firstfruits of England's new humanist maturity were seen abroad.

These traditions were still elementary and somewhat tentative. It seems that the new subjects were taken into the established framework of study without, as yet, any great sense of intellectual challenge. With the first explorations of Platonism still under way, and with the adaptation of new methods in grammar to English circumstances still a major concern, it would be surprising to find anything else. Moreover, the new studies were still the preserve of a small group largely found within the universities, close to court or ecclesiastical patronage. It is the sign and achievement of a domestic tradition that this learning becomes available to a wider group through multi-plication of contacts, and that English scholars achieve a mastery of the subject which permits extensive original thought.[1]

This perhaps is one way of describing the attraction exerted by the group which Sir Frederic Seebohm labelled 'the Oxford Reformers'. Seebohm analysed the interests of these men as something which was new not only in England but in Europe as a whole. That this work was actually a phase of a general European movement is now clear, but all subsequent study has confirmed his impression that there was an important step forward for English learning in the early decades of the sixteenth century. Perhaps most interesting since Seebohm's day are the gains from new attention given to Colet, whose contact with More and Erasmus may well have crystallized aspirations and discontents which both the younger men had felt since their university studies, respectively at Oxford and at the Collège de Montaigu in Paris.

What is less clear is the impact of these changes beyond the much-studied London group in immediate contact with Thomas More. In attempting to describe the native English humanist community we must begin with the problem of identification: who are the humanists, who are their patrons, and what are the centres where they congregate? We must also seek to discover if their interests are truly distinguishable from those of their fifteenth-century predecessors. To some extent this point was anticipated with the discussion of More's relation to Erasmus, but it will be important here to see if the evangelical interpretation of humane studies common to More and Erasmus was widespread within the humanist group in England. With these problems behind us, it will be possible to trace the unfolding of religious controversy and official policy within this influential community, and to identify the crucial strands of continuity in their thought.

[1] R. Weiss, op. cit., chs. xi and xii.

It is the business of the present chapter to suggest answers to these questions for the scholarly community outside the two universities. The results can then be compared with those obtained from a closer look at the more concentrated group of university scholars. From the production of the English presses, from dedications, from book and manuscript ownership, and from a variety of incidental information in records, evidence will be produced to suggest that Erasmian humanism in the fullest sense was the characteristic commitment of this group, a momentous development for the realm, as becomes clear with the fall from favour of Wolsey.

The first step is to trace the affiliations of the English humanist community. Starting with the well-known London group, the associations of these men will form the most natural guide through this complicated pattern of influence, leading us to schools, to the London legal community, to the royal family itself, and from there to the many patrons who usually derived their own influence ultimately from court favour: bishops and curial servants, monasteries, and aristocratic families.

There can be no error in starting with the London of More's and Colet's maturity. By the time of Erasmus's first visit to England, all the Oxford reformers but Colet had removed permanently from the university to the city of London. Early in 1504 Colet too made the break with Oxford and rejoined his friends as Dean of St. Paul's. He was the senior figure among them, a representative of the London mercantile community and sometime scholar in the schools of Rome.[1] In his approach to scriptural exegesis, and in his personal blend of Pauline Christianity with neo-Platonism, he introduced themes which shaped the views of Erasmus himself and occupied the English reform party throughout the period of the Reformation; and in his famous sermon to the Convocation of 1512 he provided the English reformers with a manifesto of their aims.

[1] Not Florence; see L. Miles, *John Colet and the Platonic Tradition* (Lasalle, U.S.A., 1961), pp. 18 f., and Sears Jayne, *John Colet and Marsilio Ficino* (Oxford, 1963).

Colet's theology seems to have combined the prevalent concern with St. Paul and neo-Platonism, already noticed in the *Enchiridion* of Erasmus, with an Augustinian emphasis which kept the philosophy in a subordinate role within the bounds of Christian orthodoxy.[1] His dislike of created matter and his emphasis on the redemptive power of Christ combined to minimize the role of the sacraments in his writing,[2] although his concern with the Eucharist and his general orthodoxy make this a less striking feature than it was in the work of Erasmus. Familiar too are the interest in mystical union, the dislike of technical theology, and the sympathy for Christian communism, all features of the devotional movements of the Low Countries. Finally, his scriptural exegesis and preaching seem to have broken new ground entirely. Reacting against the traditional analysis in terms of four levels of meaning, he stressed the essential unity of divine truth, and tended to ground this on the 'literal' meaning.[3] This in practice led to emphasis on the historical situation surrounding the birth of the New Testament, on a personal, redemptive Christ, and (in accord with his concern to return the Church to purity of doctrine and practice) on the need to reach the informed general public rather than the restricted audience of clerical specialists.[4]

The striking agreement between these views and those which were to characterize Erasmus has long fostered speculation about Colet's influence on the younger scholar during his visit to Oxford in 1499. Certainly it is clear that, whatever the exact nature of this influence, the scholars surrounding Colet were disposed to accept the Erasmian reform programme from the moment of its first promulgation. The association of Colet and Erasmus was suitably enshrined in the famous colloquy

[1] E. W. Hunt, *Dean Colet and his Theology* (SPCK, 1956), ch. 2.

[2] Miles, op. cit., p. 105 and pp. 201 f.

[3] Hunt, op. cit., ch. 4; Miles, op. cit., pp. 182 f.

[4] This aspect of Colet's teaching, and the soteriological emphasis of Colet's exegesis, is stressed by Bernard O'Kelly, 'John Colet's *Enarratio in Primam S. Pauli Epistolam ad Corinthios*: a new edition of the text, with translation, notes and introduction', Harvard Ph.D. thesis, 1960 (unpublished).

*Peregrinatio religionis ergo*, where they appear visiting together the shrine of St. Thomas at Canterbury. If we need to account for an element in English humanist activity different from the traditions of the previous century, we need look no further than this meeting of minds.

The intimate connexion between concern with religious reform and humanist education was demonstrated in Colet's own foundation of St. Paul's School, which brought the educational reforms of Italy to England.[1] More than that, his was the first 'Erasmian' foundation in the country, apparently preceding even the initiative of Lady Margaret Beaufort and John Fisher at Cambridge. The school's religious purpose was expressed in its dedication to the Child Jesus, protector and guide in youthful piety. But its purpose in the world was more novel. Colet wished the school to serve his own community of Londoners, to produce an educated laity trained in the best Latin and Greek studies and in the informed humanistic piety which would result.[2] Thus its very management was to be turned over to responsible and wealthy laymen, and Colet's choice was the Mercers' Company, to which his own family were attached.

The blessing of Erasmus on the enterprise was commemorated visibly in the verse dedication which he drew up to be hung in the proscholion. But his efforts went further. One result was the *Institutum Christiani hominis*, first published in a collection of *opuscula* in 1514, but written earlier for Colet. In form it was a Latin version in verse of a typical pietistic compendium written in English by Colet, beginning with an exposition of the Creed, and continuing with reflections on the seven sacraments, the love of God, and on the daily acquisition

[1] The view that Colet's statutes effectively proscribed pagan authors is denied by M. L. Clarke, *Classical Education in Britain, 1500–1900* (Cambridge, 1959), pp. 5–7; and is disputed also by Hunt, op. cit., pp. 2 f., and Miles, op. cit., pp. 25–26.

[2] J. H. Lupton, *A Life of Dean Colet* (1887), pp. 166–7; F. Seebohm, op. cit., ch. vi, sect. 1.

of Christian virtues.[1] With this was the *Concio de puero Iesu*, for delivery by a scholar to his fellows in the school, the *De duplici copia verborum ac rerum*, which also originated as a work done at Colet's request, and his contribution to an elementary Grammar for the school, in the preparation of which he was assisted by Lily and Colet.[2] All this was intended to permit the youth of London to imbibe together 'Christum et optimas litteras', and it is conspicuous that St. Paul's scholars in the first years of the century included such distinguished humanists as Thomas Lupset, Sir Anthony Denny (the future Privy Councillor and patron of learning), John Leland, and, somewhat later, William Camden.

A different index of the importance of this school and its subsequent influence may be found in the career of the man chosen by Colet about 1510 to direct it, William Lily. Introduced to the world of humanist learning by Grocyn at Oxford, he was a companion of More in the Charterhouse, and subsequently made a pilgrimage to Jerusalem which was followed by intensive study of Greek and Latin at Rhodes and in Rome. Here is precisely that blend of piety and scholarly aspiration which was the common muse of the Erasmian group. His *Syntax* and his work on the eight parts of speech (revised by Erasmus in 1513) were put together in 1542 to form the authorized royal Grammar of the Henrician reform movement,[3] which became a foundation-stone of classical education in England. Lily's daughter Margaret, who married her father's successor at St. Paul's School (and, after his death, a second master there), christened her children by the second marriage with the names, 'savoureusement pédantesques', of Polydore, Scholastica, and Barbara. His son George, after

[1] Allen, ii. 298, ll. 30–35; S. Knight, *The Life of Dr. John Colet* (a New Edition, Oxford, 1823), pp. 124–9.

[2] See Allen, i. 175 (intro.); Knight, op. cit., pp. 110 f.; and Erasmus's preface to the *Absolutissimus de octo orationis partium constructione libellus* (Basle, Froben, 1515) in Allen, ii. 341.

[3] Below, Chapter 7. On the spread of Erasmus's books through English schools in this period, see Clarke, op. cit.

following his father to Magdalen and the enthusiasms of the new studies, joined the allegiance of Reginald Pole and survived his exile to become a canon of Canterbury under Mary.[1]

Lily's associations will discover for us another school whose contribution, coming slightly earlier, was perhaps as momentous as that of St. Paul's. His connexion with Grocyn and Magdalen College, Oxford, leads back to Magdalen College School, which could also number among former pupils at this time Wolsey, John Claymond, Bishops Stokesley and Lee, and, as it now seems, Thomas More himself.[2] A pupil there of John Holt, More added to Holt's *Lac puerorum* of 1510[3] his own first published work, an epigrammatic salute to the book's prospective scholar reader. The Grammar itself was dedicated to More's early sponsor and patron, Cardinal Morton, and its mention serves to illustrate the signal contribution of this one school to the reform of grammar studies in England. Before Holt and Lily added to its fame, it had already sponsored the teaching of John Anwykyll and John Stanbridge, and it was soon to produce yet another distinguished grammarian in Robert Whittington.

In this direct and personal way the creed of reformed studies spread. The influence of Magdalen College School and St. Paul's would soon be felt throughout the kingdom, through their pupils and through their Grammars. Moreover, there are indications that the two schools had a continued association derived no doubt from these Oxford–London ties. For example, on the last day of 1516 a Magdalen College School master dined with two guests, a former associate, Maurice Birchinshaw, who had left the year before to teach at St. Paul's School,

[1] A. Feuillerat, *John Lyly* (Cambridge, 1910), pp. 11–14, and Zeeveld, op. cit. George Lily's works included historical accounts printed in Paolo Giovio's *Descriptio Britanniae*—the first exact map of Great Britain—and, apparently, lives of Fisher and Cranmer. Peter, a less distinguished son than George, was the father of the euphuist, John Lily.

[2] R. S. Stanier, *Magdalen College School* (2nd edit., Oxford, 1958), ch. iii. Concerning More, see pp. 58–61.

[3] *STC* 13604: de Worde.

and one Thomas Lupset. Lupset was a former pupil of Lily and a protégé of Colet, who had recently assisted Erasmus at Cambridge in his editions of the New Testament and of St. Jerome, and would shortly supervise the Paris printing of two of Linacre's translations of Galen and the second edition of More's *Utopia*.[1] In a glimpse of this sort it is possible to grasp both the intimate character of English humanist studies at this stage and the rapid progress which, to some extent at least, this very intimacy fostered.

With mention of More and Linacre we are brought back to the London community, and to the most striking influence of all, that of Thomas More's own household. It is unnecessary to ventilate a theme already so widely known, but it might be mentioned here that the association of this circle with St. Paul's School was predictably close. Lily worked with More on his translations from the Greek anthology, and in Colet's school More found a scholar tutor for his family and a future son-in-law, John Clements. Moreover, John Heywood the dramatist, who married More's niece, the sister of William Rastell, also seems to have had an association with St. Paul's School.[2]

More's City connexions have been much discussed, and form the background to an entire work on his *Utopia*.[3] There is one aspect of his professional affiliation which has not, however, received the attention which our present concern would warrant. His membership in the Inns of Court naturally bound him into that community of lay learning, which was proving to be an attractive alternative to the universities. But more specifically, his legal training and eminence brought him, in December of 1514, into a more restricted but most influential association, that of Doctors' Commons.

[1] J. A. Gee, *The Life and Works of Thomas Lupset* (New Haven, 1928), pp. 44 f., p. 58.
[2] A. W. Reed, *Early Tudor Drama* (1926), p. 61; on the collaboration of Lily and More, see Bradner and Lynch, op. cit., p. xxvii.
[3] R. Ames, *Citizen Thomas More and his Utopia* (Princeton, 1949).

Doctors' Commons was an informal association of civilians and canonists connected with the Court of Arches.[1] It was located in Pater Noster Row, near the precincts of St. Paul's, where the members owned a small house and shared a common table with other learned men outside the immediate profession of civil law. From its inception in 1509 it seems rapidly to have become a regular resort for men of influence in legal and ecclesiastical circles, and the membership record suggests truly remarkable possibilities for dining and conversation.

In May of 1511 the names of members were apparently first committed to record, and already the association included many of the important patrons of learning. Colet, Grocyn,[2] and Cuthbert Tunstall, John Yonge (Bishop of Callipoli), Hugh Oldham, Bishop of Exeter and associate of Foxe in his scheme for a trilingual college at Oxford, Nicholas West, royal chaplain and ambassador, soon to be named to the see of Ely, and Peter Gryphus, the papal tax collector, are all included. In the years following, names added are eloquent of the society's prestige and undoubted influence: Richard Sampson, the future Bishop of Chichester and Henrician apologist, at this time (1514) Wolsey's chaplain and a royal ambassador; Thomas More in the same year, as mentioned

[1] The original register of the society is Lambeth Palace Library MS. SR 136. Guildhall MS. 1353, fols. 13, 14, 17 et seqq., is a transcript with most of the names. More subscribed as follows (Lambeth MS. SR 136, f.v. 18): 'Ego T. Morus 3 die decembris anno a Christi nato 1514 admissus sum in hanc societatem et polliceor me soluturum in annos singulos 6s. 8d.' The marginal entry in a different hand is 'Thomas Morus laicus ge[nerosus]'. He would then have been about 36 years of age. See also W. Senior, *Doctors' Commons and the Old Court of Admiralty* (1922); C. Coote, *Sketches of . . . English Civilians* (1804); and *London Topographical Record*, vol. xv, ed. W. H. Godfrey (Cambridge University Press for the Society, 1931), ch. ii.

[2] Grocyn's membership, which is not mentioned by Emden, is suggested by Lambeth MS. SR 136, fol. 11. It occurs in the first section of the register where, in 1511, the names of the original members seem to have been recorded. Beside his name (in a later hand) is the marginal notation, 'mor[tuus]'. Colet's name, also in this section, is followed by his signature and oath (fol. 8), cf. Thomas More, above. The same is true of Peter Gryphus (fol. 15, 28 May 1511) and John Yonge (fol. 11, 12 Oct. 1514). Hugh Oldham's name is accompanied only by the marginal note, 'obijt' (fol. 12).

above; Andrew Ammonius and Nicholas Harpsfield in the two years following; and in 1533, within a month of one another, came Hugh Faringdon, abbot patron of Leonard Cox at Reading[1] who in November of 1539 was hanged for treason, and John Tregonwell, Principal of Peckwater Inn at Oxford and future visitor of monastic houses. Other members by 1530 included John London, the Warden of New College and another future agent of Cromwell; David Pole, nephew of Reginald; Edmund Bonner; Thomas Winter, Wolsey's much-tutored son; William Petre, future Secretary of State, and John Veysey, who succeeded Oldham in the see of Exeter and governed it (except for an interval under Edward VI) until his death in Mary's reign. In Grocyn, Colet, Tunstall and More, Ammonius and Sampson, the group included close friends and patrons of Erasmus.

In Doctors' Commons, then, we find a centre of activity which cuts across several lines of influence and patronage: the episcopacy, reforming abbots, the City itself, the universities, and, looming large beyond, the court. It is time to turn to this last arena, where all other lines converge.

We are indebted to the Spanish disciple of Erasmus, Juan Luis Vives, for an account which provides the best introduction to this side of English court life in the untroubled years before Henry's discontent with his marriage came to dominate the scene. It is an account of the Queen, Catherine of Aragon, on a familiar journey by barge from Richmond palace to the royal Brigettine house of Syon to pray. In her company is Vives, the devout and brilliant counsellor, who, as the barge returned in the late afternoon, turned the talk to the classic theme of the mutability of fortune. The Queen expressed a preference, after the many turns of fate she had already known, for a tranquil and undramatic life. If compelled, however, to choose between the extremes of adversity and prosperity, she mused, she would prefer the harder lot ('malim mihi omnia contingere asperrima et infelicissima quam secundissima'), for

[1] See p. 62.

if the unfortunate lacked consolation, real loss of spiritual integrity often visited the prosperous ('nam mihi videntur calamitosi homines egere consolatione, sed nimis prosperi mente').[1]

This scene leads us into a critical network of associations. Vives himself, who left England rather than become a party to the divorce proceedings against his patroness, seems to have acquired her protection in these years through an introduction by Thomas More.[2] To More, Vives, and Erasmus, Catherine was known as a model of feminine piety and learning. She was a member of the third order of St. Francis, and her charity and piety were as profound as her patronage of learning was generous. Her generosity permitted Vives to come to England and conclude his commentary on the *De civitate Dei*, which he dedicated to the King. In 1523 he was deterred from Alcalá by Wolsey's invitation to lecture at his new foundation in Oxford, and shortly afterward his revolutionary tract on the education of women, dedicated to Catherine herself, appeared at Antwerp.[3] Moreover, for Catherine's daughter Mary, whose tutor he was, he wrote the *De ratione studii puerilis* and his *Satellitium*.[4]

Vives was only the most widely celebrated of Catherine's scholarly beneficiaries. Linacre, Pace, and Leland, along with younger aspirants to learning, all benefited from her bounty. Both Erasmus and Vives wrote works on Christian marriage for her, and she received the dedication of Wyatt's *Plutarch* in 1528.[5] In 1523[6] Pynson published the *De libero arbitrio*

---

[1] *Literae ad Franciscum Craneveldium* (Humanistica Lovaniensia 1), Louvain (1928), Ep. 90 (from Oxford, 25 Jan. 1524), ll. 26–39. Also described by Vives in *Introductio ad Sapientiam; Satellitium sive Symbola* (Parisiis, apud Simonem Colinaeum, 1527), p. 35, no. 56.

[2] *Literae . . . Craneveldium*, General Intro., pp. xlviii–xlix; also Ep. 261, intro., a–c, on Vives's attitude to the royal divorce.

[3] *De institutione foeminae Christianae*, 1524 (NB 2167), brought for presentation to Catherine of Aragon in April 1523; on the English version by Richard Hyrde, see below, Chapter 6.     [4] Above, n. 1.

[5] *STC* 20059†, *Of the quyete of mynde*, Pynson [1528?].

[6] *STC* 24728; also 24729.

*adversus Melanchthonem*, by a Franciscan Observant, Alphonso de Villa Sancta, likewise dedicated to her.

In all of this Queen Catherine was continuing and complementing the work of the Dowager Countess of Richmond and Derby, the Lady Margaret Beaufort. Patroness of Caxton and foundress of a court school in the last decade of the previous century,[1] the Lady Margaret was the principal bridge between the humanism of the Yorkist court and that of the new age. An interest in devotional works was always inseparable from her own learned enterprises. Along with the Queen she may have commissioned an undated *Book of Prayers* from Wynkyn de Worde, and John Fisher, at her express request, published a treatise on the seven penitential psalms.[2] In 1494, again at her instigation, de Worde published Walter Hylton's *Scala perfectionis*, and, perhaps most notable of all, she was the patroness of Atkinson's version of the *Imitation of Christ*, the suppositious fourth book of which she translated herself.[3] She also made an English version of *The mirrour of golde for the sinful soul*, first published in 1522.[4] Thus there was good reason for the King's decision that it should be Erasmus who would compose the inscription for her tomb. And if we add to these titles Thomas Paynell's dedication of his version of Erasmus's *De contemptu mundi* (in 1532) to Mary, sister of the King and Dowager Queen of France, we have an interesting impression of feminine devotion at the royal court.

This devotion found other expressions. Apart from the Lady Margaret's crucial endowments at Cambridge, which are dealt with in the next chapter, the most notable was the patronage

---

[1] C. H. Cooper, *Memoir of Margaret, Countess of Richmond...*, ed. J. B. Mayor (Cambridge, 1874), pp. 45–46, 52.

[2] Ibid., p. 83, n. 4; *STC* 10902, *This treatise concernynge the fruytfull saynges of Dauyd, . . . J. fyssher*, de Worde, 1508.

[3] *STC* 23955: *A full deuout a. gostely treatyse . . .*, Pynson, 1503, 04 (2 pts.). Five more editions are recorded before 1525.

[4] The Carthusian Denis de Leeuwis's *Speculum aureum animae peccatricis*; see W. E. A. Axon, 'The Lady Margaret as a Lover of Literature', *Library*, 2nd ser., vol. viii (1907), p. 40.

of certain religious houses distinguished by the integrity of their life. This included three of the houses conspicuous in Wolsey's day for exemplary observance: the Brigettine house of Syon already mentioned, the Carthusian house of Shene down the river from it, and the Observant Franciscan convent at Greenwich. Although all three attracted the favourable attention of the humanist circle (Shene being selected, according to Erasmus, as Colet's favoured place of retirement), only Syon's rule added a concentration on learning to strictness of life. Its double community attracted postulants from distinguished families, as befitted its royal associations, and once the new foundations at Cambridge had made their impression on the university it attracted a stream of Cambridge men.[1] The Lady Margaret remembered all three houses in her bequests, and Queen Catherine was always an attentive and generous benefactor in her lifetime.

It is not therefore surprising that the largest single group of pietistic works produced in the period is associated with Syon. Dedications reveal two royal servants involved in this enthusiasm, the Steward of Syon house, Sir Richard Sutton, co-founder of Brasenose College, Oxford, and the patron of *The Orchard of Syon* (1519), and Sir John Hussey, Comptroller of the royal household and patron of *The Mirrour . . . of Christes Passion* (1534).[2] The prolific author of most of Syon's productions was Richard Whitford, the 'poor wretch of Syon', whose early career as a Fellow of Queens' College, Cambridge, had taken him to Paris as Mountjoy's chaplain and into the circle of Erasmus's friends. He received in fact the significant compliment of being chosen judge in the rhetorical competition between More and Erasmus over Lucian's *Tyrannicida*. From the time of his own first undertaking, a translation of St. Augustine's rule for the Sisters of Syon in 1525, until the dissolution of the house and his retirement in the Mountjoy

[1] D. M. Knowles, *The Religious Orders in England*, vol. iii (Cambridge, 1959), p. 213.
[2] *STC* 14553: Redman.

household, he published over a dozen treatises of a devotional and (later) controversial character, sponsored by the house but clearly intended also for the lay reader.[1]

Outside the strictly devotional sphere, the royal ladies entered into the general patronage of learning at court. The Lady Margaret had added to her pietistic publications Watson's translation of Brant's *Ship of Fools* and the edition of *Kynge Rycharde* published by de Worde in 1509, and Caxton's press worked under her general patronage. Catherine of Aragon's interest in humanistic education has already been described. It is clear, too, that in combining pietism and humanism the ladies reflected the general tone of court patronage. Linacre's edition of Galen's *De sanitate tuenda*, published in 1517 and dedicated to the King, spoke to the learned world abroad of the debt owed by English scholarship to the Crown. At least equally instructive are some surviving royal manuscripts which suggest that court taste had an Erasmian flavour. For example, some time shortly after 1508, Erasmus's servant and pupil Gervase Amoenus of Dreux presented the King with a French translation of devotional works from Latin, presumably as a bid for attention at the accession of the young monarch. In the dedication he referred to the patronage of William Blount and to his association with one Henry 'Hault', who had conceived the scheme which he was now carrying to completion.[2] The works selected are revealing. They are from the *Enchiridion* and from Pico della Mirandola's rules for the spiritual warfare of the Christian, and they conclude with Erasmus's prayers to the Virgin and to Jesus. It is not surprising then to find two other French translations from Pico the elder dedicated to Henry VII and, in a different but related vein, some dialogues of Lucian dedicated to Henry VIII.[3]

[1] On Whitford see Knowles, op. cit., p. 214; also below, Chapters 5 and 7.

[2] Allen, viii, p. xxi, and i, p. 442, n. 57. Haute, who died in 1508, was Protonotary Apostolic, and a kinsman of Queen Elizabeth Woodville (Emden). The manuscript is Royal MS. 16 E. xiv.

[3] Royal MSS. 16 E. xxiv and xxv, and 12 C. viii. Royal MS. 16 E. xxv

In the humanistic pietism of Queen Catherine and the Lady Margaret we have reached the pinnacle of this early English Erasmian patronage. The King's own education disposed him to a sympathy with the reformers' aims which was taken for granted by men like Erasmus and More, but the direct patronage of learning seems to have come primarily from the royal ladies and from a group of eminent churchmen and courtiers in close association with them. To this last group we must now turn.

Nearest to the court in point of influence, as a channel through which the humanist doctrine was made to circulate, came interested members of the episcopacy and the curialists— the prominent servants of the Government. Erasmus's own ties in England could be taken as a key to the composition of the interested episcopal party: Warham, Tunstall, Foxe, and Longland—these, with John Fisher, are perhaps the obvious names. Although Wolsey planned a school on the new design at Ipswich and provided employment for many in the reforming humanist party (Richard Pace, Thomas Lupset, Thomas Elyot, and John Clerk, among many others) he seems nevertheless to have found little reputation among them. His greatest contribution was his Oxford foundation, but his failures elsewhere made him a target for criticism, and in his fall was seen the removal of an impressive obstacle to reform.

The role played by the other bishops mentioned is too well known to need elaboration here. There are three more, however, less often included as patrons of humanism. The first, Thomas Halsey, the English Penitentiary in Rome, and after 1515 Bishop of Leighlin and Kildare in Ireland, was a member of the group on good terms with Erasmus, Fisher, and Pace.[1] More important perhaps were two courtier bishops of the old school, John Veysey and Nicholas West. Diplomatic emissaries

is in the same hand as the former, and like it contains Pico's 'Rules for the Christian battle' (in French). Thomas More had also translated these as part of his version of the Life of Pico.

[1] Allen, i. 254; also 216, l. 20.

of the King and both of them keepers of great state, they are also commemorated in the publications of the time. Veysey received the dedication of Barclay's translation of Sallust's *Jugurtha*, and West is remembered in connexion with Barclay's translation of Baptist Mantuan's *Life of St. George* and with Bullock's *Luciani opuscula* in 1521.[1] Finally in this category there is Thomas Ruthall. Royal Secretary to both Henries, Bishop of Durham in 1503 and Chancellor of Cambridge University, he received two dedications from Erasmus himself: *Senecae lucubrationes* in 1515, and the *Timon* in *Luciani opuscula*, about 1506. He was also selected to receive the important general dedication of More's translations of Lucian.

Among the curialists, lay and clerical, More's name must of course lead any list. But a variety of dedications reveal casual contact between humanists and others in the official circle, and a few examples will suffice. One of these should be another John Yonge, an intimate of Colet and a patron and correspondent of Erasmus, who dedicated to him his *Plutarchi de tuenda bona valetudine* of 1513. As Master of the Rolls, with many benefices at his disposal, he spent most of his life in the royal diplomatic service, and on his death in 1516 he left bequests to Wolsey, Warham, and Grocyn, as well as to New College (of which he had been a Fellow) and Winchester, where his education began.

Another curialist of note, Robert Aldridge of Erasmus's *Epistola . . . in tyrologum quendam* (1527), spent most of his early life between King's College, Cambridge, and Eton, where he was a master for some years. Made a canon of Windsor and Registrar of the Garter in 1534, he was raised to the episcopal bench in 1537 as Bishop of Carlisle. He enters directly into the story of Erasmus in England as the interpreter on the famous trip to Walsingham preserved in the *Colloquia*,

---

[1] STC 21626: *Here begynneth the famous cronycle of the warre, wh. the romayns had agaynst Iugurth*, Pynson [1520?]; STC 16896: *Lepidissimum Luciani opusculum*, J. Siberch, 1521. On the Barclay, see A. W. Ward, *DNB*; on Bullock's close association with Erasmus at Cambridge, H. C. Porter, *Reformation and Reaction in Tudor Cambridge* (Cambridge, 1958), pp. 31 f.

and in 1525 was one of those sent—no doubt deliberately chosen for his interests and associations—to persuade the refractory Syon community to accept the Royal Supremacy. A member of the 1539 committee to promote uniformity of belief, he supported the Act of Six Articles and ended his days, under Mary, protesting against the innovations of Edward VI.

Beyond this episcopal and curialist group, in the penumbra of the royal influence itself, there stand the aristocratic patrons. Here the Blounts were pre-eminent. William Blount, fourth Lord Mountjoy and Erasmus's principal English patron, is the man to whom the *Adagiorum collectanea* was originally dedicated in 1500. His son and successor, Charles, received the dedication of this work in the many editions after his father's death, a graceful acknowledgement of the continued humanist sympathies in the family. Charles was also complimented by Erasmus's *Livy* of 1531, and his personal tutor, Peter de Smet (Vulcanius), was perhaps selected by Erasmus himself. Moreover, Vives selected him for particular mention with the Princess Mary in his introduction to the *De ratione studii* in 1523.[1] After appearing in court as a page to Queen Catherine, he continued his father's services there after succeeding him in the title in 1534. From 1537 to 1541 he entertained the scholar Andrew Gerard of Ypres, and tried to secure Ascham as a tutor for his own son. He was also sufficiently powerful to shelter Richard Whitford after the dissolution of the Syon house and to have his continued publication tolerated.[2] Ascham and Leland (whom he seems also to have assisted) both praised his learning and character and reflect the deference accorded to the family which had brought Erasmus to England.

Next in point of interest come the Poles, who appear in print as the patrons of Gentian Hervet. The French scholar's translation of Erasmus's *De immensa misericordia Dei* in 1526 was dedicated to the Countess of Salisbury, and that of Xenophon's

[1] Vives, *Opera* (Basle, Episcopius, 1555), i, fol. 7; see Allen, vii. 2023.
[2] See below, Chapters 6 and 8.

*Treatise of the householde,* five years later, to Reginald Pole's brother Geoffrey. During this period the Countess was also governess to the Princess Mary, and to her own son Reginald, most favoured of the royal protégés abroad.

By way of comparison there is the family of Boleyn, from a slightly later period. Sir Thomas was the recipient of three dedications from Erasmus, the *De praeparatione ad mortem* (1534), the *Enarratio in Psalmum xxii* (1530), and the *Explanatio symboli* (1533). The second of these he requested himself.[1] Similarly, in 1533 he may have commissioned the anonymous translation of the last-mentioned work, the *Playne and godly exposytion of the commune crede,* in the dedication of which there is a classic exposition of the Erasmian attitude to religion.[2] Erasmus himself described Boleyn to a friend as 'egregie eruditus', so it seems that it was not simply the accident of his daughter's promotion at court which attracted the humanist's attention to the family.

Other aristocratic patronage could be mentioned, but these three families are outstanding for their deep involvement in an Erasmian blend of humanism and piety. Moreover, in citing their names, we have all but completed the list of leading Erasmian sponsors in this early period. There remains only one general category, that of the monasteries. Certain of these which contributed to the growth of the new studies in England can be discerned through the fame of the abbot. Thus John Ramsay of Merton, to whom Paynell dedicated his translation of Erasmus's *Comparation of a Vyrgin and a Martyr,*[3] was a reforming abbot elected in January 1530, after a career as Prior of the Austin canons' college of St. Mary's at Oxford. He resigned before the dissolution of the house in 1538, and after writing several devotional treatises, he ended in the Protestant camp. Hugh Faringdon (or Cook) of Reading Abbey seems to have been an enterprising educator who put the abbey's library at the disposal of the King during the debate on the divorce, and

---

[1] Allen, viii. 2232.                              [2] Below, Chapter 5, p. 137.
[3] *RSTC* 10465.5; Maitland 439 (Berthelet, 1537).

who was responsible for the upbringing of at least one noble child, James Basset, stepson of Arthur Plantagenet, Lord Lisle. His monastic achievement is best commemorated in the preface to *The Arte of Rhetoryke*, the first English work on the subject, written by the master of his abbey school, Leonard Cox, whose own subsequent career is of considerable importance. Evidently a loyal servant of Henry whose attitude to the Royal Supremacy is not entirely clear, Faringdon was indicted for treason in 1539 and executed at Reading, possibly as a consequence of his close association with the Poles.[1]

Finally, Richard Kidderminster, the distinguished Abbot of Winchcombe to whom John Longland dedicated a group of sermons in 1523, is the most notable of the three as a reformer and patron of learning. Influential at Oxford, where he intervened on behalf of the regulars, he described his own community as an 'altera nova universitas', and was himself an antiquarian of accomplishment.[2] He died before the crisis of the reign, apparently about 1531, but not before sustaining a vigorous defence of total clerical immunity against the contentions of the Franciscan champion for the Government, Henry Standish.

Apart from these conspicuous cases, monastic centres of humanism and reform can occasionally be detected through accidental contacts. Prior John Ramsay's career is illuminated by the excellent reception accorded to Erasmus during his stay at St. Mary's in Oxford, where a predecessor of Ramsay, Richard Charnock, was clearly in the front rank of the university's sponsors of the reformed studies. The coincidence is enough to draw attention to this house of studies for Augustinians at the university as a likely centre of reforming humanism by 1520. In the same way Erasmus's contacts discover an unexpected patron of learning in Richard Bere, the Abbot of Glastonbury who is better known for his magnificent building operations. In a letter of 1524 Erasmus refers to his patronage

---

[1] Knowles, op. cit., p. 175; pp. 378–9, and App. ix.
[2] Ibid., pp. 91–95; Wood, *Annals*, vol. ii, p. 21.

of Richard Pace, and associates him also with Zacharias Deio-
tarus, a continental disciple of Erasmus resident in England.[1]
Finally, Evesham monastery, in the person of Robert Joseph,
supplies, as we shall see, the most unexpected evidence of a
widespread community of aspirants to humanistic learning
scattered through a chain of Benedictine houses.

In sum, the resemblances between the situation in England
and that in other countries where the Erasmian gospel was
making its way is striking. The sponsorship for this devout
humanism comes from the highest quarters and is never far
from the royal family itself. Indeed, the King, the Lady
Margaret, Wolsey, Queen Catherine, and the Princess Mary,
along with the collective entity of Syon Monastery, together
account for perhaps half the total number of book dedications
in this early period. In the City, apart from routine sponsorship
by booksellers and publishers, merchants only twice appear
by name in these dedications. One Roger Thomye, mercer, is
joint sponsor with a bookseller of Trevisa's translation of
Higden's *Polychronicon* in 1527. The other is an anonymous
'marchaunt of London' who paid for *The boke named the royall*,
the popular devotional work published by Wynkyn de Worde
in 1507. Nevertheless the association of the London humanists
with the mercantile community is amply evident from the
careers of Colet and More alone, and from the involvement
of the Mercers' Company with St. Paul's School. Most obvious
is the concentration of important patronage in a very few
hands and the close intimacy of this sponsoring group, including courtiers, administrators, ecclesiastics, and reforming
abbots. This occasionally becomes evident in a fashion which
is the more striking for being quite casual. Thus in 1517 Henry
Kebyll, draper and citizen of London, sometime Lord Mayor
and a merchant of the Calais staple, drew up a will in favour of
his daughter, the second wife of William Blount, fourth Lord
Mountjoy. She and her husband, his executors, were to receive
the generous sum of £2,100 to purchase an estate. Appointed

---

[1] Allen, v. 1490, ll. 21–25; and iv. 1205, n. 1.

to oversee the executors, with a fee of twenty marks, was (among others) John Colet, clerk, Dean of St. Paul's.[1]

Finally, at the centre of this whole group of patrons is the King himself, the automatic recipient of attention from favour-seeking writers, but a man himself so well educated as to attract the unfeigned respect of the best of them. In the later devotion of the humanist community to the King and the dynasty these elements in the humanist tradition in England must be borne in mind.

Equally remarkable in this period is the exiguous opposition to Erasmus in influential English circles. Conservative hostility at the universities was confronted with support from the highest quarters. Only one man of stature in learned circles exposed himself as a public opponent of Erasmus, and that was Edward Lee, Archbishop of York after 1531. Yet Lee's other activities exempt him from the charge of obscurantism, however scathing Erasmus's own appraisal became. Apart from Lee's charges, the public fulminations of the irrepressible friar Standish against Erasmus's New Testament seem to have provided the only vocal opposition, and this had the effect of making obvious the powerful support he enjoyed.

In examining the pattern of patronage, then, we have really gone far towards answering the questions raised in the second part of our inquiry concerning the interests of those involved. The Erasmian bent can be discovered also in the production of English presses from the second decade onward, although in the first decade of the century the selection scarcely departs from that of the earliest English printing. Vernacular classics were reissued, while the inevitable Aesop and chronicles, along with vernacular works of piety, ballads, and 'prognostications', seemingly formed the bulk of the traffic. The Grammars of Whittington and Stanbridge declared the growth of classical education, but translations are from French, rather than from Greek or Latin. It is the appearance in 1510 of More's translation of the Life of Pico della Mirandola which ushers in a new era in the publishing trade.

[1] Bishop Kennett's collections, Lansdowne MS. 978, fol. 155.

The second decade in fact, shows some increase in humanist titles. Vergil and Plutarch (in the first edition of Erasmus's *De tuenda bona valetudine precepta*) both appear by 1516, when More's *Mery geste how a sergeaunt wolde lerne to be a frere* was issued by Julian Notary.[1] The pietist strain, with that learned association which justifies the label of 'Erasmian', is also clearly announced. In 1519 there appeared *The Orchard of Syon*, four years after the Atkinson translation of Kempis. Equally expressive was a tripartite production by Pynson in 1516, consisting of a calendar of English, Irish, and Scottish saints in English for those unable to understand Latin; the Life of Saint Bridget (which seems to point to a connexion with Syon); and Richard Hilton's 'devoute boke'.[2] Some continuity of interest behind these productions can be surmised from a translation which had appeared five years before, *The chirche of the euill men and women* by St. Bernard of Siena, with a Savonarola work of 1509. In these the links with continental reform movements become visible, and the second work must receive further attention in the next chapter.[3] Sermons by the reform party, including Colet's celebrated sermon to Convocation and Tunstall's *In laudem matrimonii oratio*,[4] on a favourite Erasmian theme, contributed the prestige of eminent churchmen, and More's nationalistic controversy with the humanist Germain de Brie was brought home to the learned public by Pynson in 1520.[5]

---

[1] *STC* 20060: *Plutarchi de tuenda bona valetudine precepta, Erasmo Roterodamo interprete*, Pynson, 1513; dedicated to John Yonge, Master of the Rolls. *STC* 24814: *Bucolica Virgilii cum commento*, de Worde, 1514. The *Mery geste* is *STC* 18091 [Anon., 1516?].

[2] *STC* 4602: *Here begynneth the kalendre of the newe Legende of Englande . . .*, Pynson, 1516.

[3] *STC* 1966: *The chirche of the euill men and women*, de Worde, 1511. The colophon attributes the printing to two Paris theologians, one of them being Noël Beda, of the Collège de Montaigu. On the Savonarola work, Chapter 4, pp. 98 f.

[4] *STC* 5545: *Oratio habita ad clerum in conuocatione, anno 1511*, Pynson [1511–12]. *STC* 24320: *C. Tonstalli in laudem matrimonii oratio*, Pynson, 1518.

[5] *STC* 18088: *T. Mori epistola ad G. Brixium*, Pynson, 1520.

By the third decade, in which these humanist reformers become involved in religious controversy and national policy, the dominance of Erasmian thought in English publication is quite obvious. Much of the matter will appear in later discussion, but an indication may be given here of the development of taste. In the classics, Wyatt's *Plutarch*, translated from the edition of Budé for the Queen, Catherine of Aragon, appeared before 1530, at about the same time as Wynkyn de Worde's *Complures Luciani dialogi a D. Erasmo in latinum conuersi*. As we have seen, Erasmus's Cambridge disciple Henry Bullock had first introduced Lucian to the English public in the early 1520's, and by the end of the third decade two English versions of dialogues by Lucian had issued from the More circle, an anonymous *Necromantia* and a version of the *Cynicus*, possibly by Sir Thomas Elyot.

In general, the growth of humanism is manifest in a decade which began with Siberch's unauthorized Cambridge edition of Erasmus's *De conscribendis epistolis* and concluded with Wakefield's *Syntagma de hebreorum codicum incorruptione*, embracing in the intervening years such works as Linacre's important *De emendata structura Latini sermonis* (1524) and the popular *Progymnasmata grammatices vulgaria*. Polydore Vergil's edition of Gildas was published in 1525, Leonard Cox's *Arte or crafte of rhethoryke* in 1524, and in 1526 there appeared two translations of Erasmus emerging from the More–Pole connexion: Gentian Hervet's *De immensa dei misericordia* and Margaret Roper's *Deuout treatise vpon the pater noster*, both from Berthelet's press.[1]

This published work in itself enables us to form some conclusions about the nature of the English humanist enterprise in this period. There are no monumental scholarly works, but there is much interest in the foundations of good grammar, in the classical tongues (with growing attention to Hebrew), and

---

[1] The Gildas, *STC* 11892: *Opus nouum: de calamitate, excidio et conquestu Britanniae*, 1525. The Cox, *STC* 5946: R. Redman; the Hervet, *STC* 10474; the Roper, *STC* 10477.

in rhetoric. In aristocratic circles romances continue to obtain patronage, with chronicles and classical history forming the background to Polydore Vergil's edition of Gildas, the best achievement of its kind at this time. French is the one vernacular language to get serious attention, Palsgrave's great *Lesclarcissement*[1] of 1530 confirming the evidence of translations. There is some small experiment in the publication of classical texts, but it seems evident that the classical editions used by Englishmen were bought or printed abroad. More important is the translation industry, in which, along with concern for piety, wisdom, and conduct, there is growing attention to satirical writers like Lucian. Complementing this is the great production of cultivated works of piety, associated above all with Syon monastery and the Lady Margaret.

In general, the English press down to the third decade of the century does reveal the leavening influence of Erasmian humanism, but its offerings predictably lag behind the appetite of the educated minority. The conservatism of the press is best indicated by its indifference to the writings of Erasmus himself. Wynkyn de Worde had found it profitable in 1519 and 1520 to reprint the *Colloquia* and the *Christiani hominis institutum in fide Iesu*,[2] but Gentian Hervet and Margaret Roper in 1526 were breaking new ground with their translations, which are the first real moves in a broader campaign directed at the English-reading public.

We see something of the motives behind this campaign if we examine the introduction of Hervet's translation. Its dedication by this old associate of Lupset to Margaret Pole, Countess of Salisbury, whose grandson Arthur he tutored, reveals that the work was done at her request. The preface which follows this tells us more about the views of the Pole circle. Hervet hopes to please and compliment his learned and virtuous patroness by making generally available the fruits of

[1] Below, Chapter 5, p. 120.
[2] *Colloquia*, *RSTC* 10450.5 (1519), 10450.7 (1520). The second work is *RSTC* 1040.52 (another edition by Pepwell in 1520, *RSTC* 10450.3).

Erasmus's 'sermon'. The merit of both author and work surpass his wit to tell, he claims, but for the sake of others than the Countess herself, he will explain that Erasmus is a man of incomparable learning in both pagan and Christian sages and doctors. A restorer of truth and learning, like Isaac recovering wells which the Philistines had corrupted, he has refreshed the 'clear springs of holy scripture'.

Like all Erasmus's works, the present one, Hervet continues, is greatly profitable, but it even surpasses his *Proverbs*, his New Testament and *Instructions to Princes*, and his many other treatises for the learned, because, like the *Enchiridion*, it is profitable to all men.

Then, in discussing God's mercy and the sweetness of free repentance and forgiveness of sins, Hervet makes an interesting observation. He notices that among men those that forgive sin have not all equal power: 'som cases be reserued to the pope and of the popes himselfe power som do put a great dout: but god himselfe is he that hath rule both in heven and in erth . . .', and there is no doubt of God's power. On the eve of the great debate in England, from the heart of the Pole circle there emerges this strong Erasmian note of purely personal pietism, elevating the private relationship between the individual conscience and its Creator above the sacramental organization of the Church.

After a lapse of one year in the publication of texts of Erasmus, the year 1528 brought two significant productions, both from de Worde's press, the *De copia* and the *Luciani dialogi*.[1] In general, however, Erasmus is still reserved to the educated minority, and for the best evidence of their interests we must turn to their writings, their associations, and—as in the next chapter—to their libraries. Some of the reasons for supposing that Erasmus's influence was great have been stated already, and the question is a vital one, for the moment the royal divorce is achieved the English bookstalls are crowded

[1] *De copia* in Dibdin, ii, p. 234, no. 330; recorded by Ames as published 9 Oct. 1528. The Lucian is *STC* 16891.

with a host of translations of Erasmus, and this phenomenon is one for which we must account. Part of the explanation is in the private devotion to Erasmus growing in the circles described here, already somewhat apparent in the Lucianism and pietism associated in the book production cited above. The rest of the answer lies with government policy, inspired by a resolve to bring Erasmus before the general public.

It is possible to illustrate both the intimacy and the evangelical interests of the London humanists from a record left through the personal idiosyncracy of a scribe's hand: the highly distinguishable hand of Peter Meghen, a one-eyed Brabantine scribe who was Colet's letter-carrier, and who seems to have circulated his services through the group.[1] In the tasks assigned to Meghen there is a vivid insight into their interests. Perhaps the most famous works copied by him are the manuscripts of Colet's own works, including those on the Epistle to the Romans and the *Ecclesiastical Hierarchies* of Dionysius.[2] With these are associated some which Colet arranged to have prepared for his father, Sir Henry Colet, the Lord Mayor of London. They are Erasmus's Latin version of the gospels of Luke and John, with the Pauline and Catholic epistles. They were set in parallel columns with the Vulgate text, and prepared by Meghen in the years from 1506 to 1509. In the latter year he copied for Colet himself Erasmus's version of the gospels of Matthew and Mark.

For an unknown sponsor Meghen produced a revised version of the Vulgate Epistles of St. Paul, evidently from a fresh

[1] See Allen, ii. 416, where (June 1516) he carries four volumes of Erasmus's *St. Jerome* to Warham. For indentification of works written by Meghen, see: A. E. Pächt in *Burlington Magazine* (vol. 84, 1944), p. 137, n. 6; Dr. R. W. Hunt in *Bodleian Library Record*, vol. iii (1950–1), p. 26.

[2] The Colet manuscripts are: Corpus Christi College, Cambridge, MS. 355, Exposition on Romans; Emmanuel College, Cambridge, MS 3. 3. 12 (James 245), Treatise on 1 Corinthians; Cambridge Univ. Library MS. Dd. 7. 3, Erasmus's translation of Matthew and Mark made for Dean Colet in 1509; British Museum, Royal MS. 1. E. v, Erasmus's translation of Luke and John, made for Colet between 1506 and 1509.

translation of the Greek,[1] and a collection in Latin of the Psalms and Canticles, which found its way later into the Lumley library. For Henry VIII himself, at the behest of another unknown sponsor, he prepared a *Canones Horoptri* in which Holbein and Kratzer also collaborated—a reminder therefore of More's patronage as well.[2]

Wolsey too used the services of Peter Meghen to devise two lectionaries, one of which survives at the Oxford foundation which succeeded his own, Christ Church, and the other at Magdalen College, Oxford, with which he had been associated as a student and Fellow.[3] By far the largest number of commissions surviving and identified, however, are associated with the name of Christopher Urswyke.

Urswyke, a civil lawyer and canonist from King's Hall, Cambridge, who became Warden of that foundation in 1485, was chaplain to the Lady Margaret, and acted as her trusted agent with Archbishop Morton during the plotting of the dynastic revolution which overthrew Richard III. From this beginning his career flourished in the strong light of Tudor favour, and he was employed in many diplomatic missions, being made Dean of Windsor in 1495. In 1502 he was given the living of Hackney, where he remained until his death in 1522.

His friendship with Erasmus is commemorated in the latter's dedication of the *Gallus* in *Luciani opuscula* in 1506. The characteristic praise of Lucian here places Urswyke's own taste in an interesting perspective. As a tie with the earlier humanist achievement in England, he commissioned Meghen to prepare

[1] British Museum Royal MS. 1. D. xi–xv, and Royal MS. 1. E. iii (psalms in Latin, of Gallican version, followed by canticles; from the Lumley Library). Cf. Bodleian Library, Corpus Christi College MSS. XIII–XIV, Gospels and Acts of the Apostles, from the Vulgate, but with interlinear version in red, from Erasmus's translation. This is true also of the second volume, containing the Pauline epistles, Apocalypse, and 'S. Hieronymi Erasmique argumentis penitus instructum'.

[2] Bodleian Library: MS. Bodley 504, dated 1528 (S.C. 2168), rules for finding the time of sunrise and sunset, the position of the sun in the Zodiac, &c.

[3] Christ Church, Oxford, MS. 101; Magdalen College, Oxford, MS. 223.

the translation of Chrysostom made by William Sellyng for presentation to Prior Goldstone of Canterbury. A copy of the same work, including other material and also in Meghen's hand, is illuminated with Warham's coat of arms on the first folio.[1]

For his personal use Urswyke had Meghen copy the canonical epistles and Ecclesiastes, each with the preface of St. Jerome; a treatise on the dignity of the human condition ascribed to St. Ambrose; and a work by the same Father on the dignity of the priesthood.[2] Ten years later, acting as executor to Sir John Huddleston, Urswyke caused Meghen to write a Latin translation of the Homilies of Chrysostom on St. Matthew and prepare a Psalter for the Cistercian community of Hailes in Gloucestershire.[3] But most interesting of all is a miscellaneous collection of homilies and religious works which must have been done by Meghen shortly before Urswyke's death. The authors represented are a significant group: writings of Chrysostom and Augustine are here associated with two significant works by Savonarola and with a (subsequently excised) pair of sermons by Luther, on preparation for the Eucharist and on the passion of Christ.[4]

In Urswyke's employment of Meghen we seem to find summarized the interests of the whole group: the early Fathers (with a characteristic emphasis on Chrysostom), Erasmus's version of the New Testament, association with a Cistercian community, and the reforming gospel of Savonarola. The further inclusion of Luther is a rare early augury of steps which

[1] British Museum, Additional MS. 15673: see R. Weiss, op. cit., p. 157, n. 7. The date is 1488. At the end is a letter from Christopher Urswyke to Goldstone. The second copy is Additional MS. 47675 (not mentioned in Pächt's list), prepared originally for Cardinal Morton.

[2] Bodleian Library, MS. Douce 110, dated 1504 (S.C. 21684). Urswyke also owned Corpus Christi College, Cambridge, MS. 346, *Augustinus de civitate Dei*, Venice, Gabriele de Pietro, 1475 (Hain +2052; Proctor, 4193).

[3] P. S. Allen, *The Age of Erasmus* (Oxford, 1914), p. 142. Also C. M. Church, *Archaeologia*, vol. lvii (1901), pp. 215–16.

[4] The Savonarola pieces are commentaries on the psalms, 'In te Domine speravi' and 'Miserere mei Deus'; see below, Chapter 6. The manuscript is in the Bodleian Library, University College MS. 40.

were clearly to be taken by some, if by no means all, of the Erasmian reforming party.

Urswyke's interest in Luther raises a question with which the present discussion might conclude: the reputation of the group for orthodoxy at this time. In general it seems clear that they were exempt from suspicion, even in the period after Lutheran works were sought out for destruction. More's licence to read heretical works so that he could reply to them was perhaps a formal recognition of tacit permission which applied throughout this select and highly placed community. The heresy prosecutions of the period do not involve the Erasmian intelligentsia, and touch even radical university graduates only when the scandal is striking. The alarm of Wolsey over his Cambridge recruits gathered in Oxford is an isolated example in this period of a 'purge' directed against a centre of studies. Colet's 'heresy trial' and the involvement of Margaret Roper in proceedings about her English version of Erasmus's commentary on the Lord's Prayer might at first glance seem to be important exceptions. Yet neither of these last two examples appears at all grave when examined closely, and they serve really to highlight the general exemption of the Erasmian community from supervision.

Colet's difficulties with Bishop Fitzjames of London are still obscure, although it seems probable that vernacular translations of the Creed and certain other prayers formed part of the charge. Yet vernacular translations of this sort were sufficiently plentiful, and it is clear that it must have been views expressed in sermons which provided the real core of the accusation. Warham's complete solidarity behind Colet rescued him from his embarrassment, and Latimer's later claim that Colet would have been in danger of burning if the King had not changed his mind is impossible to believe, and must be assigned to the rhetorical exaggeration of so much Reformation controversy.[1]

A similar episode of ecclesiastical discipline involving More's

[1] See P. S. Allen, 'Dean Colet and Archbishop Warham', *EHR*, vol. xviii (1902), pp. 303–6.

own daughter grew out of the regulation of the book trade. Leo X's Bull against Luther, which began the campaign against Lutheran books, was issued in July of 1520. It was not until the end of the decade that some efficient means was found for checking publication by turning the problem over to the Council. The list of prohibited books provided at that time, like all similar lists in Henry VIII's reign, includes strictly Protestant works, and there is no suggestion of suspicion directed against Erasmus or his fellow workers in moderate reform. However, in the intervening period to 1530, control of publication was left with the old ecclesiastical machinery originally invented to deal with Wycliffite heresy and the circulation of manuscripts. It is perhaps the breakdown of this system which involved Margaret Roper.

It is clear that by 1524 there was serious difficulty for the London ordinary, since Tunstall then and in the following year issued a warning to a gathering of London booksellers. In the autumn of 1524 it was made necessary to have episcopal approval for newly imported books, to be obtained from the Cardinal, from Canterbury, or from London or Rochester. Early in the following year Wynkyn de Worde was prosecuted for printing the heretical *Image of Love* (translated by John Gough, the bookseller and printer), of which some sixty copies were allegedly sold, interestingly enough, to the nuns of Syon. About the same time there appeared Margaret Roper's *Devout Treatise upon the Paternoster* from the Latin of Erasmus and introduced by one of the family tutors, Richard Hyrde. In March 1526 Berthelet was called before the Vicar-General for publishing works without previous approval by any of the four designated Bishops: Wolsey, Warham, Tunstall, or Fisher. The works so published were a curiously Erasmian list: in addition to Erasmus's treatise, there were Fisher's February sermon (actually against Lutheran books) at St. Paul's Cross, Gentian Hervet's translation of the *Immensa misericordia Dei*, and Berthelet's own version of Erasmus's *Dicta sapientium*. Berthelet was ordered to sell no more of these works, and to be careful to obtain the necessary approval before printing any new works in future.

It is impossible to see in this incident any apprehension about Erasmian opinion: the sympathies of the bishops involved would alone prohibit that interpretation. Moreover, the works in question soon appeared again with a royal privilege. The contemporary episode involving Syon monastery is striking, yet Berthelet, unlike Gough, was not accused of heresy, but only of an error in procedure, perhaps induced by his very conviction that these particular works could have no conceivable difficulty with the licensing authorities established in 1524.[1]

To conclude, then, it seems that the two decades after 1500 effected a marked alteration in the early humanist traditions of the previous century in England. In place of a movement heavily reliant on imported Italians at court, where the reformed study of grammar seems the most mature domestic contribution, there is a growing community of English humanists with interests of their own, and with patrons and followers in growing number reaching even into the City of London. These interests are largely centred on the Erasmian blend of classical culture and religious reform, and accommodate a wide variety of concerns, from pietism to translations from the classics. Some of the older members of Henry VII's Italian colony in London are attached to the new group, which, like its predecessor, is strongly centred on the royal court. Thus Antonio Bonvisi, More's merchant friend and patron, lives to give assistance to More's descendants when they choose to leave England rather than accept the official religious changes. More notable in the world of letters was Polydore Vergil, the official historian. He was quite in harmony with the Erasmianism of the younger generation and, like Erasmus, wrote a commentary on the Lord's Prayer which in the later

[1] Here following A. W. Reed, 'The Regulation of the Book Trade Before the Proclamation of 1538', *Transactions of the Bibliographical Society*, vol. xv (1920).

period of religious warfare was censured by Rome. Even his encyclopaedia of the origins of things, the *De inventoribus rerum*, was in part an Erasmian reform tract, which was both expurgated by Protestants and condemned by the Sorbonne.[1] In this it demonstrated the general experience of the group. With the growing impact of Protestant thought in England after 1520, these men and women were moving towards a crisis which would afflict the moderate reform party throughout Europe. In this crisis the university graduates would play a dominant role, and we must turn to the universities in this same period before attempting an account of the development of English humanism in the period of active religious change.

[1] On the Erasmianism of Polydore Vergil, see D. Hay, *Polydore Vergil* (Oxford, 1952), pp. 33–34 and pp. 65 f.

# 4

## HUMANISM IN THE UNIVERSITIES
### 1500 TO *c.*1530

FOR the English universities, the early sixteenth century was a time of profound change, not only in teaching but in structure and in relations with the Government. The dramatic episodes of the Dissolution, the divorce crisis, and the first Henrician visitation have tended to preoccupy historians, but the universities' internal growth had already led to changes as momentous as these. The collapse of the traditional lecture system conducted by regent masters was accompanied by rapid disappearance of the halls and the emergence of colleges as teaching centres, and in the government of the universities the Heads of these new collegiate establishments played an increasingly dominant role.

Associated with these changes was the introduction of humanism as a disturbing force beneath the surface of a traditional curriculum which had already been considerably modified through the dispensing power of Congregation. Again, study of religious controversy and the growth of Protestant groups has tended to obscure the influence of humanistic study, although this had been present as a leaven since the late fifteenth century. Moreover, it is at this time, before the debate on the royal divorce completed the involvement of Oxford and Cambridge in politics, that a generation of graduates appeared which included such important names as Reginald Pole, Thomas Bilney, Edmund Bonner, John Foxe, Nicholas Udall, Richard Taverner, John Cheke, and Alexander Nowell, a list which only suggests the range of their later opinion and influence.

We have as yet only an uneven impression of the atmosphere

in which these men came to maturity. Existing accounts tend to concentrate on the new foundations, the battle for privileges, and the eruption of Protestantism. For the rest it is largely assumed that the traditional curriculum held unchallenged sway, except for the small group of men who can be traced in direct succession from the apostleship of the Oxford Reformers. Both Cambridge and Oxford—and more especially Oxford—seem to be given over entirely to scholastic studies until, in a rather mysterious burst of suppressed resentment, they join the royal visitors in 1535, 'setting Dunce in Bocardo'.

A proper account of this critical period awaits a careful investigation of each of the major faculties of Oxford and Cambridge, along with a fresh study of university government. For the present, we can hope only to assemble some evidence that humanistic influence, especially in extra-official teaching, was stronger than has been thought. This humanism we find, moreover, has a markedly Erasmian bent which ties it to our central theme.

The sources of investigation must for the most part be university Registers and Grace Books.[1] Although outside London and the court, Oxford and Cambridge were the natural gathering-places of men who would shape the future of the country, they were rarely gathering-places for the records which such men left. The archives of these university communities yield a disappointing return about matters intellectual, for colleges were concerned with their properties, and Congregations with their privileges. Neither tended in the normal

---

[1] At Oxford the sources used are: Archives MSS. Registrum F (reversed) and Registrum EEE (together covering the business of the Vice-Chancellor's Court from 1506 to about 1535), Registrum G and Registrum H (registers of Congregation from 1505 to 1517 and 1518 to 1535). I am indebted to Mr. W. T. Mitchell, who is editing the registers for the Oxford Historical Society, for his assistance with these. Also C. W. Boase, *Register of the University of Oxford (1449–63, 1505–71)* (O.H.S., vol. i, 1884). At Cambridge the corresponding materials have been published. *Grace Book B, 1488–1544* (two parts), edited for the Cambridge Antiquarian Society by Mary Bateson, was issued in 1903 and 1905. *Grace Book C, 1501–42*, edited by W. G. Searle (Cambridge, 1908), contains only graces.

course of business to collect much information about studies, and on the whole we must be content with what can be prised from the interstices of administrative records. Thanks primarily to probate jurisdiction, there is a fair return drawn from book inventories. There is also the evidence of college libraries, and at Oxford at least, the chance record of a humanist monk which shows unmistakably how misleading the official record of studies can be.

The starting-point is the already well-known official provision of new foundations, and these must be briefly taken into account. At Cambridge, active humanist enterprise clearly begins with the foundations of the Lady Margaret and John Fisher, Christ's College and St. John's. It is important to recognize that the main theme of their statutes, however, is not humanism as such but the reformation of the secular clergy. It is a purpose shared by many preceding foundations, and by others less celebrated in the same period: by Jesus College, Cambridge, which received its statutes about 1514, and by Brasenose College, Oxford. The momentous innovation of the Lady Margaret and her holy and learned counsellor was the decision to bring about such reformation through the infusion of the new learning into clerical studies.

The divinity readerships at Oxford and Cambridge were the firstfruits of the Lady Margaret's association with Fisher. They were intended to give free instruction of distinguished quality in the theology schools, and were significantly to be discontinued in Lent so that both the reader and his hearers could devote themselves to preaching.[1] The emphasis on preaching was of course fundamental in this group and found its classic expression in Erasmus's De ratione concionandi.[2] In practice, the Lady Margaret Preachership was perhaps the most interesting experiment. Providing for six sermons annually in

---

[1] C. H. Cooper, *Annals of Cambridge* (Cambridge, 5 vols.), vol. i (1842), pp. 271–2.

[2] *Ecclesiastes sive de ratione concionandi* (Basle, Froben, 1535). Fisher and More both urged publication of this work, which had been in hand for some twelve years when it appeared.

London and selected points in Cambridgeshire, Hertfordshire, and Lincolnshire, the founders insisted that the holder should be a Doctor of Divinity (or at least a B.D. and perpetual Fellow of some college in Cambridge) and was to hold no benefice, in order to prevent mediocrity or negligence.

The statutes of St. John's College, in their successive revisions by Fisher, most clearly show the merging of their initial purpose with the study of humanism. The first version of 1516 is clearly derived from the statutes of Christ's College, founded in 1505. Theology is the goal of all learning, but there is now the significant addition that besides philosophy and the arts which are its most useful adjuncts, some of the scholars are to learn Greek and Hebrew.[1] In the revision of 1524 this clause is modified to provide for the selection of especially proficient scholars for this purpose, and both versions anticipate ordinary conversation within the college in Latin, Greek, or Hebrew. Moreover, both embody the wish of the founders to have the fruits of theology communicated to the people, and provide that one-quarter of the Fellows shall preach publicly in English.[2]

The final version of Fisher's own statutes appeared in 1530, enlarged generously through experience and, in all probability, the examples of Foxe and Wolsey. The foundation is increased in size and provided with two deans, in arts and theology. As before, all members are destined to holy orders. The three main designs of the founders are described as 'Dei cultus, morum probitas et Christianae fidei corroboratio'. On the teaching side there are important additions. Four Fellows are to lecture in the branches of mathematics—arithmetic, geo-metry, perspective, and cosmography, and Arabic and Chaldaic are added, rather optimistically, to the list of permitted tongues. Most important is the provision for permanent establishment

[1] The statutes of St. John's College, Cambridge, are in *Documents of . . . the University and Colleges of Cambridge*, vol. iii (H.M. Stationery Office, 1952), and J. E. B. Mayor, *Early Statutes of the College of St. John . . .* (Cambridge, 1859), where the versions of 1516, 1524, 1530, and 1545 all appear. On the present subject, see Mayor, p.375, ll. 25–29.

[2] Mayor, op. cit., pp. 313 and 377.

of Greek and Hebrew lectures within the college, the former
for juniors and the latter for seniors. The Hebrew lecturer is
definitely to be a priest and theologian, although it is provided
that the Greek Reader may be a layman.[1]

These endowments in 1530 were the first permanent provision of the kind in Cambridge, since Erasmus seems to have
lectured from 1511 to 1514 on special stipends and, as it seems,
the grant of the Lady Margaret for a Chair in divinity. Nevertheless, from about 1518 onwards the university itself provided
for fairly regular public lectures in mathematics and, presumably, in the humanities as well. In 1518 John Bryan,
Erasmus's pupil, seems to have lectured on Aristotle from
Greek texts,[2] and in the same year Fisher took steps to assure
good Greek instruction at large with the appointment of
Richard Croke as Reader in Greek in the university. The very
eloquence and apologetic force of his inaugural lecture[3]
suggests the novelty of the study in the curriculum, and his
alarmed references to the progress of Oxford in Greek studies
ironically recalls More's identical appeal about Cambridge's
advance in his letter to Oxford that same year.[4] Croke's listeners
might have thought of Foxe's institution the year before of
a public lecture in Greek for Oxford University as a whole,
included in his provisions for Corpus Christi College. At that
time, however, the post was still not filled, and Cambridge had
won the race with Croke's appointment.

Foxe's foundation was to Oxford what St. John's was to
Cambridge: the first permanent home of the new learning in
the university. However, there was one foundation which
preceded it in the first years of the century, that of Bishop

---

[1] Mayor, op. cit., revision of 1530, c. lvi, p. 250.

[2] J. B. Mullinger, *The University of Cambridge ... to 1535* (Cambridge, 1873),
p. 517, citing information from a manuscript of Archbishop Tenison (in
S. Knight, *The Life of Erasmus* (Cambridge, 1726), p. 147, n. 'a'). Also A. Tilley,
'Greek Studies in England in the Early Sixteenth Century', *EHR*, vol. liii
(1938), p. 229.

[3] *Orationes Ricardi Croci Duae*, Lutetiae Parisiorum, 1520.

[4] Rogers, letter 60, l. 216 f.

Smith and Sir Richard Sutton, and Brasenose College has its relevance to our theme. It was perhaps a less reactionary institution than has been claimed. Like Christ's College it could claim the combination of a dedicated layman and a bishop as founders, both hoping to improve the standards of the secular clergy. Sutton's associations, moreover, are important. He was Steward of the monastery of Syon, and gave generously to it both during his lifetime and in his will. As was noticed in the previous chapter, he was patron of that distinguished product of the early English press, *The Orchard of Syon*. He and Bishop Smith seem to have attracted a wider circle of interested laymen as well. Most of these were in the Bishop's employ or had connexions in the Inns of Court, and their arms were inserted in the college hall. One of them, significantly, was Sir John Hussey, patron of another Syon production, the *Mirrour . . . of Christes Passion*. The author of this work, John Fewterer, was the convent's General Confessor, and is remembered in Sutton's will by name.[1] In the light of these associations it seems legitimate to identify the lay side of the Brasenose foundation with that same pious, reforming circle which was led by the Lady Margaret.

Bishop Smith himself had risen through the patronage of the Countess of Richmond, and the general aim of his foundation, like its curriculum, closely resembles her own Christ's College. His friend and contemporary in the Countess's clientele, Hugh Oldham of Exeter, who advised Foxe to change his plan to create another monastic house in Oxford, seems to have been associated in some way in the Brasenose scheme.[2] Certainly in 1538 John Claymond, President of Foxe's new foundation,

[1] R. Churton, *Lives of William Smyth . . . and Sir Richard Sutton* (1800), App. xxii. The original is in possession of the college. It might be added that Hussey, through marriage to Margaret Blount, was closely related to the Mountjoy circle, and that Smith's great-niece Anne was a nun of Syon (ibid., p. 415).

[2] Churton, op. cit., p. 440, says that Oldham's arms were in the old library window of the college, and that Sutton's appeared over the gate of Corpus Christi College, but they are not recorded there by Wood. Cf. *Brasenose Quatercentenary Monographs* (O.H.S., vols. lii and liii, 1909), iv, p. 5; ix, p. 154; x, p. 33.

gave six scholarships to Brasenose. The scholars were to be selected by the President of Corpus Christi College, by the Vice-President, and by the Humanities Reader, and were to attend the Greek and Humanities Readers at Corpus as a condition of tenure. If there is nothing specific in the foundation to suggest that Brasenose was intended to be a home of the new studies, there is equally nothing to indicate that its founders would not have welcomed this gesture from Foxe's college. Moreover, Brasenose numbered among its members in this period Alexander Nowell, later eminent as a divine and humanist, who was admitted as B.A. in May 1536, and became a Fellow in the same year. He is said to have lectured in the university on logic from Rudolph Agricola, which suggests that as an undergraduate he had not at any rate been shielded from humanist influences.[1]

It was Richard Foxe, however, who provided the definitive institution of Renaissance education in England. His Oxford 'bee-hive' was an English adaptation of the type of trilingual college already flourishing at Alcalá. A second northern version was established in the same year, 1517, at Louvain. It was clearly intended to fertilize the whole academic community, and in this apostolic attitude it surpassed St. John's at Cambridge. Foxe's public lecturer in Greek was to read to the university three days a week from an approved grammar, with some part of Lucian, Philostratus, or the orations of Isocrates. On alternate days he was to lecture on a variety of other authors, including Aristophanes, Euripides, Sophocles, and Thucydides.

Through the efforts of the Greek lecturer and of the Latin or 'Humanity' reader it was intended that the range of classical authors available to the university public should be greatly broadened. During vacations, moreover, the Humanities reader was to give special instruction in Valla's *Elegantiae*, the *Noctes Atticae* of Aulus Gellius (both favourite works of Erasmus), and Politian's *Miscellanea*. A third Reader in theology rounded out the typically Erasmian programme by replacing

[1] R. Churton, *Life of Alexander Nowell* (Oxford, 1809), p. 7.

traditional medieval authorities with Latin and Greek doctors from the humanist canon, especially Jerome, Augustine, Origen, and Chrysostom. The omission of Hebrew prevented Foxe's college from meeting the strict trilingual standard, but his was nevertheless the most radical departure from traditional studies yet seen in England.[1]

Foxe's plans were enormously enlarged upon for the next foundation, Wolsey's own Cardinal College. There is no opportunity here to probe the problems surrounding the close relationship between these two establishments, nor is there any need. There cannot have been much more than two or three years of settled teaching between the foundation of Wolsey's college and the involvement of the humanist group in the royal divorce proceedings in 1529. His contribution had the effect, however, of increasing the concentration of talent in Oxford and spurring humanist activity there.

These foundations should be seen in relation not simply to developments at Cambridge, but to almost a century of experimentation in Oxford beginning with the university's unsuccessful appeal to Duke Humphrey to establish endowed lecturerships. Edward IV and the Lady Margaret had provided help in theology, but the university was left to manage the problem for arts as best it could. It seems to have tried to meet the demand for new studies by supplementing the lectures of masters with free public lectures on specific subjects provided by bachelors who were supplicating for their M.A. degrees. It was thus that the first known course of lectures in Greek officially sponsored in the university was provided at Oxford during the Christmas vacation of 1512 by one John Bakeham, who apparently lectured on the alphabet.[2]

---

[1] T. Fowler, *The History of Corpus Christi College* (O.H.S., vol. xxv, 1893), and *Statutes of the Colleges of Oxford* (printed by Her Majesty's Commissioners), vol. ii (1853), (10).

[2] I am much indebted to a recent study by Dr. J. M. Fletcher, 'The Teaching and Study of Arts at Oxford, *c.* 1400–*c.* 1520' (Oxford D. Phil. thesis, 1962), on the whole subject of changes in teaching in this period. On the present point, pp. 52 and 102–3.

These attempts, many of which may have escaped the sporadic attentions of the scribes of the register, were supplemented by the private teaching of such men as Grocyn and foreign scholars like Stefano Surigone and Cornelio Vitelli. More effective had been the endowed lecturerships in natural and moral philosophy at Magdalen College, which anyone in the university could attend without payment. Foxe's provisions at Corpus were a major step forward, but his bachelors were intended to make use of the Magdalen lectures in addition to those supplementary ones which he provided on his own foundation.

By the early 1520's then, the tradition behind the new studies in Oxford was respectable, although their position was not secure until the foundation of Corpus Christi and Cardinal colleges. It is important to review the efforts which had preceded these foundations, however, before we can understand More's letter to the university in 1518, or account for the other evidence of a fairly widespread devotion to the new learning which we shall shortly consider. By the middle of the third decade such men as Thomas Lupset, Juan Luis Vives, John Clements, Nicholas Kratzer, and Simon Grynaeus had all been established at Oxford as teachers. Promising younger men were also appearing. At Corpus Christi College alone, John Helyar, John Shepreve (a future Regius Professor of Hebrew), Nicholas Udall, George Ederich (a future Regius Professor of Greek), and John Morwent Reader in Greek and secretary to Bonner, all began their careers at this time.

Between 1515 and 1520 then, both universities were provided with public lecturerships in Greek and mathematics as well as in divinity, and with collegiate foundations intended to act as nurseries of the new learning. Although the provision at Oxford was rather more lavish, St. John's at Cambridge, under the guidance of Fisher and the first President, Nicholas Metcalfe, accumulated a brilliant community. Only at Oxford do we have evidence of specific authors taught by these Readers, and that list is liberal and impressive. Whether or not it was fully implemented remains uncertain, and the only really conclusive evidence for the penetration of the new learning among the members of the universities must come from their personal records. Before we turn to these, it is worth remarking once again on the closely knit community of interest which stood behind this establishment of humanism in England. We might expect never to leave the court and episcopate, but it is remarkable to notice that we are never really far from the household of the Lady Margaret.

To begin a study of the individual members and their tastes we must resort to records which are intractable and undramatic, the archives of the university courts. Even these, however, despite their prevailing concern with the established curriculum and non-scholarly matters, can be called to witness the change in atmosphere. On the whole the Oxford registers, especially those of Congregation, are the more rewarding, since graces granted to those wanting special exemptions from the formal requirements are often detailed and informative. There is too little evidence to permit any sort of reliable statistical analysis, since, apart from gaps in the records, there is no reason at either place to suppose that all the graces granted were entered. In a general way, however, certain interesting features emerge.

The first is the very considerable exchange of students between Oxford and Cambridge, and between both and universities abroad. With such migration it would be natural to expect English scholars to have some awareness of continental thought. In the decade from 1501 to 1511, the Cambridge Grace Books record fifty-five men with Oxford degrees or undergraduate experience; in the next decade, thirty-four, and in the decade ending in 1531, eighteen. Lack of comparable information at Oxford makes strict comparison impossible, but from 1505 to 1511 there are twenty-six graces recording incorporations or Cambridge experience; twenty-eight from 1511 to 1516, and from 1521 to 1531, a period corresponding to the last decade mentioned at Cambridge, fifty-nine.

Conclusions about these figures, which may include duplica-
tions, must be very tentative, and it is certain only that they
represent a small proportion of the total number involved. If
one were tempted to speculate about the apparent shift towards
Oxford in the last period, it might be partly attributed to the
interest in Foxe's and Wolsey's foundations. Seven of Wolsey's
recruits, at least, have their graces entered together.[1]

Evidence for circulation between English and continental
universities is also striking. In these first thirty years of the
century the registers record studies at, or students arriving
from, a wide range of places abroad. The most popular foreign
centre, not surprisingly, is Paris, with Louvain next. A complete
list, however, must include the names of Bologna, Turin,
Ferrara, Orleans, Angers, Padua, Salamanca, Valencia, Siena,
Frankfort, Freiburg, Cologne, Montpellier, and such general
regions as 'Normandy' and 'Portugal' (or simply, *in partibus
transmarinis*). Perhaps the most interesting private case, among
these frequently unknown migrant scholars, is Nicholas
Kratzer's arrival in 1523 from Wittenburg.[2]

In the Cambridge registers such matters fairly exhaust the
information available for our purposes. The books recorded
there are few, and the studies required of a petitioner are
conveyed always by a conventional formula. At Oxford,
however, we are slightly more fortunate. The clerks frequently
specified the task required, revealing the books being lectured
on, and it is also possible to detect the university consenting
to the removal of teaching into halls and colleges.

This latter trend confirms what we know from other sources
of the collapse of the regency system. It most commonly
appears with civil lawyers, but in time inceptors in the arts
and even theologians are instructed to read their lectures in
their own halls and colleges. A fairly typical example would be
that of John Booth, B.A., in 1516, who, having been instructed
to read *De generatione et corruptione* in the Schools, later had this
condition deleted, provided he read 'in domo sua publice, quia

---

[1] Registrum H, f.v. 143.    [2] Ibid., fol. 100 ('Nicholaus Karche').

est exiturus universitate'.[1] In 1527 one Oliver Stonynge, M.A. and student of theology, is accorded a grace of which the final condition is that he read the lectures on the Epistle of Paul to Timothy 'in sua domo'.[2]

The books mentioned on such occasions provide few surprises, but help to fill in our impression of the official curriculum. The most interesting examples occur with the grammar graces. In the first register, from 1505 to 1515, there is mention of Porphyry, a comedy of Terence, the second book of the *Aeneid*, and Sallust. In the later register Priscian is added to these, with the *Georgics*, the first Eclogue of Vergil, Lucan, and (in 1532) the satires of Aulus Persius. In theology, in addition to the aforementioned Epistle to Timothy, there is the Apocalypse and, more interesting, Melanchthon's *Logic*.[3]

Thus even the central records of the universities provide a certain amount of useful evidence. They show a considerable exchange not only between Oxford and Cambridge but with the Continent in this period. At Oxford, too, it is clear that even the official record admitted a wider variety of teaching than the statutes envisaged, and that a considerable amount of teaching, even by regent masters, was moving into the colleges and out of the schools.

At first sight the impression gained from the colleges is like that given by the university registers to this point: at most, a modest response to new intellectual influences. In the older colleges few records remain to provide any evidence about teaching, but what there is gives a conservative picture. At Magdalen (the leading humanist college of the previous century) there seems to be little that is new, except in the grammar teaching of Magdalen College School. The most rewarding document is at Merton College, in its unique *Registrum annalium*, and here there is little to challenge the

---

[1] Registrum G, f.v. 279, f.v. 281.

[2] Registrum H, fol. 168. Another bachelor, William Haynes (f.v. 181), asked to be allowed to read in his hall rather than in the Schools, 'causa est quia ibi maiorem habebit frequentiam'.

[3] Ibid., fol. 168 (grace of Anthony Frabyser).

impression given by its very conservative library. The college seems to have been exposed (however ineffectually) to a Head with humanist interests in Warden Richard Rawlyns, who in a fulsome reply to the Fellows' welcome in February 1509 referred in passing to the evil fruits of the subtle science of Scotus.[1]

The college libraries provide an obvious source of information about official attitudes, and here the answer, at both Oxford and Cambridge, is that the colleges were conservative buyers. This is not in itself remarkable; when they did buy books they invested in standard authors and reference works, and it is evident that these would tend to lag behind student taste. We need a much finer impression of reading in these three decades than college libraries can provide, and we must find it in the fortunate survival of a few booksellers' lists and in the inventories of private libraries.[2]

Among the ten surviving booksellers' lists only one is truly informative. The chance preservation of John Dorne's record of sales for the year 1520 gives a tantalizing glimpse into an Oxford of which we know very little. It is unique at both universities, in size and comprehensiveness, and, a year after More's reproof to the 'Trojans' at Oxford, it shows a significant trade in the literature of the new humanism.[3]

Dorne's most popular items are the new Grammars of Stanbridge and Whittington, along with a mass of predictable

---

[1] *Registrum Annalium Collegii Mertonensis, 1483–1521*, ed. H. E. Salter (O.H.S., vol. lxxvi, 1923), p. 382. If, as Dr. Salter suggests, the hand of the original (in possession of the college) at this point is that of Rawlyns, it is distinctive and humanistic, and seems to reappear at fol. 240 describing the visit of Queen Catherine Parr with characteristic humanist extravagance. On other evidence of humanist teaching at Merton, see below, re Robert Joseph.

[2] On college libraries in this period, see especially the important Sandars Lectures of N. R. Ker, 'Oxford College Libraries in the Sixteenth Century', *Bodleian Library Record*, vol. vi, no. 3 (Jan. 1959); and W. D. J. Cargill Thompson, 'Notes on King's College Library, 1500–1570 . . .', *Transactions of the Cambridge Bibliographical Society*, vol. ii, pt. 1 (1954), pp. 38–54.

[3] Dorne's list is in *Collectanea*, i (O.H.S., vol. v, 1885), pt. 3, and *Collectanea*, ii (O.H.S., vol. xvi, 1890), App., for additions and corrections. On sales of Erasmus, *Bodleian Quarterly Record*, vol. i, no. 7 (1915), p. 176.

material which shows the background of tradition against which the changes were taking place. Change, however, there certainly is. The great popularity of Lefèvre d'Étaples's commentaries is one bond between these Oxford buyers and the pious reforming humanists around Marguerite of Navarre. Moreover, among those authors whose works sold at least ten copies in the year we find George of Trebizond (Trapezontius, the fifteenth-century translator of the Greek Fathers and Plato's *Laws*), Theodore of Gaza (through his popular Greek Grammar), Lorenzo Valla (principally the *Elegantiae*), Jean Quentin, who in 1536 became Professor of Canon Law at Paris, and finally, Luther and Aristophanes. The sales of Luther included two copies of *opera* and some controversial works, but the single most popular item is the *De potestate papae*, of which six copies were sold in the year. Along with two copies of the *Epistolae obscurorum virorum*, these provide the best evidence of a rapid response in the university to changes in opinion abroad.

By far the most striking evidence in Dorne's list of the change in Oxford opinion is the enormous sale of Erasmus. His popularity exceeds even that of Aristotle, and his works number some hundred and fifty in a total list of about two thousand items sold. The individual titles may be arranged in order of popularity as follows: the *Colloquia* (48 copies), the *De constructione* (*De octo orationis partium constructione*, 31 copies), *Copia verborum* (17 copies), the *Enchiridion militis Christiani* (15 copies), *the Apologia* (11 copies),[1] and the *Adagia* (9 copies). In addition his edition of the New Testament and the Paraphrases, in various versions, appear seven times each.

This suggests something more than an interest in tools of the grammar trade, although the *Adagia*, the *De constructione*, and the *Copia* were primarily such works. The *Colloquia*, however, as we have seen already, was an important vehicle for teaching

---

[1] Probably his defence of his New Testament edition, in *In principio erat Sermo*, published by Froben in 1520, or his apologia against Edward Lee's attack, also published in 1520. The alacrity of Oxford buyers in acquiring these items and Luther's works is noteworthy.

his philosophy, and even the *Adagia*, intended as a ready reference to classical lore, became in the course of its evolution a mine of its author's doctrines. Above all, the *Enchiridion* was of course the classical guide to Erasmian pietism, the manifesto of the movement. In the light of the interest of Oxford scholars in these works, the smaller sale of frankly controversial works by Erasmus assumes added meaning: the four copies of the *Dulce bellum inexpertis*, the three copies of the *Moria*, and the two of the celebrated (and anonymous) *Dialogus Julii*. Equally important here is the appearance of five copies of the *Dialogi Luciani*, fruit of his association with More, and, as we have seen, a touchstone of his critical spirit. It must be linked with the four copies of Lucian in Greek sold by Dorne as an important symptom of a new and satiric flavour in English humanist taste.

At Cambridge, our fullest information about reading comes from private scholars' libraries rather than booksellers' lists. The accidents of time and survival have rendered these records of doubtful value as a basis for comparison with Oxford libraries, since, by a curious accident, the extant records at the two universities never overlap in the period from 1500 to 1547. Dorne's list seems to be conclusive evidence that there was more humanist activity at Oxford than the surviving private inventories there indicate. On the other hand, the private inventories at Cambridge are the best clue to the thriving activity in that university.

At both Oxford and Cambridge, such inventories as we have before 1521 conform to a pattern in which the library of William Grocyn sets the master example.[1] It might be designated the conservative humanist library, and it shows little departure in choice of authors (if not of texts and commentaries) from fifteenth-century tastes. Commentaries on Justinian abound; Nicholas of Lyra, Aquinas, and Ockham are typical representatives in theology; and the favourite Fathers are Jerome, Augustine, Anselm, and Bede. Classical authors also follow the medieval tradition: Aesop, Cicero, Terence, Vergil,

[1] See *Collectanea*, vol. ii, pt. v.

and Aristotle. There is one appearance of Pico della Mirandola,[1] and the vernacular is represented by the *Canterbury Tales* and various chronicle collections. Inevitably the booklists of a departing generation will lag behind the fresh thought of the day, and the contrast between these libraries and the evidence of current interests from Dorne's list is precisely what we should expect.

Thus the sudden appearance in 1521 of a markedly different sort of library inventory at Cambridge is surprising until it is realized that its owner, Brian Rowe, Vice-Provost of King's, died in his mid-thirties.[2] His Greek books include a *Luciani dialogi*, manuals (among them that of Richard Croke), and Erasmus's translation of Theodore of Gaza's primer. He seems to have begun the study of Hebrew as well, and to have collected editions of the early Fathers which included those of Erasmus, whose version of the New Testament he also had. In addition to these there was a *Utopia*, a *Libellus de donatione Constantini*, and a 'Marsilius Ficinus parvum'.

The next inventory to yield such matters also comes from a Cambridge man, William Melton, Chancellor of York. The Library of this active divine, tutor to John Fisher, includes a 'Paraphrasis Erasmi', the *Heptaplus Johannis Pici Mirandula*, a *Utopia*, and a 'Novum Testamentum ad Grecam' (*sic*) as well as an unidentified work by Valla.

On the Oxford side, the series of conventional inventories continues to 1529, when that of Edmund Burton of Balliol, made about six years after he became M.A., shows a fresh pattern. The Burton list includes the Paraphrases on the Pauline epistles and a separate paraphrase of Matthew, a Greek Demosthenes, a 'dialogus Erasmi' (possibly one of the colloquies), an 'alphabetus grecus cum theodoris', an Erasmus New Testament and his *De misericordia Dei*, a five-volume 'novum et vetus

---

[1] In 1508; see W. A. Pantin, *Canterbury College, Oxford* (O.H.S., N.S. vi, for 1941), 1947, pp. 85–87 (item 36).

[2] F. J. Norton, in *Transactions of the Cambridge Bibliographical Society*, vol. ii, pt. 5 (1958), pp. 339–51.

testamentum Herasmi', the *Spongia* and *Adagia*, and a Greek dictionary, along with more conventional books. In another Oxford inventory of this year, made after the 'secret disappearance' of one William Wodrofe from his room and perhaps, therefore, indicating a young scholar's taste, we find Greek books and a considerable number by Erasmus, beside a Hebrew alphabet, Rudolph Agricola, and, once more, Valla.[1]

Thus even by confining ourselves to the lists which happen to be available from the period before 1530, we have sufficient evidence to confirm that of the Dorne inventory. The period after 1530 provides rich humanist collections indeed, especially at Cambridge, and these give eloquent testimony to humanist activity in the universities after the great foundations of the previous decade. To avoid blurring our picture of the state of humanist taste before the period of the most active domestic controversy, however, we shall confine ourselves here to the inventories which cannot reflect buying after 1530. In general, it seems evident that while we know little in detail about the progress of humanist studies during the first two decades, the foundation of new colleges and lecturerships at both Oxford and Cambridge from 1516 to 1520 produced a new burst of interest which extended far beyond the walls of St. John's College, Cambridge, and Corpus Christi and Cardinal colleges at Oxford. Moreover, this new interest was by no means purely literary, but shows a distinctly Erasmian flavour, using the term to imply some involvement with the evangelical commitments of the *philosophia Christi*.

At this point it is worth while stopping to consider the sentiments of Thomas More in his famous letter to Oxford in 1518. It contains much more than a defence of Greek as such. His language alone would assure us of his indignation at the conservative attack on Greek studies, if we did not know from Erasmus that the attack had been reported to the King by More

---

[1] The inventory of William Melton is in *Publications of the Surtees Society of London*, vol. lxxix (1884), pp. 258–9; those of Edmund Burton and William Wodrofe, respectively, are in Registrum EEE, fols. 299–300 and fol. 303.

himself and by Pace. In the indignation which underlies his irony, it is clear that it was ecclesiastical support of the 'Trojans' which exploded his exasperation, and his letter thus bears witness to the deep association of humanism and reform in this circle.[1]

More speaks for the whole party when he states his reasons for urging the study of Greek. He argues that a humanistic education trains the soul in virtue, and suggests moreover that the study of the arts is almost the sole reason why people go to Oxford, and that secular learning too can prepare the soul toward virtue, although it is not essential to salvation. This contention merges with another favourite Erasmian theme when he asserts that secular learning is positively essential if a preacher wishes to reach the ordinary man, and not merely academically trained listeners. It seems clear that More is thinking here not of familiarity with classical tongues as such, but with the 'natural theology' of the reformers against technical scholasticism. We expect then the view which follows, that classical philosophy is a natural preliminary to Divine learning, besides its importance as background to a proper understanding of the early sources of Christianity itself.

Finally, More is alert to, and annoyed by, the veiled attack on Erasmus.[2] In every respect the letter is a statement of the Erasmian position: resentment of clerical ignorance and of an abuse of clerical responsibility, advocacy of a lay, non-technical theology, and of a return to the original sources of Christian doctrine with all the resources of good scholarship to bring this about. Similarly, there is the familiar faith in the goodness and merit of the natural rational morality found at its highest refinement in pagan philosophers.

More's considerable prestige and influence was brought to bear on Oxford problems, then, not merely on behalf of a literary revival of classical studies, but to further the prospects of the evangelical reform party. To conclude the present

[1] Rogers, 60, ll. 60 f. Regarding the report to the King, Allen, iii. 948, ll. 190–3.

[2] Ibid., ll. 172–8.

discussion we may consult two sources which provide unexpected light on the depth and influence of this Erasmian
opinion in university circles and confirm that More was
defending a movement which even when he wrote was
probably well under way. The first is a manuscript letter-book
written by an Oxford-trained monk in the years 1530 and
1531. The second is a sermon of Savonarola published in 1509.
Between them they link the English humanist effort once more
to continental humanist activity and suggest that Oxford was
more influential in this realm of opinion than other evidence
would lead us to suspect.

The chance survival of the letter-book of Robert Joseph,
a Benedictine of Evesham, gives the first suggestive glimpse
beneath the surface of the activity disclosed in more conventional
records. If one were to guess at the existence of active humanist
communities outside the Oxford of Foxe and Wolsey, the
Benedictine house of studies, Gloucester College, would not
perhaps be the first choice. Yet Joseph's letters make it almost
impossible to resist the conclusion that between the years 1521
and 1530 at least, it was a place where a monk might learn a
great deal of Erasmian humanism.

Joseph's own career may be briefly given.[1] At the time when
he was collecting his correspondence for preservation in the
letter-book, he was Abbot's chaplain at Evesham. Most of the
letters in it were written, it seems, in 1530 and 1531, when
Joseph was about thirty years of age. He was educated at the
monastery and at Gloucester College, Oxford, from about
1523 to 1529, when he was recalled to Evesham. He was back
at Oxford again from 1533 to 1538, and took his Bachelor
of Divinity degree on 23 April 1535. By 1537 he was Prior of
Gloucester College, and he was at Oxford at the dissolution of

---

[1] For this information I am indebted to Dr. W. A. Pantin, who is editing
the Joseph letter-book with Dom Hugh Aveling for the Oxford Historical
Society. I have been permitted to use their transcripts of the original in the
National Library of Wales (Peniarth MS. 119, fols. 504–735) and all references
are to the epistle numbers of the forthcoming edition. The information about
Joseph and his correspondents is from the same work.

his house in 1540. He seems to have spent most of the rest of his life assisting at the church of All Saints, Evesham, and after 1559 he acted as Vicar of Cropthorne. He died ten years later.

His correspondents were for the most part monks in the closely settled regions of the Severn and Avon. His own house, with some thirty to forty men, left no records to suggest unusual intellectual activity there, although the number of men it sent to Oxford in these years exceeded its canonical quota. Moreover, the Winchcombe of Richard Kidderminster, who is numbered among the correspondents, was not far away. Nevertheless, the presumption that Joseph learned his humanism at Oxford is strengthened by his own handwriting, which is Gothic and presumably reflects the atmosphere of his monastic teaching.

The letters themselves, almost two hundred in number, are by Joseph alone. They reveal no one Oxford master, although two or three men receive a respect which shows their intellectual dominance. Moreover, his own comments to men at Oxford show that 'good letters' could certainly be acquired there and, like More, Joseph thinks that acquiring them is a principal reason for going there in the first place. Even without the other side of his correspondence, it is not difficult to conclude that Joseph was the most determined and probably the most accomplished advocate of the humanistic epistle in his group. However, it is equally clear that most of his correspondents, even if less accomplished, were men of wholly congenial taste whom Joseph respected. They seem to have been working at Greek among themselves, and the circulation of books between them is perhaps the best witness to the range of their tastes.[1]

Thomas Hearne, who knew of the Joseph letter-book and read some small transcriptions from it, commented that '... 'tis penn'd in a pretty good *Latin* Style, and far better than

---

[1] Titles of books mentioned in the correspondence include: Budé, *Pro Asse*; Erasmus, *Moria*; Pace, *De Fructu*; and authors: More, Aulus Gellius, Homer, Theophrastus, Baptist Mantuan.

might be expected from a Man bred up in a *Cloyster*, but the *matter* of it seems to be *mean* and *trivial* . . .'.[1] In fact Joseph is a disappointing source when we think of what he might have told us, and the effusions of his neoclassicism dilute matter already slight and conversational. This very style, however, is the best guarantee of the authenticity of his training, and we gain a strong impression of what the new learning meant to one Robert Joseph, B.D., monk of Evesham.

Most urgently, it meant literary excellence. Cajoling, protesting, urging his friends onward, Joseph gives us the unmistakable impression of a man with a mission. If the love of good letters is always uppermost in his mind, there are added emphases which we associate with the humanist reformers. An Attic style is the appropriate vehicle of salutary doctrine, and virtue and sound Latin are always bound together.[2]

For Joseph, it is Oxford—'Oxonia Minerva'—which is the source of such perfection. He is maddeningly vague about the sources in Oxford from which the best studies may be imbibed, but it is clear he finds tuition readily available. Special deference to certain men reveals a master–pupil relationship. George London at Gloucester College is one such man, and an Oxford secular, Master John Goodrich, seems to be another.[3] There is a general impression that the teaching of such men was informal, the private pursuit of those who were interested, probably undertaken entirely apart from the official course of studies.

If a man had to find his own humanist teachers then, such men seem nevertheless to have been well known and available. Joseph makes special efforts to place two young kinsmen with Oxford teachers who could guarantee them the sort of instruction of which he would approve. Richard Smith at Merton is asked to take Joseph's younger brother into his service and his clientele (*tuam clientelam*). Similarly, a Fellow of Merton, Robert Taylor, was canvassed somewhat later on behalf of a cousin, John Clark, to assure the best development of his talent.

---

[1] Hearne's edition of Leland's *Itinerary*, vol. ii (1711), p. 94.
[2] e.g. Letters 27 and 68.    [3] Letters 20 and 31.

Clark, moreover, is admonished to study in terms which make it clear that Taylor was his personal tutor.[1] Such developments confirm what we otherwise know of the collapse of the regency lecture system by the end of the fifteenth century, and make it easier to understand Joseph's own success in finding humanist teaching apart from the curriculum.

In the light of this, Joseph's enthusiasm for Erasmus is not surprising. The further question is whether or not this enthusiasm extended beyond the cult of 'good letters' to the *philosophia Christi*, and the answer seems to be that, in respect of the *doctrina evangelica*, Joseph's Erasmianism was rather a pallid affair. Apart from familiar criticisms of Scotist studies, his outlook was fundamentally conservative, and there are no references to the more aggressively critical aspect of Erasmus's work. Occasional passages make the loss of his correspondents' views tantalizing, since they suggest that some of his friends had imbibed more of the intellectual content of Erasmus than had Joseph.[2] The predominant impression, however, is that the world of these monasteries beyond the Thames valley was a very simple one.

This in itself is revealing for the present theme. Despite their love of literature and the anxious circulation of news, Joseph and his friends feel far from the great affairs of prelates and politics. Two events in particular are suggestive. The first concerns the notorious heretical will of William Tracy, just brought before Oxford University for adjudication. Joseph's reaction is entirely conservative and orthodox: heresy appals him. News of the will, 'full of heretical poison', has reached him by rumour, and if what he hears is true, Tracy, like Samson, will have done more harm to the Christian religion in dying than ever he did through his pestilential contentions when alive.[3]

[1] Letters 53 and 135.
[2] As in reference to the 'usual complaint' that Oxford men undermined the discipline of a monastic house; Letter 49.
[3] Letter 71.

On another occasion Joseph was sent heretical articles which had been fixed to the wall of St. Paul's in August of 1531. Joseph is amazed at the views and at the use of Scripture. The suggestion that fasting, pilgrimages, and other familiar customs might be threatened brings only the comment that this would seek to undermine the ancient order of the Church under pretext of piety. It is enough, in Joseph's views, to follow custom and the footsteps of our fathers in the faith into the celestial kingdom.[1]

The mind of Robert Joseph, then, was conventional and unexciting. We are chiefly indebted to him for leaving a record which shows how much of Erasmus was freely—if informally —available at Oxford, and for the light this sheds on other evidence about the wide penetration of the *philosophia Christi*. Moreover, the letters suggest a religious atmosphere in which conformity to Henry's purposes would be quite natural, and Joseph himself seems to have taken the Oath of Supremacy as a path to new employment in the Henrician establishment. The cause of good letters and good religion as Joseph seems to have seen it was little affected by the issues surrounding the royal divorce. In November of 1530, for example, he wrote to a friend at Oxford for fresh news about Wolsey, doubting the rumours he had heard of his fall. He prays that all this turbulence may be dispelled and tranquillity restored, so that they may all live devoutly in the service of God.[2] The incident suggests a temperament of which it might be fair to say that patient acceptance and hope of tranquillity would seem sufficient guides amidst the great affairs of Church and State about which he was so little informed.

A final clue to the unexpected ramifications of Erasmian reform opinion in England before 1530 is Pynson's publication in 1509 of Savonarola's *Sermo in vigilia nativitatis Domini*.[3] Apart from the subject, which in itself links English with continental reform opinion, the work is unexpectedly instructive

---

[1] Letter 104.                    [2] Letter 72 (30 Nov. 1530).
[3] *STC* 21800. See Appendix I.

about bonds between the university at Oxford and a reforming circle in London, and for that reason may be most appropriately treated here. It sheds light, however, on the whole matter of the views of educated circles in the period before the royal divorce controversy.

About the author of the work, who translated Savonarola's sermon from Italian to Latin, little can be gathered apart from what he himself tells us in the preface. He was Bartholomew Gallo, evidently an Italian priest from Mutila in Istria or Otranto, visiting and studying in England.[1] In his dedicatory epistle he pays a heartfelt tribute to two priests, John Yonge of All Hallows, Honey Lane, and Stephen Dowce of Whittington College, for their hospitality and their exemplary evangelical and pastoral activity. He knows of their interest in the sermons of Savonarola, and his present gift of one of these in a language which (unlike Italian) they understand, was intended to be followed by others on pastoral subjects.

The colophon salutation was addressed to the 'learned and upright' Thomas Scrow, evidently a fellow beneficiary of Yonge's generosity. In much more humanistic tones than the dedicatory epistle it congratulates Scrow on an opportunity to fulfil his ambition to study at Oxford, an opportunity evidently provided by Yonge's patronage. Gallo's dedication is dated 8 October 1509. Both Yonge and Dowce were Wykehamists who had followed the path from Winchester to Fellowships at New College, and in 1521 Yonge was to become Warden of that college until his death. It is possible to follow these associations into an interesting series of relationships.

About Scrowe little more can be discovered. In light of the foregoing it is conceivable that he was the Thomas Scrowe admitted as a Bachelor of Arts at Oxford in June of 1511 and dispensed on 19 October from further duties on the ground that he was going abroad.[2] If so, it would be interesting to know

[1] Gallo, if that was indeed his surname, does not appear in the Patent Rolls, the *Calendar of Letters and Papers of Henry VIII*, or Allen under that name or under 'Bartholomeus'.    [2] Boase, *Register*, p. 78.

something of his intended studies, and perhaps they could be conjectured from his associations.

John Yonge, M.A. and D.D., is the most prominent figure of the four involved here. He is not to be confused with his Wykehamist namesake, the patron of Erasmus who became Master of the Rolls and a practised royal diplomatist. A Winchester scholar in 1474, Yonge was admitted to New College in 1480, again as a scholar, and became a Fellow two years later. He seems to have vacated this position in 1502 for his London benefice at All Hallows, and in turn left that in 1510 to become Master of the Hospital of St. Thomas Acon, where for a time he was host to Ammonius. He retained this post, with the Wardenship of New College, until his death in 1526. Wood describes him as one of those responsible for preparing the university's statutes for examination by Warham in 1511, and refers to him again in connexion with the search for records of privileges in 1520, in the revived dispute with the town.[1] In the year of his inception at All Hallows, he was appointed by Edward Dudley director of studies to his son Jerome, along with John Colet, Bishop Fitzjames, and Sir Andrew Windsor. In 1513 he was consecrated Bishop of Callipoli in Thrace, as suffragan to Fitzjames, but his last five years were spent in Oxford at his old college. In 1514, as we have seen, he became a member of the influential circle in Doctors' Commons. On his death he left New College a copy of St. Augustine's works in the Basle edition of 1506 and, interestingly, a Savonarola *Opuscula* published in Paris and purchased by him in the year of its appearance, 1510. This latter work, now in the Bodleian Library,[2] contains a manual for confessors, heavily annotated by Yonge, the two famous Savonarola meditations on the psalms, 'Miserere mei Deus' and 'In te Domine speravi', a meditation on the simplicity of the

[1] Wood, *Annals*, bk. i, Anno 1520; E. L. Calverley (*DNB*) and Emden. Yonge was also an executor of Richard Sutton (Churton, *Lives*, App. xxii). On Ammonius at St. Thomas Acon, Allen, i. 232, 233.

[2] Seld. 8⁰ S. 20 Th.

Christian life, and an exposition of the Lord's prayer. Most interesting of all, it includes Savonarola's sermon, 'In vigilia nativitatis Domini coram fratribus habitus'. It would be difficult to construct a more eloquent handbook of the type of pietism favoured by the devout adherents of the Erasmian creed, and in the last item it confirms directly the assertions of Bartholomew Gallo about the interests of the circle.

The remaining member of the trio named by Gallo is Stephen Dowce of Whittington College. This second Wykehamist was admitted to New College in September of 1472, eight years before Yonge, and from 1488 to 1489 he was Sub-Warden of the college. In 1496 he was collated as Rector of St. Michael's Royal and Master of Whittington College, a post which he resigned on 30 November 1509. It was perhaps this occasion which the Savonarola publication was intended to mark. He died, in May of 1518, a canon of Wells.[1]

Whittington College dated from the early fifteenth century, when Sir Richard Whittington reorganized the foundation of St. Michael Royal to provide a collegiate institution for the care and instruction of the poor. It included a Master, four Fellows (who were to be Masters of Arts), and an almshouse for thirteen poor, supervised by a 'tutor'. Since Whittington's day it had grown slightly through subsequent endowments. Dowce's predecessor, Edward Underwood, D.D., had founded the *Fraternitas Sanctae Sophiae* for the reading of a divinity lecture there,[2] and in 1481 one Gilbert Heydock, D.D., had endowed two Fellowships to be held by Doctors or Bachelors of Theology (or at least Masters of Arts) to preach and give instruction to the people.[3] The last master of this foundation,

---

[1] J. Foster, *Alumni Oxonienses*, for Thomas Scrowe. On Stephen Dowce, R. Newcourt, *Repertorium Ecclesiasticum Parochiale Londinense* (1708–10, 2 vols.), vol. i, p. 493; *Acts of Court of the Mercers' Company, 1453–1527* (Cambridge, 1936), p. 339; *Registrum . . . Mertonensis*, p. 295 (where, on 3 Aug. 1504, Mag. Stephen Dowce borrows a *De Sphaera* by Theodosius of Tripoli).

[2] Newcourt, *Repertorium*, vol. i, p. 492; also J. Stow, *A Survey of London*, ed. by John Strype (1720, 2 vols.), bk. iii, pp. 3 f. and p. 37.

[3] Newcourt, loc. cit.; there was also a benefaction in 1508 to provide

with its long tradition of charity and preaching, was Richard Smith, Peter Martyr's predecessor as Regius Professor of Divinity at Oxford, and a recusant theologian to whose career we shall have occasion to return.

The link between Yonge and Dowce[1] becomes clearer when it is discovered that these two charitable foundations, Whittington College and the Hospital of St. Thomas Acon, shared the same patron. Both were governed by the Company of Mercers, the college since its foundation, the hospital since the twelfth century. Yonge was Fitzjames's own nominee for the difficult task of rehabilitating the impoverished hospital, and his ardour and efficiency in the task won him the full support of the grateful Company.[2]

In the Acts of Court of the Mercers' Company we find further evidence of a close tie between reforming clergy in London and this influential group of merchants, who in this period were also the ruling force in the Merchant Adventurers. It was to the Mercers, of course, that Colet had assigned the trust for his school at St. Paul's. Colet himself was a member, as his father had been a leading member in the previous generation. So also was Sir Thomas More, who acted as the company's agent in negotiation with the Pensionary of Antwerp over the permanent return of their mart to that city. Moreover, the membership of William Caxton gave the Mercers a certain humanist cachet which their earnest attention to Colet's school eminently justified.[3]

In the records of Yonge's installation there is interesting evidence of his character. Bishop Fitzjames's nomination of Yonge was read to an assembly of the company's livery in

a Reader in Divinity maintained by the Clothworkers' Company (Stow, (*Survey*, vol. iii, p. 6).

[1] For an exchange of letters between Dowce and Richard Mayhew, Bishop of Hereford, in 1511, see *Diocesis Herefordensis, Registrum Ricardi Mayhew* (Canterbury and York Society, vol. xxvii, 1921), pp. 47–50.

[2] *Acts of Court*, pp. 407–8.

[3] Ibid., pp. 61, 329–35, and 537. 'Maister Thomas More, gentilman', was made free of the Fellowship on 21 Mar. 1508 (p. 320).

September of 1510 in the presence of the Dean of St. Paul's, and Yonge's reluctance to undertake the commission was overcome by insistence of the entire membership, including the hospital's brethren. He was then installed three days later, and the minutes record that 'alle the hye mass time he satt in the quere lowest beneth the yongest brother'. Later,[1] after his successful and dedicated restoration of the hospital's activity and finances, he was again reluctant to leave his post to become Fitzjames's suffragan, '. . . whiche thynge he was loth to do for fere to Renne [run] in obloquy of the people, and for that shulde lett [hinder] hym muche in seyng to the profitt of this place which he much entendith . . .'.[2]

Yonge's reforming temper was not stifled for the sake of the company's own chaplains. In 1511 he began a campaign to reduce these priests to submission to his own authority in the company's chapel of St. Thomas, and he complained of their disobedience to the Court of Assistants.[3] While the matter was under examination he forbade them the use of the chapel and ventilated his grievances, in particular their failure to come to the choir on holy days, and to take an oath of obedience to his authority. He was entirely supported by the company, although the battle does not appear to have been won in his time.

With this information at hand we might expect Whittington College to figure occasionally in the religious history of the time, as indeed it does. The career of one John Standish, for example, illustrates the present discussion. He began at Brasenose College, following the course marked out at its foundation to a probationary Fellowship at Corpus Christi College. By the time he received his Doctorate in Divinity he was a Fellow of Whittington College, but according to Wood he retained a chamber at Brasenose College, 'when he receded to the university for conversation sake with men and books'.[4]

---

[1] Ibid., pp. 375–6.

[2] Ibid., p. 408. Here Yonge would consign the future elections of the Master of the Hospital, thus the custody of the foundation itself, to the Mercers' Company directly.

[3] Ibid., p. 392.      [4] Wood, *Athenae*, i. 235–8.

He conformed to each successive religious settlement, but his record in print is consistently conservative, beginning with a tract against the protestation of Dr. Barnes (which was answered by Coverdale) and concluding under Mary with discourses against indiscriminate circulation of Scripture in the vernacular, and on the unity of the Church (dedicated to Cardinal Pole).[1]

Rather more important in confirming the evidence put forward here is the association of Whittington College with pietistic publication. In 1504 a London printer produced some supposititious homilies of Origen. In the colophon it was stated that it was printed 'In alma civitate Londonense' at the request of Master William Merryman, a Fellow of Richard Whittington's college.[2] Similarly, at some unknown date, Pynson printed a life of Becket entitled *The Lyfe of the Blessed Martyr Saynte Thomas*, which from the first words of the text may have some association with the foundation of St. Thomas Acon.[3]

The enterprise of these London reformers, clerical and lay, linked with the world of the university, combines with Robert Joseph's letter-book and other evidence gathered here to strengthen the impression of a widespread Erasmian activity in educated circles, much greater than has been commonly supposed. Certainly it is clear that the Erasmian reform programme was not simply the private office of a small minority closely gathered around the court. The casual nature of much of the evidence makes it impossible to resist the feeling that much more is concealed from us by the haphazard survival of records. It is clear too, that movements of opinion by their nature leave few traces when they are unperturbed by official interference.

With such evidence as we have for background, however, it is interesting to notice how certain associations in the City

[1] STC 23209: *A lytle treatise agaist* [sic] *the protestacion of R. Barnes*, R. Redman, 1540; STC 23207: *A discourse wherein is debated whether the scripture should be in English*, R. Caly, 1554.

[2] STC 18846: *Omelia origenis de beata maria magdalena* [W. Faques?, 1504?].

[3] Dibdin, ii. 673.

of London recur in the course of the next years of religious controversy. The church of St. Thomas Acon reappears in the murder while on his way to mass of Robert Packyngton, M.P., a Mercer known to be hostile to the clergy, who 'used daily at foure of the clock Winter and Summer to rise and go to Masse at a churche then called saint Thomas of Acres . . .'.[1] Yonge's earlier church, All Hallows, Honey Lane, comes to the attention of chroniclers when its curate, a bookseller named Garret, was (in 1526) discovered retailing Protestant books throughout the country, including Oxford and (interestingly enough) Reading Abbey. Whittington College also reappeared, apart from the career of John Standish, when three of its fellows denounced a Scot, Alexander Seton, chaplain to the Duke of Suffolk, for heresy. He recanted at Paul's Cross in 1541, but Foxe reported that one of the Fellows of the college, a John Huntington, was later 'converted to the same doctrine' himself.[2]

It is clear, certainly, that the City of London was bound to be an active centre of controversy and debate. It is also clear that the merchant interest was seriously involved in the reforming activities of the Erasmian humanist community. In conclusion, some small idea may be gained of the probable intensity of this activity, and of the intimacy of association which makes it now so difficult to trace, when it is realized that the churches just mentioned, with others equally famous in these days, St. Lawrence Jewry, St. Mary Woolchurch, and St. Stephen Walbrook, were all within a short walk of one another, and, incidentally, of the London house of Thomas More, The Barge, located just next to the Walbrook, across from the church.

[1] Hall, 'xxviii yere', p. 824.  [2] Foxe, v. 448–9.

# 5

## ERASMIANS AND POLICY:
## THE CRISIS FROM 1529 TO 1534

WITH the year 1529, the twentieth of Henry's reign, the humanist community felt that hopes long deferred were at last to come to pass. Wolsey had fallen, and his fall released a pent-up flood of Erasmian activity in which future party alignments were as yet quite indistinct. Three men in particular signalled the change in atmosphere by their new tasks. In Paris, Reginald Pole pursued the King's mission to the scholars of the university with every appearance of enthusiasm. In the royal Council, Stephen Gardiner, Wolsey's scholarly protégé, consented to become chief Secretary, conducting all communication with his former chief. And in the great offices of State, England's most famous lay scholar, Sir Thomas More, accepted the Chancellor's seal formerly held by the Cardinal Archbishop. It is More's vigorous denunciation of Wolsey in Parliament which reveals the attitude of this group to the fallen giant whose unused powers had so long delayed the cause of religious reform.

In the months that followed the hopes of the reform party were expressed in a rush of activity and writing. It is this humanist activity which truly characterizes the period, providing the setting for the great public events surrounding the divorce: the Submission of the Clergy; the Statutes of Annates and Appeals, and finally, in 1534, the Act of Supremacy. In 1535 Thomas More and John Fisher died for the cause of the Roman Primacy, and the humanist community confronted the gravest crisis it would face. It survived, divided but not shattered, and the energies of most of its members were directed into enthusiastic support of the King's policies. An era had been closed, however, a time of optimism, unanimity, and zeal which could never return. Yet the achievement of this time had momentous consequences for the future, and it is this achievement which we must now examine.

The first two or three years after the fall of Wolsey clearly reveal the scale of an evangelical reform influence in educated circles in England. The writings of the humanists were diverse, undoctrinaire, loyal, and vigorous, and the satisfaction of the leading men at Wolsey's fall from power is so apparent that it seems almost to obscure the forebodings over the divorce. Hall's report of More's speech in Parliament, supported by the record of the Parliament Roll and, in its more hostile reaches, by Chapuys, must be taken as an accurate account, however ungracious it may seem. The bitterness of his comments on 'The grete wether which is of late fallen as you all knowe' may perhaps in part reflect sympathy with the Queen's sentiments towards Wolsey, but by and large More spoke for all who were sympathetic with the need for reform. Eighteen years later Erasmus recalled that Wolsey had always feared More, although he recommended him as his successor.[1] It is easy to guess that the shrewd Cardinal saw More's worth, not only in his ability but in his conservative mind, which made him the layman best able to temper the forthcoming attack on the Church.

Erasmus's own delight at these events, made doubly agreeable by the promotion of More, was broadcast to his wide circle of correspondents.[2] Only the exile of Vives in 1528 for his sympathy with the Queen presaged the dispersal of the humanist community. From England, Chapuys reported unanimous approval of the selection of More on the day the Seal was transferred (25 October 1529), and even the Imperial ambassador's confusion about Pace's likely return to court as a consequence of Wolsey's fall is eloquent of general expectation that there would be a new order in which the humanist

[1] Allen, x. 2750, ll. 51–53; Harpsfield, pp. 38–39. On More's speech, Hall, p. 764; *Span. Cal.* iv (pt. 1), 211.

[2] Allen, as above, and viii. 2263, 2287, 2295, &c.

community would take a leading part. The character of the new order is in fact quite evident: it was to be lay and reforming. Norfolk, Rochford, and Suffolk were the leading peers, More and Gardiner the chief royal servants. Gardiner's ability and sympathies made him the ideal cleric to fit harmoniously in this group. Du Bellay, the French ambassador, reporting Wolsey's fall even before the Seal had been transferred to More, believed that the principal aim of the Lords was to attack the wealth and power of the Church, asserting that they avowed this ambition openly.[1]

Although these Erasmian aspects of the period have been considerably obscured by preoccupation with the royal divorce, they make the best account of policy and events. In the first years at least, the common concerns of the humanists are more important than their differences. For example, the disagreement of More and Gardiner on the King's 'great matter' could not disrupt their harmony on other issues. They can be found at once collaborating to save Wolsey's college, with its great promise for education and reform. This appropriately foreshadows their later co-operation in 1532, when together they resisted the King's demand that Convocation should surrender its right to legislate in matters of faith and morals. Even after the Royal Supremacy was proclaimed and Gardiner had taken the oath which More refused, More, who always insisted on the purely personal nature of his decision, was found speaking well of him.[2]

With Wolsey out of the way, the reform proposals of 1529–30 had new meaning. The limit imposed on bishops' fees for probate, the prohibition of pluralities (designed to prevent their further increase, presumably while other remedies were devised), and the penalties for non-residence and against clergy engaged in commerce, all express the Erasmian spirit. So do the

[1] *LP* iv (3), 6011: 17 Oct. 1529. On the 22nd he reported that he thought no priest would again have the Seal. See the Rastell Fragments (Harpsfield, App. 1, p. 222) on Henry's determination to have a lay Chancellor.

[2] *LP* iv (3), 6666, 6679 (7 and 11 Oct. 1529); P. Janelle, *L'Angleterre catholique à la veille du schisme* (1935), p. 152.

complaints against the system of ecclesiastical justice. Seemingly, the Church was to be purified and chastened, not paralysed. It was the beginning of a programme which might have brought about a peaceful reorganization of the sees and of the whole position of Church courts in the country, if the King's divorce had not been leading him into more radical courses. But when next Parliament met, in January of 1531, it was to impose the threat of *praemunire* on the clergy and to proclaim Henry 'Supreme Head'. For such a measure, unanimous Erasmian support could not be assumed. With the further legislation and the Submission of the Clergy, signs of serious dissension appeared, and More's resignation in 1532 foretold the coming crisis.

Nevertheless, it is important not to interpret the period simply in the light of later events. Pollard's view that 'Englishmen are singularly free from the bondage of abstract ideas, and they began their Reformation not with the enunciation of some new truth, but with an attack on clerical fees',[1] puts the matter in a different way. The concerns of the first several months after the convening of Parliament in 1529 were entirely Erasmian, with royal power being invoked to correct the failures and abuses which Wolsey's enormous power had left neglected. Within this atmosphere of acceptable Erasmian reform grew those more radical proposals augmenting royal power which were neither inherent in nor markedly repugnant to that accommodating creed. Even later, when the issue of doctrinal orthodoxy was faced and settled on the most conservative lines (it is conspicuous that Henry's 'freedom from the bondage of abstract ideas' did not impair his vigorous prosecution of heresy at every stage of his career), the Henrician Church retained its Erasmian complexion, producing schemes like those for the reorganization of bishoprics which seem to show its positive aspirations.[2] There was more in

[1] A. F. Pollard, *Henry VIII* (revised ed., 1951), p. 218.
[2] *LP* xiv (2), 429, 430 (1539), and Addenda I (2), 1457. Cotton MS. Cleo. F. II, fol. 238, 'A litle treatie called the newe additions', seems to be the

Henry's policy than the advantageous use of anti-clericalism to augment his own power. Useful as that lay sentiment was to the Government, it alone cannot explain Henry's programme, or the support which he attracted. The factor binding together the attack on clerical privilege, vernacular Scripture (not in Tyndale's heretical version, it should be noted), and the doctrinal orthodoxy of the Six Articles is Erasmianism.

For many of the men who would contribute to the formation of this new policy, Wolsey's fall produced the additional excitement of uncertainty about their own careers. Until this moment his patronage had been the broadest avenue to promotion, the source of leisure for study. For the two main households of Thomas Winter and Reginald Pole it involved reorganization and a search for fresh support. Pole, more secure than Wolsey's illegitimate son, managed to preserve his connexion with the King through to his final departure from England as a royal pensioner in 1532. Thomas Winter, stranded by his father's disgrace and death, astutely applied to Cromwell. It appears, however, that for the time being his real patron may have been, not the future Secretary, but the (at this time) much more influential Stephen Gardiner.[1]

The moment when these men would be recruited for official service was still in the future; for the present the royal nurseries were still being stocked. The records of the Privy Purse and Household show four scholar-pensioners at Oxford, two at Paris (John Mason and John Bekinsau), one at Cambridge, and another at St. Paul's School.[2] Mason had come from Abingdon and the Abbot's School to be appointed (after graduation from Oxford) King's Scholar at Paris, probably on the recommendation of Thomas More. His great career as a diplomatist would carry him into the reign of Elizabeth, and his step-daughter

heads of a tract printed by Berthelet in 1531, adumbrating parliamentary reform of the Church on markedly Erasmian lines.

[1] *LP* v. 1453, from Padua, 20 Oct. 1532.

[2] J. Payne Collier, ed., 'The Household Book of Henry VIII', *Trevelyan Papers* (Camden Soc. v. 67, 1857), pp. 136–80. N. H. Nicolas, ed., *The Privy Purse Expenses of King Henry the Eighth* (1827), Nov. 1529 to Dec. 1532.

married John Cheke.[1] Bekinsau had come to humanism through Winchester and New College, and in Paris read the Greek lectures in Francis I's royal foundation. In time his learning was brought to bear in the King's cause, with his *De supremo et absoluto Regis imperio*.[2] Maintaining these men cost the king little, however, compared with support of the household of Reginald Pole, which sustained a whole school of dependants in Italy, and with them the King's highest hopes for learned assistance.

If these men are added to the account of the humanist community in the last chapter, we obtain a general picture of the humanist scene on Wolsey's fall. It is time now to examine their activity in the period roughly down to the resignation of More from the office of Chancellor. In doing so we shall discover a marked unanimity of concern for pietism, education of the nobility, and loyalty to a monarchy apparently dedicated to Erasmian reform. In brief, the established concerns of English humanism and the close association of humanist activity with the court now bear fruit in an instinctive rallying to the King's support. It is not merely personal career-seeking which is responsible, important as that was. Humanist concern with the social order, with religious reform, and with the great matter of the 'commonwealth' clearly began in the period just described. When the extent of this concern has been exposed, we shall turn to the years from More's resignation to his execution, to see how the momentous events of these few years began to divide a hitherto united society, and how a rising bureaucrat of genius, Thomas Cromwell, turned this division to the King's—and his own—advantage.

Within four months of Wolsey's death, which occurred at the end of November 1530, the title of 'Supreme Head' had been added to the King's style. Immediately there appeared a

[1] Mason's shock at the imprisonment of More and Fisher is recorded in a letter to Starkey, 3 July 1535, printed in Ellis, 2nd ser., vol. ii, no. cx.

[2] STC 1801: Berthelet, 1546. For a further phase of Bekinsau's career, see Chapter 8.

flow of official propaganda which was destined soon to swell
to a torrent. The direction of this official publication can be
quickly described. In the first place, there is strong insistence
on doctrinal orthodoxy against the Lutheran threat. In 1528
the King's letters to Luther, published by Pynson, mark the
same aspect of royal policy as the proclamation on heretical
books of the year following: it is stern resistance to Protestantism, coupled now with increasing measures of State control
over the press. By 1530 the decisions of universities disposed to
favour the King's cause were gathered together under the supervision of Edward Fox as the *Gravissimae totius Italiae et Galliae
Academiarum censurae* and printed by the King's Printer, Thomas
Berthelet. The next year they appeared in English translation.[1]

The official apology thus combined resistance to Protestant
heresy with proclamation of learned support for the King's
quarrel with Rome. A new phase emerged with two treatises
of Christopher Saint German and *A glasse of the truthe*, by an
unknown author. Saint German's legal approach to the
problem of the Royal Supremacy was to be a cornerstone of
the Henrician apologetic, and he and Gardiner with Edward
Fox would carry the main burden of formulating a theoretical
justification in public tracts. The story of this development is
already familiar, and it is no part of the present study to deal
with political apologetic as such.[2]

More interesting from the humanist point of view is *A
glasse of the truthe*, since it introduces a vein of significant writing outside the realm of political theory. It is clear that this
work was produced under the close supervision of the King,
if not actually by Henry himself, and it represents the first fruit
of a purely humanist discussion. Concerned only with the
status of the King's first marriage and with the limits on papal
dispensing power, in its last pages it presages future developments. Lamenting the treatment the King has received from

---

[1] *STC* 14286 and 14287.
[2] See F. Le Van Baumer, *The Early Tudor Theory of Kingship* (New Haven,
1940), and the works of Pierre Janelle and Gordon Zeeveld.

Rome, the pamphlet's spokesman observes darkly that a way 'might be found well enough to end the matter honourably within the realm, if the whole head and body of the parliament would set their wits and good wills unto it'.[1] The King and Parliament should then press the metropolitan clergy to disregard their (improper) oaths to the papacy in order to bring a settlement in the realm. In his analysis of this treatise, Janelle suggested that the author had his eye on the 'advanced thinkers' of the day, meaning those inclined to Protestantism, and adduced as evidence the repeated appeals in the work to the attitude of early popes against those of their modern successors, and the attention paid by its author to the usages of the primitive Church.[2] As we have seen, however, such appeals were by no means the exclusive property of those Protestant advocates against whom Henry was otherwise taking such energetic measures. They were the instinctive arguments of the whole humanist reform group, and in *A glasse of the truthe* we have the first official utterance of (and to) this community, applied to the specific problem of the royal divorce.

The Government's interest in the treatise is sufficiently revealed by the attempt to circulate it in learned circles. A second edition was printed in 1531 or 1532, and in the latter year a French translation was issued as well.[3] About the time that version appeared, Richard Croke wrote to Cromwell from Oxford that he met with scepticism when he tried to represent it as the King's own work. Nevertheless all agree, he observed, that it has done more to advance the King's cause than all other publication and preaching. Many had been converted by it, as the bearer of the letter, a young man learned in Greek and Latin, could testify. And at this point the bearer, so recommended, is put forward as a man Cromwell might consider for support.[4]

---

[1] *STC* 11918: Berthelet [1530]: N. Pocock, *Records of the Reformation* (Oxford, 1870), vol. ii, no. cccxx, p. 418.    [2] Janelle, op. cit., p. 246.

[3] *STC* 11919; Baumer, op. cit., App. A.

[4] SP 1/71, fol. 52. Ellis, ser. iii, vol. ii, no. cxciii.

Official publication of course is the essential background for an examination of humanist reaction to the King's policies, but by concentrating on it to the exclusion of less formal productions we may gain a distorted view of an aggressive propaganda machine coercing opinion along highly theoretical lines. It is clear, however, that alongside these government pressures there was a significant offering of voluntary activity which cannot be explained in terms of an omnipotent court party. In fact, it is at this moment that the Erasmian group meet governmental need with a body of doctrine, at once apposite and ill defined, which announces the future core of Henrician belief for the ordinary Englishman.

In 1529, at the outset of our period, the first important use of Erasmus came from a Protestant exile. Clearly calculated to appeal to the English reader, the work was a translation of the *Paraclesis*, entitled *An exhortation to the diligent studye of scripture*. The translator was probably William Roy, whose name has been associated with *Rede me and be nott wrothe*, a vigorous satire of the previous year against Wolsey and the clergy. Printed along with 'an exposition on the seventh chapter of the first epistle to the Corinthians', the *Paraclesis* was published over the Protestant press signature, shared by Tyndale, of 'Hans Luft, Marburg', in fact the press of Johannes Hoochstraten of Antwerp.[1] Despite the ban on most works from this press, the *Paraclesis* soon made its way in England, clearly with tacit official approval. When it next appeared in 1534 the accompanying commentary on Corinthians had been replaced by 'An exhortacion to the study of the Gospell' taken from Erasmus's preface to his Paraphrase on St. Matthew.

The appearance in English of this basic handbook of Erasmian reform doctrine is another reason to regard the year of Wolsey's fall from power as a turning-point in the growth of English humanism. An additional instalment of the same kind,

---

[1] *STC* 10493; *NB* 2982. Robert Wyer evidently printed two editions of the *Paraclesis* in 1534, and there was another in 1548 (*RSTC* 10493.5, 10494, 10494.5).

Vives's *Instruction of a christen woman*,[1] appeared from Berthelet's press in 1529, translated by Richard Hyrde, the tutor to
More's household. He had earlier written the introduction to
Margaret Roper's translation of Erasmus's treatise on the Pater
Noster, and the new work was published posthumously, since he
died in 1528 while pursuing the King's business with Gardiner
and Fox in Orvieto. The subsequent history of his 'yong maid
Frances', mentioned in the Pater Noster preface, is symptomatic of the history of this group. She was the daughter of Suffolk
and the King's sister Mary, and in 1534 she was married again,
this time to Henry Grey, Marquis of Dorset, and became the
mother of Lady Jane Grey, whose humanist and Erasmian
education is famous.

With the following years of 1530 and 1531 we discover
a harvest of writing which forms a singularly suitable accompaniment to the official productions already mentioned.
Pietistic works, for example, include a new edition of Bona-
ventur's *Vita Christi* and the anonymous *Declaracyon and
power of the Chrysten fayth*, which, although apparently Protestant in its emphasis on salvation by faith and being 'borne
a new', contains no attacks on Rome.[2] There is a life of Saint
Margaret, de Worde's *The myracles of oure blessed Lady*, and
another anonymous work *The xii profytes of trybulacyon*.[3] More
important as evidence of Erasmian interest, the Syon circle is
remarkably active. Fawkes printed *The Myrroure of oure Lady*,
an anonymous work whose first Prologue is to the monastery
of Syon itself, and the colophon attributes the printing to the
Abbess and to the General Confessor, John Fewterer.[4]

Whoever wrote this work, we know that Richard Whitford,
the only Syon monk to publish regularly under his own name,
now brought out his *Werke of preparacion vnto communion*.
Combined with *Werke for housholders*, it appeared in successive

---

[1] STC 24856.
[2] STC 3267: de Worde, 1530; STC 5160: R. Wyer [1530?].
[3] STC 17326 (Redman), 17541 and 20413 (de Worde).
[4] STC 17542: R. Fawkes, 1530.

editions.[1] Its success is significant, since it was concerned not only with good preparation for reception of the sacraments, but with the proper Christian government of the family, a development of the ideals of More and Vives. As a handbook of family devotion, including a system of daily meditation, it was one of the most notable contributions to the Erasmian ideal in England. In the same year appeared Whitford's translation of the 'Golden Epistle' of Saint Bernard, printed by Thomas Godfrey, with the *Four revelations of Saint Birget*.[2]

The work of translating Erasmus seems to have proceeded with a blend of amateur enthusiasm and careerist zeal. From an unknown press and hand there appeared, in London, *L. Lactantii Firmiani carmen: ab Erasmo editum*, a work of the fourth-century Christian humanist and apologist, Latin tutor to Constantine's son Crispus, and the humanists' 'Cicero Christianus'.[3] The amateurs were apparently responsible also for the anonymous version of Erasmus's Latin edition of Plutarch's *The gouernaunce of good helthe*, from Wyer's press in 1530,[4] and for the interesting *The Table of Cebes the Philosopher*, from Berthelet about this time.[5] This latter work was a small triptych including, besides Cebes, Plutarch's 'How one may take profite of his ennemies', the Latin version of which had been dedicated by Erasmus to Henry VIII, and Erasmus's own 'Comfortable exhortacion against the chances of death'. It was the joint production of Sir Francis and Sir Anthony Poyntz. According to the dedication, it was made by the former at the request of his brother, and was now seen into print by the latter, presumably in memory of Sir Francis, who had died in 1528. Both were experienced royal servants, Sir Anthony being at this time on a commission to inquire into Wolsey's possessions.

However, it was a future professional translator of great

[1] *STC* 25412 (R. Redman, 1531), 25422 (de Worde, 1530), 25423 (de Worde, 1533), and several undated editions.
[2] *STC* 1911.
[3] *STC* 15118, and Allen, i. 49, l. 100.
[4] *STC* 20061.                                    [5] *STC* 4891.

importance who in 1531 provided Redman with an English version of Erasmus's treatise *Epystle in laude and prayse of matrymony*.[1] This was the work of the most prolific popularizer of Erasmus whom England produced, Richard Taverner. We shall have occasion to return to Taverner often hereafter, but the appearance of his version of the *Encomium Matrimonii* in 1531 provides a significant clue both to his early career and to the whole humanist enterprise in this period. A Norfolk man born in the very first years of the century, Taverner was one of the Cambridge recruits found by Wolsey for his Oxford college. He was likewise one of those involved in the alarm about heresy there in 1529. His career after that is in some doubt, but he seems to have gone abroad, perhaps after taking a Cambridge M.A. in 1530. Wood records his proficiency in philosophy, Greek, and divinity, and his study at some period in a Chancery Inn, the Strand, from which he entered the Inner Temple, 'where his humour was to quote the law in Greek, when he read anything thereof'. At any rate, he seems to have been abroad in 1532, for he then wrote to Cromwell as a person unknown and in great distress who would be of service. He mentions his study of English law, the loss of his former patron, and his conviction that he must first communicate with Cromwell before asking for the King's favours. His hope, he continues, is not for wealth, but rather for the service of the commonwealth.[2]

A second letter survives, written shortly after the first. In it Taverner thanks Cromwell ('o vir incomparabilis') for having spoken to the King himself in order to relieve Taverner's grave want. Moreover, at Cromwell's instigation, it seems that the Duke of Norfolk promised an annual stipend which would abundantly fill Taverner's needs.[3]

Predictably then, the dedication of the *Laude and prayse* makes public record of his gratitude to Cromwell for rescuing him from his plight, and provides a rare but important clue

[1] *RSTC* dating; *STC* 10492.     [2] SP 1/73, fol. 143.
[3] Ibid., fol. 145.

to the inception of a deliberate policy which helped to place Erasmian thought in the fore as the positive doctrine of the Henrician settlement. It is impossible to doubt from the preface that this particular work was chosen by Cromwell, or at least in consultation with him. After the complimentary introduction, Taverner goes on to reflect on the work itself and its importance to the people; he considers

the blynd superstition of men and women which cease nat day by day to professe and vowe perpetuall chastyte before or [sic] they suffyciently knowe themselues and thinfirmite of theyr nature, which thyng . . . hathe bene and is yet unto this day the rote and very cause original of unnumerable myscheues. I pray our lorde Jesu of his infinite goodnes to prouyde som spedy reformation, whan it shalbe his pleasure.

We apparently have here the very work which sealed the bargain between Cromwell and Taverner in this year. Not only does it anticipate the whole temper of the ensuing religious changes, it specifically anticipates the general assault on the religious houses. The attainment of the secretaryship was still three years away, but it is an obvious sign that Cromwell was, and was known to be, a coming man.

Taverner's translation was not alone. It appeared within months of another significant work, *An Epystell unto Christofer bysshop of Basyle concernyng the forbedinge of eatynge of flesshe*.[1] In this characteristic work on the right use of fasting as a help to 'good lyveng', an unexpectedly wider range of topical problems in the Church are treated. Although it is desirable for a commonwealth to keep good form and the traditional order, yet 'the Sabbath is made for man', and an excess of holy days keeps people from their work, which the poor can ill afford. Similarly, the observance of chastity among priests, commendable when they were few and holy, is becoming a scandal: 'there is an innumerable multytude of prestes everi-where. And among so many howe gret scarcenesse is there of them which lyueth chastely.'

[1] *STC* 10489: T. Godfray, [1530?].

In effect, the pamphlet is a plea for that basic Erasmian principle of concentration on essentials of religion, on the need to avoid mistaking permissive, man-made regulations for the heart of Christian truth. The complexity of rules for fasting is ridiculed and compared unfavourably with the liberty of the apostles, of which St. Paul spoke. Moreover the fasting law favours the rich over the poor, even to the purchasing of pardons in Rome. No one, surely, can deny that papal decrees on that subject, as on clerical marriage, are only man's law; how can anyone be bound to Hell for contravening such rules? Bishops are supposed to save men's souls, not condemn them, and papal powers should be properly used to provide equity in ecclesiastical law—exceptions for the aged, children, the poor, and others in like need. Backbiting and slander are much worse abuses than are failures with observances like these, and constitute the eating of *man*'s flesh: 'They cal them Lutherians and heretykes whiche doth eate fleshe . . .', but these same critics overlook the basic law of charity. In conclusion, there is a strong recapitulation of the need to place things of true importance to the fore, and to bind men's consciences on those matters only.

Although the translator of this work is unknown, the contemporary commissions to Taverner strongly suggest that its unknown author was working with official inspiration. Taverner himself is the link with a Cambridge scholar who, on 2 July 1533, wrote to Cromwell seeking to attract attention by a significant translation of Erasmus, this time the lives of Vitruvius and Colet. The scholar was a Martin Tindall, Fellow of King's College, Cambridge, and formerly a King's Scholar at Eton. He had taken his B.A. in 1531, about the time he acquired his Fellowship, and from 1537 to 1538 was headmaster of Eton, probably in the absence of Nicholas Udall. He later became master of the school at St. Albans. In his letter to Cromwell he observed that once Erasmus's Lives of these men were translated, '. . . thei, but speciali Collet, may walke a brode in his owne contre, where he may visite his kinffolke, his frends, his familieres, and his scoleres, or rather godsones (for full many he did regender and get to god) for all be not yet dede . . .'.[1] Appealing to Cromwell's good reputation as a sponsor of poor scholars and clients, and especially as the former benefactor of his own brother, John Tindall, now dead, he asks that Master Taverner, who last year was Master of Greek in Cambridge and is now Cromwell's client, should oversee the work. He also refers (with a significance which becomes clearer later in the present chapter) to offering the work to 'Mr. Marshall'. In brief, the episode testifies to the peculiar value of Colet to this group, and provides a precise link between Erasmus and two important members, Taverner and Marshall, of Cromwell's circle.

Enough has been said to show that already by 1531 Cromwell was emerging as a semi-official sponsor of translations from works of Erasmus which had immediate relevance to the reform of the English Church. The translations we have discussed were associated by date of publication with two other humanist works, more completely original, which in these two years of 1530 and 1531 help to demonstrate the way in which the English humanist tradition is developing its native bent. They are John Palsgrave's *Lesclarcissement de la langue francoyse*, from the press of John Hawkyns, and Sir Thomas Elyot's *The boke named the gouernour*, published by Berthelet the next year.[2]

Palsgrave's treatise on French grammar, beautifully produced and carefully edited, was a pioneering achievement in the study of vernacular language. The author was a graduate of Corpus Christi College, Cambridge, and of the University of Paris. Schoolmaster to the Lady Mary, sister of Henry VIII, he accompanied her to France when she married Louis XII, and was mentioned by More in 1516, when he remarked to Erasmus that Palsgrave was about to study law at Louvain. More interesting is a later appeal by Palsgrave to More for support

---

[1] Harleian MS. 6989, fol. 45. For his career, Sir Wasey Sterry, *The Eton College Register (1441–1698)* (1943).

[2] *STC* 19166 and 7635.

in the humanistic education of Henry's illegitimate son, the Duke of Richmond, against the opposition of clerical tutors.[1] After this long career as tutor in court circles, he was collated to St. Dunstan in the East by Cranmer in 1533.

The *Lesclarcissement* has no intrinsic reform interest, but it reveals an Erasmian link with Leonard Cox, the schoolmaster of Reading Abbey, whose own career is important in our story. Cox wrote a prefatory Latin poem to the work, as did a certain Galfridus Troy and Andrew Baynton, one of his courtly pupils. The author's own prefatory epistle to the King, to whom it was dedicated, reveals the preoccupation of the whole group with the education of the nobility. The epistle implies that the work was undertaken at the King's request, and it was protected with a patent monopoly for seven years under the Signet. Andrew Baynton's epistle 'To the young gentlemen, my lorde Thomas Hawarde, my lorde Geralde and maister Charles Blount sonne and heyre to the lorde Mountjoye his late scole felowes', provides its own link with the More–Erasmus circle. And finally Palsgrave himself, like Richard Taverner earlier, acknowledges indebtedness to the Duke of Norfolk. It is interesting as additional light on the temper of this group to discover that an extended satire on Wolsey, headed 'A brief remembrance how our Commonwealth hath been ordered since my Lord Cardinal had the chief authority', is endorsed 'The last matter found in Palsgrave's coffer'.[2]

The second Berthelet publication, Elyot's *Governour* of 1531, is a magisterial statement of the Erasmian educational and political programme, with an importance now generally recognized. Elyot's own humanist education was conducted possibly at Oxford, certainly in the More circle and the Middle Temple; and like so many others, he began his career in

---

[1] Allen, ii. 499, and Rogers, Letter 168.
[2] *LP* iv (3), 5750. The three pieces are in Palsgrave's hand and the first is signed by him. They are apparently drafts of a satirical dialogue on Wolsey's career.

Wolsey's patronage. In 1528 he obtained the wardship of a cousin, son of Reginald Pym, revealingly christened Erasmus, who was destined to be the grandfather of John Pym. His brief career as senior clerk of the King's Council had been brought to an abrupt conclusion by Wolsey's fall, and the new work was clearly an astute bid for renewed royal recognition.[1] His past career and presumably his known sympathies seem always to have tainted him as a suspect Catholic. At any rate, he was forced at one point to make open declaration of his views and to submit his books for Cromwell's inspection. The suspicion may be further explained by the recent identification of Elyot with 'Papyrius Geminus Eleates', the author of *Hermathena* and of the preface to an anti-Lutheran tract, *Propugnaculum*, published by Pynson in 1523. The latter tract itself was by Edward Powell, Canon Residentiary of Salisbury, who refused the Oath of Supremacy about this time, and was hanged with two other Catholics at Smithfield in 1540.[2]

The *Hermathena* bore two dedications to Pace. In form it was an imitation of the dialogues of Lucian, like some of Elyot's English treatises soon to be published. If accurate, the identification not only places Elyot with leading figures in Pace's circle, but shows him an almost ideally representative figure of the moderate reforming party. In the Pace circle his associates would have included Robert Wakefield, shortly to emerge as an available advocate for the King's cause, Thomas Hurskey, head of the Gilbertines in England and an intimate of Pace, and John Clerk, the Catholic writer and secretary to the Duke of Norfolk, who in 1542 translated *A Treatise of Nobility* from the French. This association with Pace's friends also makes it likely that Chapuys was correct in 1531 in placing Elyot in the

[1] S. E. Lehmberg, *Sir Thomas Elyot, Tudor Humanist* (Austin, Texas, 1960), pp. 12–13 and 49–51.

[2] C. W. Bouck, *Transactions of the Cambridge Bibliographical Society*, vol. ii, pt. v (1958). *STC* 11719 and 20140. Powell, a Fellow of Oriel College, Oxford, was an advocate for Queen Catherine and wrote a tract in her favour recorded by Stow (*Annales of England*, ed. 1615, p. 581). He was executed in 1540 for refusing the Oath of Supremacy.

Boleyn circle, since Thomas Boleyn was Wakefield's greatest patron. At any rate, Elyot was chosen in that same year to join an embassy to the Imperial court, and was subsequently commissioned to assist Stephen Vaughan in pursuing Tyndale. In 1534 Chapuys included him among those who would join an uprising inspired by the Emperor on behalf of Queen Catherine. His subsequent works are the utterances of a conservative member of the middle party, veiled criticisms of the more radical aspects of the new order, openly hostile to Protestantism.

Apart from these major works, the humanist group produced a scattering of other writings which have an Erasmian flavour. At least two Lucian items appeared in these years: an English translation of the *Necromantia* from John Rastell, possibly translated by the publisher, and in 1531 a new edition of the *Luciani dialogi aliquot per D. Erasmum uersi*. And it may have been at this time that Berthelet printed an English version of the *Cynicus*, which has been ascribed to Thomas Elyot.[1] With these appeared Colet's famous sermon to Convocation, seemingly a kind of touchstone for reform-minded Englishmen, translated by Thomas Lupset and issued by Berthelet in 1530.[2]

On the pietistic side, the indefatigable Richard Whitford of Syon added to his 1530 production the following year with Thomas à Kempis's ... *the folowynge of Cryste*, the first English version since the Atkinson translation sponsored by the Lady Margaret, which this one displaced.[3] The same year Syon produced *Pylgrimage of perfection* in a new edition.[4] The author of this treatise was identified by Whitford in *A dayly exercyse and experyence of death*[5] as 'William Bonde, bacheler of devinyte

---

[1] *STC* 16894 (Berthelet); J. Wortham, 'Sir Thomas Elyot and the Translation of Prose', *Huntington Library Quarterly*, vol. xi (1948), pp. 219–40, and Lehmberg, op. cit., p. 18, n. 40. The other two Lucian items are *STC* 16895 [1530?] and 16892 (R. Redman).

[2] *STC* 5550.     [3] *STC* 23961 (Wyer).     [4] *STC* 3278 (de Worde).

[5] *STC* 25414 (J. Waylande, 1537). Dibdin records other Syon works for these years which have evidently disappeared since, notably no. 381 (*Saint Bonaventure his lessons . . .*, in 1532), no. 382 (a 1532 edition of Whitford's *Pomander of Prayer*), and probably no. 379 (*The abbaye of the Holy Ghost* in 1531).

and one of his devoute bretherne lately departed'. Bonde was a former Fellow of Pembroke College, Cambridge, and one of the Cambridge group who joined Syon, where he died in 1530.

At this point it should be clear that the years immediately after Wolsey's fall from office witnessed a remarkable publication enterprise which truly deserves the name 'Erasmian'. It is sponsored by humanists committed to reform in Church and State. Only a small (if significant) part of this production can yet be traced to direct official sponsorship; most was the voluntary achievement of men dedicated to reform, or to advancing their careers, or to both. As to their interests, at this stage the dominant impression is one of general unanimity. Differences of taste and quality can of course be detected, as between a Taverner's eager pamphleteering in the Government's interest and the work of More himself, who by this time had wholly given himself over to the fight against Lutheran heresy. For the moment, however, latent disagreements about the King's divorce were almost invisible beneath the common solidarity against decay and corruption in Church and State. Their hope was to advance true religion and learning through vernacular treatises on education, grammar, devotion, and government, through the study of the three tongues, and through loyalty to a reforming monarch who had given new hope to his subjects with a new generation of counsellors.

The Erasmian reform movement was scarcely well begun when the King's own decision to move into radical courses threatened its survival. The Submission of the Clergy, which induced More's resignation on the plausible pretext of ill health, is an obvious parting of the ways which makes it possible to discern two currents of opinion beginning to divide the hitherto united humanist society. The one is formed by a minority of discreet but ever more intransigent opponents of the royal divorce policy, now confronted with growing radicalism in the King's circle. The second is the migration of humanists to the patronage of Thomas Cromwell, who, as we shall see, comes to his new office in 1534 with a formidable propaganda group already in his clientele.

A general idea of the range of opinion which emerged from the humanist group under the impact of the royal divorce crisis may be gained by looking briefly at the response of four celebrated scholars. The first of these is Cranmer, whose début in public life was attributed to a characteristically Erasmian suggestion that the King should consult, not courts and canonists, but 'learned' opinion. It is this which initiates the resort to theologians in England and at universities abroad, and starts a propaganda campaign based on the claim to a 'learned consensus' against the authority of Rome.

The second figure is William Tyndale. A disciple of Erasmus in his youth, he is the first of the major English scholars to turn to Protestantism. Cranmer was to follow his course, without ever finding the single-minded conviction of Tyndale. Tyndale's controversy with More is thus a symbolic prologue to the story of the middle party in England. It is also oddly appropriate that Tyndale, like More, awoke fatal displeasure in the King by conscientious disapproval of the divorce.[1]

The third figure is that of John Fisher, venerable, innocent, learned, and ascetic, who, while More was still keeping his bargain with Henry and maintaining public silence on the divorce, proclaimed his hostility abroad. Later, interrogated by the Council, he admitted having written seven or eight books against the divorce, at least two of which found their way into the hands of Chapuys.[2] The only one to be published appeared, appropriately, at Alcalá, the scholarly home of Imperial Erasmianism, in 1530.

Finally there is the enigmatic Reginald Pole, the doyen of the younger generation of scholars. Though he was willing to assist in the canvass of other scholars' views, his own at this time were kept from contemporaries and ultimately from future generations as well. His unwillingness to commit himself

---

[1] In *The practyse of prelates* (STC 24465, 1530).
[2] *LP* iv (3), 6199, 6596, 6738; v. 460.

became obvious to the King when Pole refused York, where as Archbishop he would have been an admirable member of the team which the King was creating with More, Gardiner, and, more recently, Cranmer. The 'book' by Pole on the divorce which Cranmer was set to summarize seems to have been an apologia to the King for this refusal, and whatever Henry's true opinion, he let it be the occasion for a reconciliation, agreeing to support Pole in his return to study abroad. When Pole left England in January of 1532 he had still all his benefices and the full royal pension of £100. His dissent from the King's policy had been cautiously conveyed, but there would be no further confidences until his study produced the book which finally shattered the English humanist circle.

Among them these four men, all immediately involved in the divorce controversy, defined the spectrum of opinion which was to emerge from the humanist circle. It is our task now to trace the emergence of these views, and to begin with the first symptoms of a serious rift in the group.

The warning is given in the spring of 1532, with Pole's departure for Italy after refusing the see of York, followed in May by More's resignation and the retirement of Stephen Gardiner, in disfavour, to Winchester. The successful stand of More and Gardiner in the Lords against the Submission of the Clergy had settled their fate. Even if Henry's more radical measures of the moment were being adopted only as bargaining positions with Rome, the two men who had been Henry's first choice in forming his new administration refused to be associated with them. In the next year the exposure of the affair of Elizabeth Barton enabled the Government to discredit this group in a bid for public and humanist support.

The formation of an official party of learned supporters is heralded by the timely death of William Warham, just when the aged patron of Erasmus was at last preparing a general public disavowal of the King's recent policies towards the Church. It enabled Henry, with the co-operation of an alarmed and indecisive Clement, to install in his place Thomas Cranmer, who would henceforth do the King's will from Canterbury. Cranmer's appointment seems to have begun a general rally from the Erasmian group which helped to offset the great blow to unity and prestige from the defection of More and Fisher, Pole, and (for the time being) Gardiner. The names of the King's recruits include Thomas Starkey, Richard Moryson, Richard Taverner, Leonard Cox, Thomas Paynell, John Rastell, Stephen Vaughan, Robert Wakefield, William Marshall, Thomas Swinnerton, Richard Sampson, Edward Fox, and David Clapham. It was an able committee, and for the collecting of most of it Thomas Cromwell was undoubtedly responsible.

Serious preparation of an official apologetic line had probably begun in 1533, and its main lines can be briefly sketched. The principal works were Richard Sampson's *Oratio* and the important *Opus eximium* of Edward Fox, both published in 1534. The former work, described by Janelle as 'l'œuvre d'un humaniste', contains little of theoretical importance, being written in the form of an exhortation to pious and unconditional obedience to the King. Fox's work was more significant, a repertory of arguments in favour of royal against papal supremacy, seemingly a summary of views canvassed throughout the previous two or three years.[1] Both these works emerged from several months of concentrated effort, the true story of which may never be unravelled. The Record Office and Cotton manuscripts contain most of the evidence in a vast number of anonymous tracts in various hands, many incomplete, many much corrected, almost all unidentifiable. Derby's hand is frequently present, and no doubt many others also represent royal clerks and secretaries. Tunstall's is another which provides a more direct tie to the court clergy. It is clear that it is this group which carried the burden. Sampson and Fox were both members of it, and so was Stephen Gardiner, who, after much

[1] *STC* 21681 ('R. Sampsonis oratio qua docet Anglos regiae dignitati ut obediant . . .', Berthelet, 1535?) and Janelle, op. cit., pp. 271 f. Fox is *STC* 11218 (Berthelet, 1534).

deliberation, would finally decide for the King and produce the most original work of theory to be associated with the Henrician settlement.

There is much evidence that the Government sought widely for support, from Imperialist theory to (less predictably) Wycliffite materials. The official case can also be seen in growth, from the 'Document of the year 1531', printed by Pocock, to the 1533 *Articles deuisid by the holle consent of the Kynges counsayle*, where most of the topics developed by Fox and Gardiner are adumbrated.[1] On all other matters than the Roman question, strict orthodoxy was stressed. Thus in 1532 Robert Wyer published an English version of the Articles of 7 October 1531, proclaimed by Charles V to assert his authority over the Lutheran heresy.[2] It is clear that such a work must at least have had royal approval if not actual royal sponsorship. Similarly, in 1533 there was an inhibition of all seditious preaching, which cancelled existing licences and required the issue of new ones by the episcopal conservatives, Longland, Gardiner, and Stokesley. All preachers were instructed to avoid non-Catholic doctrine and the affairs of the Prince.[3]

The need for a strong apology was pressing. In these same years the opposition to the Government was by no means silent, although it was subdued. The State Papers reveal in a variety of places that a sermon campaign, probably spontaneous, was giving the Government concern. At the same time an outspoken attack was made with the *Invicta Veritas* of Queen Catherine's brilliant chaplain, Thomas Abell, published abroad in the spring of 1532.[4] It was this work which caused the drawing up of the Articles of the following year.

At this critical time, then, the work of the More circle and of Syon is of considerable importance. William Rastell, who may be considered the unofficial publisher of the conservative group, cannot have given much comfort to the Government. In 1532

[1] *STC* 9177 (Berthelet).    [2] *STC* 5016.
[3] Lansdowne MS. no. 1045, fol. 60.
[4] *STC* 61 (Luneberge, 1532).

he brought out '. . . two fruytfull sermons' of John Fisher and More's *Confutacyon of Tyndales answere*,[1] both by known critics of the King's policy, although they were works in themselves within the bounds of acceptable doctrine. In the same year the Syon circle produced the fourth book of Whitford's translation of Kempis, treating 'specyally of the sacrament of the aulter', and the first edition of Whitford's popular *The Pype, or Tonne, of the lyfe of perfection*.[2] This pietistic work, written some years before, was now issued with avowedly controversial purpose. In the preface to his readers Whitford announced that it had been thought necessary to print it 'Bycause of these newe fangle persones whiche in dede ben heretykes. . . . Here is somwhat spoken in our commune tonge that all you may knowe all their false and subtyll deceites and the rather beware of them.' The readers are also directed to watch for his forthcoming translation of the 'Imitation'.

The year 1532 saw the printing of one more patently orthodox work on doctrine, *The Interpretacyon and sygnyfycacyon of the Masse*, directed 'to all good Catholyke persones, to knowe howe they shall devoutly here Masse . . .'. In effect it seems to have canvassed all the sacraments, and it was written by 'frere Gararde, frere mynoure of the ordre of the Observauntes'.[3] Gararde seems otherwise to have escaped notice in an order which was distinguished above all others for vocal and heroic opposition to the King's policies.

The following year was even more productive for these Erasmian conservatives. Rastell published four of More's controversial works, including the *Apology*,[4] and Whitford's *Werke for householders* was reissued in a corrected version by Wynkyn de Worde.[5] The most interesting phenomenon,

[1] *STC* 10909 and 18079.

[2] *STC* 23962 (R. Wyer) and 25421 (R. Redman).

[3] Dibdin, iii, no. 940 (R. Wyer).

[4] *STC* 18078; also the *Second parte of the confutacion of Tyndals answere* (*STC* 18080); *The debellacyon of Salem and Bizance* (*STC* 18081); and *A letter impugnynge the erronyouse wrytyng of J. Fryth* (*STC* 18090).

[5] *STC* 25423.

however, is the appearance in this year of two works by Thomas More's son John, the rather obscure figure known to us chiefly through the polite references of More's celebrated acquaintances. Erasmus had dedicated two works to him, the *Aristotelis opera* of 1531 and the *Commentarius in Nucem Ovidii* of 1524. In the next year he would receive another considerable tribute, the dedication of Simon Grynaeus in his preface to the Basle edition of Plato in Greek.

Although it is amply clear that John More was overshadowed by his awesome relationship, in this year, 1533, at the age of twenty-four, he himself produced two learned translations which are unusually revealing about the concerns of the circle. The first was an English version of Damião de Goes, *The legacye or embassate of prester John unto Emanuell, Kynge of Portyngale*, published by William Rastell. The work itself, according to the preface, was brought to him by a 'special familiar friend', presumably from Antwerp, where the Latin version was published the autumn before.[1] Written by a devoted admirer of Erasmus, it combined an account of the Christian kingdom in Ethiopia, awaiting union in common cause against the Moslem and pagan world, with an appeal to Catholic Christendom by the exiled Archbishop John Magnus Gothus of Uppsala, whom Goes met in Danzig when Gothus was in flight from Lutheranism in Sweden. The work was dedicated to the archbishop, Goes urging that steps should be taken to send missions to the Lapps as potential allies complementary in the north to the Ethiopians in the African east.

The whole work reflects preoccupation with the disintegration of Christian unity, combined with exhortation to tolerance of inessential differences of observance when agreement can be reached in things necessary to salvation. It thus embraces the

---

[1] STC 11966. *Legatio Magni Indorum imperatoris Presbyteri Joannis ad Emanuelem Lusitaniae regem, Anno Domini MDXIII*, Grapheus (Antwerp), 1532. On Goes, see Bataillon, *Études sur le Portugal au temps de l'humanisme* (Coimbra, 1952). I am greatly indebted to Professor Francis M. Rogers of Harvard University for drawing my attention to the wider significance of More's translation.

theme of *adiaphora* which was so much developed by Melan-chthon, but which was common to the entire Erasmian commu-nity as something fundamental to both reform and Christian unity. John More's preface also seems to emphasize the natural law principles and the exploration motif which are so conspi-cuous in the *Utopia*. In fact, the whole account of the fabulous kingdom becomes a description of a somewhat bizarre Chris-tian Utopia. The appearance of this singular work in the More circle at precisely this moment is striking evidence that their unease was finding veiled and skilful expression. Moreover, it struck upon an interest already expressed in England. In 1520 John of Doesborowe in Antwerp had published a small volume, *Of the new landes and of the people founde by the messengers of the kynge of portyngale*,[1] containing an account of the semi-fabulous kingdom from the reports of the Portuguese ambassadors.

John More's other translation, also published in 1533, was *A sermon of the sacrament of the aulter*[2] by Frederick Nausea, preacher in the cathedral at Mainz and later Bishop of Vienna, a prominent Catholic champion, with Cochlaeus, against the Protestant reformers. It provides confirmation, if any were needed, of the conservative purpose of the Goes translation.

The activity of the More circle in these years did not end here. At the turn of the year 1533–4 Rastell published the work which finally aroused the Government, the *Answere to the . . . poysened booke* (of John Frith).[3] The coincidence of publication of this treatise by More with More's imprisonment was more than Cromwell could overlook, and although Rastell managed to avoid serious consequences, he deemed it prudent to withdraw from his printing career.

The *Answere* did not appear alone. Three devotional works were published, at least two of which can be connected once again with Syon. One is of uncertain origin, the *Deuout treatyse*

[1] STC 7677. Compare with the Protestant work *The original and sprynge of all sectes and orders* (STC 18849, Nicolson, 1537).

[2] STC 18414 (W. Rastell).

[3] STC 18077; actually published before Christmas of 1533. See Rogers, letter 194.

*called the Tree and xii frutes of the holy goost*, for an unidentified 'relygious woman' by an anonymous author.[1] The general spirit of the work would make attribution to Syon seem plausible. Certainly the house produced a posthumous work of William Bonde, *A deuoute treatyse for them that ben tymorouse and fearefull in conscience*, intended, 'yf yt be well red ouer and folowyd . . . [to] brynge y reders out of all scrupulosite of conscience and sarvyle feare and brynge them to the holy feare and love of almyghty God'.[2]

With Bonde's work appeared that of a confrère, the Confessor General John Fewterer, whom we have met more than once already. Fewterer, like Bonde, had been a recruit for Syon from Pembroke College, Cambridge. An intimate of More, Fisher, and Houghton, he was an 'ambiguous figure in his last years', finally yielding to the King. His present work was a translation of *The myrrour or glasse of Christes passion*, published in December 1534 by Redman.[3] The dedication is very revealing. Made to Lord Hussey, diplomat, soldier, and royal councillor, it provides a direct link, through that gentleman's earlier associations, with the group of reforming laymen associated in the foundation of Brasenose College. In 1533 Hussey had been made Chamberlain to the Princess Mary. In 1534 Chapuys suggested that his loyalty to the King was wavering, and in January 1536 Hussey asked to be excused from the forthcoming Parliament on grounds of ill health. He was present when it met, perhaps in response to strong intimations of royal disfavour if he should be absent, but his wife Anne, daughter of the Earl of Kent, was sent to the Tower at the same time for calling the Queen Dowager's daughter 'Princess'. Although he remained apparently loyal during the 1536 risings, in the spring of 1537 he was arrested for complicity in the Lincolnshire rising, and, over pleas of ignorance of the whole affair, was convicted and executed.

---

[1] *STC* 13608; 2 colophons: (i) R. Copland, 1534; (ii) R. Copland and M. Fawkes, 1535.        [2] *STC* 3275: M. Fawkes [1534?].
[3] *STC* 14553; Knowles, op. cit., p. 213.

One final work completes the picture of this conservative humanist response to the King's challenge. Published also in 1534 by William Rastell, it is *A letter of a yonge gentylman*, by Germain Gardiner.[1] Outspokenly conservative, it managed narrowly to avoid open confrontation of the King's cause by attacking the heresy of Frith and the whole Protestant community at Cambridge. It was written by Stephen Gardiner's nephew, and in part forms a defence of the Bishop of Winchester's pains to convert the Protestant advocate he had condemned. As a work clearly aimed at the younger generation of university graduates, however, it reveals the sense of crisis in the humanist community. Its author, significantly, was one of those involved later in the conspiracy to overthrow Cranmer.

It is clear from this that the Government had reason to press its humanist supporters for publication, and it is against the background of the conservative writing we have just examined that we must now see the active policy of recruitment upon which Cromwell embarked in the years 1532 to 1534. Foxe long ago pointed out that Cromwell 'always retained unto him and had about him such as could be found helpers and furtherers of the [gospel]; in the number of whom were sundry and divers fresh and quick wits, pertaining to his family, by whose industry and ingenious labours, divers excellent ballads and books were contrived and set abroad, concerning the suppression of the pope and all popish idolatry'.[2] Certain select members of his circle have been studied in the related problem of political apology, but the Paduan recruits from Pole's household, important as they are, by no means do justice to the breadth of Cromwell's scheme.

The first humanist to come to view after Richard Taverner was a man won over from the Queen's cause. This was Robert

[1] STC 11594.
[2] Foxe, p. 403. On Cromwell's plan of campaign, see Janelle, op. cit., pp. 204 ff. He cites (p. 205, n. 1) *LP* vi, no. 1486, a memorandum of the Council for 2 Dec. 1533, Cotton MS. Cleo. E. VI. 317. However, he clearly refers to *LP* vi, no. 1487, which he quotes and which is Cleo. E. VI. 312.

Wakefield, canonist and Hebrew scholar, who had numbered among his pupils Reginald Pole, Pace, and Thomas Hurskey, the head of the Gilbertines in England. In 1519 he had been Professor of Hebrew at Busleiden's College at Louvain, and from there had migrated to St. John's, Cambridge. A varied career in England and on the Continent finally led to an invitation to succeed Reuchlin at Tübingen, where he introduced the study of Syriac and Arabic. Early in 1523 he was appointed by Henry to teach Hebrew at Cambridge, and the next year was made a royal chaplain.

His patrons included Thomas Boleyn and John Fisher, and by the time he and Pace were consulted about the divorce he had published his *Oratio de laudibus trium linguarum*, delivered in Cambridge in 1524, and was preparing the *Syntagma de hebreorum codicum incorruptione*, which appeared about 1530.[1] Initially he favoured the Queen, but was soon won over, perhaps (as Wood says) 'courted by fair promises'. Certainly the influence of Pace must have been important, and the *Kotser codicis*,[2] published about 1532, was the result. It placed the impressive scholarly authority of Wakefield behind the proposition that the King's first marriage was prohibited by law both natural and divine. Appended to it were Pace's letter of 1527 commending Wakefield to the King for his learning, and a letter from Wakefield himself to the King, pleading his initial ignorance of the carnal intercourse alleged between Catherine and Prince Arthur, by way of excuse for having begun as her defender. He also promises an answer to Fisher's book defending the marriage. Like Pace's letter this is dated 1527, and both are dated from Syon.

The second official recruit to appear in this year is Stephen Vaughan. Although no humanist, his connexions and activities are important. He was one of Cromwell's closest friends and most reliable agents, and at this time was King's Factor in Antwerp. His background was mercantile London, possibly

[1] *STC* 24944: de Worde [1524] and 24946 (de Worde).
[2] *STC* 24943 (Berthelet [1532?]).

including St. Paul's School. His father's connexion with the Mercers' Company adds interest in light of the connexions of that guild exposed above. His early association with Cromwell may have come from this business world, and by 1524 he was in Cromwell's service. He seems to have adopted Protestant reforming views very early, and by 1525 was feeling the uncomfortable attentions of Thomas More for his heterodox opinions. In 1531 he was charged by Henry to persuade Tyndale to return to England and retract his views, and it is this activity which is our major concern.[1]

Early in 1532 there was an exchange with Cromwell which is slightly mystifying. Two letters dated 22 and 26 January reveal that he has been given the task of writing a book of some sort for Cromwell, and that the task is a very uncongenial one. He is insistent that his authorship be kept secret, if possible even from the King. In part this may be because Cromwell has called 'hasty' for it, and it is a complicated matter 'in a daye or twain to be well stody[ed]'.[2] It is clear that he has promised the work to the King, and finds the matter repugnant, since it may bring him in discredit among those 'by whome I have had my lyvyng'.[3] Pollard assumed the work to be one on commercial matters, certainly the subject on which he was an expert. The existence of an entry among Cromwell's documents for 1533, for 'Articles devised by Mr. Stephen Vaughan for a Commonwealth', suggests that it might have had a slightly broader purpose, and that Cromwell had compelled his old friend to contribute to the high political discussions in his clientele.[4]

Although the work cannot be more closely identified, it is interesting to know of this activity because of Vaughan's negotiations with Tyndale, which occupied him through 1531 and 1532. Vaughan's best efforts with his outspoken friend were unavailing, and finally drew upon him the royal displeasure. Tyndale's reply to More, which Vaughan had sent before

[1] Ellis, ser. iii, vol. ii, letters cxciv (to Henry VIII) and cxcvi (to Cromwell).
[2] Cotton MS. Galba B. x, fol. 2.      [3] SP 1/69, fol. 82.
[4] LP vi. 299, p. 137.

publication in an effort to appease Henry, had the opposite effect to the one intended. But the whole episode, taken in conjunction with the above commission to write a treatise on the 'Commonwealth', with others to secure copies of Ockham's *Dialogues* and the Latin text of Melanchthon's Augustana Confession for Cromwell,[1] is significant background to the publication in England of a translation of Erasmus's *Enchiridion*, a matter with which we must deal separately.

The next year, 1533, saw further additions to the circle of Cromwell's writers. At the beginning of the year, Berthelet, already King's Printer, offered his services to Cromwell, thereby doubling his connexion with official policy.[2] Thomas Starkey, from Pole's Padua household, addressed a legal opinion on the divorce to Henry, in a bid for attention which was followed by a treatise on the nature of true policy. In December Richard Moryson, also in Pole's service, wrote to Cranmer for patronage. And finally, one of the few known direct commissions from Cromwell was issued in 1533, that to William Marshall.

The work of Starkey and Moryson has been clarified already by Zeeveld. The best-known work of Marshall is his translation of the *Defensor Pacis*, which appeared in 1535 but, as the correspondence of April 1534 makes clear, was ready in 1533.[3] It was only one of several important tasks for Marshall. In his first letter to Cromwell he mentions an accompanying translation of Valla 'on the Donation of Constantine': 'Surely I thinke there was never better boke made and sett forthe for the defasing of the Pope of Rome than this.'[4] This work was immediately sent to press, and appeared the same year under the imprint of Thomas Godfray.[5] It included the text of the

---

[1] STC 12510: *Disputatio inter clericum et militem* (Berthelet [1531?]; English editions 12511 and 12511a). Also Janelle, op. cit., pp. 262, 277. For the Melanchthon, Ellis, ser. III, vol. ii, no. cxcvi, dated 19 June 1531.

[2] *LP* vi. 72 (25 Jan. 1533).

[3] STC 17817: Wyer for Marshall, 1535. Compare Baumer, op. cit., p. 44, n. 27. SP 1/83, fol. 58.

[4] SP 1/83, fol. 57.                         [5] STC 5641 (1534).

Donation, Valla's treatise on it with a preface by Ulrich von Hutten, and Nicholas of Cusa's opinion on the Donation written for the Council of Basle, and concluded with the comment of 'Antony archebysshope of Florence on the same donation . . .'.

After introducing this work to Cromwell, Marshall's letter continued: 'Erasmus lately wrote a worke upon our comen Crede and ten commaundements dedicate to my lorde of Wilshire, whiche I wille have from the prynters assone as god sendeth to me money wherewith to sett theym and assone as I can gett theym to be bounde I wolle sende to you a cople.' And he concludes his plea for £20 with 'I trust you wolle lyke the translation of the saide two bokes, they have coste me bothe labor and money and that largely'. The identity of the translator of the Valla treatise on the Donation, then, as of the *Playne and godly exposytion of the commune crede and of the .x. commaundementes*,[1] seems clearly to be William Marshall of the *Defensor Pacis*.

The date 1533 on his translation of Erasmus's *Symbolum Apostolorum* confirms that lack of funds had delayed the release of a work already printed when he wrote to Cromwell. The title preserves the fact that Erasmus's work was done at the request of Thomas, Earl of Wiltshire, father to Anne Boleyn, and in its content it was entirely apposite to the needs of the Government. Its instructive purpose, its critical discussion of the various versions of the Creed (in which Erasmus draws upon the Greek Fathers), and its view of the Church were all of great contemporary interest. On the last matter Erasmus suggested four criteria for the discovery of the true Catholic Church which were entirely satisfactory to the Henricians: the authority of the early Councils, an approved company of divines labouring to bring forth truth from Scripture, breadth and compass, and purity in manner of life. Faith and charity

[1] *STC* 10504: (R. Redman [1533]). On another phase of Marshall's work for Cromwell, see G. R. Elton, 'An Early Tudor Poor Law', *Economic History Review*, 2nd ser., vol. vi, no. 1 (1953), pp. 65–67.

are exalted above all other virtues, and are held to lead naturally to good works.

In addition to these productions, Marshall refers in another letter to Cromwell[1] to a work, *De veteri et novo deo*, which he hopes to have in the press immediately after Easter. This must be the historical attack on the authority of Rome by Joachim von Watt, which appeared under the imprint of Byddell, dated 15 June 1534: *A worke entytled of the olde god and the newe*, by 'Hartmanius Dulichius', with the English translator unidentified.[2]

A range of taste and content eminently becoming to a disciple of Erasmus appears in the work of another court translator of this time, Thomas Paynell. In 1532 there appeared his version of Erasmus's *De contemptu mundi*, a work again clearly acceptable to the royal religious policy.[3] The dedication to Henry's sister, 'the moste noble quene Mary dowager of France', recalls the translator's career. A former Austin friar and canon of Merton, he was pensioned in 1538 with £10 annual stipend.[4] His Oxford studies at the humanistic house of his Order, the Priory of St. Mary the Virgin, included medicine, and his first published work was the *Regimen sanitatis Salerni* of 1528, dedicated to John de Vere. About the same time he published Agapetus's *The preceptes teachyng a prynce*, dedicated to William Blount. This latter work is on a sufficiently obvious Erasmian theme, and it marked him as a suitable recruit for court service. In 1529 appeared his translation of a French devotional work, the *Assaute and conquest of heuen*, just before the great tide of pietistic publication in 1530. His efforts seem to have attracted the desired patronage, since in 1539 he

---

[1] SP 1/83, fol. 58 (1534).

[2] *STC* 25127: the editors attribute the translation to 'W. Turner'.

[3] *STC* 10471 (RSTC dating). The other works of Paynell mentioned here are: *STC* 21596 (*Schola Salernitana*, Berthelet, 1528); *STC* 193 (Agapetus; RSTC gives dating 1528–30); *STC* 862 (*Assault*; Berthelet, 1529); *STC* 923 (St. Augustine, J. Cawood).

[4] *LP* xiii (1), 963. A licence to export woollen cloth was issued the following October, *LP* xiii (2), (*g*) 734, no. 20.

attended the Frankfort Diet with Christopher Mount.[1] He later became a royal chaplain and stayed in the favour of all Henry's successors. An undated volume of twelve sermons of St. Augustine, translated by Paynell, commemorated his original vocation.

In the Hatfield manuscripts, apparently unnoticed by Pollard,[2] is his Commonplace Book, an epitome of the tastes and enthusiasms of this characteristically moderate humanist. It is dated 1553. The first extract on the first folio is from the *Moria Erasmi*, and it forms a suitable clue to the contents. After a variety of extracts on matters ranging from the nature of the Eucharist to the epistles of Ovid (in English), there follows 'The exposytone uppon the psalme 127 by the famus and lerned doctor Martyne Luther of Wyteberge translated owt of Latyne in to Englyshe by Thomas Paynell Esquyre'. This confirms earlier evidence that the English humanists imitated the first friendly response of Erasmus himself to the German reformer, without commonly being led to accept his more radical principles. The other contents of the Commonplace Book are sufficient evidence that Paynell could not be counted a dogmatic Protestant, but an arresting mark of his conservative connexions occurs midway through the manuscript, where his arms are coupled with those of the Throckmortons.[3] This suggestion that Paynell was aligned with the more conservative humanistic patronage is confirmed by two works of uncertain date, both dedicated to the Princess Mary: *A compendius and a moche fruytefull treatyse of well liuynge*, and his *Sayinges of al Scripture*, a collection of 'common-places' which

---

[1] *LP* xiv (1), 490 (10 Mar. 1539).

[2] In his article on Paynell in the *DNB*; Hatfield MSS., Cecil Papers, v. 332.

[3] Sir George Throckmorton was imprisoned by Cromwell in 1540 for denying the Royal Supremacy, and later released through the mediation of Catherine Parr. His deposition (*LP* xii (2), 952) provides interesting evidence of the activity of the conservative group, including Fisher, More, and Reynolds at Syon, in enlisting the support of a Member of Parliament against the royal divorce and the legislation on Appeals, Annates, and the Supremacy. Throckmorton's younger brother Michael became Pole's devoted secretary.

doubtless owes much to the accumulation in the Hatfield manuscript.[1]

Paynell's book continues with reflections on the commonwealth, on policy and the rule of kings, which recall his translation of Agapetus. Epitaphs, medical recipes, a fragment on 'Pasquyllus', and epigrams mostly from classical sources conclude the work. Among the last items are some of considerable interest. There are twelve lines on 'T. Morus cancellarius Anglie' and various religious poems, including 'The complaynt of a synner repentyng hys former abuses', with English versions of the 'Veni creator spiritus', Pico's 'Carmina de immensa Misericordia dei', and the psalm 'In te Domine speravi', reflecting precisely that blend of humanist piety and lay devotion which had been found in Pico by More. Under the reign of Mary, it would be Paynell who would prepare the index of More's *English Works*.

To the contribution of Thomas Paynell, whose career as an Erasmian translator was just beginning in 1533, we can add that of Leonard Cox, the humanist schoolmaster of Reading Abbey. In 1534 he wrote a letter to the publisher John Toy which confirms once more Cromwell's liking for translations from Erasmus.[2] Writing on 13 May from Reading, he says:

Goodeman Toy I hartely commend me to you and to your good wife and here I have sent you the paraphrase of Erasmus with the Epistle of Saint poule to Titus, and my preface made, as you can bere me recorde, but sodaynly, wherefor it can nott be but easy. Neverteles I wyll desyer you to shew it unto the right wurshipfull master Cromwell and in any wise to know his pleasure whether it shall abrode or nott. If his mastershipp think it meate to be prentid I shall if it so pleas him either translate the work that Erasmus made of the maner to pray or his paraphrase uppon the first and second epistles to Timothe or else such works as shall pleas his mastershipp and dedicate also my suche labours to him.

[1] *STC* 1908 (T. Petyt, [1545?]); 19494 (T. Gualtier at the costes of R. Toye, 1550).
[2] SP 1/84, fol. 24.

Repeating that he would not have it appear at all without Cromwell's foreknowledge, he adds,

I am also a translating of a boke which Erasmus made of the bringing upp of children, whiche I entend to dedicate to the said Master Cromwell and that shortly after Whitsontide.

The conclusion of Cox's letter is equally informative. Remarking that Cromwell is Recorder of Bristol, he says that if he finds him pleased with this work, he intends to ask him to obtain the free school there for him, a scheme which apparently came to nothing. His attitude is a sufficiently obvious demonstration of the reputation Cromwell carried in such circles, 'For thowgh I have many goode masters in the cawse yet I had lever have his favour then all the others.'

It could not be made more amply clear that Erasmus was known to win Cromwell's favour. Of the works referred to only one can be positively identified, the *Paraphrase on Titus*, which appeared about 1535 from the press of John Byddell, perhaps acting for Toy.[1] The offer to translate the *Modus orandi Deum*, which had appeared in 1524 and was clearly a central work of Erasmian pietism, seems not to have been accepted; at least no such publication has been recorded. The paraphrases on the epistles to Timothy apparently had to wait for the great project of Catherine Parr, when the work was done by John Olde. The book which Cox was in course of translating when he wrote on 'the bringing up of children' seems either to have disappeared or to have remained unprinted. Since Whittington had already in 1532 produced a translation of *De ciuilitate morum puerilium libellus*,[2] it would seem that Cox was probably referring to the *De pueris instituendis*, which was published by Froben in 1529.

At any rate, the letter suggests that Cox's willingness to act for Cromwell in this way may mark him as the unidentified translator of some of the Erasmian material to appear in the next year or so. There are three or four such works, ideally

[1] *STC* 10503.          [2] *STC* 10467.

suited to Cromwell's purposes. In 1534 Berthelet produced an English *Bellum*, and Copland (for Byddell) printed the 'Funus' from the *Colloquia*, with its extended satire on clerical greed at the death-bed.[1] Even more pointed was the 1535 *Dyalogue bytwene Jullius the seconde, Genius, and Saynt Peter*.[2] Even with the author in doubt, the *Julius Exclusus* was probably the most widely known satire against a secular and political papacy and, like the other two works appearing here, was brilliantly timed to serve the purpose of the English Government.

Apart from these heavier thrusts, there was a variety of supporting work by Erasmus. The years from 1532 to 1534 also saw a 'sermon' on the marriage at Cana urging proper rather than meaningless devotion to the Virgin, *A Treatise perswadynge a man patientlye to suffre the deth of his frende* and, another reprinting of Hervet's translation of the *De immensa misericordia Dei*.[3]

There may have been a conservative use in 1535 of Erasmus from the press of Robert Wyer, *An Epistle concernynge the veryte of the Sacrament of Christes body and bloude*.[4] This was a translation of Erasmus's prefatory epistle to his edition of a treatise by the twelfth-century Cluniac monk Alger, *De veritate corporis et sanguinis Dominici in Eucharistia*, which had appeared at Freiburg in 1530. The whole tone of the work is ortho-dox, and seems clearly intended by its sponsor to reprove the growing irreverence toward the Mass which was to be observed in England.

By this time Cromwell had a choice of several hands for his translating work. A glimpse of what one can assume to be characteristic duties on his behalf comes from a letter of Ralph

[1] STC 10449 and RSTC 10453.5 (5 Jan. 1534). *Funus*, translated 'at the request of a certayne gentleman', had perhaps been chosen with the notorious Hunne affair in mind. A lost translation of the *Exsequiae Seraphicae* (Dibdin 1408) may also come from this period.

[2] STC 14842 (J. Byddell, 1535). An edition a year earlier is noted by A. F. Allison and H. M. Nixon in *The British Museum Quarterly* (vol. xxiii, 1960/1).

[3] RSTC 10508 dates the 'Sermon' 1533 (Wyer); STC 10510 and 10475.

[4] STC 10490, 1535, or 1538? See p. 176, n. 2.

Sadleyr, his servant and later Secretary of State.[1] In it he reports
that he has followed Cromwell's instruction and 'taken out
theffects of the boke and letters which ye sent me yesterday
and in every boke and letter in laten I have enclosed theffects
of the same in englisshe and the same do sende herin accord-
ingle'. The exertion needed to keep up with Cromwell's
demands for summaries and reports is suggested by Sadleyr's
illness and fatigue on this occasion, when he is prevented from
appearing with the reports in person. It also suggests the kind of
system which enabled Cromwell to maintain an informed campaign of publication in addition to all his other activities.

Even with this, the full account of his agents is incomplete.
At least two names must be added. The first is that of Thomas
Swinnerton, described by Bale as studious in good arts and
letters from his youth. He had taken up the Protestant cause in
England under the assumed name of John Roberts, and in 1534
his *Mustre of scismatyke bysshopes of Rome* appeared, printed
by Wynkyn de Worde for John Byddell.[2] The contribution
which this work made to the historical theme of the earlier
Valla translation suggests that it was let through the ban on
Protestant writing with evident purpose. Included with it,
moreover, were instructive accounts of the lives of Hildebrand
and Henry IV. Suspicion that the work had unofficial coun-
tenance is heightened by evidence two years later that Swinnerton was familiar with Cromwell's translating circle. In
dedicating a guide to popular interpretation of Scripture, *The
Tropes and Figures of Scripture*, to Cromwell, he regrets that it
had not been done by a more learned man, like 'good master
Moryson'.[3]

The last recruit is none other than John Rastell, whose *New
Boke of Purgatory*, attacking Simon Fish, had provoked a reply

[1] SP 1/85, fol. 94. Compare SP 1/80, fol. 114, where Vaughan recalls
Christopher Mount being set to work in Cromwell's house to translate German
chronicles (1533). Also Cromwell's accounts, e.g. *LP* vi. 717 and 1448.
[2] *STC* 23552.
[3] The manuscript in the State Papers is E 36/193. The reference to Moryson
is scored through (f.v. 4).

which converted him to Protestantism. A long letter to Cromwell as King's Secretary in October 1534 reveals the predica-
ment and projects of this convert from the More circle.
He has sent a work to Cromwell for approval which he hopes
now to improve with the addition of new authorities, if Cromwell will grant him time before printing it. He also wishes
to have the royal approval, and proposes, with authority which
his printing experience must have justified, that ten to twelve
thousand copies, distributed among the shires, could be done
under the cost of £100, and that he trusts 'it wyll do as grete
good as any lytyll boke that hath bene yet put abrode'.

Pleading moreover for some preference in the printing of
future works, his own living having been so diminished by
his work 'of the kyngs causis and opposyng of the popes
usurpyd auctorite', he suggests a scheme which touches a policy
soon to be adopted as a major feature of the reformed Henrician Church.

Also yf it lyke you I have devysed certeyn prayers in Englisshe to
be put in primers of dyvers sorts of small prose whereof some of them
be imprintyd all redy in a lytyl primer which I did send unto to
[sic] the court which be to bryng the people which rede them from
the beleve of the popes naughty doctrine, for I do consyder that the
most parte of the people be loth to bye any such boke, and yet yf
they be gyffyn to them they wyll skantly rede them.

He urges that four or five thousand such could be printed for
not more than £1,000, and that by combining this reading
with their church attendance the people could be converted
and brought 'to the ryght beleve and do as much good as the
prechyngs do'.[1]

With all this evidence for the deliberate direction of translation and of the marked interest of Cromwell and his scholars in
Erasmus, it is not surprising that the most important group of
translations of Erasmus to appear in English was published in
the years of his power. Among all of them, one in particular of

---

[1] SP 1/85, fol. 132. Also A. W. Reed, *Early Tudor Drama* (1926), pp. 24 f.

outstanding import requires special attention, and that is the *Enchiridion*. Appearing from the press of Wynkyn de Worde dated 15 November 1533, it far surpassed in popularity, measured in editions, all other works of Erasmus.[1] By February of the following year the same printer had reissued it in a corrected version, and in 1538 another edition came, again from Byddell. Editions are recorded for 1541, 1544 (two), and 1548. Before the end of Edward VI's reign, there were two more editions by Day, for separate publishers, Veale and Toy. There are few if any works, outside the realm of Scripture and liturgy, with such remarkable popularity, and it is clear that the success of the *Enchiridion* in the learned world was repeated in England with the vernacular-reading public.

It seems that this translation was that which Tyndale is known to have made.[2] Its appearance in England, where Tyndale's works were ordinarily anathema to the King, has scarcely been commented upon. Nevertheless it does require explanation, since it is clear both that it was associated with matter normally proscribed by Henry yet, despite this, officially tolerated. In the light of the above evidence of Cromwell's interest both in Erasmus and in Tyndale, and of the abortive attempts of his Antwerp agent Stephen Vaughan to ingratiate Tyndale in the King's favour, it is plausible that the text was conveyed to Cromwell by Vaughan in a final attempt to revive Tyndale's cause with a work which was sure to please the King. At any rate, its appearance is a landmark in the Erasmus campaign, both through its unique popularity in English and because of its universal importance as the accepted handbook of Erasmian pietism.

The *Acts and Monuments* provides two suggestive comments

[1] *STC* 10479 (printed for John Byddell). The revised *Short Title Catalogue* lists nine editions before 1552: 1534, 1538, 1541, 1544 (2), 1548, 1551 (? 2).

[2] J. A. Gee, 'Tindale and the 1533 *Enchiridion* of Erasmus', *PMLA*, vol. xlix (1934), pp. 460–71; and J. F. Mozley, 'The English *Enchiridion* of Erasmus, 1533', *RES*, vol. xx (1944), pp. 97–107. For another view of the appearance of this version see E. J. Devereux, 'Some Lost English Translations of Erasmus', *The Library*, 5th ser., vol. xvii, no. 3 (Sept. 1962), p. 257.

on this Protestant sponsorship of the *Enchiridion*. The most
direct is the testimony that Alderman Humphrey Monmouth,
who was tried by Stokesley on twenty-four articles including
that of giving aid to Tyndale, lent certain of his books to others,
the *Enchiridion* among them. They were 'desired by sundry
persons, as by the abbess of Denny, by a friar of Greenwich, and
by the father confessor of Sion . . .', none of whom supposedly
found fault with Tyndale's books.[1]

The second episode is the recantation of one Thomas Topley,
Augustine friar at Stoke Clare, who was converted by Coverdale and Richard Foxe, priest of Bumstead, and tried by
Tunstall in 1528. His recantation shows that already at the
beginning of our present period of discussion Erasmus was
regarded with suspicion by the conservative party as a pre-
cursor of heresy.

All Christian men beware of consenting to Erasmus' Fables, for
by consenting to them, they have caused me to shrink in my faith,
that I promised to God at my christening by my witnesses. First, as
touching these fables, I read in 'Colloquium', by the instruction of
sir Richard Foxe, of certain pilgrims, who, as the book doth say,
made a vow to go to St. James, and as they went, one of them died,
and he desired his fellows to salute St. James in his name; and another
died homeward, and he desired that they would salute his wife and
his children, and the third died at Florence, and his fellow said, he
supposed that he was in heaven, and yet he said that he was a great
liar. Thus I mused of these opinions so greatly, that my mind was
almost withdrawn from devotion to saints. Notwithstanding, I consented that the divine service of them was very good and is; though
I have not had such sweetness in it as I should have had, because
of such fables and also because of other foolish pastimes. . . .[2]

Later in his testimony Topley referred to 'communing together'

---

[1] Foxe, iv. 618. The others mentioned are 'Pater Noster' (of Erasmus?),
'De libertate Christiana', and an English Testament. Cf. *LP* xii (1), 842,
information against a commissary who, among other offences, had accused
a priest for construing Erasmus's Paraphrases to his scholars, and for this had
dismissed him from keeping his school.

[2] Foxe, v. 40; taken from Tunstall's Register.

with Coverdale about the works of Erasmus, and upon confession being unnecessary if contrition was present. He read 'Wycliffe's Wicket', on the advice of Richard Foxe, and was finally persuaded to change his views through Coverdale's preaching on the Eucharist. The whole episode demonstrates an undoubtedly characteristic use of Erasmus by the Protestant party, and suggests that the conservatives were justified at least in suspecting that his satires did much to weaken the imaginative hold of many popular religious observances.

Apart from all this translation so closely linked with Cromwell, the English humanists continued with their characteristic concerns in these years. Thomas Elyot's *Pasquil the playne*, *Saint Cyprian*, *Knowledge which maketh a wyse man*, and *Isocrates* elaborated the doctrines expounded in the *Governour*, combined with covert criticism of Henry's divorce and its attendant consequences.[1] A humanist of great future importance, Nicholas Udall, appeared for the first time in print with extracts from Terence for educational purposes, and Whittington produced some Cicero. Educational works are again conspicuous, with a second edition of Leonard Cox's *Arte or crafte of rhethoryke* and Giles Duwes's *Introductorie for to lerne Frenche*, a work dedicated to the Princess Mary by one of her tutors.[2] Gentian Hervet published *Xenophons treatise of the householde*,[3] a translation done at the instigation of Geoffrey Pole, the unhappy agent who exposed the entire Pole–Courtenay relationship to the royal displeasure a few years later. Finally, among further devotional works, two of undoubted humanist origin were Thomas Lupset's *Treatise of charitie* and *A compendious treatyse, . . . the waye of dyenge well*, both from Berthelet.[4]

It is clear, then, that the years from the fall of Wolsey to the execution of Thomas More were momentous for the

[1] On Elyot's conservatism see, for example, the Preface to *Of the Knowledge which Maketh a Wise Man*; on his covert criticism, S. E. Lehmberg, 'Sir Thomas Elyot and the English Reformation', in *Archiv für Reformationsgeschichte*, vol. xlviii (1957), pp. 91–111.

[2] *STC* 5947 (R. Redman, 1532): *STC* 7377 (T. Godfray, [1534?].

[3] *STC* 26069 (Berthelet, 1532).    [4] *STC* 16934 (1534) and 16939 (1533).

English humanist community. As the publications last cited prove, fundamental interests had not changed. Activity, however, had been sharply affected by the swift-moving events of the day: first by the excitement of the new promise of reform, then by the controversy over the divorce, and finally by the direct patronage of Thomas Cromwell. The turning-point is the year 1532, when the appearance of distinguished opposition to the King's policies, followed within a year by the decisive break with Rome, made the creation of a royal apologetic a matter of urgent necessity. It seems that it was in these months that Thomas Cromwell decided to supplement the theories put forth about the King's relationship to the English Church with a substantial body of Erasmian matter in translation, which associated the King's designs with the cause of humanism and reform.

By the year 1533 Cromwell must also have been apprehensive about a discreet publication campaign from influential conservative humanist quarters. His response was prompt. In part this challenge was met by the flood of sponsored translations which we have noticed already, but it seems possible that there was also a decisive, immediate step. This move, which started a chain of events which finally resulted in the execution of More and Fisher, was the arrest of Elizabeth Barton, the Nun of Kent. Her story is sufficiently familiar to require no repetition here, but the importance attached to her prosecution by the Government and the exaggerated efforts to involve others in her fate are better understood when the above publication of the years 1532 to 1534 is examined. Her familiar sponsors in the years from 1527 to 1532 had been precisely those societies responsible for this conservative publication, with Syon at the centre. Like her Spanish counterparts, the mystical *beatas*, Elizabeth Barton was received throughout the network of Erasmian pietism, from the 'spiritual élite of London and its environs'[1] to the Courtenays in Devonshire. In

---

[1] Knowles, op. cit., p. 184. For a roll-call of the Nun's influence, see *LP* vi. 1468.

denouncing her as a fraud and a traitor the Government not only discredited opponents of great prestige, but acquired evidence which could be put to useful purpose, if need be, at a later date.

As the first open move against that part of the humanist reform party which was hostile to the King's course over the divorce, it marks decisively the end of a brief summer of confidence and co-operation. It also foreshadows the prosecution of More and Fisher, to which it made an important contribution. With that, the conservative Erasmians were driven underground or abroad, and the field was left largely to those moderates who rallied to the Government's support.

# 6

## OFFICIAL ERASMIANISM: THE WORK
## OF CROMWELL, 1535 TO 1540

ON 22 June 1535 John Fisher was executed under the provisions of 26 Henry VIII c. 13, and on 6 July Thomas More followed him to the block. In the midst of shocked protests from abroad[1] one voice in particular was awaited with impatience by the King and by the whole English humanist community. At last in late May of 1536 Reginald Pole gave over his work on the divorce to the faithful messenger of the scholarly group abroad, Michael Throckmorton, and he delivered it to the King. It was the first polemic fruit of More's martyrdom.

Like More himself, Pole rested the argument on the problem of Christian unity, and placed the onus of demonstration on the King's defenders. In doing so, Pole, like More, naturally by-passed the whole argument about corruption and reform, where both of them were long committed, to pursue the issues already raised about spiritual authority. From this point forward those issues dominate the public debate.

Back in London, Cromwell's new recruit from Pole's own household, Richard Moryson, was set to work to make an abstract of the *Pro ecclesiasticae unitatis defensione*. His grateful admission in 1536, 'I am a grafte of your Lordshyps own setting, if I bring forth any frute, I knowe who may clayme them',[2] serves as an appropriate introduction to the work of the official

---

[1] The common reaction seems to have been amazement and horror at Henry's action, coupled with inability to share the martyrs' views of the importance of the Royal Supremacy. This seems to have been Erasmus's own reaction: see Allen, xi. 3048 and 3049, and App. II below. Melanchthon also saw More's execution as a blow 'to our order' which would favour extremists: *LP* ix. 222 and 1013.

[2] *LP* x. 975 (ii); *SP* 1/113, fol. 210. The careers and writings of Moryson and Starkey, fully explored by Zeeveld, are not dealt with here.

writers in this period. Of the group in Italy when Pole finally made his views known, George Lily and Thomas Goldwell followed him to the reforming circles about the Theatines in Rome. John Friar and Edward Wotton, like Richard Moryson and Thomas Starkey, had already returned to England and adhered to that decision, Wotton finally becoming physician to the King. Protest against the King's policies would of course have been impossible for anyone who had decided to stay in England, but the response of the English humanist community to the King's policies can hardly be explained purely in terms of career-seeking or reluctant compliance. The reply to Pole had to be made, and before long the challenge of the northern rebels likewise had to be met, and Cromwell's band of writers lent their best energies to both tasks.

At the same time the Government began to provide formularies for the faithful in Henry's Church, and the Erasmian strain in official thinking here becomes very conspicuous. Royal injunctions on Church reform, primers for popular devotion, and (after long delay) provision of an approved translation of the Bible are all fruits of this work. It was a natural development of the reform thinking which developed in the period before More's death. Despite the shock of that event, it is clear that the central enterprise of the English humanist community continued without interruption.

The main concern of the present chapter is to show how the energies of many of these men were harnessed to the needs of the Government. At the same time, the voluntary activity of the humanist community carries on the direct tradition of the Erasmian group before the deaths of More and Fisher, and in the yearly production of the English press there is ample evidence of general consent in the work of the Government, a compliance which was utilized with great energy and intelligence by Cromwell for the official formularies of faith, for propaganda treatises, and for a host of semi-official pietistic works which for the ordinary man, no doubt, were the important part of the Henrician settlement.

The heroic solitude of More and Fisher is apparent at the moment of their execution. It was soon clear that to most of their fellows their stand seemed as radical as did that of Luther. The reaction of More's family and of the conservative humanist group which later became identified with the Catholic cause is the subject of a later discussion. For the moment a prologue to the achievement of Cromwell's propaganda industry might be found in the career of one of the lesser figures in the aristo- cratic circle of translators.

Henry Parker, Lord Morley, was a member of the con- servative Erasmian group, and a man eminently sympathetic to More's own position. In the work of this industrious and mediocre man it is possible to see how little impression the stand of the martyrs of 1535 made on the average member of this circle. A tireless translator of classical and pietistic works throughout the whole period of this study, his greatest pro- duction came in the period of Cromwell's power and it forms a running commentary on the momentous events of the day. The son of a Yorkist Privy Councillor, he was introduced to court in 1516 as Gentleman Usher to the King. An embassy in 1524 to the Archduke Ferdinand revealed his dread of Lutheran opinion, and it is conceivable that his later devotion to the Princess Mary, even during her disgrace, was formed in the literary society around Catherine of Aragon. His wife, Alice St. John, was a granddaughter of the Lady Margaret and he was himself a familiar member of her circle.

In the period after the divorce, however, he seems to have been close to the Boleyns as well, and his daughter Jane married George, Lord Rochford, brother to Queen Anne. While Anne was still Marchioness of Wiltshire he presented her with his earliest known translation, 'The Pistellis and Gospells for the 52 Sondays in the yeare'.[1]

Willingness to accept Henry's religious changes was signified not only by his signature in the Lords' petition to Clement VII concerning the divorce, a fairly routine affair, but by his pursuit

[1] Harleian MS. 6561.

of Cromwell's favour in 1535 and 1539. In the former year this grandsire of prominent recusants and loyal friend of the Princess Mary sent Cromwell a greyhound, and, more interestingly, in February of 1539 he sent him Machiavelli's *History of Florence* and *The Prince*, recommending particularly the passages which he had marked on the position of the papacy in Europe.[1] He participated in the christening of Prince Edward, and in 1550 supported the prosecution of Somerset. On 25 November 1556 he died at his home in Essex. Although his career in print was slight,[2] he left behind him a unique collection of manuscript translations, dedicated  to royal and notable persons. Together they form an invaluable record of the interests of this loyal, devout, and—if uninspired—eminently Erasmian personality.

His gifts to Henry might properly begin the list: Plutarch's 'Story of Paulus Emylyus', a 'Life of Theseus', from the Latin of Lapo Birago (written some time between 1543 and 1547), 'Scipio and Hannibal', from the Latin of Donatus Acciaiuoli (written some time between 1521 and 1534),[3] and finally, one of the fifty *Novellini* of Massucio of Salerno. The subject of this last work was the betrayal of Frederick Barbarossa to the Sultan by Alexander IV. In the preface he quotes Seneca (to Lucillus), that 'faythe is the sure fundation of mans breste', and concerning bad faith, he finds it exemplified by the 'false Antecriste Alexander the iiijth bysshope of Rome', and hopes Henry will enjoy this tale of the wicked Pope and the good Emperor. He adds a salutation and good wish for Queen Catherine Parr, 'and that hope of this youre realme to cum Prynce Edwarde youre sonne' (fol. 3r-v).[4] Finally he provided Henry with Paolo Giovio's 'Commentaries on the Turks'.[5]

---

[1] *LP* viii. 957; xiv (1), 285 (Ellis, ser. iii, vol. iii, no. 278).

[2] *STC* 19211: *Exposition and declaration of the psalme Deus ultionum dominus*, Berthelet, 1539. Evidently also a verse translation of Plutarch's 'Trionfi'; see *DNB*.

[3] Bodleian Library, Laud MS. Misc. 684; British Museum, Royal MSS. 17 D. II and 17 D. XI.

[4] Royal MS. 18 A. LXII.                     [5] Arundel MS. 8.

For Cromwell, Parker translated Plutarch's 'Life of Agesilaus',[1] in which he compared the careers of Agesilaus and
Henry VIII, and for the Duke of Somerset, presumably about
1548, he translated a commentary on Ecclesiastes.[2] The preface
to this last work acknowledges his daily indebtedness to the
magnanimity of the Duke in 'maynteynyng of the true
preachers for the conducting of alle the whole bodie of this
Realme to the purenes and synceritie of the gospell', and concludes with a compliment of the King-to-be, who is appointed,
he is sure, to restore 'God's temple'.

The rest of his known dedications are to the Princess Mary.
They were clearly made throughout the period after 1535, and
include at least one made when she became Queen. In these the
pietistic and orthodox strain is clearly evident. The last of
his works, an apparently original collection of 'Miraculous
examples in support of the doctrine of Transubstantiation',[3]
deplores the late heresy and praises Mary and 'your dear
husband our lord and king'. In the prologue he traces the
progress of heresy from the denial of the Pope's authority to
the final questioning of the 'sanctum sanctorum', the Eucharist
itself. Reviewing the history of heresies, he recalls in connexion
with Luther his own embassy to Ferdinand, King of the
Romans, and the horror of the Peasants' Revolt. In the midst
of these reflections, which were undoubtedly common to
many conservative survivors of the reign of Edward VI, his
lifelong interest in Italian emerges with reference (again in
connexion with Luther) to the Koran, 'lately translated into
Italian'.

Hoping for a restoration of plenty, peace, and good religion
under Mary's guidance and the wise counsel of Cardinal Pole,
he turns to recall the household of the Lady Margaret, which

[1] Phillips MS. I, 313, cited by Sidney Lee, *DNB*.

[2] Royal MS. 17 D. XIII. The catalogue of Royal Manuscripts speculates that
the work is by Morley's son, on the ground that its 'Protestant tone' is inconsistent with the tenth Lord's career under Mary and his role in the prosecution of Somerset in 1550.

[3] Additional MS. 12060.

he knew as a boy, and his account serves as a moving testimony to the alterations and continuities of English humanism in two generations. By now, Parker thinks, there cannot be six others alive who knew her, and he claims that before her death Fisher showed him that he had written her life, a work which Parker supposed that Queen Mary now has and which he would dearly love to see. The Lady Margaret's daily devotions, her good humour and hospitality, her zeal for the Church (he recalls that she often said she would be 'a launder' to those fighting the Turk) commended her to all those who knew her, great and small.

This redolent floure, this precious margaryte is past from this worlde, not as other ffloures be that to day be fayre, and tomorowe withered and drye, but this our fayre floure as long as the sea hath fyshes, and the skye twinkling starres, untyll the sounde of the last trompet shall call all creatures to Judgment, her fame, her honour, her liberalitye, her prudence, her chastytye, and her excellent virtues shall be commendyd for ever.[1]

There are six other works dedicated to Mary. Seneca's eighteenth and ninety-second epistles, striking the general theme of resignation to sudden and unpredictable calamity and acceptance of the will of God, are sent as his yearly gift to her 'to accept as for this tyme', not that the matter of them 'anything apperteynethe unto you', but for others suffering hard fortune.[2] The second, the preface of St. Athanasius to the Psalms, was made from the Latin version of Angelo Poliziano.[3] Erasmus also is, inevitably, included. The work chosen was an appropriate compliment, the 'Paean Virgini Matri dicendus',[4] in the preface to which Parker deplores the decay in devotion to the saints in Heaven and especially to the Blessed Virgin, and hails the Princess as 'the secunde Mary of this worlde in vertue grace and goodnes'. He promises all his prayers for the removal of all plagues of 'hevynes and sorowe'.

[1] Ibid., fol. 23.                    [2] Royal MS. 17 A. xxx.
[3] Royal MS. 17 C. xii.              [4] Royal MS. 17 A. xlvi.

This note of protest at the new order of things is understandably dropped in the one translation for Mary we can trace to the reign of Edward VI. It is from Cicero, the *Somnium Scipionis*,[1] dedicated to her as 'suster to oure moste redoubted and victoriouse Sovereign lorde kyng [*inserted*] Edwarde the syxt . . .'. He anticipates her surprise, since she is accustomed to receive either 'sum notable worke concernyng sum christen doctours wrytyng in the Laten tonge, or elis sum of their worke by me translated into our tounge . . .'. He thinks she knows this work already, and that she will agree that it would benefit those whose life shows them to be of 'Epicurus sect', since it proves immortality of the soul and the justice of reward in Heaven, and puts to shame himself, a professed Christian. The Erasmian note in such respect for the Stoic code of the pre-Christian world is heard also in his reference to the work's usefulness for 'theym that muche commende vertue and folow it nothynge all'. It is interesting to reflect that the gift was probably made within a year or two of his presenting Seymour with the 'Exposition of Ecclesiastes', with its preface of distinctly Protestant tone.

Two final gifts provide information about the tastes of the Princess Mary herself. In the preface to John of Torquemada's exposition of the thirty-sixth psalm, 'Noli emulari', which he followed with an English sonnet version of Maffeo Vegio's poem 'Orpheu sileto', he recalls an occasion at Hovesden, where the Lady Mary had commended this particular psalm, with reason (as he feels), since it shows how soon the sinner is foresaken 'of and frome the false felicite of thys worlde'.[2]

Finally, a double gift couples a work of the scholastic most acceptable to the pious humanist circle, Thomas Aquinas, on the suitable theme of the 'Angelic Salutation to the Blessed Virgin', with St. Anselm on 'The Stature and Forme and lyfe

---

[1] 'The dreme of Sypyon', Royal MS. 18 A. LX.
[2] Royal MS. 18 A. xv.

of ouer blessed Lady and of Ouer Saviour Christe Jesu'.[1] In this
Prologue he compliments her Latinity, saying:

I have sene one prayer translatyd of youer doynge of Sayncte
Thomas Asquyne that I do ensuer youer grace is so well done, so
neare to the laten, that when I loke uppon yt (as I have one of the
exemplar of yt) I have not only mervell at the doinge of yt, but
farther for the well doynge set yt as well in my boke or bokes as also
in my pore wyfes, youer humble beadwoman and my chyldern,
to the entent to gyve them ocasion to remember to praye for youer
grace . . ., a myrrour to follou.

There is again the faintest allusion to her present discontents in
his prayer that 'He that for ouer redemcion was borne of the
Virgin saue and preserue your grace this newe yere in helthe
and honor, as to a kings daughter aparteynithe . . .'.

Lord Morley adds no great lustre to the literary history of
sixteenth-century England, as even the cited extracts will show,
but his indefatigable activity in translating is a unique source of
information about the attitudes of one lay member of Lady
Margaret's humanist nursery during the difficult times of
religious change. His unwavering devotion to the Princess
Mary, even at times when such loyalty must have risked disfavour, silences the accusation of mere trimming which his
persistent compliments to those in power might otherwise
imply. He was no intellectual giant, and it is easy to imagine
his consternation if he had known the attitude Reginald Pole
would have taken to his gift of Machiavelli to Cromwell.
However, it seems clear that throughout this period a conservative humanist and pietist group continued to meet and
write in the private court of Henry's eldest daughter, and, as
we shall see, it was part of the achievement of Catherine Parr
to bring this group back to the centre of affairs. From the
happier world of Henry's final days which she created, it was
an easy step for the uncomplicated humanist piety of Henry
Parker to the more radical but still essentially Erasmian

[1] Royal MS. 17 C. XVI.

atmosphere of the first months of Edward VI's reign. It is clear, too, from his final work that, for him as for Gardiner, the later experience of the Royal Supremacy during the Protectorship was needed to persuade him that a religious settlement based on the King's government of the Church was ultimately unacceptable.

Many years later, Robert Parsons preserved an anecdote about a certain courtier, possibly Sir Francis Bryan, which demonstrates exactly the same temperament in dispute with a court lady 'somwhat forward in the new ghospell'. To this lady, who disliked the Articles of 1536 and their attribution 'to a mortall knigs [sic] devise', Bryan was said to have replied, 'Truly (madame) I will tell you my conceyt plainely. Yf we must needs have devises in Religion, I had rather haue them from a King, then from a knave, as your devises are. I meane that knave, Friar Martyn, who not yet 20 yeares agone was deviser of your new Religion, and behaved himselfe so lewdly in answeringe his Maiestie, with scorne, and contempt, as I must needs call him a knave. . . .' And adducing the basest motives for Luther's 'new tricks of Religion', Bryan is made to say, 'I would rather for my part, sticke to the deuisinge of a King, that hath maiestie in him, and a counsell to assist him (especially such a King as ours is) then to a thousand of these companions putt together.'[1]

Parsons probably obtained this story from Sir Francis Inglefield, Privy Councillor to Queen Mary, who is cited in his next chapter as the source of information on the trial of Joan of Kent, and 'divers other particularityes which in this chapter and the former are touched by me'. At any rate it has a ring of authenticity as an (unintentional) representation of the views of many men, in and out of court, who preferred the King's reforms to the radical stand either of More or of Luther. It was

---

[1] STC 19416: A Treatise of three Conversions of England, from Paganisme to Christian Religion, [St. Omer], 1603–4, pt. 2, ch. 11, sects. 17 f. A. F. Allison and D. M. Rogers, A Catalogue of Catholic Books . . . 1558–1640, Bognor Regis, 1956, no. 640.

in this loyalty that Cromwell and Henry found the indispensable support for the Henrician settlement.

The official formularies of faith which appear now for the first time form the background against which humanist production must be seen. The cautious and occasionally bewildering development from the Ten Articles of 1536 and Cromwell's Injunctions of the same year, through the 'Bishops' Book' (thrashed out between a commission of ecclesiastics, the King, and Cranmer, and given unofficial approval in the summer of 1538) to the Injunctions of Cromwell in September 1538, has been frequently examined. Through the whole period there was the presiding influence of the negotiations with the Germans, although even at the height of agreement Lutheran influence on Henrician doctrine was kept comparatively slight.[1] In any event, the Act of Six Articles concluded this period of experimentation with a return to Catholic orthodoxy which dominated the official formularies of the Henrician Church until the King's death in 1547.

For our present purposes, it is advisable to turn from the traditional preoccupation with possible Protestant influence in this period to the Erasmian aspects of Henry's reforms, which may be thought to have attracted the support of that very important class of scholars and intellectuals now rallying to the King's cause. It was precisely because there was promise of such reform, not because of hopes that the King would lead England into the Protestant camp, that this support was forthcoming. At the beginning, the Ten Articles of 1536, with their clearly provisional character, cannot be examined too closely for evidence of the King's ultimate intentions about the religious settlement, even supposing his own mind was clear about these. Nevertheless, in one way they do exhibit a basic characteristic of the future Erasmian settlement, in the distinction drawn between 'articles necessary to our salvation' and 'certain other

---

[1] E. G. Rupp, *Studies in the Making of the English Protestant Tradition* (Cambridge, 1947), pp. 122 f.; C. W. Dugmore, *The Mass and the English Reformers* (1958), pp. 106–9.

honest and commendable ceremonies, rites and usages now
of long time used . . .'. It is the 'adiaphoristic principle' attributed by Zeeveld to Starkey, which, however, was instinctive
to the whole approach of Erasmus and his followers, including
many others besides Melanchthon.[1] It provided the best reply
to the problems of unity and authority which had been raised
by More, Fisher, and Pole.

   More interesting are Cromwell's Injunctions of 1536 and
1538, in which Erasmian reform is very clearly the chief inspiration. The placing of the Bible in English in the parishes, with
matters of controversy referred not to the clergy as such but
to the 'better learned', the reduction in holy days and the dis-
couragement of pilgrimages and devotion practised with images,
the required family instruction in the Pater Noster, Creed,
and Ten Commandments, and the provision that beneficed parsons with sufficient income must support a scholar at a university
or grammar school—all these provisions form the real foundation of the Henrician settlement and early establish its character,
at a time when diplomacy abroad and episcopal disagreement
at home obstructed a more permanent formulary of faith.

   With *The Institution of a Christian Man* or 'Bishops' Book' of
1537, a conservative statement of principle designed to unite
the episcopal bench (or at least conceal differences within it),
the Erasmian basis is again evident. Acknowledging that the
contents are all based on the 'true meaning of Scripture'—a
phrase which avoids Protestant commitments—the *Institution*
is once more based on the notion of 'necessary doctrine' drawn
from the great Christian epitomes of faith, the Commandments,
Creeds, and Pater Noster. The four sacraments omitted in the
Ten Articles are restored. Although invested with less dignity
than the three held to be founded by Christ, they are held to
be 'approved by the common consent of the catholic church',
a criterion which explicitly revived tradition along with
Scripture as a touchstone of authenticity.

[1] C. L. Manschreck, 'The Role of Melanchthon in the Adiaphora Controversy', *Archiv für Reformationsgeschichte*, vol. xlviii (1957), pp. 165–81.

The commentary on the Creed's ninth article, on the 'Holy Catholic Church', touched for the first time on the issue of unity raised by More and Pole. The reply follows Marsilian principles, emphasizing that the various national Churches in England, Spain, France, or 'in any other realm' enjoy no difference in superiority, and that 'the unity of this one catholic church is a mere spiritual unity'. It seems likely that this notion of affiliation through 'one faith, hope and charity' and the same ministry of sacraments was in effect another aspect of the adiaphoristic emphasis. Certainly, the notion of essential belief and permissive local observances was the strongest answer to Roman insistence on the Petrine Supremacy yet found. It preserved the idea of a learned consensus based on apostolic practice with a standard for criticism and reform of the medieval Church.

The *Institution* of 1537 was of course only a provisional settlement, and the King's own decisions on doctrine, except for the Six Articles reasserting conservative Catholic practice, were to be postponed until the *Necessary Doctrine and Erudition for any Christian Man* in 1543 (the 'King's Book'). However, even at the end of our present period, in 1540, and after the Six Articles of 1539, the essentially Erasmian character of the nascent Henrician Church was already clearly detected by foreign observers. Marillac, writing to the Constable of France in May of 1540, asserted that the King kept all final decisions on doctrine to himself, and that he was told that a book would soon appear sanctioned by Parliament, where every man might learn what he was to believe, and doubtful points would be decided by neither German nor papal views, but by the authority of the early Christian Church.[1]

The great usefulness of an appeal to a scholarly consensus is

[1] Public Record Office MS. 31/3/10, Baschet's Transcripts, f.v. 123: 'que bientost sortira un livre authorisé par le Parlement, auquel tout ce qu'on doit tenir en la dite Religion, sera déterminé non selon les doctrines des Allemans ny du Pape mais de la vérité conforme aux Conciles anciens de l'Eglise, par ou ils estiment que le dit sieur leur Roy sera connu, et connu par le Roy son bon frère, pour tel qu'il est inquisiteur et amateur de la seule vérité . . .'.

evident at every step of the way, but perhaps most conveniently demonstrated with the *Institution* of 1537, which was known by all to be a first attempt at common agreement. In the weeks which preceded its publication it is clear that not only the bishops but the administrators had a hand in its creation. Cromwell, Wriothesley, and Richard Moryson were among the laymen involved, and in the sacramental question opinion was sought not only from Dr. Buckmaster, the Vice-Chancellor of Cambridge, and Dr. Edmunds, Master of Peterhouse, who had been proved at the divorce proceedings to be well disposed to the Government, but from Dr. Richard Smith, the conservative Regius Professor of Divinity at Oxford.[1] The State Papers also yield a treatise on the seven sacraments by Richard Moryson,[2] unquestionably prepared as background.

Since in this way the *Institution* represented a broad consensus of learned opinion, clerical and lay, its immediate transmission to Reginald Pole[3] assumes added significance. Pole's connexions of course were markedly with the reforming party still, and in light of his legatine mission to Flanders in support of the Pilgrimage of Grace, this manifesto by the Erasmian group in England might have been taken either as challenge or ground of conciliation; at any rate, it was to seem a mark of unity. Even Cranmer, answering protests that the book had restored 'ceremonies, pilgrimages, and purgatory', defended it by the assertion that only 'old, good usages are restored, such as those of the primitive Church'.[4]

This brief examination of the official formularies of the period introduces an important related problem, the production of an official translation of the Bible. From 1525 onward the popular version of Scripture in English was Tyndale's New Testament, whether in its primary, corrected, or pirated edition. All were specifically condemned by Henry's Government before and after the break with Rome. In 1530 a commission appointed to consider the need for an English translation

---

[1] *LP* xii (2), 403.          [2] *LP* xii (2), 405 (ii).
[3] *LP* xii (2), 620.          [4] *LP* xii (2), 846, (i) (7 Oct. 1537).

had reported unfavourably, but the question could scarcely be closed with an heretical version still finding an eager market. In 1534 the Canterbury Convocation petitioned the King for an English Bible, and it seems likely that from that time forward both Cromwell and Cranmer were anxious to provide one. In the next year Coverdale produced the first complete version of both Testaments in English, printed on the Continent but evidently intended to be tolerated in England. In 1537 the second edition reappeared with a royal licence, but at the same time Tyndale's version was reissued, only slightly refurbished, as the 'Matthew Bible'. In 1538 Coverdale provided a fresh version of the New Testament with an accompanying Vulgate text, which went through five editions in 1538. Finally, in September of 1539, there appeared the Great Bible, Coverdale's official government version for the rest of the reign.

At first sight it must seem remarkable that on this basic principle of Erasmian reform the Government was for so long content to make do with borrowed Protestant Scriptures, when here above all the exercise of officially sponsored learned opinion would have been most appropriate. In explanation at least four things must be considered. An attempt to get a consensus of scholarship, from the bishops at least, was made by Cromwell and Cranmer in 1534–5, by distributing chapters of the New Testament for translation.[1] The lack of co-operation was clearly overwhelming, as Cranmer's famous comment over the Matthew Bible admitted: he felt the bishops would only agree by Doomsday.[2] Secondly, it seems likely from the succession of attitudes adopted in royal injunctions that the King himself was very much of two minds about the desirability of distributing vernacular Scripture, so the royal support essential to obtain a consensus was doubtless lacking.[3] Thirdly, the

[1] A. W. Pollard, *Records of the English Bible* (1911), pp. 196 f.
[2] Ibid., pp. 214–16; *LP* xii (2), 434 and 512.
[3] The only bishop known to have completed Cranmer's assignment was Stephen Gardiner, the learned conservative and former colleague of More. Stokesley of London flatly refused to bring 'simple people into error'. Pollard, *Records*, loc. cit.

project of translation was recognized to be an arduous and
long-drawn-out affair, probably even more time-consuming
if a board of scholars was employed, so the experiment had to
be made with existing translations, if the attempt were to be
tried at all. Coverdale's employment was, after all, the employment of a learned scholar of judicious and moderate opinion,
a man far removed from the shrill Protestant dogmatism of
a Joye or a Frith. Finally, it must be noticed that Cromwell
did make one attempt to rescue the Matthew Bible, when
its character as thinly disguised Tyndale became obvious, by
placing the matter in the hands of one of his humanist writers,
Richard Taverner.

The Matthew Bible of 1537 seems to have been introduced
by Cranmer as the best version he had yet read, and one with
presumably fewer heretical associations than the version under
the name of Miles Coverdale. Cromwell evidently had ordered
the latter Bible printed even before he became Vicar-General
in 1534, but the King would give it no official sanction. It was
simply allowed to circulate, and the fulsome dedication to
Henry must have been intended in part to give it an air of that
official approval which it manifestly lacked. It was in any case
at best a translation of translations, and it was not until the
reissue of 1537 by Nicholson that the title-page claimed a royal
licence. By that time Cranmer had discovered the version of
'Thomas Matthew'.

Whether or not Cranmer was aware that this was really in
large part the work of Tyndale, edited by his old colleague John
Rogers, is not clear; it is remarkable that the tendentious matter
it contained did not inhibit him or Cromwell from seeking
(and getting) a royal licence. Conceivably they might have
framed it as a threat to speed the bishops toward agreement.
At any rate, when the controversial nature of the work became
clear, Cromwell apparently moved to withdraw it and substi-
tute a modified version, for which Richard Taverner was made
responsible.

The Taverner Bible was so soon displaced by the 'Great

Bible', also of 1539, that it has been scarcely noticed. As the only direct venture by the Erasmian humanist group into biblical translation, however, it deserves attention here. It is clear that Taverner was rushed into action so abruptly that anything more than revision was impossible, but his command of Greek was nevertheless important. He revised the Matthew Bible throughout, the Old Testament with reference to the Vulgate, and the New Testament with reference to the Greek, presumably of Erasmus's edition. He also suppressed the quire containing Tyndale's tendentious prologue to the Romans, and moderated Protestant readings and annotations throughout.[1] Thus Rogers's attacks on clerical celibacy, on purgatory, and on fasting were all eliminated, as was the comparison of the Pope to Anti-Christ, with a consequent change in tone from a distinctly Protestant work to a moderate and characteristically Erasmian compromise.

In general his revision of the text was in the direction of brevity, the New Testament often relying on almost verbatim translation from the Greek. His own views on the matter can be obtained only from his prefatory dedication to the King. Here, after offering great praise to Henry for putting forth the 'unspotted and lyvely worde of God', he observes that a truly faultless translation is so difficult 'That I feare it can scarce be doone of one or two persons, but rather requyreth bothe a deper confarrynge of many lerned wittes togyther, and also a iuster tyme and longer leysure' for accurate appraisal of the problem. The request to undertake this revision, he points out, came to him from the printers 'for default of a better lerned', and it seems clear that both the request and the recommendation of the scholar must originally have come from Cromwell. He concludes with a plea for understanding of the shortcomings of which he must have been all too well aware:

But now though many faultes perchaunce be yet left behind un-castigat, either for lack of lerning sufficient to so gret an enterprise,

[1] H. H. Hutson and H. R. Willoughby, 'The Ignored Taverner Bible of 1539', *The Crozier Quarterly*, vol. xvi (1939), p. 170. STC 2067.

or for default of leasure, I trust your maiestie . . . will pardon me, consyderynge (as I haue alredy declared) how harde and difficile a thinge it is, so to set forth this worke, as shal be in al pointes faultles and without reprehension.

At the time when Taverner was set to work on this, in the midst of one of his busiest periods of official translation, Cromwell was working anxiously to secure a satisfactory revision of the Coverdale Bible to answer the demand of his own Injunctions for a Bible 'of largest volume' to be set up in the parishes. Perhaps it was uncertainty about this venture, suddenly made precarious by the unexpected capitulation of Francis I to the ecclesiastical authorities in Paris, which prompted the production of Taverner's version as an emergency measure.[1] At any rate the Paris Bible was entirely the work of Cromwell and Coverdale, there being no record of the 'dyverse excellent learned men' who supposedly assisted the latter. The famous title-page, possibly Holbein's work, which showed Cranmer distributing the Bible to the clergy and Cromwell to the laity under the supreme governance of the King, was a pictorial expression of the spirit of the official royal reform to date. The Royal Supremacy, the elevation of the laity to an estate equal with the clergy, and the scholarly return to apostolic authority (expressed in the claim, unfortunately false, to revision 'after the veryte of the Hebrew and Greke textes') epitomized the Henrician settlement.

With this appraisal of the official formularies of Cromwell's period in mind, it is possible to turn to the greater body of writing emanating from the humanist group under his immediate or indirect influence. Here it is evident that the coincidence of royal policy with the traditional interests of the Erasmian community in England, already noticed in the period after Wolsey's fall from power, is exploited on an enormous scale. The Government leads where they are inclined to follow, and induces a large group of official writers to flood the

[1] *LP* xiii (2), 1085, the inhibition issued by the French Inquisitor-General to Regnault and his associates, 17 Dec. 1538.

countryside with Erasmian literature wholly complementary to the official settlement.

Three general categories of writing can be described. The first is the mass of secondary works associated with the official religious formularies already described, including sermons, primers, and publications like the 1536 translation of the Augsburg Confession. The second category, already well known to historians of the period, is the core of frank propaganda produced to meet the challenges of the day—the papal summons of the Council of Mantua, the Northern Rebellion, and the conspiracy of the Courtenays. And finally, there is the whole penumbra of apologetic and pietistic work, hitherto unnoticed, which served to confirm the Erasmian character of these early steps to a settlement by informing the taste and conscience of the whole reading public. The relationship of the three types of writing is best seen when followed year by year.

In the category of secondary works bearing on the religious settlement the year 1535 brought three which concluded the apologetic about the Royal Supremacy: Gardiner's *De vera obedientia*, William Marshall's translation of the *Defensor Pacis*, and Christopher Saint German's treatise on '. . . the power of the clergye, and the lawes of the realme'.[1] These were undeniably the major works of apologetic, and, as the petitions of the Pilgrimage of Grace revealed, the writers were seen by the Government's opponents as their chief concern. The views shaped by Gardiner, and the adoption of Marsilius as the semi-official theorist of the Henrician Supremacy have long been known. Two lesser but like works of 1535 command more particular attention here, each from the Cromwellian humanist circle. The first is *A Treatise concernynge divers of the constitucyons prouynciall and legantines*, published by Thomas Godfray and translated by Leonard Cox. The second, more momentous, is *A goodly prymer in Englyshe . . .*,[2] printed by John Byddell for

---

[1] STC 11584 (Berthelet), 17817 (R. Wyer for W. Marshall), and 21588 (T. Godfray).
[2] STC 15988. C. C. Butterworth, *The English Primers* (*1529–1545*)

William Marshall, translator of the *Defensor Pacis*. Its appearance marks the first identifiable venture of a government agent into the realm of liturgical devotion.

The printer's colophon for this primer is one which will draw our attention several times in the literature of the next few years. The name of William Marshall seems likely to point to the authorship of the work, since Marshall's career as a practising printer remains without any other evidence than these very devices. At any rate, we have seen that his translation of the *Defensor* (similarly identified in the colophon to that work)[1] was directly commissioned by Cromwell. In fact, it is one of the few works whose whole genesis can be traced. The nature of the primer makes it impossible to doubt that it was similarly commissioned, or at least blessed. Indeed, its appearance is strongly reminiscent of the circumstances surrounding Taverner's commission to revise the Bible of 'Thomas Matthew'.

Its contents, although sharply critical of much existing devotion and filled with dire warnings about the spiritual dangers in traditional primers, nevertheless steer a rather reluctant middle course. The emphasis throughout is on the proper and devout use of most of the traditional form of worship, including devotion to the saints and the Blessed Virgin. The Litany is here restored, preceded by a lecture on the author's (or editor's) intentions, in which he denies any wish to disapprove of more than abuse of such prayer. After the Litany, Savonarola's meditation on the psalm 'Miserere mei Deus' is incorporated, and the remaining contents alternate traditional and Lutheran materials.[2]

This Byddell–Marshall primer of 1535 was the first completely English primer to gain any wide circulation, and on its

(Philadelphia, 1953), where the more radical earlier version of Marshall's primer is dated and analysed, ch. 6.

[1] 'R. Wyer for W. Marshall.'

[2] Butterworth, op. cit., ch. x. H. C. White, *Tudor Books of Private Devotion* (Madison, Wisconsin, 1951), pp. 91–101. On the Lutheran content of the primer, see Butterworth's App. I.

colophon it bore the royal monopoly of printing for five years. This presumably was Marshall's reward for his industry, and for providing an indispensable instrument of devotion and instruction. The distinctly Erasmian character of the work is made clearer in the revised edition printed late in 1537. In the Calendar of Saints' Days at the beginning of this work, under the date of July xii, 'Saints Nabor and felix' are deleted, and in their place stands 'Erasmus of Roterdame desessed, 1536'. It is the first open canonization of Erasmus as the patron of the Henrician establishment.[1]

The Byddell–Marshall primer stood alone in the field of vernacular primers produced in England until four years later steps were taken to produce something like an official version. Cromwell this time commissioned John Hilsey, Bishop of Rochester, and his book, dedicated to Cromwell, appeared the same year from the press of John Wayland.[2] The same year an adapted version was published for the use of children, also bearing Hilsey's name.[3] In this primer much emphasis was laid on obedience to the Prince, and the Litany was reduced even further than in the 1535 version. The emphasis throughout was on full instruction of the faithful, and on all matters of doctrine its position was conservative and traditional. It was, in fact, a true fulfilment of the Erasmian spirit of the settlement.

It is clear then that the years 1535 and 1536 brought major developments not only in official apologetic but in the positive affirmations of Henrician reform. Alongside these official treatises, devotional works, and steps toward the securing of a vernacular Bible, there was a great penumbra of publication which served to elaborate the expression of humanist opinion in these years of crisis. Two of these works were referred to in the last chapter: the *Julius exclusus* and Cox's *Paraphrase on*

---

[1] *STC* 15998, sig. C. The episode has a Protestant parallel in Joye's commemoration, in his condemned *Hortulus Animarum*, of 'Saint Thomas Hitton', the Protestant martyr.

[2] *STC* 16009 (1539).

[3] *LP* xiv (1), 1329; *STC* 16011. White, op. cit., pp. 104 f.; Butterworth, op. cit., p. 190.

*Titus.* A third translation of Erasmus appeared about 1535 from the familiar press of 'J. Byddell for W. Marshall', *A lytle treatise of the maner and forme of confession.*[1] The appearance of this orthodox and pietistic work at this moment and under such sponsorship clearly shows the difficulty in attempting a simplifying or sectarian analysis of the Government's religious position in these years. It stood side by side with two other tracts by Marshall the same year, one of which, translated 'from the Latin of the Strasbourg preachers', maintained that'pyctures and other ymages are in no wise to be suffred in churches'. The other, recalling the social concerns of the humanists,[2] was *The forme and maner of subuention for pore people practysed in Hypres.* The former work with its frank iconoclasm seems at first far from the atmosphere of Erasmus's treatise on confession, but it had an obvious relation to Cromwell's forthcoming campaign to clear the churches of most of their inheritance of medieval devotions. At that, the spectrum of opinion established by these works is no wider than Erasmus's own views, the unique usefulness of which to the English Government is by now becoming very apparent.

The next year, 1536, brought the downfall of Anne Boleyn, a new Act of Succession, and the Pilgrimage of Grace. Little in the way of secondary works appeared to elaborate the religious settlement, except a translation, again by Richard Taverner, of the Augsburg Confession. Cromwell's commission was again behind the work, which was entitled *The Confessyon of the fayth of the Germaynes in the councell,* together with the *Apologie of Melanchthon, who defendeth with reasons invincible the aforesayde confessyon.* . . .[3] In part this event must be seen in the light of current negotiations with the Lutherans, in part as evidence of Cromwell's willingness to employ moderate Protestant opinion

---

[1] *STC* 10498.

[2] *STC* 24238 (f. W. Marshall, 1535) and 26119 (T. Godfray, 1535). See Elton, above, p. 137, n. 1.

[3] *STC* 908: dedicated to Lord Cromwell. Also this year two sermons, *STC* 16795 and 22575.

where convenient.[1] But Zeeveld has also pointed out that this work coincided with another publication of this year by an English humanist, Thomas Starkey, which introduced the first fully developed discussion of an Erasmian principle elaborated by Melanchthon, the principle of *adiaphora*.

Starkey's work, written the previous year, was *An exhortation to the people instructynge theym to unitie and obedience*.[2] Here the principle of 'things good, things ill, and things indifferent' was fully applied to English religious problems, to the question of papal authority (held to be a thing indifferent), to General Councils (things useful, subject to the confirmation of princely authority), and to the Royal Supremacy (a thing good within the general sphere of ecclesiastical matters not essential to salvation). Although it seems slightly generous to credit Starkey with introducing this Erasmian principle to an English humanist world already thoroughly imbued with it, there is no question of its central importance. It was not only a device to account for and define Henry's authority over the Church, but an answer to the challenge from Pole about Christian unity.

The appearance of Starkey's *Exhortation* coincides with a new stage in official apologetic, provoked by the Northern Rebellion in that year. In addition to the official answers to the rebels in Lincolnshire and Yorkshire, there were two important pamphlets by Richard Moryson, *A remedy for sedition, . . . concernynge the true and loyall obeysance, that Commens owe unto their prince . . .*, and *A lamentation in whiche is shewed what ruyne cometh of seditious rebellyon*.[3] Published with an anonymous 'panegyric of Henry as abolisher of popish abuses',[4] these works are the only part of the considerable output of tracts during the period

---

[1] There are several Lutheran treatises in these years, one at least (*STC* 16963) associated with William Marshall. Also *STC* 16962 (1534), 16988 (1535?), 16999 (1537), 17000 (1538), all recalling the charge in Cromwell's attainder, that he dispersed 'false and erroneous books' through the shires, causing some to be translated into English.

[2] Not in *STC*: Berthelet, 1536. See Baumer, op. cit., App. A.

[3] *STC* 20877 (Berthelet, 1536) and 15185 (Berthelet, 1536).

[4] *STC* 13089a (no title or publisher), 1536–7.

when the Pilgrimage of Grace seemed a dangerous threat. Both Starkey and Moryson were involved, with others as well, probably including Tunstall. Moryson's tracts are not rich in invention or political theory, but they were effective for their immediate purpose. They reflect the atmosphere of Padua in their citations from Jerome, Vives, and Erasmus, but probably the most significant contribution they made was the first (unacknowledged) incorporation of the work of Machiavelli.[1]

With the year 1537, the year of the Bishops' Book, the official apologetic turns to a new problem, the calling of the General Council of Mantua. The immediate result was an explanation of the English refusal to participate after Henry VIII's earlier appeal to a Council, and it was issued in two versions, an English *Protestation that neyther his hyghenes nor his prelates is bound to come to Mantua* and the Latin *Illusrissimi* [sic] . . . *regis, senatus populique angliae sententia de eo concilio quod Paulus episcopus Romae Mantuae futurum simulauit.*[2]

The religious settlement was supported with the official treatises *A declaracion of the seremonies a nexid* [sic] *to the sacrament of baptyme* and *The pater noster, the crede and the comaundementes, in englysh*, from the press of John Byddell.[3] In addition, two works recalled the sharp division on the episcopal bench. One at least must have been published with Cromwell's authorization, Latimer's *Sermon . . . to the clergie, in the convocation (9th June)*, from Berthelet, dated 23 November.[4] The other, published on the Continent, came from the pen of the Scottish reformer Alexander Alesius, who was called into the 1537 Convocation by Cromwell to give his views on the sacraments, to the delight of Fox and Cranmer and the consternation of the conservative group, London, York, Lincoln, Bath, Chichester, and Norwich.[5]

---

[1] Zeeveld, op. cit., pp. 187–9.
[2] *STC* 13090 (Berthelet, 1537) and 13082 (Berthelet, 1537).
[3] *STC* 6455 (London?, 1537) and 16820 (1537).
[4] *STC* 15286 (1537).
[5] *STC* 292: *Of the auctorite of the word of god agaynst the bisshop of london* [Leipzig?, 1537?]; *LP* xii (1), 790.

It is not possible, however, to associate the humanist group as such with any of these measures. Apart from some reissues of established works, the production, if small, is interesting. From his home with the Mountjoys, Richard Whitford, the 'wretch of Sion', issued two new pietistic works, and re-edited an old favourite, the *Werke for householders*.[1] It seems clear from the letters of the royal visitor to Syon, Thomas Bedyll, that Whitford had been very firm in refusing to acknowledge the Royal Supremacy, but his connexion with the Mountjoy family, and, presumably, the purely pietistic character of his writings, seemingly protected him from government prosecution. From the dissolution of the convent to his death he remained with the family of Erasmus's old patron, William Blount. The new works published in these years suggested no diminution of his energies or powers; they were *A dayly exercyse and experyence of dethe* and *A dia-loge . . . bytwene the curate and the parochiane for preparacion unto howselinge*.[2]

In the same vein were two new translations of Erasmus, *An exposicyon of the xv psalme*, from an unknown hand, and Thomas Paynell's *The comparation of a virgin and a martyr*.[3] This latter work was dedicated 'to the ryght worshypfull Master John Ramsay, lorde priour of Merton', of which house Paynell was a canon. Two years later, Paynell would add to these the equally Erasmian sermon of Saint Cyprian on the Lord's prayer.[4]

The final work of 1537 which bears on our theme is a curious production issued from the Protestant press of Nicholson at Southwark. Entitled *The original and sprynge of all sectes and orders*, 'by whome, whan or were they beganne . . .',[5] it was translated anonymously from the 'hye Dutch', and enters our story as a Protestant comment on the theme of John More's earlier work on the kingdom of Prester John. The contention

---

[1] *STC* 25425: Newly corrected, R. Redman, 1537.
[2] *STC* 25414 and 25416 (both J. Wayland, 1537).
[3] *STC* 10495 (Wayland, 1537) and *RSTC* 10465.5 (Berthelet, 1537).
[4] *STC* 6156 (Berthelet, 1539).                    [5] *STC* 18849.

that John More's translation work was essentially a conservative religious tract arguing for Christian unity on an adiaphoristic basis is confirmed by this treatise, which was evidently thought by the Protestant group to be sufficiently important to be translated into English. Referring in the preface to the present diversity of Christian sects, the writer attempts a twofold rebuttal of the Catholic charge that unity had been disrupted. The first assertion is that Rome itself is but one among many such divisions, an argument with obvious relevance to the official apology in England. The second is that a wide diversity of sects has always been the normal condition, not only of Christendom, but of Judaism: '. . . yf thou reade diligently, thou shalte thynke it no maruayll, that ther is now suche contencyon and diuision in the worlde, in as much as ther was no tyme, no age, no generacyon sence the begynnynge but alwaye ther hath ben some sectes, some diuersite of opinion, and some sundrye maner of belefe in the same'.

The body of the work is divided into three sections, considering (1) 'Orders, sectes or religions under the byshop of Rome', (2) 'Faythes and sectes of Christendom only, besyde all other', and (3) 'Sectes and supersticions of the Jewes or Hebrues'. Under the first heading all the religious and monastic orders are listed as 'sects', with the Armenians, Greeks, Georgians, and others, including the 'Indian faythe'.

With his discussion of this 'Indian' sect, the author presumably turns to an earlier Portuguese production about Prester John and the 1514 embassy of Matthew the Armenian to Lisbon on behalf of the Negus of Ethiopia. His account of the Ethiopian Christians includes the observation that 'They knowe ther is an head byshop of Rome, but the cause that they obey hym not, is the great distaunce from hym'. On the whole the treatise is very moderate concerning the Roman claims, adducing the withdrawal of religious from the world as the peculiar sign of errancy. 'Christe knoweth how nedeful the true Christenmen be in thys world' is the reproach, which (with the above observation concerning the 'Indian' attitude to Rome) suggests an Erasmian rather than a distinctly Protestant attitude in the writer.

The following year, 1538, brought with it widespread icono-clasm, sponsored by Cromwell, and the execution and arrest of the Courtenays on charges of treason. It was in this year, too, that the negotiations with the Lutheran divines seem to have reached a final impasse, especially on questions which would seem negotiable on Erasmian principles but on which Henry himself stood fast: communion in both kinds, private Masses, and celibacy of the clergy. The achievement by Paul III of a ten-year truce between Francis I and the Emperor had prompted a fresh series of negotiations, and when they failed there was need for a continental alliance to offset the still pressing French–Imperial combination. It was this combination of circumstances, with the geographic situation of Cleves against the Imperial Netherlands, which produced Cromwell's negotiations for a marriage alliance, not with a doctrinaire Lutheran but with the sister of the essentially Erasmian Duke William V of Jülich-Cleves.

Since the reputedly staunch Protestantism of Cleves is an historical tradition which flourishes almost without question,[1] it is worth observing here that the ecclesiastical history of the duchy in the early sixteenth century is a classic of Erasmian moderation. The father of Duke William and of Henry's Queen Anne, Duke John of Cleves, had imposed a completely Erasmian reform on his duchy with the Church Ordinance of 1533. He inherited the active reforming policies of his father-in-law, Duke William IV of Jülich-Berg, refused to enforce the Edict of Worms in his territories, and prohibited Luther's writings as 'vain, wrong and heretical'. One of the authors of this Church Ordinance, Conrad von Heresbach, was tutor of William V. Heresbach was a friend and admirer of Erasmus, and Erasmus himself was consulted about the conduct of reform in the duchy.

---

[1] e.g. F. G. Emmison, in his recent biography of the eminent Erasmian figure Sir William Petre, *Tudor Secretary* (1961), calls the Cleves marriage a 'Lutheran union' (p. 44).

Shortly after his accession in 1539 William V inherited the region of Geldern-Zütphen, which interfered with Imperial interests in the Low Countries. As a result he sought alliance with the Schmalkaldic League against Charles V, but he regarded the Church Ordinance of 1533 as binding throughout his life. His opposition was crushed by Charles in a brief campaign during the summer of 1543, after which Cleves was firmly bound to the Catholic interest. In 1538, however, this diplomatic alliance, far from being Protestant, represented a distinct repudiation of the doctrinaire Lutheran party.[1]

The Cleves marriage alliance and the final failure of the negotiations with the Lutherans in 1538 is probably responsible also for the appearance at that time of a distinctly anti-Protestant work by Erasmus, the *Epistle concernynge the veryte of the Sacrament of Christes body and bloude*, published for an unknown translator by Robert Wyer.[2] It is one of the great humanist's most orthodox productions, and at the outset he recommends the example of Berengarius in submitting to the judgement of the Catholic Church on the question of the Eucharist. The recipient of the original was Balthazar Mercklin, Bishop of Constance and Imperial Vice-Chancellor, to whom Erasmus dedicated his edition of the *De veritate corporis et sanguinis Dominici in Eucharistia* by the twelfth-century Cluniac monk, Alger.[3] The interest of the work for England, apart from its distinct assertion of traditional sacramental doctrine, was perhaps in its reference to popular practice. After invoking the judgement of the Church, Erasmus declares characteristically that the great subtleties about the doctrine are best left to those

[1] On the religious policies of the Dukes of Cleves see J. P. Dolan, C.S.C., 'The Influence of Erasmus, Witzel and Cassander in the Church Ordinances and Reform Proposals of the United Duchees [*sic*] of Cleve during the Middle Decades of the 16th Century', *Reformationsgeschichtliche Studien und Texte*, Heft 83 (Münster, 1957).

[2] *STC* 10490: the editors suggest the date 1535, but E. J. Devereux has pointed out that the reference to Erasmus's death and the imprimatur 'ad imprimendum solum' demanded by the 1538 Proclamation are evidence for a later dating.

[3] Freiburg, Jo. Faber Emmeus, 1530.

fit to deal with them, 'But as unto the laye people it doth suffice yf they do belieue that after the wordes of consecracion be once by the mynyster [*sic*, translating, "Vulgo satis est credere post consecrationem illic esse verum corpus et sanguinem Domini . . ."] spoken ouer the creatures of breade and wyne, that there is incontynent the very body and bloude of our sauyour Christ . . .'. Erasmus also rebukes disorder at the supreme moment of the elevation, recalling that the custom of the primitive Church was universal prostration, and concludes with an exhortation to priests to bear in mind this exalted function in reforming their own lives.

The translator of the work, in an epistle 'to the deuoute and good Christian Reader', seems above all anxious to invoke Erasmus's authority for the traditional doctrine of the Eucharist, and with it for a devotional attitude at Mass. As evidence of Erasmus's own reverence, the translator points out that he had translated the liturgy of St. John Chrysostom and had dealt with the Mass very reverently in the *De sarcienda ecclesia concordia*, the *Enchiridion*, and in the Paraphrase of the second chapter of St. John. All of these references to the work of Erasmus, like the careful citation of the source of the translation ('in the great volume of all his Epistles, pagine 1577'), show both the translator's thorough acquaintance with Erasmus's writings and his conviction that an appeal to Erasmus's authority would be both popular and impressive to his readers.

Apart from this, the internal crisis of 1538 prompted a new apologetic work by Moryson, his *Apomaxis calumniarum, confitiorumque*. Directed against the enemies within, the *Apomaxis* probably had its roots in an earlier answer to the criticisms of Cochlaeus and Reginald Pole.[1] The chief preoccupation of the year, however, was not the Courtenays but the continued need for an apologetic reply to the Council of Mantua.[2]

The interrogation of the Courtenay circle itself did, however,

---

[1] *STC* 18109 (Berthelet, '1537', but the dedication is dated 12 July 1538). Cf. Zeeveld, op. cit., pp. 158 f.

[2] Notice *STC* 23407, 24237, 13080, 13081.

shed some light on the attitude of humanist patrons who were
out of sympathy with the Government. It was alleged against
the Countess of Salisbury that she forbade her tenants to read
the New Testament in English, 'or any other new [books]
which the Kynges Hynes hathe pryvelyged'.[1] The deposition
of Sir Henry Owen, Kt., revealed similar alarm at 'these new
English books',[2] and the same attitude can be discovered in
the visitation of Woburn Abbey.

Here the records are more rewarding with detail about the
reading of the deponents than are those concerning the Courtenays. In an examination in May 1538, at which Sir William
Petre presided as one of the three commissioners, it became
evident that the Abbot, Robert Hobbes, a friend of Lord Grey
of Wilton, was strongly disaffected towards the Government's
religious policy.[3] A clerk of the district, Sir John Mylward of
Toddington, had written a treatise supporting the Roman Supremacy with the views of divers Church doctors, *De potestate
Petri*. In a later account the doctors he cited are listed, at least in
part: they include among others Augustine, Jerome, Ambrose,
Chrysostom, and Cyprian. Milward, then, ranks as a learned
conservative, closely associated with the monastic community
in which he sought critical advice about his work. He seems
also to have written another work about a monk of the house
who had forsaken the habit, but of neither treatise does there
seem to have been any trace for the commissioners.[4]

The inquisition of Woburn Abbey produced yet another
acknowledgement that the propaganda campaign of Cromwell's humanists had not gone unnoticed. Abbot Hobbes
was charged with having said, among other indiscreet remarks,
'though the Lord Privy Seal seems to be the maintainer of these
wretched heretic books that he set forth *cum privilegio regali*,
neither the King nor he knows the pestilent doctrine that is in

---

[1] Testimony of Johanes Ansard: *LP* xiii (2), 817, p. 326.
[2] Ibid. 831 (2) (iii).
[3] *LP* xiii (1), 981 (i); Knowles, op. cit., pp. 373 f.
[4] *LP* xiii (1), 981 (i), (ii) and (iv).

them'.[1] The royal privilege noticed both by the Courtenays and Abbot Hobbes was not, of course, an endorsement of the contents of the work, but a grant of monopoly. The confusion worried the Government, however, as is made clear by the addition of 'ad imprimendum solum' by the Proclamation of 1538. Finally, it is perhaps not an abuse of the evidence to see in these very generously phrased condemnations protest not only against the frankly official apologetic and doctrinal works, but against the whole broad output of translation which we have been discussing.

In concluding with Woburn, it may be noticed that the King's great friend the poet Sir Francis Bryan, to whom Wyatt and Lord Berners dedicated works of their own, was High Steward of the abbey and was described by the Abbot of Woburn as his 'trusty friend'.[2] Bryan's physician, moreover, Doctor Redechin, was alleged to believe that the Supremacy had no basis in Scripture. The abbey seems to have had interesting associations, and it is illuminating to find the same preoccupations—with clerical abuses, scriptural authority, and the learning of the early church fathers—in these conservative circles as among the humanists who were prepared to accept Henry's policy. Once more the essential unity of spirit and continuity of interest from the pre-Reformation community of Erasmian learning is made apparent.

And once more the humanist publication of the year confirms this impression. The appearance of Elyot's Dictionary was the chief event not only of this year, but perhaps of the whole period of Cromwell's dominance, so far as learned enterprise is concerned. The preface to the Dictionary (exalting Henry's position and his genius in disputation with the heretic John Nicholson) describes Henry's personal interest in the work and his decision to assign it to the supervision of the Lord Privy Seal, 'chief patron of virtue and cunning' after the King. On the bookstalls it accompanied appropriately Erasmian works. Pietism was represented there by Richard Wyse's *A consolacyon*

---

[1] *LP* xiii (i), 981 (2), p. 363.        [2] Ibid., p. 362.

*for chrysten people* and by an anonymous translation of St. Martin of Braga, entitled *The rule of an honest lyfe: Here unto is added the Encheridyon of a spyrytuall lyfe.*[1] Once more Erasmus was invoked, with the anonymously rendered *Preparation to deathe, a boke as deuout as eloquent,* published again and perhaps translated by the King's Printer, Thomas Berthelet.[2] Richard Taverner also reappeared on the scene, this time with a translation of the *Loci communes* of Erasmus Sarcerius, *Common places of scripture ordrely set forth.*[3]

This last work has additional interest because of the associations of the author. A Protestant reformer of the party of Melanchthon, Sarcerius had been a pupil of Peter Schade at Fribourg, and was at this time in the service of Prince William of Nassau-Dillenburg. His *Methodus divinae scripturae locos praecipuos explicans* of 1528 was translated by Taverner at the King's instigation,[4] and he himself was invited to apply to the King for reward. One of the last evidences of Cromwell's activity is a letter from Christopher Saint German in which, after a discussion of private concerns, he reports that he cannot get any copies of Sarcerius's *De locis communibus.*[5]

The publications of the next year, 1539, are eloquent of the continued sense of insecurity both at home and abroad. In October the marriage treaty with the Duke of Cleves was signed, and it was not until the next spring that there were signs of Imperial alienation from France over the issue of Milan. Until that time the situation abroad looked ominous, especially with the proposed official visit of Charles V to Paris, and Henry turned his energies to supervising the fortification of the realm. He was supported from the unofficial chancery of Cromwell with two more works from the pen of Richard

[1] STC 26063 (J. Waylande, 1538) and 17500 [1538?].
[2] STC 10505: the *De praeparatione ad mortem* of 1534.
[3] STC 21753 (J. Byddel, 1538; also incorrectly entered under 'Desiderius Erasmus' as 10465).
[4] LP xiv (1), 496; Erasmus Sarcerius to Henry VIII, 10 Mar. 1539.
[5] LP xiv (1), 1349; presumably the 1538 *Loci aliquot communes theologici* of Sarcerius.

Moryson, *An exhortation to styr all Englyshe men to the defence of theyr countreye* and *An inuective ayenste . . . treason*.[1] The latter work received in fact three impressions in the course of the year, sufficient evidence both of official alarm and of public interest. This time the immediate subject was the recent Courtenay conspiracy, . . . *the great and detestable vice treason, wherein the secret practises and traiterous workings of theym that suffrid of late are disclosed . . .*, but the further intent to unite the country behind the King in the face of prospective attack is amply evident.

These two manifestoes were accompanied by another timely production, evidently translated by John Gough the printer himself. This was John LeMaire's *The abbreuyacyon of all generall councellys*, designed to strengthen the Government's argument against the papal claims to dominate General Councils.[2] Richard Moryson seems also to have had time for a private bid for royal favour, for in addition to the official work which had occupied him in the past three or four years as the leading pamphleteer in Cromwell's domestic campaigns, he now published a flattering work timed to coincide with Henry's military preparations. This was a translation of Sextus Julius Frontinus, *The strategemes, sleyghtes and policies of warre* from the press of Berthelet.[3]

The prefatory dedication to the King is a striking example of the extravagant heights to which Moryson's adulation of Henry could rise. Hailing the King's love for 'this your noble empyre', a reminder of the imperial theme so conspicuous in the royal statutes, he expresses a wish to assist in the ceaseless work of the monarch for his people. He cannot indeed see how he could wish greater comfort to all Englishmen than that which they would gain if they should see how 'your grace spendeth all the hole day'. After referring to the treason of Sir Nicholas Carewe, he recalls that he had long wanted to dedicate something to Henry, but that hitherto all his 'trifles' had been too mean.

[1] *STC* 18110, 18111 (Berthelet).
[2] *STC* 15453 (J. Gough, 1539): cf. 21308.    [3] *STC* 11402 (1539).

Now, weak and imperfect as this one also is, he is prepared to offer it because of the King's desire for the safety of his people. 'I coulde not, but for a season a courtayne drawen betweene my weake eies and the resplendent beames of your most clere maiestie, folow fervent desire and humblye offer unto your hyghnesse this my rude translation. . . .'

Stressing the importance of 'policie' over sheer strength in war, he offers this handbook for the use of Henry's captains. For, he adds, warming to the sense of imminent national peril, 'Peace is to be refused, whan tyme forceth men to warre. Wherfore I have besydes this my translation, in an other tryfle of myn, exhorted al my contrey men, peace laid aside, to prepare for warre, that if nede constrein them to it, they may be redy to entertayne false frendes, worse than enmies, accordyng to their desertes.' He hopes in future and at a happier time to be able to serve Henry with 'delectable liquour' rather than this cup of 'troubled water', and wishes him long life, to the comfort of all his subjects, and 'to the destruction and deth of al popery'.

The sense of national emergency revealed by these works is vivid. Tunstall's sermon before the King on Palm Sunday was also published in an attempt to rally the country.[1] But other plans of the humanist community happened in this year to produce predominantly literary and pietistic works, which make an oddly tranquil accompaniment to the Government's fiery proclamations.

The first such event was the publication of two new works by Sir Thomas Elyot, the revised *Banquette of sapience*, a collection of moral sayings gleaned from antiquity and the early Christian Fathers, and *The castel of helth*, dedicated to Cromwell. Pietistic works also were offered by the government printer in his reissue of Elyot's translation of two very significant Erasmian works: *A swete and deuoute sermon of mortalitie of man*, by St. Cyprian, was printed with *The rules of a christian lyfe by*

---

[1] *STC* 24322 (Berthelet, 1539).

*Picus erle of Mirandula.*[1] And, as mentioned already, Berthelet also printed Paynell's translation of St. Cyprian's sermon on the Lord's Prayer.[2]

The rest of the year's humanist production is given over to a voluminous contribution by Richard Taverner. Since 1536 Taverner had been Clerk of the Privy Seal, and in this year he received a sizeable grant of ecclesiastical lands in Lincolnshire.[3] His duties seem to have provided plenty of time for literary activity, for to that already mentioned he now added four books which clearly represented work over a considerable period.

Two were concerned with lay religious instruction, the *Epitome of the psalmes or briefe meditations*, translated by him and dedicated to the King in an interesting preface, and *A catechisme or institution of the Christen religion*,[4] which was reissued in the following year. The dedication of the former work confirms what was already evident about the ground of Taverner's official position:

. . . more than thre yeares passed, my verye good lorde and olde mayster my lorde Privie seale for such qualities as he thought to have espyed in me . . . preferred and delyuered me up unto your graces service, and sythens that tyme, to thintent he wolde make me the more hable and mete to serve your highnes in my callyng, hath enured me with dyverse translacions and other exercises.

This particular contribution to the pietistic cause was apparently deemed important enough to be published twice in the same year by different printers.

Closely resembling the *Epitome of the psalmes* in general character is his *Catechisme or institution of the Christen religion*,

[1] *STC* 7630 and 7643, both from Berthelet. On Elyot see Lehmberg, *Elyot*, pp. 129–31 and 132–47. The Cyprian is *STC* 6158.

[2] *STC* 6156 (1539).

[3] Book of Augmentations, leases of 30 Hen. VIII, calendared in *LP* xiv (1), 1355 (p. 607).

[4] *STC* 23709 (1539); 2748 and 23710, two separate editions from Bankes the same year. The author of the *Epitome* was Wolfgang Capito, the correspondent of Erasmus turned Lutheran.

which like the *Epitome* may be a by-product of his revision of
the Bible, which also appeared in this year. At any rate, it seems
that in the realm of official pietistic writing Taverner occupied
as important a place in Cromwell's bureau as did Moryson
with popular political apologetics.

Finally, in the closely related sphere of translating Erasmus
himself, Taverner apparently found time for two works which
probably derive from his personal tastes, the *Prouerbes or
adagies with newe addicions gathered out of the Chiliades of Erasmus*
and his *Garden of Wysdom*.[1] The latter work was issued in two
parts, the first looking forward to further publication, the
second thanking his readers for the interest which had made it
possible in the midst of the 'sondrye occupations' which had
postponed its appearance.

Together these works form one of the greatest repositories
of Erasmian adages and classical wisdom made available to the
sixteenth-century English reader. Like all the rest of Taverner's
work of this kind, it derives entirely from Erasmus, although
this indebtedness is not always acknowledged.[2] The *Proverbes
or adagies* acknowledges the *Chiliades* and the *Mimi Publiani*, and
Taverner, like Robert Burrant in his *Preceptes of Cato*[3] at a later
date, added his own to the comments of Erasmus, usually to support the Supremacy and the Henrician settlement. Reverence
for the Prince and a concern to avoid disorders in the commonwealth go hand in hand with an enlarged scriptural content.

In the *Garden of Wysdom* there is a more original departure
in manner. Taverner here abandoned the form of comment
upon a Latin adage and produced a work entirely in English
prose. The material, however, comes chiefly from the *Apophthegmata* of Erasmus, like Udall's independent work of 1542,[4]

---

[1] STC 10437 (R. Bankes, 1539) and 23711a. See Devereux, n. 2, below.

[2] C. R. Baskervill, 'Taverner's *Garden of Wisdom* and the *Apophthegmata* of
Erasmus', *Studies in Philology*, vol. xxix (1932), pp. 149–59. On the complex
bibliographical history of these productions, see an article by E. J. Devereux
forthcoming in *The Library*.     [3] STC 4854; see below, Chapter 7.

[4] STC 10443 (Grafton, 1542). For collation of Taverner's with Erasmus's
references, see Baskervill, op. cit., p. 156, n. 11.

and incorporates some fifty odd of the nearly six hundred names in the original work. In several passages allusions praising the King are added, with other reflections on contemporary problems, and in this way the work was turned into a valuable compendium of moderate humanist opinion about contemporary affairs.

Taverner's productivity and popularity were never greater than in this period, and his continued production of books through the year of his patron's fall, 1540, serves to suggest that the English humanist enterprise would survive this apparent calamity as well. Indeed, the only discernible change in the complexion of English publication is a sharp drop in official apologetic treatises. The Royal Manuscripts collection, however, provides a treatise whose prospects of publication (if publication was ever intended) were certainly diminished by Cromwell's fall. It is a project devised by Richard Moryson for the codification of English common law into Latin. With it is a treatise on tenures and services intended to exemplify Moryson's proposals.[1]

Although no precise date can be attached to these two works, they seem to derive from the last decade of Henry's reign, and they reveal at the very least the enthusiasm of members of the Paduan circle for civil law studies and the results which these could produce when they returned to consider the English scene. The treatise was a product of Moryson's leisure hours intended (like his translation of Frontinus) to contribute something useful to Henry's divinely ordained ministry to his own people. It suggests that the common laws 'of this your Realm, that nowe be unwritten, myght be written; that nowe lye dispersed and uncerteyn, myght be gathered together and made certeyn; that nowe be in no tonge myght be reduced into the Latyn tonge'.[2] It is the confusion, delay, and expense of legal recourse which Moryson fears, for he finds that in England law

---

[1] Royal MSS. 18 A. L and 11 A. XVI. The former is briefly noticed by Zeeveld, op. cit., p. 233.

[2] Royal MS. 18 A. L, f.v. 3.

does not bring concord and peace as it should, but rather produces discontent with civil government. In this respect it compares unfavourably with two exemplary codes, that of Rome and that of God for Israel, expressed through Moses.[1]

Finally, the confusion of tongues in English law, embracing Saxon, British, Italian, Latin, French, English, and Greek, could be eliminated by turning the whole into the eminently suitable tongue of Latin. 'For albiet our owne in other thyngs be very parfet and plentious, yet for that lawes have certeyn termes which never cam into our tongue and are emonge the latynes easily expressed, the latyn tongue muste needes be moche apter playnly to set out lawes.' Admitting some possible defects here, Moryson insists that there is no other legal language 'so copious that is used commonly among Christen men'.[2]

Taken thus far, Moryson's treatise seems to have a confined purpose, vaguely sinister in light of the English legal tradition, as a tacit plea for opening English law to a 'reception' of civil-law principles. In fact, however, this neglected treatise turns abruptly to the much broader theme of the Prince's service. Moryson, it develops, is less interested in imposing a uniform Latinity on the law courts than in improving the education of the profession. The practitioners of law should know 'other sciences and artes liberall', and for this they must know Latin. How, without it, can they learn logic, 'of all sciences the chiefest'? Or how know its ground and principles without philosophy? Or without knowledge of God's law? Lawyers in England now spend all their time pursuing only their private profit, instead of studying good letters, and, what is worse, they will actually try to prevent a young aspiring lawyer from acquiring such knowledge, 'as though good letters and the lawe coulde not agree in one parson'.[3] What we have here is in fact a repetition in the smaller sphere of the humanist circle of the entrenched conservatism of the world of scholastic learning. The parallel is the more apparent from Moryson's own illustration. Why should the established lawyers take this

---

[1] Royal MS. 18 A. I, fols. 5-6.   [2] Ibid., fols. 6ᵛ and 7.   [3] Ibid., fols. 7ᵛ-10.

attitude? He cannot say, unless it is for the same reason as that which moved the abbot, 'who wold his novyces to be no better lerned then hymselfe'.[1]

Behind this resentment is the new ideal of humanist service to the commonweal. If lawyers were more learned, they would soon learn other arts and be better able to serve the King both at home and abroad, where he is now constrained to employ bishops and doctors, 'who be chiefly ordeyned to preache and teache Goddes worde, for lacke of layemen lerned to execute that office, wherby ther dueties resteth undone, and a great nomber of your poore subiectes for lack of teachyng be ignoraunt in the knowlage of God, in ther duetie of obedience to hym, your Grace and your lawes'.[2]

Finally, such learning is an indispensable weapon against the Bishop of Rome, 'subvertour and suppressour of all godlynes'. Here Moryson observes that Irish scholars studying in England, who in all other things were 'verie asses', excelled in canon law, being able to rehearse more texts by heart 'then auncient students and olde fathers in this Realme'. From this, Moryson concludes, Rome draws her great strength in Ireland.[3]

Warming to this subject, Moryson makes a revealing digression on the need to extirpate Roman principles from English religion. The evils of Rome should be 'daily by all meanes opened, inculked and dryven into the peoples' hedes, tought in the scoles to children, plaied in plaies before the ignoraunt people', sung by minstrels, and published in books in English 'purposely to be deuysed to declare the same at large'. Such works are indeed 'to be born withall, yea though som thyng in them be to be mysliked'.[4] Admitting the difficulties in writing against the papists perfectly, Moryson proposes an annual feast of thanksgiving for deliverance from the Roman yoke, since 'this Pharoah' is not yet dead, and he elaborates his proposal for popular plays as well, presumably to offset the effect of the traditional popular religious drama. Against the background

[1] Ibid., fol. 10.  [2] Ibid., fol. 11–11$^v$.
[3] Ibid., fol. 13.  [4] Ibid., fols. 15–16.

of this argument of Moryson, John Bale's *Kyng John* assumes new significance.

Apologizing for this digression, Moryson concludes with an appeal to Henry to undertake his project of codification in order to emulate Justinian. It becomes apparent here that the emulation is to be carried to considerable lengths. 'The same reason, the same lawe of nature that was among the Romanes is emong us.'[1] English laws, although they differ in form and handling, 'be made of that matier that ther lawes be. . . . So it is not impossible but easy to tourne the matier of the cyuyl lawes into ours, and yet in no poynte change any of ours.' As an example of what is to be done, he submits a 'rude plat' in Latin on land tenure and services.

This then was Richard Moryson's contribution to the 'threat', if such it was, of a reception of civil law in England. As we have seen, he was inspired less by a conscious admiration for the authoritarian aspects of the Roman code than by a feeling that here the new generation of educated laymen would find an entrée both to a work of learning and to the opportunities of royal service. It is significant that in the year of Cromwell's fall, not long before he wrote this treatise, Richard Moryson also published at the press of Berthelet a translation of Vives's *An introduction to wysedome*.[2]

Apart from these matters, the humanist output of the year of Cromwell's fall from power was much as it had been throughout his supremacy. There is Elyot's interesting *Defense of good women*, regarded by many as a thinly veiled defence of Catherine of Aragon,[3] and certainly as an assertion of the feminine ideal of the humanist–pietist community. Whittington's translation of the *De civilitate morum puerilium*[4] reappeared, having first been published eight years before, and there were

[1] Royal MS. 18 A. L, fol. 24.

[2] *STC* 24847 (1540); also 1544, with possibly two editions in 1550.

[3] *STC* 7658 (Berthelet, 1545). See Lehmberg, *Elyot*, pp. 174–7, and Foster Watson, *Vives and the Renascence Education of Women* (1912), pp. 211–12. *Pasquil the playne* was also reissued in this year (*STC* 7673).

[4] *STC* 10468 (J. Byddell, 1540).

probably four separate editions of Savonarola's meditation on the psalm 'Miserere mei Deus'.[1]

Besides this, the production of Erasmus expanded with three new works. Richard Taverner, continuing his transcriptions, published (in Latin and English) *Flores aliquot sententiarum, the flowres of sencies gathered out of sundry wryters by Erasmus. . . .*[2] The contents of this work came chiefly from a small addition to the *Dicta Sapientum e Graecis*, and its character and dedication to the 'florentissima pubes Britannica' place it in the list of educational works.

Two anonymous translations supplement this, each of considerable interest. The first, *A dialoge or communication of two persons, newly translated into Englishe*, published in these years probably by John Byddell,[3] is the first of the Colloquies to appear in English, the subject being 'The pylgremage of pure devotyon'. No more suitable product of Erasmus's pen could have been found for Cromwell's purposes. The Injunctions of September 1538 had decreed the suppression of the cults of saints and of shrines, and Erasmus's famous account of his visits to Walsingham and Canterbury were an obvious choice for translation. The influence of the colloquy can even be traced among the Articles of Inquiry given to the King's Commissioners visiting Walsingham, and in the official Declaration of Faith issued in 1539.[4] The clumsy and verbose prologue 'To the reder' strikes a belligerent note against false and ungodly devotions, but at least two aspects of the work suggest that it is not merely a Protestant tract in disguise. One is the deliberate reference to the recent rebellions and to the need for loyalty to the Prince, 'whome thou arte so straytly commaunded to

[1] *STC* 21793, 21794, 21795, and 21795a, the last two by Byddell for William Marshall.

[2] *STC* 10445 (Ex aed. R. Taverner, R. Bankes, 1540). This year also saw his 'Epistles and gospelles' in separate publication (*STC* 2967).

[3] *STC* 10454; evidently part of the propaganda provoked by the Pilgrimage of Grace. Cf. H. de Vocht, *The Earliest English Translations of Erasmus' Colloquia, 1536–1566* (Louvain, 1928).

[4] de Vocht, op. cit., pp. xlvi–xlviii.

obaye', to avoid 'domage of a publike weale, whiche above all vices is noted most to be abhorred'.

The second suggestion of official sponsorship is in another recommendation of a middle way, or at least of obedience to the established order, in the attack on images in the Churches. Noting the value of Erasmus in exposing false and idolatrous devotion to images, where they are used 'contrary to the immaculate scripture of gode', the anonymous translator equally with his chosen prophet condemns the 'arrogancye' of 'the pryuate judgment of certayne that of theyr owne brayne wolde cast out images of the temple, with out a comen consent and authoryte'.[1]

The last anonymous work has an interest greater than its brevity would suggest. It is a translation of Erasmus's sermon 'Of the chylde Jesus', written for delivery by a scholar of Colet's school at Saint Paul's and styled by the translator 'To be pronounced and preached of a chylde unto chyldren'.[2] Recalling thus the first years of English reforming humanism, it comes also within the category of the works already noticed which were intended to provide special instruction for the young, a major feature of the reform movement as it was shaped by the English humanist community.

The Erasmian output of 1540 did not end with translations of the master. One of the most characteristic works, a translation of Henry Cornelius Agrippa's *The commendation of matrimony*, published again by Berthelet,[3] introduced a new scholar to the scene. David Clapham dedicated this work to Cromwell's son Gregory, in terms which suggest that he may have occupied a position something like a tutor in Cromwell's household. Moved, as he claimed, by his 'vehement affection' for Cromwell's heir and by admiration for his great diligence towards wisdom, he chooses this work because of the exemplary marriage of Gregory. The sacramental character of the marriage bond is emphasized in a way which suggests a

---

[1] Preface, fol. iiij.        [2] *STC* 10509 (R. Redman, [1540?]).
[3] *STC* 201 (1540).

markedly conservative attitude on the sacramental controversies. Clapham refers to the exemplary education provided
for Gregory by his father, and then expands this theme in a very
interesting way. About the elder Cromwell he says:

And surely his care in that behalfe hath not been onely for you, but
for manye other: yea the thing that he specially wisheth and desyreth
is, that the youthe of this hole realme of England shulde be brought
up vertuousely, namely the noble mens chyldren, in good litterature,
and the other after theyr abilities, wyttes and aptenes, in sciences and
craftes, wherby they shall highly profite themselves, to the great
advancement of the common weale, and above al thinges, he wolde,
that with theyr lernyng of good letters, sciences and craftes, wherby
. . . they shuld be ernestly taught, obedyence to god, to the kynges
hyghnesse, and to suche rulers and lawes, as his maiesty shal ordeyn.

It seems quite possible that we have here an authentic record
of opinions in the Cromwell circle on the vital question of
reforming English education. The concern is hardly surprising:
we know already from another tutor that the young Cromwell
was brought up on Erasmus.[1] Wood records nothing of Clapham's connexion with Cromwell, attributing to him travel and
studies in the civil law, with unknown degrees. Perhaps not
unexpectedly, he was a member of Doctors' Commons and
became a noted proctor in the Arches, where he won the
notice of, among others, William Cecil. His present interests
were confirmed two years later, with the publication of
Agrippa's *Treatise of the Nobilitie and excellencye of Woman
Kynde*.[2]

It is appropriate to notice here, then, three other works of
educational purpose in 1540. John Palsgrave published his
version of Fullonius's *Acolastus*, put into English 'after such
maner as chyldrene are taught in the grammer schole' and
dedicated to the King.[3] Robert Whittington issued *The Paradox*

---

[1] Ellis, ser. iii, vol. i, letter cxxiv (p. 344).
[2] *STC* 203 (Berthelet, 1542). Bale also recorded a translation of Erasmus's
*De matrimonia*, perhaps a confusion with Taverner's work (*STC* 10492).
[3] *STC* 11470 (Berthelet, 1540).

*of M. T. Cicero*,[1] and the third work came again from Richard Taverner, *Catonis disticha moralia cum scoliis Erasmi*.[2] Like the *Flores* of this year it was taken from the *Opuscula aliquot* of 1514, and was intended to be 'in usum Anglicae iuventutis'. In the same volume was Taverner's *Mimi publiani*, with the English phraseology much revised, and the *Flores* once more, somewhat revised. The preface was dedicated 'to the tendre youth of Englande', and, as in his earlier works, Taverner followed the Latin epigram with an English version of Erasmus's commentary and occasionally an addition of his own.

Two other works published in 1540 require brief mention. One is the reissue, the first since it appeared in 1529, of Richard Hyrde's version of Vives's *The Instruction of a Christen Woman*. Interestingly enough, the dedication to Queen Catherine was not suppressed. Even if this was an oversight, which seems scarcely likely in the house of Henry's official printer, it makes a surprising coincidence with the appearance in this same year of More's *Boke of the fayre gentilwoman*, which was printed by Robert Wyer.[3] The author's identity was only thinly veiled behind 'Tho. Mo.'

On the eve of his fall, Thomas Cromwell received the dedication of a pietistic work written, evidently, by a grateful country gentleman of Essex. It was *A commemoration of the inestimable graces and benefites of God*, from the press of Berthelet.[4] The author, John Pylbarough, describes himself as Cromwell's 'servaunt' in the preface, and he appears to be otherwise unknown to the literary historians of England. However, in the State Papers he is recorded three times in 1540–1 on Commissions of the Peace in Essex. His work on the graces of God, 'infused through the bryght lyght of the knowlege of his holy word, in our moste dradde Soveraygne lorde Henry the eight, . . . composed on the psalm, Benedictus Dominus Deus Israel',

---

[1] *STC* 5313 (J. Redman f. R. Redman, 1540).
[2] *STC* 4843 (In aed. R. Taverneri per R. Bankes, 1540).
[3] Maitland, no. 522*b* (p. 439); uncontroversial early verses.
[4] *STC* 20521.

seems to be the only record of this bond with Cromwell. In itself it is minor item, but as a symptom of the Secretary's wide connexions in the realm, and of the pietistic forces which he had succeeded in channelling and using to the ends of the Government, it is a suitable subject on which to conclude the period of his career.

His fall seems to have deprived us of at least one interesting work. Leonard Cox, the humanist schoolmaster of Reading Abbey, was in correspondence with Cromwell in the spring of 1540, when he dedicated to him his edition of Lily's Grammar, published in the same year.[1] On 23 May he wrote another letter which reveals that Thomas Berthelet was the intermediary in this bid for the Privy Seal's attention, which had been rewarded by Cox's acceptance 'into your service', with 'further promise of your speciall benevolence'.[2] Cox promises his best service, and apologizes for not yet having called in person to thank Cromwell, a fact explained by the place of the letter's origin, Caerleon in Wales, where ultimately he kept a school. However, he hopes by Michaelmas to bring Cromwell 'a farre better worke then that which I have dedicate to yowe all redy, and that uppon rhetorike which I entende to entitle erotemata rhetorica'. He hopes further to provide a work so distinguished 'that the world shall alwaies be myndefull of your singulare beneficence not to me onely but to all that be studiouse of good lernyng wherein I will neither spare busy studie and labour nor coste on books'. For the future he promises regular production. 'And ons [sic] every yeare I intende during my life by Goddes grace to set abrode one thing or other to the perpetuall praise of your lordeshippes most excellente vertues and the commune profite of students.'[3]

---

[1] STC 15604 (Berthelet, 1540).

[2] SP 1/160, fol. 79.

[3] Ibid., fol. 80. W. S. Howell, Logic and Rhetoric in England, 1500–1700 (Princeton, 1956), pp. 94–95, points out the implicit connexion of Cox's 'erotemata rhetorica' with Melanchthon's Erotemata Dialectices, and considers the possibility that Cox was influenced by William Paget's Cambridge lectures on Melanchthon's rhetorical theories. See below, Chapter 8, on Paget.

Cox's Erasmian production had only begun, but this particular work cannot be traced either among his known publications or in earlier lists by Bale and Wood. More interesting than his vanished work on rhetoric, however, is the additional evidence in his letters of the way in which Cromwell recruited the men who produced the vast publication which had already supplied the spiritual content and apologetic of the Henrician settlement. And, like the rest of Cromwell's recruits, Cox was to find an active career ahead in Henry's final years and under Edward his successor.

On 28 July 1540 Cromwell was executed after an Act of Attainder which included a general charge of circulating heretical works through the realm. Two days later the Supreme Head, with judicious discretion, put to death three Lutheran and three papal martyrs, to show that in the realm of doctrine nothing had changed. In retrospect, it is clear that Cromwell's propaganda extended far beyond the political treatises which first attracted scholarly attention. As his contemporaries knew, he was at the centre of a great publication programme in which popular doctrinal works were the main theme. The influence of these ideas can be traced also in the official and semi-official formularies of the early Henrician Church, and the keynote is always Erasmian reform.

His agents were for the most part men of second-rate ability. The Taverners and Coxes, like the two—Starkey and Moryson —recruited from Pole's household, were not original minds, but they were men with talents admirably suited to the Government's purposes. The Lord Privy Seal was in close touch with greater intellect in Elyot and Cheke, but such men were never strictly his pensioners. In this period, however, they seem to stand for the central tradition of English humanist activity. And whether dealing with a Taverner, a Starkey, or a Cheke, one is conscious of the continuity of humanist concern from the period before More's death. Like the earlier humanists, these men are for the most part active laymen dedicated to the service of the Prince and the pious pursuit of secular careers.

They write, like their predecessors, on piety, education, and government. They engage, like their predecessors, in controversy on matters of public and political moment, and their energies and enthusiasm create the positive doctrine of the Henrician settlement.

The completely Erasmian character of the resulting official and quasi-official publications of these five years before Cromwell's death is surely the most striking single aspect of the royal provision for England's faith. The attack on clerical power and independence is combined with careful provision for lay devotion, and the agents, voluntary and professional, range in conviction and character from Richard Whitford to Richard Taverner. Taverner is the most productive contributor. Clearly he is Cromwell's principal propagandist in this phase of policy, and his own words suggest that he may be the unacknowledged translator of Erasmian works like the 1535 *Julius exclusus* and *Epistle concernynge the veryte of the Sacrament of Christes body and bloude*, whose important bearing on the moulding of public sentiment needs no emphasis. Certainly the sudden explosion of Erasmian works in these years speaks for itself, in the context of royal policy and the earlier devotion to Erasmus revealed in humanist circles. Even when Protestantism is ventured, it is commonly the moderate and conciliatory doctrine of Erasmus's disciple Melanchthon, or his own pupil Erasmus Sarcerius, which is put before the English reader.

This in itself speaks for the essential continuity of English humanist opinion to this point in the religious controversies of the day. But one or two additional matters call for special comment. Interest in Savonarola, a marked concern of the Erasmian community everywhere, was early a property of the English group, as has been seen from time to time. In this period, however, a sudden propagation of Savonarola repeats in smaller scale the more conspicuous circulation of Erasmus. Moreover, the writings in question are the paired meditations on the Psalms, 'Miserere mei, Deus' and 'In te Domine speravi'. Here is matter of special import. Savonarola's meditation on the 'Miserere' was one of the most poignant and widely circulated documents of the pre-reform period, and its propagation throughout the reform circles of sixteenth-century Europe has been the subject of special study.[1] As in England, it was usually associated with the second work, which was unfinished at the time of his death. The Marshall Primer of 1534 introduced the 'Miserere' into England, and in 1535 it was incorporated into the revised version associated with Byddell. It was also picked up in 1538 by the Salisbury Primer. Apart from its appearance in the numerous editions of these Primers, it appeared alone, and may have undergone four editions in the single year of 1540. Finally, both meditations were included by Redman in 1535 in his collection of *Prayers of the Byble*, where they were associated with devotional material from Erasmus and from Protestant sources.[2]

Similar evidence of continuity of opinion is found in the work of Sir Thomas Elyot through this period. His Latin–English Dictionary was his great achievement, perhaps the only really major work of scholarship published in these years. His *Defence of Good Women* and *Bankette of Sapience* were dialogues on themes familiar in the conversation of the humanist coteries surrounding Catherine of Aragon, who was herself recalled by the first of these treatises. *The Castel of Helth*, dedicated to Cromwell, showed a desire to make more widely known the interest in medicine which he evidently acquired from Linacre himself, and in its general attitude to a careful physical regimen announces a concern which would soon be given more original form in Ascham's *Toxophilus* (the *Governour*, indeed, had already lamented the decay of proficiency in the longbow). Similarly, the St. Cyprian and Pico della Mirandola publications in 1534 carried on pietistic themes which are easily discovered

---

[1] M. Bataillon, 'Une source de Gil Vicente et de Montemor . . .', *Études sur le Portugal*, pp. 197–217.

[2] C. C. Butterworth, op. cit., ch. viii, and in *The Library*, ser. 5, vol. vi (Dec. 1951), pp. 162–70. For editions, see STC 21790–6, 21798, and 21799. Nineteen editions of the Salisbury Primer are listed to 1540 (STC 16001–18). The Redman *Prayers* is too scarce for an estimate of its circulation.

in the earlier interests of the humanist group. The dedication
of the first of these to Elyot's step-sister in religion, Susan Feti-
place, recalled More's dedication of his own translation of Pico's
Life, which had been dedicated to another nun, Joyce Leigh,
the sister of Archbishop Lee of York.[1]

This phase of Elyot's work recalls another voice heard in
these years, that of Thomas Lupset, whose works were
published posthumously by the King's Printer, Thomas
Berthelet.[2] Like Elyot's writing irenic and conservative, Lupset's works had a deeper spiritual quality combined with the
common concern with education and the state of the commonwealth. Lupset's death in 1530 had removed him from the scene
before his reaction to the national crisis in Church and State
could be known, but his dislike of heterodoxy and social dis-
turbance is amply clear in his writings, linking him with More,
Gardiner, and Elyot. Nevertheless, this former intimate of Pole
and highly regarded disciple of the first phase of the domestic
humanist tradition, who had taken up the cause of Erasmus
in England against Lee, was unmistakably committed to the
reform doctrines of the whole group. In his *Exhortation to
yonge men*, appearing now for the first time, he struck a characteristically Erasmian note on Scripture reading. Disapproving
of the new writers of 'flittering workes' who lacked both
judgement and learning in their approach to the early Fathers,
he urged the young man seeking 'to walke in the pathe way that
leadeth to honeste and goodnes' to immerse himself in the New
Testament. However, he urged him in doing so to 'submit your-
selfe to the expositions of holy doctours; and euer conforme
your consent to agre with Christes church'. More than that,
'Your obedience to the universal faith shal excuse you before
god, although it might be in a false belefe. . . . Surely, . . . it is
your parte to obey, and to folowe the church. . . . I exhorte
you to meddel in no point of your faith other wise then the

<hr>

[1] Lehmberg, *Elyot*, p. 129.
[2] *STC* 16934: *A compendious treatyse, teachynge the waye of dyenge well*, 1534;
16936: *An exhortation to yonge men*, 1535; 16939: *A treatise of charitie*, 1533.

church shal instruct and teache you.'[1] He recommends Jerome
and Chrysostom, Aristotle's *Ethics*, Plato's *Republic*, Cicero and
Seneca as guides and counsellors in this study, and in conclusion
he adds: 'Mo bokes I wyll not aduyse you, for your soules
study, to rede, thanne these: excepte hit be Enchiridion, that
Erasmus wrytethe, a worke doubtles, that in fewe leaues con-
teynethe an infynite knowlege of goodnes.'[2]

Mention of Lupset recalls Thomas Starkey's *Dialogue between
Cardinal Pole and Thomas Lupset*, concluded about 1535 in the
final months of his chaplaincy in Lady Salisbury's household.[3]
Here the whole theme of the well-ordered Christian society
and the duty of the humanist to the commonwealth was
discussed in a Socratic dialogue which is a lasting monument
to the royal school maintained through Pole in Padua. It
continues therefore the concerns of More's *Utopia* and Elyot's
*Governour*. It is a reminder, too, that Elyot himself had not
forgotten this problem. He had raised the question of responsible counsel to the King in *Of the Knowledge which maketh a
wyse man* in 1533, and, with more pointed reference to the
contemporary scene, in *Pasquil the Playne* in the same year. He
returned to it now with *The Image of Gouernance*, an account
of the life of Alexander Severus, the original of which had
come to him from the Erasmian court of Charles V.[4] Of these
last three works by Elyot, the *Pasquil* alone revealed some
originality of thought and attitude. It recalls a Roman tract,
*Dialogus Morphorii et Pasquilli*, sent by Bonner to Cromwell
late in 1532, and may have been suggested by Cromwell as an
inspiration for a useful piece on the Government's behalf. If so,
the result is interesting, for it seems clearly to express deep disapproval of the recent fruits of counsel in the kingdom, and

[1] Gee, *Lupset*, p. 244, ll. 9–28.  [2] Ibid., p. 245.
[3] Text in *England in the Reign of Henry VIII* (E.E.T.S. Extra Ser., nos. xxxii
and xii, 1878 and 1871).
[4] *STC* 7664 (Berthelet, 1541). The author, Archbishop John Maria Puderi-
cus, was a Neapolitan noble, member of the Royal Council and Imperial
chaplain who died in 1525. See H. H. S. Croft, *The Boke named the Governour*
(1880, 2 vols.), vol. i, pp. cxlv f.

more particularly, of the royal divorce. The role of the meddling flatterer is assigned to a Protestant, and Germany is reproved for having 'kicked agayne her mother', the Catholic
Church. Perhaps there is some significance in the fact that this
work, first published anonymously in 1533, was reprinted in
1540, the year of Cromwell's fall. At any rate, in the winter of
1534 Elyot had been compelled to satisfy Cromwell that his
prolonged association with the More circle had not weakened
his loyalty.[1] As he was a man of private means who had come
to maturity before the disruption of the humanist circle, Elyot's
remains a more independent voice among Cromwell's humanist writers than that of Starkey. Yet both men accept the royal
polity and contribute their learning to the King's cause.

In short, in the five-year interval defined by the executions
of More and Cromwell, the Henrician commonwealth had
been given a definite character. It was an Erasmian polity, and
a capacious mansion which could contain most opinions except the extremes of Protestantism and a rooted attachment
to Rome. The shaping of this settlement was the work of the
humanist community recruited by the astute genius of Thomas
Cromwell. It was a legacy which would survive his death. Yet,
although the militant organization of propaganda was achieved
by policy, Cromwell seems to have made use of sympathies
and interests which were abundantly supplied by the first years
of English humanism in the days of Erasmus and More, and here
the evidence of continuity is remarkable. The *media via* of the
Henrician settlement was to many not simply a compromise, but
the fulfilment of a positive tradition rooted in the cause of Erasmian reform. It is this which explains the loyalty of the intelligentsia through so many uncertainties. Sceptical of traditional
theology, indifferent to a venal Rome, and loyal to a reforming
monarch who seemed determined to preserve what they felt to be
the essentials of Catholic orthodoxy, they contributed their learning and energies to formularies of faith and the devotions of the
faithful in the hope of realizing the Erasmian dream in England.

[1] *LP* vii, 1559 (Elyot to Cromwell, 20 Dec. 1534).

# 7

## THE LAST YEARS OF THE REIGN:
## THE ROLE OF CATHERINE PARR

CROMWELL'S death could no more pass unnoticed by English humanists than could that of More. Yet despite the view that it posed a problem of 'what was going to happen to scholarship', English humanism seems to have continued on a comparatively unperturbed course. It is not even true that 'Cromwell's fall closed the direct avenue of approach from study to court'.[1] The Secretary's own recruits were maintained as before, not abandoned. Leonard Cox continued as a schoolmaster at Reading until 1546, then travelled extensively abroad before returning to his English career. Richard Taverner was put in Gardiner's custody at Cromwell's fall, but soon returned to favour, and in 1545 was returned as Member of Parliament for Liverpool. Some time after 1545 he is found writing a letter (from Hampton Court to Parker as Vice-Chancellor of Cambridge) which shows him involved with the universities in the service of the King, and in that year he reissued his *Proverbes or adagies* from Erasmus with additions from both Latin and English proverbs, declaring in his prologue the 'love I beare to the furtheraunce and adourment of my natyve countrey'.[2] Paynell likewise continued in favour, and only William Marshall leaves no certain trace in this period. Dedications reveal a predictable shift in aristocratic patronage to individuals currently in high favour, but the interests of the patrons are much as before.

Thus, although there is nothing in the last years of Henry's

---

[1] Zeeveld, op. cit., p. 234. The 'spirit of policy-making' (p. 239) involved more than political matters, as the circle around Catherine Parr shows.

[2] *STC* 10438 (Whitchurch).

reign to match the closely knit body of official propagandists which Cromwell had organized, the avenues of promotion were still open to the able humanist willing to serve the State. If the writers of these years do not entirely imitate the activities of Moryson and Starkey, it is because the basic apologetic had been stated, and the problems which Cromwell had tried to meet with his group of publicists were not revived. By 1540 the official political and religious doctrine was supplied. It was time for a new generation to appear, a generation which had come to intellectual maturity in the atmosphere of the Henrician settlement. This generation found appropriate patronage, not in a Machiavellian Secretary of State, but in a noble lady of irenic temperament and sincere attachment to humanist learning, Queen Catherine Parr. It is in her circle, which revives the traditions of her royal predecessors Margaret Beaufort and Catherine of Aragon, that the Erasmian spirit finds new shelter and influential support. In preparing the world inherited by the generation which was to come, her influence during Henry's last years was probably decisive.

An investigation of the humanist circle around Catherine Parr and of its effect on policy will be the main concern of the present chapter. Before turning to her learned royal nursery, however, it will be instructive to glance over the humanist publications of these years, to discover the context of writing in which her own patronage flourished. Even a cursory survey reveals that the preoccupations of the English humanist community were unaltered by Cromwell's fall and the marked conservatism of Henry's religious policy.

Patriotic treatises might take first place, since the rally to the Crown had been of such decisive importance from 1535 onward. Hall's and Harding's Chronicles, Leland's great undertaking, Elyot's *Image of gouernance compiled of the actes of Alexander Seuerus*, all with different inflexions, show the way to the future cult of Tudor kingship.[1] Two minor works illustrate the success

[1] *STC* 12720a (Berthelet, 1542) and 12767 (Grafton, 1543) for Hall and Harding; Elyot was *STC* 7664 (Berthelet, 1541); fragments of Leland's work

Cromwell's propagandists could claim: they are the nearest thing in the period to a rallying treatise like those issued by Starkey and Moryson, and their very insignificance bespeaks the present security of the Government. One was a translation of Jacopo di Porcia's *Preceptes of warre*, published by Whit-church at the time of the Scottish campaigns, and the other was Thomas Paynell's translation of Felicius's *Conspiracie of Lucius Catiline*, dedicated to the King.

Di Porcia's *Preceptes*, translated by one Peter Betham, was consciously modelled on earlier work. In the dedication to that 'polytike counsaylour' Sir Thomas Audeley, the translator recalls Moryson's version of Frontinus as a model, showing in action what is here taught in theory. He also admires Moryson's English style, and concludes with a discourse, anticipating Ascham's complaints of the following year, about the use of 'inkhorn' terms. He concludes that it is best to follow Chaucer and other old writers in using plain English, and compliments Wyatt as 'a worthy flower of our tongue'.[1]

Paynell's translation came in the year of the Lincolnshire Rebellion, on which it was in all probability intended to com-ment. It is far removed from the vehement exhortations of Moryson, and the dedication's main purpose is to enlarge on the already familiar theme of the divine obligation of obedience to 'our gouernour'. Like others before, he feels obliged to do all in his power to assist the King against the unthinkable sin of rebellion: '. . . what man is he, nay what monstruous beast, that wolde ones thynke to rebell ageynste, or wylfully disobey your regal power, lawes, ordinances, and expresse commaunde-ments?' God will not suffer such to prevail against 'his ymage in erthe, a kynge', and he feels that if any in the past might have done so, it would surely have been Lucius Catiline. Yet even he with all his advantages failed, as the reader will here learn,

appeared at intervals from 1542 to the end of the reign, mostly in poems and commemorative addresses, but his greatest work remained unknown, of course, until it was taken into the custody of Cheke.

[1] *STC* 20116 (1544).

for Paynell has translated this work 'speciallye for this intente, that all that be unlerned may se, if god amonge the gentiles wold not suffer riottous rebelles to overrunne rulers and distroye common weales: howe moche lesse then wyll he suffer them to preuayle ageynste a chrysten prynce, his veray image in erthe?'[1]

The theme of devotion to the prince, then, was well on its way to becoming a literary mannerism. There is other evidence in these final years of the reign that Erasmian sentiments were becoming deeply embedded in the English humanist tradition. One of the most marked is the concern with the status and education of women. Already announced by Vives and the More circle, this interest is shown in a conspicuous production of treatises about 1542, almost heralding the King's marriage with Catherine Parr in the year following. A variety of works like Christopher Goodwin's *Maydens dreame*, Edward Gosynhill's *Prayse of all women*, and Robert Vaughan's *Dyalogue defensyue for women agaynst malycyous detractoures*[2] reflect the appearance of what amounts to a new literary theme. The most ambitious of these works, perhaps, was David Clapham's translation of Cornelius Agrippa's treatise, *Of the nobilitie of woman kynde*.[3] Education in general received fresh attention in 1542 in the form of an approved royal edition of William Lily's Grammar. Here royal paternalism reached a new height. In the preface to the *Introduction of the eyght partes of speche*[4] the King admonished 'all schoole-maisters and teachers of grammer within this his realm' that this work, compiled for their sake, is to be used alone, 'and none other'. The education of the

---

[1] *STC* 10751 (Berthelet, 1541). It is of a piece with Edward Walshe's *The office and duety in fightyng for our coun'rey* (1545; *STC* 25000), Cheke's translation of Leo V 'on the sleights and policies of war' (recorded by Ascham in the *Toxophilus*), Anthony Cope's version of Livy, *The historie of . . . Anniball and Scipio* (1544; *STC* 5718), and Edward Seymour's *The late expedicion in Scotlande* (1544; *STC* 22270).

[2] *STC* 12047 (R. Wyer for R. Bankes); *STC* 12102 (W. Myddleton); 24601 (Wyer for Bankes).

[3] *STC* 203.

[4] *STC* 15605 (Beerthlet): cf. Butterworth, op. cit., pp. 251 f.

youth of the realm is a matter of the most fundamental concern to the commonweal, he continues, and it has hitherto been hindered by the great diversity of Grammars and systems of instruction. Now all are urged to work, for God, King, parents, and themselves, 'and moche avaunce the common weale of your countrey'. Happily, the royal sponsor himself could point to a model of industry and pious application in his family, and all are urged to take as an example the noble Prince Edward, 'nowe almost in a redynesse to rounne in the same rase of lernyng with you'. The work concluded with Lily's *Carmen de moribus* and Erasmus's *Institutum Christiani hominis*, the inspiration for all such works. The effective monopoly of Erasmus over English educational theory and practice was with this work made official.[1]

Finally, in our survey of humanist publication from 1541 to 1547, we can point to the same continuity in pietistic works. Erasmus himself was made to contribute, with a new edition of his *Preparation to deathe*, a new colloquy, *The epicure*, and, most important, a compressed version of the ever-popular *Enchiridion*, provided by Coverdale.[2] This last work, although apparently printed in Antwerp, is the most powerful evidence yet of the real popularity of this handbook, which was presumably too loquacious and extensive for the general public which it was now beginning to reach.

Continued interest in Chrysostom is another feature of the pietism of these years. Lupset's version of *A sermon that no man is hurted but of hym selfe* was issued by Berthelet in 1542.[3] Cheke's first published work in the following year, two homilies of Chrysostom with Greek and Latin texts,[4] dedicated to the King, coincided with his appointment as royal tutor. And at about the same time another St. John's Cambridge man, Sir Thomas

---

[1] Nicholas Udall, soon to be involved with the royal project for translating the Paraphrases, in 1542 published a translation of Erasmus's *Apophthegmes* for the needs of 'studious youth'. *STC* 10443 (Grafton).

[2] *STC* 10506 (Berthelet, 1543); 10460 (Grafton, 1545); 10488 ('Adam anonimus, Ausborch', 1545).

[3] *STC* 14639.          [4] *STC* 14634 (Wolfe).

Chaloner, published an English translation of one of these same homilies edited by Cheke, and dedicated it to Sir Anthony Denny.[1] Early in the next reign he would be responsible for the first English version of *The Praise of Folly*. Finally, in 1545 there appeared Chrysostom's *De providentia Dei ac Fato orationes sex*.[2]

The list of pietistic publications could be further extended,[3] and one more name might be included for its particular interest. In 1541 Richard Whitford produced his first new work in four years, *Dyuers holy instrucyons necessarye for the helth of mannes soule*,[4] 'newly made and set forth by a late brother of Syon Rychard Whitforde'. In the protection of Mountjoy, this disciple of the More circle continued his reforming mission, discreetly evading all issues of controversy. Whitford's preface to the reader is, however, an interesting document, revealing that anonymous heretical works had been circulated by insertion in earlier editions of his own *A dayly exercyse and experience of death*. He apologizes in the present preface for setting forth his name on the title-page with a precise list of contents, but offers this excuse for seeming lack of humility: 'For (of a certente) I founde nowe but very late, a worke ioyned and bounde with my pore labours and under the contentes of the same volume and one of my workes that was named in the same contentes lefte out, in sted whereof was put this other worke that was not myne.' If Whitford had been flattered by this testimony to his own popular authority in the realm of spiritual counsel, he does not show it.

[1] *STC* 14637 (Berthelet, 1544). Denny also received the dedication of Paynell's translation of St. Cyprian on the Lord's Prayer. Chaloner also translated Gilbert Cousin's *Of the office of seruauntes*, dedicated to Knyvet (*STC* 5879; Berthelet, 1534).

[2] *STC* 14630 (Wolfe).

[3] e.g. Paynell's translation of St. Bernard (*STC* 1908; Petyt [1545?]) and John Clerk's *Opusculum plane diuinum de mortuorum resurrectione et extremo iuditio* (*STC* 5408; J. Herforde, 1545), dedicated to Henry, Earl of Surrey. Clerk was a close associate of Pace in Italy and secretary to Thomas Howard, with whom he was later arrested.

[4] *STC* 25420 (Myddleton).

For so the heretykes do use to sende forthe theyr poyson amonge the people, coured with suger. For they seme to be good and deuout workes, and be in very dede very starke hereses, as of late I sawe a boke and worke of the archeheretyke Luter, translate into Englysh worde for worde, and I sayde that boke was against the kynges honour, bycause he had (by hys noble worke) condempned hym for an heretyke. Be you ware therfor of all suche fatherles bokes, that nother haue the name of the auctour, nor of the translatour.

It is interesting that Whitford, who in a second preface revives his former signature as 'the olde wreche youre assured bedeman late of Syon', appeals here not to the many proclamations which had condemned Luther's books among others, but to the King's *Assertio*, which had earned him the title 'Defender of the Faith'. Public recollection of those associations and inevitably of the *Assertio*'s now very embarrassing defence of the Roman primacy was about as much as Whitford could venture under the vigilant eye of Henry's Council.

Whitford's was a voice from the past, still vigorous in the altered circumstances of Henry's final years. In 1545 the English press produced a work which can scarcely be fitted into any of the foregoing categories, and which looks toward the future of English humanism and education. It takes us also to the chief matter of the present discussion, the court circle of Catherine Parr.

The work in question was Roger Ascham's *Toxophilus*.[1] Its unique character as an educational treatise combined with a meditation on the state of the realm is too well known to be developed here. Apart from its declared purpose, the *Toxophilus* is a mine of information about Ascham himself, his friends and patrons, and the stock of classical learning which they presumably shared. Since Ascham's career spans the period from Fisher's day at St. John's, Cambridge, to that of Catherine Parr at court which heralds a new generation of English humanism, some slight attention to Ascham's own background will form a useful introduction to this latter subject.

[1] *STC* 837 (Whitchurch).

The first important matter is Ascham's account of the private schooling which was the foundation of his own scholarly training. It suggests that if we had more information of the kind we might discover that the English gentry had been affected by the new enthusiasms much earlier than we can otherwise guess. It was Sir Humphrey Wingfield who had provided this upbringing, a man, in Ascham's words,

> To whom, next God, I ought to refer, for his manifold benefits bestowed on me, the poor talent of learning which God hath lent me; as for his sake do I owe my service to all other of the name and noble house of the Wingfields, both in word and deed. This worshipful man hath ever loved and used to have many children brought up in learning in his house, amongst whom I myself was one.[1]

The account of Wingfield's manor school, and of the archery bows brought by him from London at term-time, reveals a world of private civility which was the real inspiration of Ascham's ideal for English education. His very preface, 'To all Gentlemen and Yeomen of England', reveals this, a conception of education which was a natural development of the earlier ideas of Colet and More with their more urban outlook. Finally, there is the familiar theme of devotion to the national cause, with education seen in a Platonic light as the instrument of moral regeneration. *Toxophilus*, in accepted dialogue form —'this English matter, in the English tongue, for Englishmen'— contained 'a pastime honest for the mind, wholesome for the body, fit for every man, vile for no man, using the day and open place for honesty to rule it, not lurking in corners for misorder to abuse it'. For England's future Ascham sees no better hope than that provided by the example of his own early benefactor. 'Would to God all England had used, or would use, to lay the foundation after the example of this worshipful man, in bringing up children in the book and the bow by which two things the whole commonwealth, both in peace and war, is chiefly ruled and defended withal.'[2]

---

[1] Ed. Giles, ii, *Toxophilus*, p. 135.    [2] Ibid.

Behind the appearance of this work is a story which is immediately relevant for our present purpose. In Ascham's letters we have the best record of the course of English humanism in the period immediately after Cromwell's fall. The first important fact which emerges concerns his sponsorship. The patronage which supported Roger Ascham is surprising to anyone who conceives of Cromwell as the exclusive agent in fostering English learning in these years. The centre of Ascham's life, of course, was St. John's College, Cambridge, the creation of John Fisher and the Lady Margaret Beaufort. The extraordinary influence and vitality of this foundation is nowhere better demonstrated than in the personal world of Roger Ascham. William Bill, John Cheke (the master to whom Ascham was so devoted), John Christopherson and George Day, William Cecil, and Thomas Smith—all were contemporaries at St. John's, and all were men to influence the world of Elizabethan England.

In this milieu, so often identified with the Protestant interest in the English Reformation, Ascham's choice of sponsors is significant. In part it may have been suggested by his Yorkshire origins. It is evident, however, that he sought support consistently, not from the radical humanist party, but rather from learned, conservative clergy. George Day and, more important, Archbishop Lee of York, sometime Erasmus's antagonist, provide the essential patronage to the time of the latter's death, Lee with a pension of forty shillings which formed a major and indispensable part of Ascham's income.

On Lee's death in September 1544, Ascham had to seek new patrons. He seems deliberately to have avoided the opportunities of court propaganda for more conservative sponsors. The most interesting episode concerns another old Erasmian connexion, one with the Mountjoy family. On the instigation of Redman of St. John's, Ascham had been put in the position of having to reply to an invitation (apparently unsolicited) from Charles Mountjoy, son of Erasmus's pupil and patron, to represent him at court and teach his son. The reply, in which he rejects the post, suggests that the Mountjoy household still had at least the name of a centre of patronage.[1] Moreover, it is clear here for the first time that Ascham had a positive aversion to the political hazards of Henry's court, a very understandable view in a man of scholarly temperament, certainly by the year 1544. Finally, to both Mountjoy and Redman, he protests his commitment to Archbishop Lee, who at the time of writing was still alive.

The conclusion of the letter to Redman foretells the future and suggests that his dread of court life is not, after all, complete. He begins with the unexceptionable statement that his present regimen is the nightly examination of God's word, with reading of Plato, Aristotle, and Cicero, 'which is a veritable handmaid and attendant', and he proposes to spend the rest of his life in that study. However, if he had the opportunity, through Lee's intercession, he would like nothing better than to spend a few years abroad with one of the King's ambassadors. It also becomes apparent that he has assisted Redman in one of the pressing matters concerned with the formation of religious policy, and regrets any impression that this might have been merely to further his own advantage. It is clear, then, that Ascham's attitude to public service was at least ambivalent, and that the ideal of service to the State held attractions for him personally.

In fact, the matter was solved differently. The first unexpected opportunity occurred at Cambridge, with the need to fill the Regius Chair of Greek in 1544. Ascham's campaign was mounted probably through Cheke and certainly through Sir William Paget, and was supported best of all by his own qualifications. In a letter to Sir William Paget he refers to the other solution to his problems, one which was evidently quite original. He says that he has just written for His Majesty a book 'On the art of Shooting', which is presently in press, and that he hopes it will be evidence of his love for his country and

---

[1] Ascham's praise of the Mountjoy household is rather qualified (Giles, i, letters 19 and 20).

no mean memorial to his learning.[1] This was, of course, the *Toxophilus*, one of the most symptomatic works of English humanism to emerge in the period since More's death. His character references are mostly St. John's men—Redman, Nicholas Ridley (of Pembroke Hall), and, above all, Cheke. Paget helped with the *Toxophilus*, so Ascham must have made his impression.

The *Toxophilus* is the best evidence that Ascham was seeking court favour, and in the time-honoured way of an eye-catching treatise. This one, however, was supremely safe in being neither political nor religious, except for its incidental purpose of improving the country's archery. He presented the work in person to Henry in the summer of 1545, and the way seems to have been well prepared. Both the Duke of Norfolk and Paget wrote letters on Ascham's behalf; Essex (William Parr) and Gardiner sponsored it in Council.[2] From his correspondence at the time it is clear that Cheke also (perhaps his principal intermediary throughout) introduced him in the circles around the Queen's nursery. Whatever his disavowals of political ambition, his début at court had been made, and made successfully. The King showed his pleasure with an annuity of £10, one-quarter of the stipend of the desired Regius Chair at Cambridge. The next year his financial problems were further eased, when he received the post of Public Orator at the university.[3]

The breadth of Ascham's sponsorship at court is remarkable, and almost suggests that he was being put forward as a man of promise jointly by the Parr circle and the conservative groups. His failure to reap immediate reward in the form of office possibly contradicts this, but his success certainly bore great promise for the future. The presentation of the *Toxophilus* also introduces one of the most remarkable forays which Ascham made at this time—his cultivation of Stephen Gardiner.

It would seem that he approached Gardiner directly over the

---

[1] Giles, i. 22 (p. 52).    [2] Ibid. i. 32 and 34.
[3] Ibid. i. 46.

*Toxophilus.* A letter written evidently in the summer of 1545 seems to thank the Cambridge Chancellor for his support of the work in introducing it in Council, and it is accompanied by the protest that he values Gardiner's opinion on it above all others. Setting forth his motives in writing the work, he explains his desire to establish a model of English prose free of bizarre importations from other tongues, and his personal desire to show that his interests in archery at the expense of graver occupations are by no means wasted. Finally he acknowledges his wish to secure some patronage, and asks Gardiner to intercede with the King. The greatest reward he could have would be royal support for studies in Italy and overseas, and in acknowledging this as the target at which the book aims, he appeals to Gardiner as a 'unique patron of letters' and as his university's Chancellor.[1]

Ascham clearly succeeded in making his good impression. Shortly afterward Norfolk, seemingly through Gardiner, asked Ascham to supply a tutor for his son's children, and Ascham was able to oblige.[2] His reputation with the conservative party at court was clearly well established, and the importance of this for the peace of mind he craved and for his future career will soon become apparent.

The next phase of Ascham's apparently highly organized attempt to improve his fortunes involved an approach to Sir Anthony Denny. Sir Anthony was a St. John's man, distinguished there for his scholarship, and a former pupil of William Lily at St. Paul's School. He had made great efforts on behalf of the college's associated school at Sedbergh,[3] and at this time was closely associated with the Parrs and with Cheke in the education of Prince Edward. Ascham's approach here combines with other evidence to show that he was thinking the 'royal nursery school' might be the most congenial situation he had yet discovered.

A former pupil, and one much loved, William Grindal, was already in this situation through efforts made by Ascham and

[1] Ibid. i. 34 (p. 81).    [2] Ibid. i. 44.    [3] *DNB* and Giles, i. 15.

Cheke when he missed a Fellowship at St. John's. Ascham's letters of this period to him, and after his visit to court (in the summer of 1545) to Barnaby Fitzpatrick, the Prince's favourite fellow pupil, to the Countess of Pembroke, to Sir John Astley, and to the Lady Elizabeth herself show his unmistakable desire to keep his memory alive there.[1]

The most revealing correspondence, however, is that with Cranmer, showing Ascham in the process of acquiring indispensable reputation with the Prince's godfather and with the more radical side of the closely balanced council. The pretext is slender: the need for a dispensation from fasting and abstinence to accommodate the demands of Ascham's undoubtedly frail physique. But the letter in which he makes the petition clearly has other purposes. His plea is supported by reference to the authority of Herodotus about the customs of Egyptian priests, with a hitherto uncharacteristic complaint about 'popish nonsense', and with an extended account of the university which would leave Cranmer in no doubt about his (presumably) unknown correspondent's learning or his reform sympathies.[2]

With characteristic deftness, Ascham follows this letter with two more intended to alert Ponet and Grindal to his new venture, giving the former a hint that it might be well to borrow a Greek Gregory of Nazianzus from the Archbishop in his name.[3] His immediate reward was prompt production of the necessary dispensation, for which Cranmer himself paid the cost of sealing. Ascham's grateful thanks were accompanied by a promise of repayment through constant study.[4]

When the King died, Ascham was still at Cambridge, but his lines to court influence were open, and it was not long before he

[1] Giles, i. 38, 40, 41, 42, and 45. In this connexion his out-of-season birthday poem for Prince Edward (i. 30) might also be noticed.

[2] Ibid. i. 27, p. 66: 'Et hic inique comparatum est, ornatissime praesul, ut quum tot superstitionum genera ab Egyptiis, quod facile probari potest, primum ad Graecos deinde ad Romanos redundarunt, post in nostra tempora per sentinam illam Papisticam derivata sunt. . . .'

[3] Ibid. i. 28 and 30.                                    [4] Ibid. i. 29.

was called to the service of the new King. The time spent on examining his career to this point seems to be justified by at least three considerations. In the first place, the record Ascham has left us is unique; no other humanist of the time has left his early career so well or so eloquently documented. Secondly, it illustrates the tastes and tactics pursued by a humanist of very different disposition from the exuberant pamphleteers Cromwell culled from Pole's Padua household, and especially the contrast between a man like Moryson, who admired Machiavelli, and one who hated him as Ascham did.[1] But given that contrast, the remarkable thing is their basic agreement in scholarly taste and devotion to the commonweal. Opposed on the one hand to the shattered group of recusant humanists and on the other to the militant Protestants who had turned all their energies into religious debate, Ascham and Moryson share more characteristics than they dispute.

Finally, Ascham's career is the best introduction to the new situation at court after Cromwell's execution. New problems and a new atmosphere (in which the close fighting of factions mingled with the irenic influences surrounding the upbringing of the royal children) had all made a new approach necessary, and that approach we can see vividly demonstrated by this promising humanist Fellow of St. John's. We must now turn to the court circle which both attracted and frightened Roger Ascham.

It was the royal school which was attractive as the intellectual centre of the court, and in this Thomas Cromwell had an unacknowledged tribute. The creation of Prince Edward's establishment was perhaps his last major contribution to the Henrician settlement, and it occupied him during much of 1539. He worked, of course, with the Prince's godfather, Thomas Cranmer. At the same time they were both involved in the foundation of new bishoprics, and the two projects had something in common. Cranmer and Cromwell were concerned that the new deaneries and colleges of prebends should

[1] *The Scholemaster*, ed. Giles, iii, p. 163.

have Readers of Divinity, Greek, and Hebrew, and should be stocked with students for ecclesiastical promotion later: 'So every bishop should have a college of clergymen under his eye.'[1] This was at least the plan, and it was taken directly from the common programme of humanistic reform of education and religion.

Under the vigilant eye of the King, the same two worked to provide the long-awaited heir with the most propitious environment England could afford, and the results must be taken as a declaration of policy. It was humanistic and mildly Protestant, with the Erasmian tinge of the Melanchthon party which was coming to characterize the new generation. In charge as Chamberlain was the senior figure, Sir William Sidney, cousin to the King's sometime brother-in-law, Charles Brandon, head of the Suffolk clan. His wife's sister, Sybel Penne, was the Prince's dry-nurse.

The second-ranking figure, Sir Richard Page, succeeded Sidney in July of 1544, when Sidney, presumably wishing for an easier post, succeeded Sir John Cornwallis as Steward in the princely household. Page's wife was Elizabeth Bourchier, widow of Sir Edward Stanhope, and mother by him of Anne, Countess of Hertford.

The Lady Mistress of the household was Lady Bryan, who occupied the same post successively to the Princesses Mary and Elizabeth. She was Margaret, sister of John Bourchier, second Lord Berners, and wife of Sir Thomas Bryan. The Almoner, Dr. Coxe, became the presiding officer over the Prince's early education, and in the changes of 1544 was promoted to the post of Dean.

This was the establishment as Cromwell left it,[2] and it seemed to function smoothly during the Prince's infancy. It could not become important as a political and humanist centre, however, until the Prince's intellectual formation became

[1] Strype, *Cranmer*, Book I, ch. xix, p. 107.
[2] For this reconstruction of the Prince's household, see J. G. Nichols, *Literary Remains of King Edward VI* (1857, 2 vols.), vol. i.

important, and before that occurred another major personality had entered the picture. On 12 July 1543 the King married the twice-widowed Catherine Parr in a ceremony presided over by Stephen Gardiner. The following December, for the first time recorded, Henry had all his three children together in the same household. It was the most eloquent expression of his last Queen's influence, which brought some peace and harmony to the final years of his life.

Catherine Parr was already, by virtue of her own connexions, a member of the court circle just described. Her brother William, soon to become the Earl of Essex, was married to a Bourchier, and her sister Anne was married to William Herbert, the illegitimate son of Pembroke who was granted the title by Edward VI. Anne had entered Jane Seymour's court and assisted at the christening of Edward VI. The dominant figure in the group, however, was Catherine herself, not merely through her position, but in virtue of her learning and personality.

She was herself a moderate Protestant. Her household after the death of her second husband, Lord Latimer, had become the resort of Coverdale, Latimer, and Parkhurst. Her religious views as expressed in her own writings, however, are much closer to the generic pietism characteristic of the whole Erasmian pre-reform generation than to any dogmatic allegiance, and her love of scholarship and learning are very well attested. She was in fact the sort of person who could reunite the royal children in a common bond of domestic affection, infused with the learned pietism in which all three were freely engaged.

Her first measures were to reorganize the royal nursery. Shortly after the December family reunion Catherine was made Regent during Henry's absence in France, and at the same time the household was removed to Hampton Court. Sir William Sidney was replaced as Chamberlain by Sir Richard Page, as we have seen, and Dr. Coxe was made Dean. Most important, this venerable tutor was assisted by an outstanding humanist and scholar, John Cheke of St. John's, Cambridge, 'as a suppliment to Mr. Cox both for the bettere instruccion of the Prince, and the diligent teaching of suche children as be appointed to attende uppon him'.[1]

Dr. Coxe's temper may be judged from the vigorous letter to Paget in October of 1546, protesting against the recent proclamations for burning books, of which the effect was 'eradicare lolium cum tritico'. Earlier in the same month he had complained to Paget about the shortage of livings for able clerks, and the added threat to good learning and religion posed by the dissolution of colleges and chantries.[2] The selection of Cheke was probably inspired both by his own pre-eminence and by his long-standing connexions with the court through Dr. Butts, the King's physician. In the previous year he had published his translation of the homilies of Chrysostom, his first work, but his reputation at Cambridge seems to have been due not simply to the scholarship which gave him the first appointment as Regius Professor of Greek, but to his whole success in exciting and adding to the humanist traditions of St. John's College. Ascham is an eloquent and possibly partial witness to his role, which, if less unique than his devoted pupil repeatedly made it out to be, was certainly outstanding. His selection as the Prince's tutor suggested that the princely establishment was to be of considerable intellectual distinction, and the additions which were soon made confirmed this impression.

The Queen herself undertook the general charge and is clearly the creative force behind the augmented school. It was intended, as the above citation mentions, not merely for the royal children, but for such members of the nobility as gained admittance. In this it followed a pattern established earlier for the Duke of Richmond, when the Queen's brother, William Parr, had shared Henry Fitzroy's studies under Richard Croke and John Palsgrave. This kind of school was of course provided throughout the country wherever a wealthy noble was

[1] J. G. Nichols, *Literary Remains of King Edward VI*, vol. i, p. xxxix.
[2] SP 1/226, fol. 16 (*LP* xxi (2), 321) and SP 1/225, fol. 185 (*LP* xxi (2), 260).

concerned to provide a teaching establishment. But the royal nursery, especially sustained with such distinguished instruction, could not but have special significance.

According to his own journal, Edward's serious education began at the age of six, in the year of Catherine Parr's reorganization. Within a year Cheke's abilities were reinforced by Ascham's brilliant pupil, William Grindal, described as 'the best Grecian among them'. His special duty was to act as tutor to the Lady Elizabeth, a post in which Ascham himself was to succeed him. John Belmaine, a French tutor with distinctly Protestant views, Thomas Sternhold, Groom of the Robes of Henry VIII and author of the metrical version of the Psalms dedicated to Edward VI, and Sir Anthony Cooke appear to have completed the establishment. Cooke, like Cheke a man in his thirties and possibly a Cambridge graduate, was linked to the circle by his marriage relationships. His wife was Anne, one of the daughters of Sir William FitzWilliam,[1] and his eldest daughter, Mildred, was William Cecil's second wife, as Cheke's eldest, Maria, was Cecil's first. His daughter Anne, famous for her learning and like her father a translator of materials of reform interest,[2] married Sir Nicholas Bacon, to become the mother of Sir Francis.

The nursery school was completed by the noble children who were taught with Prince Edward: Henry Brandon (the young Duke of Suffolk), Lord Thomas Howard, Giles Poulet, Lord Lumley, and Lord Mountjoy—all seem possible members. Brandon with his younger brother Charles went to Cambridge in 1550, and both died the following year of the 'sweating sickness'. In 1549 Ascham was tutor to both, and their death was a widely lamented loss. Edward's own favourite, already mentioned, was Barnaby Fitzpatrick, the hostage cousin of the Earl of Ormonde, and it seems likely

---

[1] No relation to the Earl of Southampton; a London merchant who had risen in court service through Wolsey's sponsorship.

[2] *STC* 18766: Ochino, *Certayne sermons*, J. Day [1550?], collaborating with Richard Argentine.

that Henry Lord Hastings, later third Earl of Huntingdon, a cousin of Reginald Pole, was also 'bred up in his childhood with King Edward'.

Besides the influential families thus associated with the royal nursery, there were those Ladies in Waiting nearest in confidence to the Queen herself. On 20 May 1546, writing to his sister Mary, who was with the Queen, Edward sent his salutations to Lady Tyrwhit, Lady Herbert, and Lady Lane: precisely those ladies who would soon be involved in the attack on Catherine Parr's circle from the conservative camp.

The scene lacks the drama—and, incidentally, the information which might thereby have been supplied—of a widespread purge of moderate opinion. In the final years of Henry VIII's reign, however, three or four campaigns were mounted which closely resemble a conservative attempt at such a purge. Viewed together, they seem unquestionably part of a larger scheme to dislodge this influential circle from its position around the Prince, and they therefore provide some background to the final struggle for power in the Council of the dying King in 1546.

The problem was dissident opinion in influential aristocratic circles. The attack on the Courtenays in 1540–1 had effectively silenced the stronghold of conservative humanist opinion, and in the following years Henry turned with equal vigilance to opinion on the religious 'left'. It was a pattern characteristic of the attempts to preserve Henry's very personal ecclesiastical settlement on the basis of the Royal Supremacy, and the instrument of attack was Stephen Gardiner. The movement foundered, however, when it reached the person of Catherine Parr herself, and it seems likely that Gardiner's over-reaching in that matter was the immediate cause of his fall from influence in the last year of Henry's reign.

There were foreshadowings of future events as early as 1541. The Lincolnshire Rebellion and the execution of the seventy-four-year-old Countess of Salisbury, the last and most pathetic victim from the Courtenay clan, attracted attention to conservative discontents. Two other events, although little noticed, suggest that the Government's vigilance over aristocratic opinion was more widely extended. Lord Lisle, the bastard son of Edward IV who had kept Calais for Henry, was imprisoned in the Tower without formal charges, and there died. The episode is mysterious, but the State Papers reveal the Lisles associated with pietistic circles.[1] The same year, in the first commission to make inquest under the terms of the Six Articles, a heretic priest was discovered in All Hallows, a chaplain to the Duke of Suffolk. This 'Scottish Man', one Alexander Seton, was denounced, as it happens, by three Fellows of Whittington College.[2]

The year 1542 seems to have passed without spectacular prosecutions, and the attention of contemporary witnesses was almost entirely absorbed by the Scottish war and the fall of Catherine Howard. The following year, however, another heretic was brought to recant, one widely connected with the lesser gentry, while at Windsor appeared the first evidence that very highly placed circles might be tainted with dangerous opinion.

The Protestant heretic was Thomas Becon, a prodigious producer of widely circulated pamphlets, who seems to have been nurtured in the very neighbourhood of Canterbury. His first appearance with a patron of rank is in 1538, when he is associated at Ipswich with Thomas, Lord Wentworth of Nettlestead. In 1541 he was evidently apprehended for the first time by Bonner's commission in London, and recanted. Immediately afterward he went into Kent and changed his name, his dress, and his habits: where before he had preached, he now wrote and published. That same year his first work appeared under the name 'Theodore Basile', *Newes out of heauen*, dedicated to 'Maister George Pierpount'. The following year, 1542, there were no less than eight new works by him, almost all with dedications to gentry related more or less directly to Sir Thomas

---

[1] e.g. *LP* xiii (1), 1338, where the book referred to sounds very like the *Enchiridion*, and xv, 1030, letter 36.

[2] Foxe, v, pp. 448–9.

Neville, to whom one of them, *A Christmas bankette*, was dedicated. In 1543 there were three more works (in addition to reprints), Sir Thomas Wyatt and Lady Anne Gray being the most prominent recipients of his attentions.

Not all Becon's 'patrons', it seems, necessarily knew beforehand of the honour thus paid to them, but certainly some of them were occupied in keeping him at work in Kent, possibly with the knowledge, or at least the tacit consent, of Cranmer. The works themselves were highly tendentious, if not overtly Protestant, and in 1543 he was forced to make an extended public recantation clearly designed to destroy his prestige. For the rest of the reign he found shelter in an itinerant life in the midlands, hiding with the scattered Protestant gentry and 'teaching divers gentlemen's sons'.[1]

The career of Becon, and his blatantly successful ways with the gentry, may have added to the alarm of the conservative party. At any rate, by 1543 a new temper was in the air. The act 'For the Advancement of True Religion' restricted Bible reading and condemned unauthorized translations, and the King's Book showed the world abroad as well as the populace in England that the Henrician Church was to be much more orthodox than earlier formularies had seemed to suggest. On 12 July the King married Catherine Parr, and almost at once a major heresy-hunt burst forth at Windsor.

The immediate occasion for this affair was the arrival of Dr. London of New College as a canon of Windsor. This gentleman, whose appearances in the history of the time are frequently tinged with the ridiculous,[2] had already made his conservative opinions clear in his own college, and he now discovered a

---

[1] For Becon see D. S. Bailey, *Thomas Becon* (London and Edinburgh, 1952), where his connexions with the gentry are thoroughly worked out. The works cited above include *STC* 1739, 1713, 1731, 1738, and 1756 (in order). On 4 May 1543 the Council decided on a general inquiry into 'all abuses and enormites off religion' in Kent (Dasent, *Acts of the Privy Council*, N.S., i, 1890).

[2] For a reappraisal of London's character, see Knowles, op. cit., pp. 354 f. On the whole episode, Foxe, v. 464–97, and James Gairdner, *Lollardy and the Reformation* (1908–13, 4 vols.), vol. ii (bk. iv, cap. 3), pp. 375 f.

circle at Windsor which he thought important enough to bring to the attention of Gardiner.

The thing which requires explanation is the comparative unimportance of the people over whom such great perturbation was shown. An organist, John Marbeck (albeit a great one), a singer (Robert Testwood), a tailor (Henry Filmer), a priest (Anthony Peerson), and a minor lawyer (Robert Bennett) were scarcely worth the scandal of collective martyrdom. It is clear from the investigation, however, that they were thought to be useful in snaring larger prey.

The first evidence is Gardiner's repeated and prolonged examinations of John Marbeck. Marbeck had been preparing an English Bible Concordance, and had translated some letters of John Calvin for a friend. It was the Concordance which fascinated Gardiner, less because the work was dangerous in itself than because, as Marbeck's own account makes clear, Gardiner felt he was not capable of doing such work alone, and must have had the direction of a better-educated sponsor. It is significant that at the same time Gardiner and Wriothesley were preparing articles for their first unsuccessful attack on Cranmer.

The investigation of the group, however, yielded other information. One of the original suspects, Anthony Peerson, seems to have had friends at court and even within the Council. It was Dr. London's pursuit of these, presumably on very slender evidence, which proved his downfall. Immediately after the Windsor burnings, the accusers found themselves under examination by the Council, and London himself was judged perjured. The list of pardons issued on 31 August tells that those implicated were all associated with the Privy Chamber.[1] Sir Philip Hoby, the diplomatist, half-brother of the translator of Bucer and Castiglione,[2] was involved, as was

[1] Dasent, op. cit., vol. i, pp. 97–98, 101.

[2] Sir Thomas Hoby (1530–66), who was married to Elizabeth, third daughter of Sir Anthony Cooke. In 1574 she married John, Lord Russell, second son of the second Earl of Bedford. She translated a French treatise on the Eucharist (D.N.B.).

his wife, Lady Elizabeth, daughter of Sir Walter Stonor. Thomas Welden of Bran, Berkshire, Sir Thomas Caverden of Bletchingly, Surrey, and Elizabeth his wife,[1] Edmund Harman of Langley, Buckinghamshire, with his wife, and Thomas Sternhold complete the list. Added to these were William Snowball, Yeoman Cook for the King's Mouth, of New Windsor, and his wife Margaret, like the others said to be maintainers of Anthony Peerson, the most active and radical propagandist of the group burnt at Windsor.

The failure of this attempt to purge the court of heretics, with Henry's loyal support of Cranmer, must have deterred the conservative group from another similar campaign. Two years later, however, after the last unsuccessful attempt against Cranmer (in 1545), a new opportunity presented itself. The occasion was the reappearance of a particularly aggressive heretic from the north, Anne 'Askew' Kyme of Yorkshire, who in the course of her imprisonment and examination seems to have offered the conservative group the temptation of repeating the episode of Elizabeth Barton, reversed this time against the radical party.

Anne Askew, who had disavowed her marriage and removed to the Protestant circles in London, was first apprehended and warned by Bonner in 1545. The following year she was arraigned once again, and this time behaved so obstinately that it was not possible to ignore her clearly unrepentant disposition. Moreover, it seems that she had aroused suspicion for other reasons. Just previously, Dr. Edward Crome, compelled to recant at Paul's Cross for a sermon at St. Thomas Acon against the sacrifice of the Mass, had undergone examination which

---

[1] Caverden is associated with the *Preceptes of Cato the Sage with annotacions of D. Erasmus of Roterodame* (R. Grafton), translated by Robert Burrant. The 1545 edition is known only through the copy in the J. P. Morgan Library, New York. The 1553 edition is *STC* 4854. In that year Taverner reissued his own version, *Catonis disticha moralia ex castigatione D. Erasmi* (N. Hill, *STC* 4844). In his dedication, Burrant hails Caverden as the embodiment of Cato's 'politique wysdome'. Like Taverner, he infused the work with contemporary allusions.

showed the drift of events. 'This Doctor Crome, after his committing, while he was in warde at Greenewych, in the court, under my lord Chauncelor, accused divers persons as well of the court as of the cittie, with other persons in the countrey, which putt many persons to great troble, and some suffred death after.'[1]

The exact identity of those named by Crome remains hidden, but this testimony of Wriothesley's chronicle sheds light on the treatment of Anne Askew. On this second examination she was subjected to the full rigours of torture, an extremity which is not recorded at any other time in the period. On 16 July she was burned at Smithfield, while Nicholas Shaxton, arraigned at the same time, recanted in a public sermon.

The examination of Anne Askew by the Council was a full-dress affair. Gardiner presided, with John Dudley, now Viscount Lisle, and Lord Parr, the Queen's brother, who evidently urged her to confess that the sacrament was 'flesh, blood and bone' of Christ. She then replied in a fashion which did their own credit no good, that 'it was a great shame for them to counsel contrary to their knowledge'.[2]

This allusion to knowledge of opinion at court was clearly the crux of the matter. She was examined thereafter by several bishops and councillors, including Bonner and the penitent Shaxton. It was known that she had received aid from important persons in prison, and was questioned closely about that. Asked if 'my lady of Suffolk, my lady of Sussex, my lady of Hertford, Lady Deny and lady FitzWilliam' were involved in the sect, she refused to identify them. She was maintained in prison, she claimed with open impudence, by her maid's collections among the apprentices of London, but she finally identified Lady Hertford and Lady Denny as persons from whom, according to the messengers, she had received gifts of ten

[1] *Wriothesley's Chronicle*, ed. W. D. Hamilton (Camden Society, 1875), pp. 166-7.
[2] Foxe, v, p. 544, following Bale's account: see *Select Works*, The Parker Society (Cambridge, 1849), pp. 195-246.

and eight shillings respectively. A racking, with Wriothesley and Rich presiding, seems to have extracted nothing more.

It is clear that the affair of Anne Askew is the true introduction to the attack on Catherine Parr which followed shortly. The events narrated by Foxe can be placed in 1546 as the year after the King's return from Boulogne, and in his own narrative they follow the affair of Anne Askew, although the events concerning the Queen are not dated and clearly ran over a period of several weeks.

It appears that the Queen's habit of reading Scripture, with 'divers well learned and godly persons' to instruct her, had been extended to include her ladies and gentlewomen, especially during Lent. The reading occupied an hour in each afternoon, with sermons often touching on abuses in the Church. The Queen did not scruple to discuss such matters with the King, and according to Foxe it was fear of this influence which aroused the conservative party—Gardiner, Wriothesley, and others. As the King's health declined and his disposition worsened, opportunity to undertake this exceedingly dangerous exposure apparently offered itself. 'The sharpness of the disease had sharpened the King's accustomed patience, so that he began to show some tokens of misliking, and contrary unto his manner, upon a day breaking off that matter [of the Queen's discourse] he took occasion to enter into other talk, which somewhat amazed the queen. . . .'[2]

On her departure, Gardiner evidently took the opportunity of the King's ill humour to question her freedom in such high matters. 'Besides this, that the religion by the queen so stiffly maintained, did not only disallow and dissolve the policy and politic government of princes but also taught the people that all things ought to be in common. . . .'[2] The conservative concern for public order so familiar in Gardiner's views gives this the ring of authenticity. The rest of the story as told by Foxe clearly conceals as much as it discloses. Gardiner, it is claimed, secured the King's promise of immunity, 'that his

[1] Foxe, v, pp. 553 f.          [2] Ibid., p. 556.

Majesty should easily perceive how perilous a matter it is to cherish a serpent within his own bosom'. Foxe himself suggested that the King acted with double purpose, granting them leave to draw articles against her, 'to see, be like, what they would do'. A search was made of the books in her closet, unfortunately not specified by title, and charges were drawn also against the ladies closest to her, the same three to whom the young Prince had sent his greetings through his sister Mary—Lady Herbert, the Queen's sister, Lady Lane, her cousin, and Lady Tyrwhit. Foxe is inconsistent in his account of the exact purpose of the prosecution, whether it was intended to involve all four ladies at once, or to use the royal companions to incriminate the Queen under examination. At any rate, the conclusion of the strange episode has the air of elaborate contrivance, presumably invented by the King himself.

After a regular visit by the Queen during this period of secret investigation, according to Foxe, '. . . it chanced that the King, of himself, upon a certain night after her being with him, and her leave taken of him, in misliking her religion, brake the whole practice unto one of his physicians, either Dr. Wendy or else Owen, but rather Wendy as is supposed, pretending unto him, as though he intended not any longer to be troubled with such a doctress as she was . . .'.[1] He declared that the Queen was in grave danger, and told him the whole story, insisting on secrecy.

At this point, the Bill of Articles against the Queen, subscribed by the King's own hand, was permitted to escape the custody of one of the councillors and taken 'by some godly person' to the Queen. The consternation it induced in her was sufficiently great to warrant the King's dispatching his physicians to attend her, and the faithful Wendy reported his conversation with the King as he was no doubt intended to do. After a visit from the King, Catherine Parr returned the visit that same evening accompanied by the three suspect ladies, and reconciliation was effected. Pleading her unfitness to hold

[1] Ibid., pp. 557–8.

views on deep matters of religion at all, she protested that her husband's wisdom was her only anchor under God. 'Not so, by St. Mary,' quoth the King, 'you are become a doctor, Kate, to instruct us (as we take it), and not to be instructed or directed by us.' Denying this, the Queen claimed to wish only to learn from him and to distract him from his infirmity, and submitted her views to him entirely. 'And is it even so, sweetheart,' quoth the King, 'and tended your arguments to no worse end? Then, perfect friends we are now again, as ever at any time heretofore.'[1]

Foxe's contention that the whole scheme was a lesson by the King to the Gardiner group cannot conceal the King's real anger at the Queen's independence of opinion, or his great jubilation at his victory. It is also difficult to share Foxe's enjoyment of the macabre joke, which looked on the surface so like a revival of the fate of earlier Queens, although none of those were tried for heresy. That Henry was in a very conservative frame of mind on religious matters was evident from a hundred indications, perhaps none more revealing than the evidence that the most radical reforms that Cranmer dared suggest, even in Gardiner's absence, were the pulling down of rood crosses and the suppression of a few added ceremonies.[2] At the same time it is clear that while Gardiner was nervous about the possibility that the Queen held heretical views, what disturbed Henry was her apparent independence of mind. Once she submitted, he apparently lost interest in her views, and her establishment, both at court and in the royal nursery, was unthreatened.

The whole episode received interesting treatment two generations later by Robert Parsons, reporting recusant traditions.[3] Parsons, unlike Foxe, directly connects the incident of Anne Askew with the attack on Catherine Parr. According to

[1] Foxe, v, pp. 559–60.

[2] Notice also Henry's letter to Mary, Queen Regent of the Netherlands, *LP* xxi (1), 1098 (20 June 1546).

[3] Parsons names Sir Francis Inglefield, Privy Councillor to Queen Mary, *A Treatise*, p. 593.

Parsons, Henry was informed that Anne Askew 'did in secrett seeke to currupt diuers people, but especially weomen, with whome she had conversed; and that she had found means to enter with the principall of the land, namely with Q. Catherine Parr herselfe, and with his neeces the daughters of the Duke of Suffolke and others. . . . And by her confession he learned so much of Q. Catherine Parre, as he had purposed to have burned her also, if he had lyued.' Parsons also adds the information that the principal charge against the Queen was formed from the books discovered in her closet, 'brought or sent her in by Anne Askue. Whereof the witnesses were, the Lady Herbert, Lady Lane, Lady Tyrwitt, and others. And by that occasion was the said Anne Askue putt to the racke, for the discouery of the truth.'

This is the only occasion in the reign when a circle of aristocratic pietism is subjected to inquiry. If behind the King's rather brutal pleasure in the episode we can detect a determination to protect his Queen, it scarcely seems possible to conclude, with Foxe, that he was therefore sympathetic with doctrinaire Protestantism. What does seem likely is that the Queen's 'Protestantism' was little more than a general patronage of reform which embraced the moderate Protestantism of men like Coverdale. About her own views we have no evidence except the works she wrote and patronized, and those, as we shall see immediately, were purely Erasmian in character. That this must have been known to Henry, and that he must have approved it, is obvious; the collapse of the attack seems if anything to admit failure to associate any of these highly placed persons with opinions which would have disturbed seriously the established Erasmianism of Henry's reformed Church.

The most important achievement of this group, apart from providing a new avenue to preferment and a centre of humanism at court, was the education of the Prince himself. Edward's firm and rather narrow Protestantism has a dogmatic quality which it is hard to describe as Erasmian. To the extent that it is necessary to find another explanation than his extreme youth and premature promotion to power, it may lie with two of his tutors, Dr. Coxe and John Belmaine, and of course with the influence of Cranmer.

His pietism, however, was the common property of the wider group, and the surviving records of his humanist education show influences which were first felt in the English court under Catherine of Aragon. The two humanists who seem, from his own references, to have formed a staple of his early education were Erasmus and Vives. The *Colloquies* and the *Satellitium* were evidently close to his hand, for frequent reference in quotation. In addition, in the early letters, till 1547, the young Prince refers to Cicero, Cato, and Aristippus, and, of course, the Bible.[1]

The other works known to be directly associated with the group confirm this picture of a non-dogmatic, humanist pietism. First come the works of Queen Catherine herself, first published in 1545. *The Prayers styrring the mynd vnto heauenlye medytacions*, published by Berthelet in June, were immediately reissued.[2] This was followed on 6 November by an extended version, *Prayers or medytacions, wherein the mynd is stirred, paciently to suffre all afflictions here.*[3] This collection proved to be one of the most frequently reprinted pietistic works of the day, going through at least five more editions by 1548. The elaboration of the title is the best clue to its character: '[Prayers . . .] wherein the mynd is stirred paciently to suffre all afflictions here, to set at nought the vayne prosperitee of this worlde, and alwaie to longe for the euerlastynge felicitee: Collected out of holy woorkes by the most vertuous and graciouse Princesse Katherine quene of Englande . . . .'

---

[1] J. G. Nichols, op. cit., e.g. letters XVII and XX. Also Butterworth, op. cit., p. 251 and notes 10 and 11, concerning the *ABC*, Lily's Grammar, and Erasmus's *Institutum*, specially printed and bound by Berthelet for Edward's use in 1543.  [2] *STC* 4818.

[3] *STC* 4819 (Berthelet), and 4820–4. Strype, on evidence which is unclear, credits Catherine Parr with translation of Savonarola's exposition of Psalm 51 (Strype, *Edward VI*, pt. 1, cap. xvi, p. 206).

The principal achievement of Catherine's pietistic spirit is *The lamentacion of a sinner*, published by Whitchurch on 5 November 1547 and reissued the next year.[1] It was printed 'at the instaunt desire of the righte gracious ladie Caterin Duchesse of Suffolke, and the earnest requeste of the right honourable Lord William Parre, Marquesse of North Hampton', and the preface adds another interesting sponsor, William Cecil, perhaps the true agent behind its publication. Claiming that he himself had taken much profit from the work, and that he wished to make it available to every Christian, Cecil states: 'Here mayst thou see one . . ., a wife to hym that was a kinge to realmes, refusinge the worlde wherein she was loste, to obteyne heauen wherin she maye be saued.' It was principally aimed, it seems, at other noble ladies: 'And to all ladies of estate I wishe as ernest minde to folow our quene in vertue, as in honour; . . . so shall they (as in some vertouse ladies of right high estate it is with great comforte seene) taste of this fredome of remission of this everlastyng blisse. . . .'

The *Lamentacion* itself seems the unmistakable record in the Erasmian vein of a deep religious experience, the nearest approach to later Protestantism being the emphasis on faith alone; but that itself was a possible Erasmian preoccupation until the Council of Trent made it the exclusive property of the Protestant party. This theme is echoed in another possible surviving work in the Cecil Papers, an anonymous religious poem in French ascribed to her. In this the author comes to Christ, penitent:

> Saint Paul a dit que Justifiez sommes
> Par foy en Christ et non par œuvres d'hommes
> Ny de la loy, car si aucun se fie
> Que c'est la loy seulle qui Justifie
> Donc faudroit il dire que Christ souffrit
> La mort en vain quand pour nous il s'offrit.[2]

More interesting is the next phase, in which the author,

[1] *STC* 4827, 4828.        [2] Cecil Papers, vol. 314, f.v. 19.

expounding the theme that God is Charity, turns to contemplation of Christ crucified—the very theme of the widely
circulated pietistic tract by that name which was placed on the
first Roman Index in May of 1549. Contemplation of the cruci-
fixion with the heart is recommended as the best key to understanding charity, for in Christ crucified one can see the great
beauty of the soul better than in all writings:

> Ce crucifix donc est le livre enquoy
> Dieu a enclos ce que contient la loy
> Et a escrit briefve conclusion
> De ce qui sert pour ma salvation.[1]

There are no allusions to the Protestant reformers or any
peculiar Protestant tenets. In its emphasis on pietism, trust in
Christ, and non-sacramental devotion the poem is a classic
production of Erasmian piety.

Court pietism did not stop there. Prince Edward's tutor,
Sir Anthony Cooke, produced a translation of St. Cyprian
on prayer, probably in these years. A fulsome dedication to
Henry VIII as 'pastor of the people'[2] introduces the work,
which he feels will have a chance of being read by those who
will not read the New Testament itself in English. The Erasmian note is evident in what follows:

Chrisostome treatythe of the same matter very devowtly and
ornatelye, and as towching the argument thereof, nothing varying
from Cipryane. Whereby it apperethe that in these menys days this
godly exercise was not myssused as it hathe ben syns. But Chrisostome ys moche in the apparrell of wordes, and not so furnyshed
with the testemonyes of Scripture. So that in this I think to the in-
dyfferent reader, he ys not egall with Cypriane.

If the treatise were only better known, Cooke feels, devout
prayer would be restored to its true place in the Christian life,
whereas now, because a few pray superstitiously, many pray
but little.

[1] Cecil Papers, vol. 314, f.v. 25.
[2] SP 6/12, fols. 14–35, fol. 16 and 17 cited.

Works by the Princesses complete the picture of the royal nursery's pietistic production. The first, already mentioned as a New Year's gift in 1545 from the Princess Elizabeth to her stepmother, was a translation of Marguerite of Navarre's *The Mirrour or Glas of the Sinfull Soul*.[1] Here was a classic of the French Erasmian movement, emanating from its greatest patroness and now offered to her present English counterpart, Catherine Parr. It seems the clearest evidence that these royal English pietists were well aware of the interests of their continental cousins and saw themselves in the same role.

In addition to this work, the Princess Elizabeth also composed an elaborate version, in Latin, French, and Italian, of Catherine Parr's *Prayers or Medytacions*, dedicated to the King and dated 3 December 1545.[2] It was probably about this time too that she prepared a French translation of Erasmus's *Dialogus fidei*, also for Henry VIII.[3]

Another work is testimony to the genius of Henry's last Queen for producing an atmosphere of harmony. Although it was not published until the next reign, it is appropriate to mention here that on the Queen's suggestion the Princess Mary turned her own considerable scholarly abilities to the great project which was Catherine Parr's monument, the translation of Erasmus's Paraphrases on the New Testament. The section of the work which she began was concluded (when illness interrupted and the King's injunctions pressed for the work) by Master Francis Malet, D.D. Although it is difficult to be certain, it seems likely that the four gospels were assigned and begun by the accession of Edward, under whose royal authority the work was carried to completion. Nicholas Udall's dedication of the gospel of St. John to Catherine Parr is perhaps the best concluding comment on her domestic success:

When I consider, most gracious Quene Katerine, the greate noumbre of noble weomen in this our time and countreye of Englande,

---

[1] *LP* xix (2), 794.          [2] Royal MS. 7 D x.
[3] Well attested by visitors who saw it in the Whitehall library; see W. B. Rye, *England as seen by Foreigners* (1865), pp. 133, 165, 171, 282.

not onelye geuen to the studie of humaine sciences and of straunge tongues, but also so throughlye experte in holy scriptures, that they are hable to compare wyth the beste wryters as well in endictynge and pennynge of godlye and fruitfull treatises to the enstruccion and edifiynge of whole realmes in the knowleage of god, as also in translating good bokes out of Latine or Greke into Englishe for the use and commoditie of suche as are rude and ignoraunte of the sayd tounges, I cannot but thynke and esteme the famous learned Anti-quitee so ferre behynde these tymes, that there cannot iustelye bee made any comparison betwene them.[1]

The Paraphrases must be reserved for later treatment, but it is appropriate here to notice that they were undoubtedly conceived as part of the apparatus of Henry's final religious settlement. In 1543 the Act for the Advancement of True Religion and the publication of the King's Book, *A Necessary Doctrine and Erudition for any Christen Man*,[2] ended any doubts about the conservative and orthodox character of its doctrine. Within that framework, however, there was much room for reform opinion to work creatively. The King's Book itself was an achievement of conservative reform, with careful and instructive statements on doctrine, as in the treatment of Transubstantia-tion which was greatly expanded from the 1537 version. The product of some three years' canvass of episcopal opinion and of Henry's own vigorous examination and scrutiny, it was un-mistakably a definitive treatment, at least for Henry's lifetime, of all the issues which he cared to discuss.

The King's Book was not alone. With it went *An exhortation unto prayer*, also published by Berthelet[3] and evidently intended to provide a popular handbook of the new religious practices in the form of a devotional guide. The *Exhortation* was 'thoughte mete by the kynges maiestie, and his clergie, to be redde to the people in every churche afore processions', with Cranmer's litany to be sung at the same time. This was followed

---

[1] *STC* 2854: *The first tome or volume of the Paraphrase of Erasmus upon the newe testamente* (Whitchurch, 1548), preface to the Gospel of St. John.
[2] *STC* 5168 (Berthelet).
[3] *STC* 10619; cf. Butterworth, op. cit., p. 247.

by instruction on the need, manner, and subject of prayer, with new prayers 'set furth and used in the vulgar tunge, for styrring the people to more devotion'.

In 1545 the King's Primer,[1] like the King's Book, supplanted an earlier Cromwellian innovation, the Hilsey Primer of 1539. In the new version, which appeared from Grafton's press dated 29 May, there are extensive revisions. The most striking feature is the altered Calendar, with almost no commemoration of saints. This change is reflected likewise in the Litany. The text of the old Litany survives only as far as the invocation of the celestial hierarchy; after that, replacing the traditional roll-call of saints, there begins a series of homiletic petitions for the needs of the Church.

Despite many alterations, the Primer was still recognizably the familiar instrument of English lay devotion, with more non-scriptural prayers and a diminished penitential emphasis. Of the new prayers, the longest and most interesting is a translation from Erasmus's *Precationes aliquot*, in which the governing theme of petition for the penitent and needy Church has obvious application to the situation of the Henrician body. It includes, moreover, a lengthy and timely exposition of the divinely ordained, hierarchically ordered society.

Preceding the whole was Henry's vigorous Injunction establishing the work as the only one authorized in his dominions. Here also is specific interest in the instruction of youth in English in the elements of their faith, a complement to the official *A.B.C.* also set forth in this year by royal command.[2]

These then were the elements of an official vernacular system of worship and instruction which was to be supplemented by a vernacular liturgy. The first experiment in this last important work was tried in May 1544, a Litany for public worship which was intended as a first instalment to an adaptation of the

---

[1] STC 16034 (Grafton); LP xx (1), 661; Butterworth, op. cit., ch. xix.
[2] STC 20: *The ABC set forth by the Kynges majestie* (W. Powell, [1545?]).

whole *Processionale*.[1] Ultimately this work was abandoned for the project of the Edwardian Prayer Book, but it is final evidence that in Henry's most conservative last years the programme of Erasmian reform, far from being abandoned, was bearing its first important fruit in public worship. It is clear that Erasmus's Paraphrases were seen by the Queen as an ideal complement to this whole programme, and one which further demonstrates the original fount of ideas from which the Henrician settlement drew much of its inspiration.

It seems then, that English humanism was directed, after the fall of Cromwell as before, from the court, but that the nature of this direction had changed. Instead of the professional propaganda circle of Cromwell's day there is the group of distinguished humanists collected by Catherine Parr to provide instruction for the royal children, and for her own friends and associates, in learned pietism. Her favour provided even surer promotion than did that of Cranmer, who is perhaps a more obvious successor to Cromwell.

The achievement of the Parr circle was entirely in harmony with the 'necessary doctrine' view which marked the last phase of Henry's religious policy, and it reached from the important official formularies of the Henrician Church to the publication, in the last complete year of the reign, of the entire works of Thomas Lupset,[2] the universally admired and conservative exponent of the Erasmian humanist tradition in England. The perpetuation of Erasmian patronage at such a high level in these critical final years of Henry's reign was a momentous influence on both court and letters, as the attack on the Queen herself testified. And Catherine Parr's decision to sponsor a complete translation of the Paraphrases of Erasmus is the most appropriate symbol of the link which she forged with the religious settlement of the early years in Edward VI's reign.

[1] See F. E. Brightman, 'The Litany under Henry VIII', *EHR* 1909 (xxiv), pp. 101–4, and E. C. Ratcliff, 'The Liturgical Work of Archbishop Cranmer', *Journal of Ecclesiastical History*, vol. vii (1956), pp. 189–203.
[2] *STC* 16932: *T. Lupsets workes* (Berthelet, 1546).

# 8

## ERASMIANS AND POLICY
## UNDER EDWARD VI

THE Protestant policies of England's Government from 1547
to 1553 were the first serious threat to the traditions of evangelical humanism established during the reign of Henry VIII.
Those traditions, as we have seen, maintained a moderate
position between the rival orthodoxies with remarkable con-
sistency, drawing on the early Erasmian humanism which
had been made domestic in the period before religious strife.
In part the adoption of this position was clearly expedient, and
the utility of an Erasmian outlook amid the vicissitudes of
Henry's own religious policies was never more clearly demonstrated than by Cromwell's own propaganda enterprise. At the
same time, the close interaction of Government policy and
spontaneous reform sentiment indicates that this policy met a
need felt throughout the humanist community. The fundamental Henrician position, even in its most conservative phase,
combined orthodox doctrine in essentials (papal supremacy
being defined as an error) with sweeping changes in other
spheres: in vernacular Scripture and liturgy, in education, and
in the popular observances of late medieval religion. In this
fashion it became the most complete fulfilment of the Erasmian
programme which Europe had yet seen. Only in the drastic
treatment of monasticism and, more important, in the break
with Rome were there issues which a conservative Erasmian
would find difficult. It is clear that few, initially at least,
thought these issues important enough to risk the martyrdom
which was Henry's price for dissent. The doubts raised by the
Conciliar struggle and the venal morality of Rome, placed
beside the efficiency of Henry's Government and the powerful

sentiment of loyalty to the King himself, combined to enlist the support even of men like Gardiner behind Henry's policy. They were happy to co-operate provided doctrinal purity were preserved in the practice of the faith, and there was always the prospect of renewed negotiations with a chastened papacy. In the meantime it must have seemed to many, including those like Thomas Elyot who were fearful of Protestantism and uneasy at the King's career, that the best immediate course was to support Henry to maintain order, and to further such immediate reform projects as the Government was prepared to sponsor. The few martyrs claimed for Rome came, significantly, from the very centres where the new learning and strict religious observance had made the deepest impression.

Now this solution was threatened, and with the accession of a boy king the whole structure of the Supremacy tottered. For conservative Henricians like Gardiner, Tunstall, and Bonner, the problem of ecclesiastical supremacy vested in a minor was an embarrassment they were ill prepared to face. With the victory of the radical faction in the Council their rather reluctant loyalty to the Henrician ideal was strained to the breaking-point, and for them the accession of Mary was nothing short of providential. In a chastened mood, they were prepared to accept a final use of the Supremacy to restore the bond with Rome and orthodoxy. For these men and many of like conviction, the original insistence of More and Fisher that the Roman primacy was essential to maintain purity of doctrine and the integrity of the Church had by then been unmistakably vindicated, above all by the confusions and bleak opportunism which passed for reform under Edward VI.[1]

The reign of Edward, then, saw the formation of two rival views about the events of Henry's reign, each in retrospect

---

[1] Cf. Lacey Baldwin Smith, *Tudor Prelates and Politics* (Princeton, 1953), ch. ix. Five Henrician bishops survived to the accession of Elizabeth: Heath, Kitchen, Tunstall, Thirlby, and Bonner. With the exception of Kitchen, they all refused (like the rest of the Marian episcopate) Elizabeth's revived form of the Supremacy. Kitchen twice voted against it, but later took the oath and retained his see of Llandaff. Smith, op. cit., p. 287, n. 23.

denying the essential Erasmianism which had been its guid-
ing spirit. The strict Protestant interpretation, fixed for ever
under Mary in the exile communities which fostered Bale and
Foxe, saw all Henry's reform as at the very least Protestantism
*manqué*.[1] The recusant exiles in turn reviewed their own mar-
tyrology and, divorcing More from Erasmus, established an
approach which was exemplified by the work of Robert
Parsons. Here Henry was a monster, and the English martyrs
died for a posthumous Tridentine Rome.

In an atmosphere like this it might seem probable that the
middle position would disappear altogether. Yet under Edward,
the Protestantism which the English humanists adopted was
closer to Melanchthon than it was to Luther, and they never
found it necessary to disavow their past. Outside the realm of
doctrine, they maintained their sympathies and traditions
intact. The persistence of a personal and undoctrinaire pietism
was one manifestation of this, and the general welcome
accorded to moderate Protestant scholars from abroad was
another. Peter Martyr at Oxford, Bucer at Cambridge, the
learned Hebraists Fagius and Tremellius, with John à Lasco,
Peter Alexander, and Matthew Negelinus all stood for the
traditions of sound learning and linguistic excellence which
were already native to England. Ascham's admiration for
Sturmius and his assistance to Cheke in supplying information
about the continental adiaphorists[2] betray the sympathies of
these English humanists when they examined continental
Protestantism.

This is not to deny that under Edward the country was
flooded with Protestant literature, some of it of a most sectarian variety. Neither is it intended to obscure the vigorous
Protestantism of such men as Ponet and William Thomas,
or of such youthful exponents of humanist achievement as

[1] Foxe claimed both Henry and the non-Catholic victims of his persecution
as Protestant champions: for an example of the difficulties this posed him,
see vol. v, bk. ix, p. 696. Cf. Parsons, *Three Conversions*, pt. 2, ch. 11 (p. 550).

[2] Strype, *Cheke*, p. 53, and Giles, i (2), 108 (p. 219—to Cheke, 11 Nov. 1550,
from Augsburg).

Lady Jane Grey or the young King himself. With few exceptions, however, the humanists maintained a moderate attitude which the Government was content to respect. The worst moment for them came with the vigorous and destructive visitation of the universities. Moreover, the Edwardian Government too had its limits in heterodoxy, as the burning of Joan Boucher for Arianism showed. It must also be remembered that in the end most, like Cheke and Ascham, were willing to make the same accommodation with Mary that they had made with the régime of the Protector.

Thus the Erasmian traditions of English humanism continued without much real alteration even when the leading figures had abandoned the Henrician compromise for Protestantism. In these same Protestant humanist circles it is possible, for example, to see the old ideal of the 'necessary doctrine' emerging. In 1549 the university disputations of Peter Martyr against Dr. William Tresham of Christ Church at Oxford and the similar disputations on the Eucharist at Cambridge, both held before the King's commissioners, preserved this ideal at least in form. Perhaps more significant because of its essentially private character was the eucharistic debate held two years later, at the houses successively of William Cecil and Richard (now Sir Richard) Moryson. In learned circles, seemingly, the channels of discussion were not completely closed, and it is interesting that it was the leading Catholic spokesman at these last meetings, Dr. Feckenham, who as Dean of St. Paul's in 1556 combined with Pole to prevail upon Cheke to return to the unity of the Church.[1]

It is the work of this concluding chapter to illustrate the consequences of this persistent attitude of humanist moderation. The first fruit was the approved settlement of religion in 1549–50. In the first Prayer Book, with its accompanying formularies and devotional works, the Henrician proposals for a wholly vernacular Church were achieved still largely within the

[1] Temporarily, as it proved; Strype, *Cheke*, p. 11 and pp. 70 f. (on the eucharistic debates).

Erasmian tradition. It is only with the second Prayer Book and Cranmer's more radical phase that this solution is abandoned.

Secondly, the continuity of humanist thought bore fruit in a variety of works which, echoing the same interests as before, carried English letters to a new level of maturity. By the death of Edward VI it seems doubtful if any reaction but a vigorous and persistent assertion of religious censorship could have altered the established course of English letters, nourished from the well-springs of humanism established in the early years of the century. At the same time, the story of the English humanist community is not complete without an account of the conservative humanists, caught between the English Government and the reactions of Tridentine Rome, yet concerned to make known another version of these events.

The Prayer Book of 1549, with the Ordinal of the following year, was Cranmer's first statement about the form the English Church should have. Except for the drastic alteration of the canon of the Mass, there was little in the Prayer Book which could not be regarded as the realization of an Erasmian attempt to make the form of worship more instructive to the people. Even Cranmer's treatment of the Breviary was affected by Cardinal Quiñones' Erasmian reform of the Roman Breviary.[1] Moreover, the principle of periodic exhortation to the people was shared with continental reformers outside Protestant circles, and realized the common emphasis on instruction apart from the performing of a rite. Some of the most original elements, like the order for evensong, show a remarkable insight into the related problem of encouraging lay participation in a part of Church life which had become a most vivid symbol of clerical monopoly.

The Prayer Book, by combining all the previous rites except

---

[1] E. C. Ratcliff, 'The Liturgical Work of Archbishop Cranmer', *Journal of Ecclesiastical History*, vol. vii (1956), pp. 193–4. Cranmer's adherence to Erasmian reform principles is so much a conspicuous influence in his development as to make imperative an examination of his theology in this light.

ordination into one volume, also provided a common handbook of devotion which could be shared by clergy and laity alike. However, its close association with religious ceremony reduced its value compared with that of the traditionally popular primer as an aid to private devotion, and it is doubtless because of this that the old primer, now deemed too traditional to be useful, was revised. In 1553, a year after the appearance of the more patently Protestant second Prayer Book, a revised primer under the royal authority was published by William Seres. The basic material of the old primers was removed, and the whole work was closely assimilated to the second Prayer Book.[1]

By this time, however, Cranmer's productions had become quite specifically Protestant. The earlier Prayer Book pointed the direction of his movement, especially in its attitude to the sacrificial aspect of the Mass, as did the Ordinal of 1550. At that time, however, it was associated with another work inherited from the court of Catherine Parr which placed the new religious settlement in a much more traditional light. This was the complete translation of Erasmus's Paraphrases on the New Testament.[2]

The origins of this work have already been discussed. Officially, the translation was authorized by royal injunctions of 1547 requiring parsons, vicars, and curates within a year after the visitation to provide the Paraphrase 'upon the Gospelles' in English, set like the English Bible in some accessible place in church, 'whereas their parishyoners may moste commodiously resorte unto . . . and read the same'.[3] Significantly, the earlier provisions for the maintenance of scholars at university from the income of benefices worth over £100 a year were repeated here, the Erasmian classic being thus associated with a general programme to raise the level of clerical instruction.

---

[1] *STC* 20373; H. C. White, op. cit., pp. 119–21.

[2] *STC* 2854: E. Whitchurch, 1548–9.

[3] *STC* 10088: *Iniunccions geuen by the moste excellente Prince, Edwarde the .VI*, Grafton, 31 July [1547].

That the Paraphrases were also intended for the edification of the clergy was not left in doubt. All clerks under the degree of Bachelor of Divinity, within three months after the visitation, were to own a New Testament in Latin and English as well as the complete Paraphrases of Erasmus. To ensure that they would 'diligently study the same, conferring the one with the other', the bishops and ordinaries were required to examine them, a provision which echoes the annual Lenten examination of parishioners on the elements of the faith.

The work itself, published in two volumes in 1548 and 1549, represents effort divided between the two reigns. The earliest section completed appears to be Nicholas Udall's translation of the Paraphrase on Luke, the preface to which is dated 30 September 1545. This is mentioned in his general introductory dedication to the Queen, which also forms a prologue to the uncredited translation of Matthew, described as 'procured' by her. In his 'Preface unto the Kynges Maiestee' Udall says that all he can claim as his own is the Paraphrase on Luke 'and the digestyng and placyng of the texte throughout all the ghospelles, and the actes (except the ghospel of Marke), to thentent the unlearned readers maie percieve where and how the processe and circumstaunce of the paraphrase aunswereth to the texte, and how it ioyneth therwith'. The translator of the Paraphrase on Matthew may thus be left to conjecture.[1]

The gospel of St. Mark was translated by one Thomas Key, described by Strype as a 'Registry of Oxford',[2] on the suggestion of Henry's physician, Dr. Owen. The gospel of St. John was, as noted already, the work of Princess Mary, and there survives a letter from Catherine Parr praising her work and urging her to put it forth in her own name.[3] Udall's explanation of the illness and urgency which caused her to leave it to Dr. Malet for final preparation places the date for

[1] Udall's statement in his introduction to Acts, that he did not know the person responsible for the translation of Matthew, would seem to exclude Catherine Parr herself, who was suggested as the translator by Strype.

[2] Strype, Memorials, ii (Edward VI), pt. 1, p. 46.

[3] Cotton MS. Vespasian F. III, no. 35, fol. 37.

conclusion of the first volume after the issuing of the Injunctions for the Visitation of 1547. With its appearance, the requirements of the first part of the Injunctions, to provide the Paraphrases on the gospels for the laity, could now be met.

Nicholas Udall was the general impresario for the first volume, providing the dedicatory epistle to King Edward and (by virtue of her dominant role) the Queen Dowager, with a Preface to the Reader and prefaces to St. Luke, St. John, and to the Paraphrase on the Acts of the Apostles which concludes the volume. Apart from his testimony to the influence of Catherine Parr, there is incidental interest in his conception of the work. In the first preface, in praising Henry's reformation of the Church, the elements he cites are the abolition of the papal primacy, the destruction of all 'sects of cloisterers', of all 'counterfeit religion' and of idolatry, with (above all) the setting forth of Scripture in English. In Udall's mind Henry's work was a wholly Erasmian achievement.

On the crucial question of the Roman primacy, Erasmus is specifically called to witness.

Neither dooeth any wryter more wittily, more earnestely, more aptly, more finely, more substancially, more piththily [sic], more plainly describe and peyncte out the unsurped estate, preeminence, and pompe of the bishop of Rome then he dooeth: as well in all other places where iust occasion offreeth itself, as also directely (though under a preatie coulour) in the eleuenth chapitur of the Euangeliste Marke.[1]

The implication that Erasmus was a schismatic from Rome is thus neatly introduced. The eleventh chapter in question inveighs against pomp and display of wealth, and begins by comparing the humility of Christ's entry into Jerusalem with the pomp of the clergy:

With his dignitie compare me a bisshop of one temple, whiche hath bought the priesthode or prelacie lastyng but for one yeare

---

[1] 'The preface vnto the kynges Maiestee', Sig. B3. There are some half-dozen variants of STC 2854, vol. i. References in this chapter are correct for Bodley 0096 Th and Huntington 82526.

of a wicked and heathen kyng, for a fylthy sume of moneye. Compare the bare heade of Jesu, with his tyarre, or myter, all glysteryng and shyning with golde, and precious stones. [fol. lxxi$^v$; sig. 2M5$^v$]

In case the reader should miss the allusion, a marginal instruction informs him that 'The bishop of Romes pompe is couertly described'. The parable of the fig-tree is similarly taken to point a contrast between the barrenness of official religion and that of the true believer, and the point is sharpened by the unfavourable comparison of priestly pride and pomp with the humility and poverty of Christ:

How muche Jesus defyeth suche bisshoppes, this one thing playnely declareth, because he commaunded all that coloured and stately priesthode, with the temple thereof, utterly to be abolished and destroyed. For these be they by whom euen nowe in our dayes, Jesus (who will be thonly heade of priesthode) is slayne in his menbres [sic]. He seketh for these ministers, that maye bring vnto him the Asse, that maye couer the foale with theyr mantels, that maye strowe the waye with Palme boughes, and with godlye acclamations and cryinges, knowleage that the kyngdom of the gospel promysed of the prophetes is come and presente. [fol. lxxii; sig. 2M6]

Finally, the meditation on Christ's entry into Jerusalem raises the theme of the Church itself, and a tacit reference to Rome must have been automatic for the good Henrician:

What would he nowe do if he sawe his spousesse the churche (whiche he washed with his owne precious bloud, to make her cleane vnto himselfe, without any spot, or wrinckell) so to be arayed, polluted, and defiled with all manoure of fylthynesse, and that by the very bishops the rulers of the same. Who have not only cattell, and piggions to sell, but also all holye thynges, which in very dede, can neyther be bought, nor solde for monye. He seeth it undoubtedlye, although he winke thereat for a season. Neyther shall such personnes therfore escape unpunished, because god of his great lenitie and gentlenesse suffreth them, to thend they should repent, and cum to amendement. [fol. lxxiii; sig. 2N]

On the two most famous texts adduced in favour of the

Petrine supremacy, the English Erasmians could also take comfort from Erasmus's commentary. On Matthew xvi (verses 13–19) the famous reply is rendered:

> . . . thou arte very Peter, that is to say a sound and a sure stone, not wauering hither or thither with sundrie opinions of the vulgare sorte: and vpon this stone of thy profession wil I buyld my churche, that is to say, my house and my palace. . . . [fol. lxx; sig. M4][1]

The power of the keys survives Erasmus intact, but the whole passage is compatible with a Conciliarist view of the Petrine authority.

Similarly at John xxi (verses 13–19), the injunction to 'feed my lambs', Peter's role is exemplary only, and the commission of the keys is interpreted thus:

> And he specially spake to Peter, utterly to put away the remembraunce of his deniyng Christe, and to notise that he should haue the hiest and chefe place in the ministerie of the ghospell, that did passe other in excellencie of charitie towardes the flocke of the Lorde. And therefore, by hym, whom Jesus knewe to be of a more feruente mynde then the reste, he would expresse to all the Apostles and theyr successours, a proufe of a true and a perfite shepeherd. And in dede Peter is wount at other tymes also, to be as a mouth of the Apostles, and by hym the Lorde woulde haue it knowen and to be heard what the other also would openly confesse: for bicause, by the expressed voyce of this man, the publique confession of the whole churche did but a late tyme before, deserue a promyse of the keyes of the kyngedome of heauen. [fol. cxvi^{r-v}; sig. T8^{r-v}][2]

---

[1] Cf. *OO* vii. 92F to 93A: '. . . affirmo, te vere Petrum esse, hoc est, solidum lapidem; non huc aut illuc vacillantem variis opinionibus vulgi, et huic saxo tuae professionis, superstruam ecclesiam meam: hoc est, domum et palatium meum. . . .'

[2] Cf. ibid., fol. 47C: 'Petrum autem potissimum alloquitur, quo memoriam abnegationis aboleret, significans illum in Evangelico ministerio principem locum habiturum, quo caritate in gregem Dominicum praecelleret caeteris. Per hunc igitur, quem noverat caeteris ardentioris animi, voluit omnibus Apostolis, et horum successoribus, specimen veri perfectique Pastoris exprimere. Solet autem et alias Petrus velut os esse Apostolorum, et per hunc audiri voluit Dominus, quid caeteri quoque profiterentur. Siquidem hujus voce edita totius Ecclesiae professio, jam pridem promeruerat sponsionem clavium regni coelestis.'

The conclusion of the section might also be cited for its tacit application to the official apology:

The lord Jesus would haue these thynges with so greate dyligence powred into the myndes of his disciples, because he knewe there would rise men, that should not for the loue of Jesus, but for theyr owne commodities sake, take cure of christen people, or rather inuade and with violence take cure vpon hande: whiche maner of persons woulde in stede of shepeherdes, playe the tyrauntes, and robbe altogether. [fol. cxiiii; sig. T9][1]

Apart from such passages, Udall's prefaces also reveal suggestive notions. Toward the end of his first preface, to the King, he expressed the hope that the distribution of Scripture and of such works of enlightened commentary will bring into being 'one folde and one shepehearde', perhaps the basic underlying theme of the entire Henrician reply to the accusations of More and Pole.[2] The attitude to Erasmus himself is entirely characteristic: he will be favoured by all lovers of the truth and the Gospel, as one

whose doctrine the moste and best parte of all Christian Royalmes and vniversities hath euermore allowed and iudged to be consonaunt to the trueth ... ['... unto the Reader'; sig. B7 r-v]

The 'ornateness' of his style also is defended as a hallmark of authority, for

who wryteth more ornately then the Greke divines Basilius, Gregorie Nazianzene, Theophylactus, Chrysostome: who in latine more elegauntely then Lactantius, Hierome and diuerse others. [sig. B7v]

Erasmus is thus incorporated into the pantheon of great Church Fathers, and this seems to express the actual attitude of these reformers to the man who provided continual inspiration and scholarly support for their every undertaking. Equally,

---

[1] Cf. ibid., fol. 648B: 'Haec Dominus Jesus tanta diligentia voluit esse inculcata discipulorum suorum animis, quod non ignoraret exorituros, qui non amore Jesu, sed sui commodi gratia curam populi Christiani susciperent, vel arriperent potius, qui pro Pastoribus agerent tyrannos ac praedones.'

[2] Sig. B5.

Erasmus's dislike of any threat to Christian unity and his tenacious adherence to Rome is passed over in silence, while full play is given to those aspects of his writings which favoured the Henrician position and reform. Of these, of course, there were many. Erasmus's dislike of schism and of Lutheran doctrine and his irenic disposition seem to have played a greater part in his loyalty to Rome than did his opinion of Rome's authority,[1] and it was clear from the first that the English conservatives could find little counsel in his writings for the difficult question posed by Henry.

Finally, Udall suggests a characteristically ordered conception of society and of the obligation of public service, which rounds out the Henrician theme of patriotic reform:

> The partes of deuout readers are with immortal thankes to receiue and take the fruicion of honeste and godly studies: the office of learned men is without deprauyng or derogacion of other mennes diligence, and without any arrogancie on their owne behalfes, to emploie their good talentes to the publique behouf of their countrey, and to the fertheraunce of godly knowelage: the office of everie studious and diligent wryter is to haue his yie directed to the publique utilitee onely, and than to thinke his upright well dooynges a sufficient price and rewarde of theimselfes. . . . [Preface 'To . . . Quene Katherine dowagier . . .', sig. C1ᵛ]

The new atmosphere of Edward's reign is evident immediately in the sponsorship of the second volume in 1549. The place of Catherine Parr is now taken by Anne Seymour, Duchess of Somerset, and the whole tone of the prefaces suggests a more Protestant attitude. Coverdale introduced the work with another dedicatory preface to King Edward, and it is to be presumed that he was responsible for the subsequent Paraphrases on Paul's epistles to the Romans, Corinthians, and Galatians. Ephesians, Philippians, Thessalonians, Timothy, and Philemon were all translated by John Olde at the instance of the printer, Edward Whitchurch, and he acknowledges a

[1] See, e.g., Allen, viii. 2263, ll. 5 ff. Erasmus to Cuthbert Tunstall, Freiburg, 31 Jan. 1530.

special debt to the 'devoute woman of God, the Duchesse of Suffolke'.[1] Titus was reissued in the translation of Leonard Cox, whose account of the matter shows that the old school-master of Reading Abbey school was still busy with reforming causes, in particular with translation of two treatises by 'Marke the heremite'. He had thus made use of the time during which his preaching was stopped under the general prohibition of the Council. John Olde reappears as the man who reminded Cox of his former translation, undoubtedly to help fill the gap in material needed to complete the second volume. In order to contribute 'my farthinge into the treasorye of the lorde' Cox has revised it, and dedicates it to John Hales, 'whome I knowe to love gods worde synceretly [sic] and unto whome I know-ledge my selfe to be moste hyghlye bounde of all men, as unto the chefe and onely socourer of myne olde age . . .'.[2]

After this epistle and an unacknowledged translation of the Paraphrase on the Epistle to the Hebrews, John Olde dedicates to the Duchess 'certain of Paules epistles, whiche were lefte un-translated for lacke of payne takers in that matter, forsomuche as the learned menne appoynted to thys purpose of translacion, had finished their limited taskes before: and now at the like request I have made the like enterpryse to translate the Canony-call Epistles of S. Peter, Jude, James and John'. His 'speciall good friende' Edward Whitchurch was again apparently responsible for bringing this about, and the Protestant associa-tions of the work are made amply clear in his further acknow-ledgement of Latimer's friendship, and of the Warwickshire living he had obtained from the Duchess. It is therefore interest-ing to see that, for the first time, the praise accorded to Erasmus is qualified by a suggestion of lack of trust. Lamenting what he calls the 'devilles diligent preaching prelacie', he feels

[1] Sig. C2. Compare Dasent, *Acts of the Privy Council*, 10 July 1546 (p. 479), where Olde, chaplain to Lord Ferrers, confesses he had been 'of a light dis-posicion concerning matiers of religion', but being repentant, is dismissed with a lesson.

[2] Sig. 4E2. John Hales was probably the brother of Sir Christopher, the Attorney General.

only limited confidence in Erasmus's aid in redressing their influence:

. . . Erasmus in these epistles is a ready strong interpretour in many necessary places: in all I am not hable to affirme, knowing that he in his life tyme, was a manne subiecte to infirmitie and imperfeccion according to the naturall condycion of manne: as he himselfe speaketh of the great Doctour, S. Hierome: *Homo erat, et falli poterat et fallere.* A Manne he was, and might bothe be deceaued and deceaue. [sig. 1ᵛ]

Finally, the work was concluded by adding Leo Jud's Paraphrase on the Revelation of St. John, by Edmund Allen, described by Strype as 'a learned minister of the Gospel'.[1]

Taken together, the prefatory remarks in the second volume suggest that the project for translation suffered a sharp check from lack of direction after the death of Henry, and that it was continued under the sponsorship of the Protestant party at court. The doubts of conservatives at using Erasmus thus to educate the public in scriptural matters were soon made clear. Stephen Gardiner, whose public career began with the preparation of a salad for Erasmus, had come by now to regret many of his earlier enthusiasms. On the eve of his deprivation and incarceration, he was prepared to denounce the Paraphrases both for their intrinsic defects and for the tendentious translation which they had received. He felt, moreover, that they contradicted the doctrine taught in Cranmer's homilies, and that the homilies themselves were at variance with the 'doctrine of parliament'.[2]

As for Erasmus, Gardiner warns Somerset that his later teaching was far different from that of the Paraphrases written twenty-six years previously, 'when his pen was wanton'. Erasmus is dangerous in his attitude to princes, and in taking on himself in his comments the person of the apostles and even of Christ. In general, 'whatsoever might be spoken to defame

---

[1] Strype, *Memorials*, ii, pt. 1, p. 47.
[2] J. A. Muller, *The Letters of Stephen Gardiner* (Cambridge, 1933), letter 130 (to Somerset from the Fleet, 14 Oct. 1547), p. 382.

princes' government is not left unspoken', and he teaches nothing about the duties between Christian men. As for doctrine,
it is handled 'so wantonly' that he predicts great confusion,
and cites in particular the views expressed on the Eucharist,
on marriage of the clergy, and on remarriage after putting a
wife away for adultery. Gardiner also criticizes Erasmus's
teaching that 'everye man must cum to the high pricke of
vertue, or . . . be extremly nought . . .'.[1]

The Prayer Book of 1549 proved to be only a temporary
solution for Cranmer and the Edwardian Government, but the
Paraphrases were retained even in the most Protestant final
years of the reign. It is not surprising then to find that the
humanist production of these years retains the character of that
under Henry. As before, the interest is in devotional works,
in the acceptable moralizing of classical authors in translations
(which now begin to be printed in quantity), and in original
works of antiquarian and grammatical scholarship. There are
only a very few tracts, and these follow the Henrician pattern:
defence of public order and of Erasmian ecclesiastical reform.

The participation of humanists in frankly Protestant under-
takings is exceptional in the light of earlier humanist work.
As suggested above, however, their enthusiasm here is for
moderate and humanistic Protestantism, and examination of
their work tends to confirm rather than to contradict the
impression of an essential continuity of tradition. Apart from
their personal associations with the refugee reformers in
England, the published works are revealing. The Protestant
reformers whose works now attract the English humanists are
Melanchthon (as before), Bernardino Ochino (probably the
least humanistic of the group), Oecolampadius, Bucer, John
à Lasco, and Zwingli.

This selection clearly reflects the situation of the English
Church itself. Cranmer's proposals in 1548 to mediate between
the dissident branches of the reformed community had attracted

---

[1] Ibid., p. 386: '. . . which differeth far from the teachinge of the homelies,
and from the truthe also.' Cf. letters 133, 135, 136.

the most distinguished advocates of that policy from the Continent. John à Lasco, Martin Bucer, and John Oecolampadius, each disappointed by negotiations between Luther and the Swiss group and likewise confronted with the resurgence of Imperial power, found in the English Church a natural host for their views. With Peter Martyr, Bucer's old colleague, the Edwardian Government collected the most distinguished continental adherents of a reformed position which was expressly intended to mediate between the extreme Protestant camps.

The only important exception to this pattern is the interest in Zwingli, but it seems uncommon. The most enthusiastic advocate of the Swiss reformer in England was Master Richard Argentine, an Ipswich physician and Cambridge graduate, whose translations of Zwingli's works appeared in 1548 and 1550.[1] Calvin also appeared in English in 1550, with Somerset's translation from the French of Calvin's letter to him,[2] and the library records of the period show that the reception of Calvin's works in England occurred about this time.

Interest in continental reformers was a natural accompaniment to the intellectual growth of the English humanist community; and in the views of Calvin especially, English readers may be supposed to have discovered a natural development of the whole Erasmian notion of a Church dominated by laymen. Apart from that, the interest of the continental exiles in these Swiss reformers would be sufficient in itself to account for this new colouring of English reform opinion. Cheke's *De obitu doctissimi doctoris M. Buceri*, published in 1551 on the death of the scholar at Cambridge, serves as a general tribute of the English humanists to these Protestant scholars.[3]

In the larger context of other humanist work, this interest in dogmatic Protestantism seems an aspect of the earlier

[1] *STC* 26136: *Certeyne preceptes*, Ippeswich, A. Scoloker, 1548; *STC* 26137 (Seres and Kele, 1550).
[2] *STC* 4407: E. Whitchurch, 1550.
[3] *STC* 5108: R. Wolf.

Erasmian tradition in England, rather than a development which pushes it aside. Even in the region where one might logically expect a new dogmatism to emerge, that of tracts in defence of government policy, the work of the humanist community follows along the old lines. Nicholas Udall's unpublished 'Answer to the Commoners of Devonshire and Cornwall', written in response to the risings of 1549, is the nearest approach to Moryson's and Starkey's work for Cromwell.[1] A reasoned point-by-point reply to the petitions of the rebels, it breaks no new ground and makes its appeal to expediency and to concord through obedience. Cheke's 'True subject to the Rebell', of the same year, has much the same theme,[2] and Ponet's writings of 1549, which can be interpreted as at least being appropriate to the crisis, also cover familiar ground of the Henrician period. His *Defence for mariage of priestes, by Scripture and aunciente writers* was joined to the translation of Ochino's *A tragoedie or dialoge of the uniuste primacie of the Bishop of Rome*, a work written in England which now survives only through Ponet's version.[3]

Apart from this brief flurry of apologetic, the continued production of Erasmian works of pietism is perhaps the most obvious link with past traditions. Catherine Parr's *Lamentacion* was reissued in various forms, to become a classic of Tudor devotional literature.[4] Versions of the psalms continued to appear, with an offering by Wyatt providing perhaps the most obvious connexion with the world of humane letters.[5] The *Enchiridion* continued to be a mainstay of publication, as was Chrysostom.[6] The *Common places* of Erasmus Sarcerius in

[1] N. Pocock, *Troubles connected with the Prayer Book of 1549* (Camden Society, N.S., xxxvii, 1884), pp. 141 ff.; Royal MS. 18 B. XI.

[2] *STC* 5109: *The hurt of sedicion*, J. Daye and W. Seres, 1549.

[3] *STC* 20176: R. Wolf, 1549; *STC* 18770, [N. Hill] f. Gwalter Lynne, 1549.

[4] *STC* 4827 and 4828, Whitchurch, 1547 and 1548.

[5] *STC* 2726: *Certayne psalmes called the vii penitentiall psalmes*, T. Raynold and J. Harrington, 1549.

[6] *STC* 14638: *A sermon of pacience*, N. Hyll for J. Shefelde, 1550; *STC* 14642: *A treatise concerning the restitucion of a synner*, R. Calye, 1553.

Taverner's version reappeared in 1553,[1] and the pietistic writings of Thomas Paynell supplied a personal link with Henrician devotional literature. In 1550 he published *The piththy* [sic] *and moost notable sayinges of al Scripture, after the manner of common places, very necessary for al those that delite in the consolacions of the Scriptures.*[2] This work, the largest of its kind to date, with obvious bearing on the old prescription of vernacular study of Scripture, was significantly dedicated not to the more popular Protestant patrons of Edwardian letters but to 'the right excellent and most gracious Lady, my Ladye Maryes good grace'. In his dedicatory prologue, moreover, he praised her devotion to godly learning, her liberality to those 'whiche diligently do exercyse themselves in the spirituall and morall study of the sincere worde of God', and her 'begnignitie' to him, 'bountefully to me declared', which forces him to publish it in her name. Coming as it did on the eve of the Council's attack on the private household devotion of the King's Catholic sister, it was a striking assertion of the breadth of the tradition of learned pietism in England.

Closely related to these works were the first English concordances, in 1550. John Marbeck's harrowing task finally came to a happy end with the publication of his *Worke wherein by the ordre of the letters of the A.B.C. ye maie redely finde any worde conteigned in the whole Bible.*[3] In his dedication to Edward VI, Marbeck described himself as he had to Gardiner and Bonner, as having 'never tasted the swetnes of learned letters, but altogether brought up in your highnes College at Wyndsore, in the study of Muciske and pleiyng on Organs, wherin I consumed vainly the greatest part of my life'.

The same year a more truly humanist work, translated from the concordance of Bullinger, Jud, and Pellican, was dedicated to the Duchess of Somerset by one Walter Lynne.[4] Although a little remote from the English humanist scene as such, the

---

[1] STC 21754: Hyll.
[2] STC 19494: T. Gualtier at the costes of R. Toye, 1550.
[3] STC 17300: R. Grafton, 1550.     [4] STC 17117: G. Lynne, 1550.

concordances of 1550 are a natural development of the emphasis on the vernacular Bible, and a complement to the Paraphrases: Gardiner's hostility to both works gives them an association which is not purely circumstantial.

Not surprisingly, Erasmus himself makes new appearances. A Protestant apologist, Nicholas Lesse, gleaned Erasmus's *Annotationes* for comments on St. Paul, and produced *The censure and judgement of Erasmus whyther dyuorsemente betwene man and wyfe stondeth with the lawe of God*.[1] Although no immediate contemporary reference is apparent, *The Censure and judgement* surveys the whole problem of divorce, from citations of early Fathers permitting a man to remarry after putting his wife away for adultery, to the question of papal dispensing power. Lesse himself, a citizen and merchant of London and friend of Bale, seems otherwise to have confined himself almost entirely to translation of Protestant works.

More important by far is Edmund Becke's *Two dyalogues* '. . . one called Polyphemus or the gospeller the other dysposyng of thynges and names'.[2] Here once more an English Erasmian turns to the *Colloquia* for a definite controversial purpose, and this time it enables us to identify a scholarly Protestant working consciously to preserve a position between two extremes.

Edmund Becke's great preoccupation seems to have been the re-editing of earlier English versions of the Bible. A deacon ordained by Ridley in 1551, he seems to have brought to his task some learning and rather more sincerity and industry. The Matthew Bible, Taverner's version, and Tyndale's New Testament all came under his purview, appearing in new editions from 1549 to 1551.[3]

Becke's attitude to reform may be gleaned from the present dialogues, and from his third work, a theological discourse in verse form justifying the execution of the Anabaptist Joan

[1] STC 10450: Wydowe of J. Herforde for R. Stoughton [1550?].

[2] STC 10459 ('Cantorbury', J. Mychell [1550]. Edited, with introduction and notes, by H. de Vocht in *The Earliest English Translations of Erasmus' Colloquia*, Louvain and London, 1928; *Humanistica Lovaniensia*, 2).

[3] de Vocht, op. cit., pp. xvi–xix.

Boucher.[1] It is a complement to the first of his chosen dialogues, the *Cyclops*, which was written by Erasmus during a time of profound irritation with the intellectual and moral failures of some of the reformers, shortly after Basle was visited by a wandering Anabaptist preacher.[2] In ridiculing Anabaptist extravagance, Erasmus nevertheless makes several references to abuses in the Church of Rome, and the utility of the tract to Becke in the England of 1550 scarcely needs comment.

The second colloquy, the *De rebus ac vocabulis*, is an extended reflection on pretence, concluding with the portrayal of base-born scoundrels who masquerade as knights in order to realize their profligate ambitions. Again the timeliness of this discussion in the midst of growing discontent with the conduct of England's domestic affairs under the boy King is fully apparent. Becke's translations too, with their inclusion of such traditional oaths as 'by saynt Mary' and discreet omission of reference to debasing of coinage, suggest a combination of loyalty to the young King with dislike of Protestant radicalism which one would expect from the English humanist circle.[3]

Apart from these, there are three remaining pietistic works with a distinctly humanistic sponsorship. The first is the famous *Miroir de l'âme pécheresse* of Marguerite of Navarre, recently translated by the Princess Elizabeth. Her version, supplied to John Bale and retitled by him *Godly medytacyon of the christen sowle*, was published in 1548.[4] The second is William Thomas's *The vanitee of this world*, which appeared in the same year as his history of Italy.[5] The third, published in 1548, is similar in character, and in some ways the most interesting. It is a translation by Sir Francis Bryan of Bishop Antonio de Guevara's *A dispraise of the life of a courtier and commendation of*

---

[1] *STC* 1709: *A brefe confutacion*, J. Day, 1550.

[2] de Vocht, op. cit., p. xi.

[3] On Becke's other work, H. Pope, *English Versions of the Bible* (1952); W. J. Heaton, *The Bible of the Reformation* (1910), ch. xvii; F. F. Bruce, *The English Bible* (1961), pp. 83–84.

[4] *STC* 17320 [Wesel, D. van der Straten].

[5] *STC* 24023: Berthelet, 1549.

*the life of the labouring man.*[1] Bryan dedicated the work to William Parr, now Marquis of Northampton, and in his prologue describes how he had found it so enjoyable himself that, partly at Parr's request, he had decided to turn it into English. He adds the hope that it will also please Parr's sister, the Queen Dowager, which places the completion of the work before September 1548.

The book itself came from the Erasmian circles of the Spanish and Portuguese episcopate, and was a more profoundly spiritual treatise than its title would suggest. An eloquent and elevated discourse on the spiritual dangers of a worldly court life compared with the superior virtue of a life in the country, it formed a harmony of moral and pastoral meditation which was a natural medium for humanistic expression. Predictably, classical precepts are as evident as Christian precepts, and the authorities cited come primarily from the former category. But the whole work is conducted in an unmistakably religious tone, with a gravity which is strongly reminiscent of Catherine Parr's *Lamentacion*. At the conclusion, where 'the auctour taketh his leaue of the worlde with great eloquence', the renunciation of court life has really assumed the proportions of a lay monasticism:

Farewell world, forasmuch as one can nor may trust of ye nor in the. . . . Farewell world, for beyng in the, we forget our infancy, and our grene age, with out experience: our youth in vices; our middle age in turmoilyng and busynes: our olde age in lamentacions, and all our tyme counted together in vaine hopes.

O worlde uncleane, I conjure thee thou filthy worlde, I pray O thou worlde, and protest against thee thou worlde, that thou neuer have part in me, for I demaunde nor desire nothyng that is in thee, neither hope of any thyng in thee, for I have determinined [*sic*] with myself that *posui finem curis, spes, et fortuna valete.* I have finished worldly cares, therefore hope and fortune farewell.

This remarkable statement of disillusion with the career of worldly service, so unlike the characteristic note of loyal

[1] From the French of Antony Alaygre: *STC* 12431: Grafton, 1548.

enthusiasm, recalls the opening strains of Erasmus's *Enchiridion*. It is no less remarkable for coming from a veteran of Henry's reign whose authority on this subject might be regarded as magisterial. Bryan throughout Henry's lifetime had been his closest friend and constant companion. His reputation for dexterous manœuvre, if necessary at the expense of his kin, had earned even Cromwell's disapproval. His close association with the humanism of the court is well attested, and his own reputation as a poet placed him in the esteem of his contemporaries in the same rank as his friends Wyatt and Surrey. Wyatt, as already mentioned, dedicated to him one of his satires on the practices of court life, a work which clearly foreshadows the present one. Finally, he was closely associated with the literary work of Lord Berners, and was the instigator of that other translation of Guevara by Bourchier, the *Golden Boke of Marcus Aurelius*.[1]

Whatever the truth may be about Bryan's own attitude of mind, *A dispraise* is unmistakable evidence of the importance of the pietistic tradition in these aristocratic circles, and of their awareness of similar associations on the Continent. To that degree it provides an appropriate introduction to the manuscript treatise by Edward Courtenay from the same period, his translation of the Italian *Beneficio di Giesu Cristo Crocifisso*.[2]

Devotion to the theme of Christ Crucified was a conspicuous tradition in Dominican spirituality, and had included such distinguished exponents in previous generations as St. Catherine of Siena, Savonarola, Tauler and Eckhard, and St. Vincent Ferrer. It was also present in the *philosophia Christi*, suitably modulated to the more tranquil key of that creed. The *Beneficio*, whose authorship has recently been traced to Benedetto Luchino of Mantua, appeared about 1543, and was soon proscribed by the Italian Inquisition as a handbook of reformed

---

[1] *STC* 12436: Berthelet, 1535.

[2] Cambridge University Library MS. Nn. iv. 43. On the *Beneficio* see B. Croce, 'Il "Beneficio di Giesu Cristo Crocifisso"', *La Critica*, vol. xxxviii (1940).

doctrines. In the hands of Edward Courtenay, the only son of the condemned Henry Courtenay and of a daughter of William Blount, it was both a bond with the Erasmian pietistic tradition and a patent attempt to pacify the suspicious régime of Edward VI. Courtenay's mother, the Marchioness Gertrude, although imprisoned and attainted with the other members of the family in 1538, had subsequently been pardoned, and always remained a loyal friend of the Princess Mary. On Mary's accession she became a Lady in Waiting. Edward, however, as the sole Courtenay heir and a great-grandson of Edward IV, was specifically exempted from the amnesty of Edward VI in 1547 and was not in fact released until August 1553.

Courtenay's translation, 'The Benefit of Christ Crucified', is dedicated to Anne Seymour, Duchess of Somerset, by 'the sorowfull captive', with a protest that he is being made to suffer for the guilt of his father, of which he was personally entirely innocent. Referring to the solitude of his imprisonment, he makes the astute observation that it has deprived him of influences which might redound to his own benefit:

But also am I continuallie have bene [sic] depriued of this worldlie libertie, secluded and shut up in prison within the wallis from the compaine allmoste of all men, speciallie from suche of whome and bi whose godlie conuersation i shoulde or mought have conceiued or lerned anni either godlines or ciuilitie.

His Italian he claims to have learned 'by my noune studie', and his highly individual spelling, even in an age of widely various practice, suggests that his incarceration at the age of some thirteen years had indeed been a deprivation. The dedication concludes with a pathetic plea for the intercession of the Duchess, 'that by the same your godlie and pitefull meanes it may pleas my Lordis grace of his manyfolde and habundaunte goodnes, to deliver me out of this miserable captivitie and to vouchesafe to take me into his howse as his gracis seruant'.[1]

That the work reached the King cannot be doubted, for he

---

[1] C.U.L. MS. Nn. iv. 43, f.v. 3.

left on its pages the manuscript annotations, 'Faith is dede if it be without workes; Your louing neueu, Edward', and 'Live to die and die to live again; Your neueu, Edward'.[1] His pious sympathy, however, did not produce Courtenay's release. More interesting is the question of how Courtenay secured the 'trattato utilissimo' in the first place, but in the absence of evidence conjecture seems profitless. It is enough that someone in the English court felt that of the many possible approaches to the King, this one, through the most celebrated contemporary Erasmian treatise on personal devotion, would be the most likely to bring Edward Courtenay his longed-for liberty.

It is clear, then, that the Erasmian tradition of the previous reign persisted in the devotional literature of Edward's. It might be briefly noted that the same continuity can be observed in the secular morality of these years. Richard Taverner's moralistic collections from Erasmus, Elyot's *Image of governance*, Baldwin's *Treatise of morall phylosophie*, and Richard Moryson's translation of Vives all reappeared in fresh editions. Moreover, Thomas Paynell added to the English Vives canon with *The office and duetie of an husband*.[2] Taken together, these titles suggest that this aspect of the Erasmian faith was as popular under the Protestant Government of Edward VI as it had been during the Henrician régime.

There are two other works in this category which have importance far beyond that of those just mentioned. It is in this period that the *Praise of Folly*[3] and More's *Utopia* were first translated for the benefit of the English public. The former work, undertaken by Sir Thomas Chaloner, was the climax of translation activity which had almost certainly grown from his association with Cheke, Walter Haddon, and other scholars. It was remarkably appropriate that the most popular work of the moralizing, Lucianic Erasmus should receive its classic translation from the son of a London mercer, a St. John's man quite possibly, and a royal servant who

[1] C.U.L. MS. Nn. iv. 43, fols. 4ᵛ and 92.
[2] *STC* 24855: J. Cawood [1553?].  [3] *STC* 10500: Berthelet, 1549.

preserved his welcome at court under Henry, Edward, Mary, and Elizabeth. A lesser specimen of the hardy breed of Petre and Cecil (whose executor he was), Sir Thomas Chaloner concluded his literary career with the *De republica Anglorum instauranda* published in 1579.[1]

It was within two years of the *Praise of Folly* that Thomas More's greatest original production, the *Utopia*, also appeared in English, translated by Ralph Robinson, 'Citizein and Goldsmythe of London, at the procurement and earnest request of George Tadlowe, Citezein and Haberdassher, of the same Citie', and dedicated to William Cecil.[2] Cecil was in fact a former schoolmate of Robinson at Grantham and Stamford grammar schools. Robinson had gone on to Corpus Christi College, Oxford, where he was elected a Fellow in June 1542. Later he seems to have removed to Cecil's service in London.

The *Utopia* itself, despite its authorship, was a work clearly acceptable to the Erasmian community at any time. In the preface Robinson makes apology for More's obstinate religious views in terms which indicate how much of More's range and complexity would be suppressed in the later Tudor traditions about him:

> This only I saye; that it is much to be lamented of al, and not only of us English men, that a man of so incomparable witte, of so profounde knowlege, of so absolute learning, and of so fine eloquence, was yet neuerthelesse so much blinded, rather with obstinacie then with ignoraunce, that he could not, or rather would not, see the shining light of godes holy truthe in certein principal pointes of Christian religion; but did rather cheuse to perseuer and continue in his wilfull and stubbourne obstinacie euen to the very death: This I say is a thing much to be lamented.

The attitude of English Erasmian opinion to More's stand, both at the time of his martyrdom and later, could not be better expressed. By way of contrast, the emphasis of the other tradition about More, to which we shall return shortly, is

[1] *STC* 4938: in ten books, the first five dedicated to William Cecil.
[2] *STC* 18094: A. Vele, 1551

sufficiently suggested by the title of the next More translation to appear in England, shortly after the accession of Mary: *A dialoge of comfort against tribulacion*.[1]

The appearance of the *Utopia* under Cecil's sponsorship points to the growing influence of the Secretary of State in the world of English humanism. His association with the influential and productive St. John's community is already clear, and the dedications of the day suggest that he was coming to occupy a position something like that of Cromwell earlier, at least in the estimate of young humanists wishing to make their way in the world. Once more Roger Ascham provides the fullest account of the adaptation of Henrician humanist learning to the circumstances of the new reign, and it is evident that in bridging the gap between Henry's late years and the court of the Young Josiah, Cecil's influence was of paramount importance. In 1551 and 1552, in the midst of Ascham's journeys in the retinue of Richard Moryson, his letters to Cecil reveal his continued indecision about a life at court, as well as his pride in the English achievement. As Edward's reign draws to a close, he finds it prudent to reopen his association with Stephen Gardiner and to dissemble his Protestantism,[2] but his fundamental interests are always the same. He longs for Cambridge, even as be bewails the ills which beset the university through the vicissitudes of religious change, but above everything else is the expressed desire 'to do good service to the common wealthe':

And in very deed, too many be pluckt from thence [Cambridge] before they be ripe, though I myself am withered before I be gathered, and yet not so for that I have stood too long, but rather because the fruit which I bear is so very small. Yet seeing the goodly crop of Mr. Cheke is almost clear carried from thence, and I in a manner alone of that time left a standing straggler . . . I may yet be thought somewhat fit for seed, when all you the rest are taken up for better store, wherewith the King and his realm is now so nobly served.[3]

[1] STC 18082: R. Tottel, 1553.    [2] Giles, i (2), 158.
[3] Ibid. 145 (to Cecil from Brussels, 24 Mar. 1553). Letter 140 provides a

Ascham's careful cultivation of Cecil during this period is a reminder that the essential continuity of humanist opinion reflected, and in some degree depended upon, a continuity in patronage and sponsorship. The careers of Cecil, Smith, Paget, John Ponet, and others reveal the extent to which powerful patrons were entrenched, indispensable to any Government. The same applied to great families. If the Courtenays were crushed, the Mountjoys carried on, as did the Bourchiers, the Bryans, and the Parrs. Representative of this continuity in aristocratic humanism was the household of Henry Fitzalan, twelfth Earl of Arundel. His two daughters by his first wife Catherine, daughter of Thomas Grey, Marquess of Dorset, were both famous for their classical learning, and his library formed the nucleus of the famous collection of his son-in-law, John Lord Lumley. Lumley was himself educated in the Earl's household, and one of his achievements of those years, a translation of Erasmus's *Institutio principis Christiani*, is preserved in the Royal Manuscript collection.[1] The same collection contains a Latin translation by John Ratcliffe, Arundel's stepson, of a subject favoured also by Princess Elizabeth, Queen Catherine's Prayers.[2] The Earl's younger daughter, too, the Lady Mary Fitzalan, left considerable evidence of her Greek studies and her humanistic achievement in his domestic school.[3]

The household of the Earl of Arundel may be placed alongside the better-known Dorset household which produced the learning of Lady Jane Grey, or beside Ascham's account of his own education of the Princess Elizabeth, to illustrate the successful penetration of aristocratic circles by the humanist ideals of education.[4] Here the Erasmian ideals of the early

glimpse of the deeper roots of Cecil's influence with these men, when Ascham recalls Cecil's assistance with a difficult passage in Demosthenes, while at Shene.

[1] Royal MS. 17 A. XLIX.  [2] Royal MS. 7 D. IX.

[3] Royal MS. 12 A. I–IV: the last of the four is jointly signed by the Lady Mary and her fellow pupil John Ratcliffe. Compare with 17 B. XVIII, a homily of Basil of Caesarea, translated from the Greek by Mildred Cecil, Burghley's second wife and Sir Anthony Cooke's daughter, about 1550.

[4] Giles, i (2), 110 and 114.

reformers were immune from the shocks of Government
policy and religious change, and under this protection the
humanist mentality of Tudor England by mid-century had
developed. Love of the classics, a religion personal, undogmatic,
and patriotic, with a public philosophy devoted to the service
of the Prince and the 'commonweal'—these were the articles
of the creed. It was expressed in public service (including the
service of the Church), teaching, and the translation of classics.[1]
That faithful bellwether, Roger Ascham, exposed the ideals
of his fellows in a long letter to the learned Protestant John
Sturmius from Cambridge in April of 1550.[2] In a general
account of the state of England he praises the protection of true
faith provided by King, Council, and Canterbury and boasts
that in the study of Scripture they follow the ancient Fathers
('where they do not wander from scripture'), setting most store
by St. Augustine. Although there are differences in religious
opinion, the learning, generosity, and lack of bitterness of those
who disagree leaves hope that if these questions are pursued
in love, Providence will yet bring them all to the truth.

Closely linked to Ascham's pride in the English Church
is that in English education. Even his admissions are clearly
intended to give the best impression of the state of the English
universities. Professing ignorance of classical studies at Oxford,
he recalls meeting an Oxford man at court who, by preferring
Lucian, Plutarch, and Herodian, Seneca, Aulus Gellius, and
Apuleius, seemed in both tongues to show 'too much regard
for a time of decline and decadence'. This is followed with his

---

[1] It would burden the present account unduly to attempt to present the
humanist achievement outside the strictly Erasmian sphere. It is, however,
relevant to notice the maturing of the translation enterprise, with Herodian,
Tertullian, and Thucydides all making first appearances in English in 1550
(STC 13221, 23916, and 24056). Leland's great work was also under way in
these years; an Italian Grammar appeared in 1550 (STC 24020); and
Estienne's great dictionary was adapted for English use in a trilingual edition
(STC 10555). Finally, Wilson's *Arte of rhetorique* of 1553 (STC 25799) was
a significant achievement: see W. J. Ong, *Ramus, Method and the Decay of Dialogue* (Cambridge, Mass., 1958), pp. 125 and 275, and W. S. Howell, op. cit.,
ch. 2, sec. 1, and pp. 98 f.               [2] Giles, i. 99.

account of the education of his royal pupil, Princess Elizabeth, and again the account is revealing. He states that the Princess began the day with the New Testament in Greek, followed by the orations of Isocrates and the tragedies of Sophocles, whence he expected her to acquire not only purity of speech but a cast of mind suitable for her royal position and for the contingencies of chance which might befall one so placed. On the religious side of her instruction, it is in keeping with the essentially Erasmian flavour of this court Protestantism that Cyprian and Melanchthon's *Loci Communes*, with 'other works of like nature', were the guides in doctrine. The letter includes an interesting reference to Elizabeth's contempt for the slavish imitators of Erasmus, who cannot rise above the citation of proverbs.

With so much evidence of the continuity of an Erasmian humanist tradition among the English scholars who accepted the decisive break with Rome, it is time to turn to that other section of the humanist community which secretly or openly repudiated the Henrician settlement, to see how its interests fared. Here we find the birth of a separate tradition about the events of Henry's reign, which forms a complement to the domestic version. The natural tendency of English scholars to concentrate on the figures whose work led to the Elizabethan flowering of thought and letters has tended to obscure the importance of the learned opposition under Henry and Edward VI. An awareness of it is essential, however, if we are to understand not only the Government's policy, but the complexity of the English response to the Henrician settlement and of its disruptive impact on the learned world.

It is worth recalling at the outset that the most distinguished humanist opinion in the divorce controversy was on the side of the Queen. Not only More and Fisher, but Richard Reynolds, Polydore Vergil, Vives, Tunstall, and Erasmus himself were hostile to or at least sceptical of the King's case.[1] To these names

[1] On Erasmus's scepticism, his letter to Boniface Amerbach, 1530: Allen, viii. 2256.

of course could be added that of Tyndale, whose views (like those of Luther) are a reminder that the King's 'great matter' cut across the lines of religious differences.

Nevertheless, for reasons that we have seen, few members of the Erasmian community in England were prepared to oppose the King to the death. Indeed, it is plain that for most of the English humanists More's martyrdom was an inexplicable, personal decision. More's own anxiety to avoid burdening their consciences left his followers with no reasoned apologetic, and many must have shared the hurt bewilderment of Thomas Starkey at More's apparent desertion of the cause of royal reform.[1] At the same time, the stature of those who did die for the tie with Rome was enormously impressive, and after 1535 the English humanist community had no one left to approach More, Fisher, and Reynolds in their combination of intellectual distinction, learning, and spiritual authority. It would be natural, then, to suppose that Henry's ruthlessness left its legacy of disquiet in England as it did on the Continent, and some of the evidence for this we have examined already. A closer examination will show that the opposition to Henry's policies in the learned community was far more widespread than has been commonly supposed.

The isolation of More within his own immediate circle of family and friends was apparently complete. More eloquent than any official pamphlet was the failure of his own daughter, Margaret Roper, to grasp his purpose. No one, it seems fair to say, more fully shared More's confidence than she did, yet her recorded opinions are closer to those of her mother than they are to More's. She took the oath her father refused, so the general compliance of More's family in Henry's demands is scarcely remarkable.[2]

In general, the views of More's family are symptomatic on

---

[1] Cotton MS. Cleopatra E. vi (Starkey's draft), fols. 379 f., printed by S. J. Herrtage, *England in the Reign of Henry VIII*, pt. i (E.E.T.S. Extra Series 32, 1878), pp. xxxiv–xxxviii.

[2] Rogers, letter 202.

the conservative side. Loyalty to the heroic family martyr was of course unimpaired by acquiescence in the Royal Supremacy. Margaret Roper gathered her father's relics with the same loving pains that marked Margaret Clements's efforts on behalf of the starving Carthusians in Newgate. Yet at some later date she tried to obtain the services of the distinguished Protestant humanist Roger Ascham as tutor to her children.[1]

Within a decade of More's death, however, the family did make a conspicuous declaration against the King's policies, and the occasion was significant. It was the famous 'Plot of the Prebendaries' against Cranmer. In the first years after Henry's rupture with Rome the humanist group at large had found the papal supremacy a doubtful need, if not a positive obstacle to a renewal of the Church in England. A decade later, it seems that a conservative faction is beginning to define itself, through common awareness that the Royal Supremacy might be used to introduce Protestant doctrine. If this surmise is correct, the More family in 1543 anticipated the changing attitude of the whole conservative group in the reign of Edward VI. At any rate, involved in trials before the Council in 1544, along with Germaine Gardiner and the King's former scholar-pensioner John Bekinsau, were More's son John and his surviving sons-in-law William Daunce and William Roper, with such other associates of the Chelsea family circle as John Heywood, husband of Joan Rastell, John Larke, the parish priest, and a family chaplain, John Ireland. Of these, Gardiner and the two priests alone refused to submit and were executed at Tyburn.[2]

Outside the family, in the universities, there were other scholars whose conservative views would ultimately lead them

[1] Thus before Christmas 1544, when she died. See Giles, i (2), 166 and below, p. 267. The son, Thomas, matriculated later at Louvain; H. de Vocht, *Acta Thomae Mori* (Louvain, 1947), p. 110, n. 4.

[2] Roper's role is doubtful, but he had earlier been committed to the Tower for aiding distressed Catholics, notably Bekinsau. See *Roper's Life of More* (E.E.T.S., 1935), p. 117, and Harpsfield, p. 89. Giles Heron was executed in 1540 with six others, including a priest and a lawyer, accused of plotting with Pole.

into recusancy. All presumably took the Oath of Supremacy either in virtue of their offices or as Fellows of their colleges (Richard Whitford's seems a rare case of successful refusal, made possible by the protection of the Mountjoys[1]). A brief canvass of their quality is instructive.

The list might begin with Richard Smith, D.D., who was appointed by Henry first holder of the Regius Professorship in Divinity at Oxford. In 1537 he was made Master of Whittington College, and he was commissioned to assist in the preparation of *The Institution of a Christian Man*. At the end of the reign he published a defence of the orthodox view of the Eucharist and of the Mass[2] in time to run headlong into the religious changes of the succeeding reign, when he was made to publish in recantation. By 1549 he had fled to Louvain, where he was made Professor of Divinity, and he concluded his career as first Chancellor and Professor of Theology at Douay.

Associated with Smith in the Oxford Regius Chairs were two other prominent recusant scholars, John Harpsfield and George Etherige. Harpsfield came to the office by way of that conspicuous avenue of learned recusancy, Winchester and New College, which he attended in company with his brother Nicholas, the biographer of More. After studies in arts leading to theology, he seems to have been lecturing on the new foundation as early as 1541. As evidence of his learning, the Royal Manuscripts contain a Latin translation of the Commentary of Simplicius on the first book of Aristotle's *Physics*, and a version in Greek hexameters of the first book of the *Aeneid*.[3]

When the King's College was refounded once more as Christ Church in 1546 it seems that Harpsfield was succeeded in his position by George Etherige, formerly a scholar and Fellow of Corpus Christi College, Oxford. Eminent in many

---

[1] Knowles, op. cit., pp. 218–19.     [2] *STC* 22815 and 22820.
[3] Royal MSS. 12 F. v and 16 C. viii (with George Etherige). John Harpsfield and his brother both spent twelve years in the Fleet for recusancy under Elizabeth.

fields, including mathematics, Hebrew, Greek, and medicine, he was apparently deprived late in 1550 and restored to his chair by Mary. Under Elizabeth his hall in Oxford became a centre for Catholic gentry at the university. His known works include Greek poetry, musical compositions (including a setting for a shortened form of the Psalms in Hebrew verse), a Latin translation of the works of Justin Martyr, and a work on Paulus Aeginetus, dedicated to Walter Mildmay.

As a final representative of this learned group at Oxford, there is John Morwen of Corpus Christi College. Related to the second President, Robert Morwen, whose conservative religious views were well known, he was noted for his Greek scholarship and was appointed Reader in Greek in the college. Later, as Bonner's secretary, he came into prominence under Mary, and his pupils included two of special interest: John Jewel, the learned Elizabethan divine and apologist, and Mary, daughter of Margaret and William Roper. It would be pleasant to know the Roper family views on the respective merits as tutors of Morwen and Roger Ascham, whose letter to Mary, as Mrs. Stephen Clarke, tells us of her mother's attempt to secure his services as well. That Morwen's teaching and the family tradition bore fruit is evident from Harpsfield's assertion that Mary Roper was

very well experted in the latine and greeke tonges; she hath very hansomely and learnedly translated out of the greeke into the englishe all the ecclesiasticall storye of Eusebius, with Socrates, Theodoretus, Sozomenus and Euagrius, albeit of modestie she suppresseth it, and keepeth it from the print. She hath also very aptly and fitly translated into the saide tonge a certaine booke that Sir Thomas, her grandfather, made vpon the passion, and so elegantly and eloquently penned that a man would thinke it were originally written in the saide englishe tonge.[1]

[1] Harpsfield, p. 83. Harleian MS. 1860 seems to be the original copy of the translations from Eusebius presented to the Princess Mary. Royal MS. 13 B. x, a Latin translation of a portion of a Greek Menology, is dedicated by Morwen to Princess Mary, c. 1547–53.

At Cambridge, it is not surprising to find the tradition of recusant humanism also stemming from the foundations of Fisher and the Lady Margaret. St. John's predominates, with John Seton, D.D., holding perhaps the first place. He was the recipient of one of Leland's *Encomia*,[1] a Fellow of St. John's, and successively chaplain to Fisher (whom he attended in the Tower) and to Gardiner. His known works include a Latin panegyric of Queen Mary, but his most important contribution was a work on logic, the *Dialectica*. First published in 1545, it apparently received wide currency also in manuscript, and became the standard treatise in England through the annotations and edition of another St. John's man, Peter Carter. Like Wilson's work pre-Ramist in approach, the Dialectics formed 'the first response in English logical theory' to Rudolph Agricola's *De inventione dialectica*.[2]

Seton appears in 1542 along with Thomas Watson as one of the appellants against the Mastership of John Taylor, Bishop of Lincoln, an outsider to the college and a man strongly sympathetic to Lutheran views.[3] The episode reveals a common bond of northern origins between these conservatives, and, in Watson, introduces another learned recusant divine. Watson became a notable Catholic controversialist and was described by Pollard as 'perhaps, after Tunstall and Pole, the greatest of Queen Mary's bishops'. He was an intimate of Ascham, Cheke, Redman, and Thomas Smith in those golden days of St. John's scholarship later recalled with such emotion by Roger Ascham.[4] His classical attainment was greatly admired by Ascham, especially his tragedy *Absalom*, written during the period of their close association at Cambridge. His later literary work included a translation of the *Odyssey* now lost, and a version of a sermon by St. Cyprian. It is also significant that he assisted in the sessions at Richard Moryson's house on the question of the Real Presence.

[1] *Joannis Lelandi Antiquarii de Rebus Britannicis Collectanea* (Oxonii, 1715), App. A (vol. v), p. 182.
[2] Howell, op. cit., p. 49.     [3] Mullinger, op. cit., vol. ii, pp. 39–40.
[4] *The Scholemaster*, ed. Giles, *Works*, vol. iii, e.g. pp. 232 f.

In terms of immediate influence, John Christopherson may have surpassed both Seton and Watson in the St. John's group. A member of the college during John Redman's ascendancy, he alternated between St. John's and Pembroke Hall, which seems to have been his original home in Cambridge. He was one of the original Fellows of Trinity College by its foundation charter in 1546, and 'one of the first revivers' of the study of Greek in the university. The college supported his Edwardian exile, and in return received the dedication of his translation into Latin of Philo Judaeus, a work done while he was at Louvain. Under Mary he became the Master of Trinity College and Bishop of Chichester. His other works include a tragedy, *Jephthah*, translations of Greek ecclesiastical histories, and a Latin version of Plutarch's *De futile loquacitate* dedicated in manuscript to the Princess Mary in the reign of Edward VI.

This brief picture of conservative St. John's humanists may be concluded with mention of Ralph Baynes, the Marian Bishop of Lichfield and Coventry. A Fellow and a university preacher, he was famous in Cambridge as a public opponent of Hugh Latimer. His humanistic studies also were distinguished, since during his exile under Edward he was appointed Professor of Hebrew in Paris. Described as a pioneer in Hebrew studies in England, and learned also in Latin and Greek, he wrote an introduction to the Hebrew language, published in Paris in 1550, and a compendium of the classic thirteenth-century treatise on Hebrew grammar, the *Sefer Michlol* of David Kimhi.[1]

The most distinguished member of this distinguished group, however, was John Clements, husband to Margaret Giggs, who had grown up in More's household. Clements's early training was in that citadel of reformed studies, St. Paul's School, where he was a pupil of Lily. Here, presumably, his association with More began, and with rapid progress in his classical studies he was able by September 1516 to assist Colet with his

---

[1] *Compendium Michlol*, Paris, 1554. Baynes also published *Prima rudimenta in linguam Hebraicam*, Paris, 1550, and *In proverbis Salamonis*, Paris, 1555.

Greek.[1] From his position as tutor in the More household he moved to Wolsey's service, and was appointed the Cardinal's first Reader in Humanity. He seems to have left almost at once to study medicine at Louvain, having been succeeded at Oxford by Lupset. Both men later helped with the Aldine edition of Galen, and in 1528 Clements was admitted to the London College of Physicians, of which, in 1544, he was elected President. On the accession of Edward VI his household became the focus of recusant migration to Louvain. As the only Englishman who could wear the mantle of Linacre, his prestige in the humanist community was probably unsurpassed, and both he and his wife received the tribute of one of Leland's *Epithalamia*.[2]

It would be difficult and unrewarding to attempt a complete catalogue of English humanists whose views in the later years of Henry's reign moved towards the Catholic side, as did those of Ascham and Cheke toward the Protestant. Others could, of course, be mentioned,[3] but enough has been said to show that in both universities a divergence of opinion did occur within the framework of the Henrician settlement which was likely to lead to open rupture once the Royal Supremacy turned to overt Protestantism. The conservatives, no less than the other group, were fortified with distinguished scholarship and show the same Erasmian preoccupations: translations from the classics and early Fathers, language and grammar study, pietism and religious controversy, poetry, music, and medicine. Unlike the later generation of recusant scholars which included Nicholas Sander, Thomas Stapleton, Edmund Campion, and Robert Parsons, they were all in their productive years under Henry's rule, and in the first period of Catholic exile under Edward VI they established the precedent and, to a large degree, the tradition of recusant learning and apologetic.

[1] Allen, ii. 468, ll. 11–12; 388, ll. 173–5.      [2] Leland, op. cit., p. 109.
[3] Like Nicholas Wilson, imprisoned with More and remembered in Leland's *Encomia*, or John Clerk, the associate of Pace and secretary to the Duke of Norfolk.

In this labour of exiles we discover the concluding phase of the pre-Reformation humanist movement in England. The main current of English thought has been revealed as continuously Erasmian, shaping under Edward VI into a moderate Protestantism, a shift recorded for all time in that great monument of English Erasmian reform, the official translation of the Paraphrases on the New Testament. The greatest English Erasmian of all, Thomas More, is of course a touchstone figure. When the domestic tradition about More emerges, after initial silence, it is not More the collaborator of Erasmus who is enshrined in the pages of Foxe, but More the 'Persecutor' ranged against the 'Martyrs'; the More who, although well versed in tongues, is 'a little too much given to mocking'. And it is only More the wit who is allowed to survive in print, in the *Fayre Gentlewoman* and in his greatest work, the *Utopia*. In his preface to that work Ralph Robinson, as we have seen, said the most that could be said of More's apparent betrayal of the royal programme.

If the exponents of the domestic tradition can be accused of partiality, what of the heirs of More abroad? The chief gathering-place was Louvain, and John Clements showed the way in July of 1549. In Louvain they found, close to England and in a Catholic region with Imperial traditions, the first great northern trilingual foundation and associations with Erasmus, More, and Vives. Assisted by More's old merchant friend Antonio Bonvisi, the Clementses gathered about them the Rastells and Nicholas Harpsfield, with such learned associates as Richard Smith and John Christopherson. The exile community at Louvain was ostentatiously avoided by Ascham in his foreign travels, and he wrote of his English host in Louvain that 'He is loved with all, and regarded with the best; nor doth not use the company of J. Clement and Rastall, which, to see a mass freely in Flanders, are content to foresake, like slaves, their country'.[1]

What version of the matter did these learned exiles put

[1] Giles, i (2), 116, p. 248 (to Mr. Edward Raven, 1551).

forth? The possible sources of information about this would include their accounts of More's trial and death, biographies of More written by them, and the great monument of their common loyalty, the Marian edition of More's *English Works*. Only the second and third of these can give us certain evidence. We are still much in the dark about the first accounts of More's martyrdom, and we are on safer ground with the *English Works* and the two biographies written while that great edition was in preparation, those of Roper and Nicholas Harpsfield. The materials gathered in the *Works* seem to have been collected by the entire group and preserved principally by the final editor, William Rastell. Rastell's career (like that of John Clements) flourished in the later years of Henry's rule, and despite the outward conformity of the More circle to the Henrician régime, it is easy to imagine the concern felt for this private archive. It was the bond of their common identity as they moved from initial bewilderment to a growing sense of unease and finally into exile in protest against the implications of the Royal Supremacy.[1] Under Mary they had their opportunity to publish, and it took the form of an astonishingly compendious edition of those works which could most quickly be grasped by their fellow countrymen, those written in the vernacular. Appropriately, the index was compiled by that veteran of Henrician controversy, Thomas Paynell. For the Catholic exiles under Edward VI, after all, Paul III's offer of a Cardinal's hat to Erasmus was a more recent memory than the death of More himself.

Rastell's Preface to Queen Mary would serve as the common preface to all recusant accounts of More. He is commended for his eloquence, great learning, moral virtue, and his 'trewe doctryne of Christes catholyke fayth'. Naturally, the editors esteemed most highly More the martyr, the confuter of that very movement of heresy which by now had convulsed

---

[1] On the Louvain exiles' preserving More's letters, A. W. Reed, *Early Tudor Drama*, pp. 87–89, and his introduction to *The English Works of Sir Thomas More* (1931), vol. i, pp. 6 f.

Europe and shattered Christendom. Did this lead them to distortion?

So far as is known, they omitted none of More's English works. In including even his occasional pieces, they provided one of his last recreations, an ironic poem on the dangers of a 'pedlar' meddling in theology which is remarkably in tune with the weary comment made by Erasmus on learning of More's imprisonment, that he wished More had left theology to the theologians. By confining the edition to English works Rastell had escaped the obligation of publishing most of More's non-apologetic and non-religious writing, but this was scheduled for the later edition of Latin works, and the English collection was a natural and legitimate answer to the vernacular Erasmianism of the King's party. The Life of Pico della Mirandola is one interesting clue to More's earlier preoccupations with humanism and reform, but the image of the *English Works* (including, as it does, the writing against Lutheranism) is predominantly one of great and militant orthodoxy based on profound piety and on humanism.

It is in the correspondence of this edition that we first find evidence of direct distortion. Almost all the English letters of More which survive were in this collection, but there were significant omissions. John Palsgrave's letter, attributed to 1529, in which he appealed to More for assistance in the education of the Duke of Richmond against 'our shavyn folk who wold in no wyse he schoulde be lernyd', is the first of these. As it is now among the State Papers, separate from the rest of the collection, it is conceivable that it was unknown to Rastell, and no certain importance can be attached to the omission.

More certain is Rastell's intent with two letters concerning the Nun of Kent, both omitted from the *English Works*. The first of these[1] is More's letter to Elizabeth Barton herself, in which he made clear his refusal to hear anything 'of princes or of the realme', reminded her of the part played by a Carthusian (alleged to have prophetical powers) in the treason of the Duke

[1] Rogers, letter 192.

of Buckingham, and of the scandal so brought on religion, and exhorted her 'onelye to common and talke with eny person highe and low, of suche maner thinges as maye to the soule be profitable for you to shew and for them to know'.

The second letter, from the text of which the first is taken, was written to Cromwell by More. Burnet's accusation that Rastell suppressed it was almost certainly correct.[1] Here More states in explicit terms his distaste for 'the lewde Nonne of Caunterburye' after the recent revelations about her career. He gives a characteristically judicious account of his relations with her, in which he quotes the previously mentioned letter, explains his generally unfavourable impression, and congratulates Cromwell for exposing her deceit:

> Wherin you have done, in my mynde, to your greate laude and prayse, a verye meritorious deed in bringinge forthe to lighte suche detestable ypocrisie, wherebye everye other wretche maye take warninge, and be ferde to sett forthe theire owne devilishe dissimuled falshed, under the maner and color of the wonderfull worke of God. . . .

Two other English letters are known which were not included by Rastell. The first of these, unknown until the eighteenth century, is a moving appeal by Lady More to Cromwell in May 1535 for financial aid.[2] The second, which is found in the same manuscript collection in which the others used by Rastell are gathered (Royal MS. 17 D. xiv), is her appeal a few months earlier to the King himself. Like the appeal to Cromwell, this letter to the King now seems to add to the pathos of the family's situation once More had been imprisoned. If Rastell suppressed it, it must presumably have been through desire to avoid publishing the heart of her plea for her husband's pardon: 'his offence ys growen not of eny malice or obstinate mynde, but of suche a longe contynued and depe rooted scrupple, as passethe his power to avoyde and put awey . . .'.[3]

Although in absence of direct proof that Rastell knew of these letters we can only conjecture about their omission, there is at

[1] Harpsfield, pp. 344-5; Rogers, letter 197.
[2] Rogers, letter 215.  [3] Rogers, letter 212, ll. 36-39.

least a strong probability that he wished to avoid any suggestion that would show disharmony of opinion within the Catholic camp. This conjecture is confirmed by editorial changes which are susceptible of proof.

More's letter of 5 March 1534, in which he protested his innocence in the affair of the Nun to Henry VIII, was altered to replace his phrase 'the wykked woman of Canterbery' with 'Nunne of Canterbury'.[1] Even more extensively altered was the letter which he wrote to Cromwell on the same day, which is so invaluable for the history of his religious opinions. Once again his phrase 'wykked woman' was replaced by 'the nonne'. But the most striking distortion is the omission of a long and, for the Catholics, embarrassing passage on Anne Boleyn. More has been protesting his incompetence to decide the grave matter of the King's marital status, and continues:

. . . so am I he that among other his Gracis faithfull subgiettis, his Highnes being in possession of his mariage and this noble woman really anoynted Quene, neither murmure at it, nor dispute uppon it, nor neuer did nor will, but with owt eny other maner medlyng of the mater among his other faithfull subgiettis faithfully pray to God for his Grace and hers both, long to lyve and well and theyr noble issue to, in such wise as may be to the pleasure of God, honor and surety to theym selfe, reste, peace, welth and profit unto this noble realme.[2]

Rastell's version of the same passage is as follows:

. . . so am I he, that among other his graces faithful subiectes, his highnes being in possession of his mariage, will most hartely pray for the prosperous estate of his grace, longe to continue to the pleasure of God.

At the time of More's writing, in March 1534, Queen Catherine was of course still alive, and the Louvain group clearly found intolerable the apparent condoning of the second marriage, especially since Catherine of Aragon's daughter, now Queen, was patroness of the edition they were preparing.

[1] Rogers, letter 198.      [2] Rogers, letter 199, ll. 191 ff.

Finally, Rastell made a rather inconclusive attempt to explain away the important letter of More to Margaret Roper from the Tower.[1] In this letter More refers unmistakably to the pain which her attempts to dissuade him from his stand on the Supremacy had caused him. Rastell added a preface explaining that her letter was secretly intended to ingratiate her with Cromwell, 'that she might the rather gett liberties to haue free resorte unto her father . . .'. The letter to Alice Alington, however, indicates that Margaret Roper's opinions went deeper than Rastell's editorial comment suggested. Whether More or Margaret wrote this letter, it is clearly an eloquent testimony to the literary achievement of the whole More circle, and may have been intended to circulate in manuscript, exploring for the benefit of that group all the doubts which troubled them.[2] Margaret Roper is represented in earnest and sorrowful disagreement with her father, and the dialogue dwells at length on the objections which could be brought against More's views. The result is an eloquent apology in which More urges the right—and duty—of each to follow the dictates of his own conscience. He also hints at recent changes in the opinions of some he had formerly counted as supporters of his views, and, for the last time, he refuses to divulge the exact reasons for his stand: 'But Margaret, for what causes I refuse the othe, the thinge (as I haue often tolde you) I will neuer shewe you, neither you nor no body elles, excepte the Kynges Highnes shoulde lyke to commaunde me.'[3] Few documents even from the life of Thomas More can rival this for drama, when the confrontation of the two is presented with such skill, and More, who teasingly refers to his daughter as 'mother Eve', learns from her that she has herself taken the oath which he refuses.

The fact that this letter was left intact, and the general faithfulness of the collection in Rastell's edition, must be taken into

[1] Rogers, letter 202 (p. 508).

[2] In a circular letter at the time of his imprisonment, More told his friends that he was forbidden to see anyone but his daughter Margaret, and referred them to her for information about his needs. Rogers, letter 204.

[3] Rogers, letter 206, ll. 470–3.

account. There was no attempt to misrepresent More's general position; such partiality as can be detected seems intended to emphasize the solidarity of the group as a whole. Palsgrave's letter may have been suppressed to prevent an impression that More's support could be sought against the conservative clergy, and it is clear that they wished to exclude the evidence that he strongly disapproved of Elizabeth Barton's later activities and fully endorsed her arrest. But above all it seems that they did not want it known that More's most intimate associates in the family circle itself could not understand his views on the Royal Supremacy.

Apart from this, Marian publication suggests that the repudiation of Erasmus and the attempt to dissociate More from him was a product primarily of the second exile and not of the period of revived Catholic power in England. Of the two biographies which complement the *English Works*, that of Roper is so brief that we can overlook the omissions from More's early career. Harpsfield's work is more important, and although in his own account of More's education and marriage he makes no direct mention of More's literary work or of his relationship with Erasmus, he adds to Roper principally from the correspondence of the two men. After an outline of More's career the friendship is introduced, if only briefly, in connexion with More's writings. The epigrams and the Brixius affair are also mentioned, because More is 'herein slaundered' by some Protestants, and the *Utopia* is said to bear 'the pricke and price of all his other latine bookes of wittie invention'. It is something, but it is not a great deal, although Harpsfield does say plainly, when speaking of More's classical scholarship, that 'the said Erasmus of all men in the world [most] delighted in the companye of Sir Thomas More, whose helpe and frendshipp he muche used when he had any affaires with kyng Henrye the eight'.

A full investigation of these later recusant traditions would take us beyond the bounds of the present subject,[1] but it is

[1] See Appendix II.

perhaps relevant to observe that the general pattern of English publication under Mary does not differ radically from that which has been described under Henry VIII and Edward VI. If anything, it conforms to the rather subdued Erasmian tone which is found in Harpsfield. In particular, pietism emerges as before in Kempis, Chrysostom, Cyprian, and Savonarola, with a revised vernacular primer and devotional works by the anti-Augustinian writer, St. Vincent of Lerins, fortifying the Erasmian position within the conservative tradition.[1] The Queen's own respect for the views of her cousin Reginald Pole makes this adaptation of the Erasmian programme perhaps predictable. For that reason, it is interesting to see that in 1554 the authority of Erasmus himself was proclaimed by Mary's Government for the traditional doctrine of the Eucharist, with the publication of *The epistle sente unto Conradus Pelicanus*.[2] This was a trenchant repudiation by Erasmus of the view, reportedly spread openly by Pellican in Basle some three decades earlier, that Erasmus held heretical views on the Eucharist like those held by Oecolampadius. If it is a conservative Erasmus who is thus presented by the Marian presses, what seems remarkable is that Erasmian publication continued at all in the light of the Catholic reaction which was under way on the Continent: the general condemnation of Erasmus's works by Paul IV followed a year after the death of Queen Mary and Reginald Pole. The publications of her reign, including the great *English Works* of Thomas More, form a last glimmer in a Tridentine Catholic world of the (as it now seemed) far-off humanistic reform movement to which England had contributed so much.

Within recent years a distinguished historian of Tudor England wrote as follows about certain figures at the court of

[1] STC 23966 (Kempis, 1556); STC 14642 (Chrysostom, 1553); STC 6159 (Cyprian, 1556); STC 24754 (Vincent of Lerins, 1554); STC 16060 (*An vniforme and catholyke prymer* 1555); STC 21796 (Savonarola, 1558).

[2] STC 10491: Cawood, 1554. See Allen, vi. 1637.

Edward VI who have come into our story—Thomas Smith, Cheke, Ascham, Sir Anthony Cooke, and the whole St. John's Cambridge group associated with Cecil:

We are aware of the presence of these men at Court and aware of their sympathetic attitude towards religious reform, but we have no means of measuring their influence upon public policy. There can be no doubt about the fighting Gospellers—about Hugh Latimer, or John Hales. They never hesitated to proclaim their views. But certainly the rest of them were of a different calibre, better politicians no doubt, but much less fervent crusaders. At this critical juncture, when Latimer was thundering from the pulpit his magnificent sermon on the plough and Hales was composing his discourse on the Common Weal, the best that Cheke could produce was a pamphlet against sedition and the best Cecil could produce was a colourless, uninspired comment on the Lamentations of a Sinful Soul.[1]

Verdicts like this on leading figures of the early Tudor period are sufficiently familiar. Behind them lie, as implicit presuppositions, the doctrinal definitions created by Reformation controversies and the predominantly Protestant sympathies of nineteenth-century historians. But even orthodoxy is an organic growth, and men of one age cannot be condemned as venal for their failure to anticipate the commitments of a later generation. For the Erasmian community of the early sixteenth century the positions most ardently contested by battalions of post-Lutheran theologians were frequently peripheral to their own concerns: perhaps the issue of religious authority is the most striking example. Yet they had solid commitments of their own, and in England, for reasons which we have tried to demonstrate, these commitments became the central tradition of the religious settlement. To say this is not to deny the other roots of the Henrician Church in Conciliar theory, in the past struggles of the Crown with Rome, and in plain expediency. It does assert the role of a positive doctrine of reform, derived

[1] Conyers Read, *Mr. Secretary Cecil and Queen Elizabeth* (1955), p. 43.

from the finest flowering of intellect and spirit in early Tudor times, which initially at least attracted to the King the unanimous support of the reforming laity and clergy.

The Erasmians of the court of the Young Josiah were thus the inheritors of a domestic tradition of humanistic reform which had been established firmly under Henry VIII. What Henry's private intentions were cannot be directly shown. However, there is the foregoing evidence that his policies could be represented as Erasmian reform measures, that deliberately they were so represented, and that this interpretation was apparently adopted by the vast majority of the educated men of the kingdom. Despite the shock of losing such pre-eminent figures in the world of learning and religion as Thomas More and John Fisher, Richard Reynolds, John Houghton, and Reginald Pole, the humanist community at large accepted the royal divorce and the break with Rome.

As the Government moved into more radical courses, a distinguished minority of the humanist community repented of compliance in the Royal Supremacy, and under Henry's successor they found themselves ready to accept exile rather than assist in perpetuating it. Most, however, moved easily into an accommodation with humanistic Protestantism which, for a time at least, moderated the incipient radicalism of the royal minority after 1547. Under Mary the roles of the two groups were reversed, and with Elizabeth the Protestant exiles returned to contribute an important element to her own religious establishment. In that age, when high politics and the new Protestant orthodoxies greatly complicated the religious scene in England, the older Erasmian tradition continued to make itself felt. A representative figure is Bishop John Jewel. His important *Apologia ecclesiae Anglicanae*, as the Catholic writer Richard Verstegan noted, was translated from Latin 'into English by A. B. with the comendation of M. C. which twaine were sisters, and wives unto *Cecill*, and *Bacon*; and gave their assistance and helping hands, in the plot and fortification

of this newe erected synagog'.[1] It was the continued influence
of people like these learned daughters of Sir Anthony Cooke
which provided a plausible reform tradition native to the
country and suspicious of all competing orthodoxies—a positive,
humanistic programme for that peculiar English church settlement which, as Verstegan observed, was 'participant of some
newe heresies, and yet not consonant to any one religion els'.[2]
Whenever this peculiar element emerged, in a John Jewel or a
Lancelot Andrewes, a humanistic bent, a patristic emphasis,
a laicism and an aversion to dogma would identify a tradition
which is rooted in those early centres of reform opinion we
have discussed here: the universities, the mercantile circles of
London, and the domestic schools and salons of the aristocracy.
To that degree the tradition recalls those secret streams of
learning and evangelism which flowed beneath the more
obvious landmarks of Reformation debate, which drew their
vigour from the writings of Erasmus and his friends, and
which coursed through England as through the rest of western
Europe in the years of common effort before the disintegration
of Christian unity in the West.

[1] *A Declaration of the True Causes of the Great Troubles* ... ([Antwerp?] 1592),
p. 12 (*STC* 19400; Allison and Rogers, op. cit., 844). Jewel's *Apologie* ... *in
defence of the Church of England* (1562) is *STC* 14590.

[2] Verstegan, loc. cit.

# APPENDIX I

*Sermo Fratris Hieronymi de Ferraria In vigilia Natuitatis domini coram Fratribus suis recitatus.* Richard Pynson, 1509

THE following texts present the dedicatory prologue and concluding letter attached to the *Sermo* by the translator, with abbreviations expanded and some simplification of the punctuation. They are taken from the only known copy of the work, which is in the British Museum, catalogue number 224. g. 30 (*STC* 21800). For comment on the text, see above, pp. 98 f. Thomas Scrow does not appear in Venn or Emden, or in T. F. Kirby's *Winchester Scholars* (1888), so it seems unlikely that he was a fellow Wykehamist with Dowce and Yonge.

This particular work of Savonarola does not seem to have had wide currency. It was not part of the reform literature commonly circulating in Spain and Portugal; see Bataillon, 'Sur la diffusion des œuvres de Savonarole en Espagne et en Portugal, 1500–1560', in *Mélanges de philologie, d'histoire et de littérature offerts à Joseph Vianey* (1934), pp. 93–103, and, by the same author, *Études sur le Portugal au temps de l'Humanisme* (Coimbra, 1952), pp. 197–217.

I have noticed the following editions prior to Pynson's publication:

1. *Sermone fatto a suoi fratri nella vigilia dello Pascua di natale, sopra la natività del nostro signore Jesu Christi*, Firenze, s.d.; Hain 14402 and Reichl. 1383. These are presumably the titles numbered 212 and 213 in L. Giovanozzi, *Bibliografia delle Opere del Savonarola* (Edizioni dei Secc. XV e XVI, Firenze, 1953), dated 1495.

2. *Expositio orationis Dominice et sermo in vigilia nativitatis Domini*, Ascensianus, 1510.

P. Ginori-Conti, *Bibliografia delle Opere del Savonarola*, vol. 1 (Firenze, 1939), records the same editions as Giovanozzi in numbers 66 and 67. Both record the Pynson edition, as 69 and 215 respectively, and both record a Venice edition of 1556 as the next appearance of this work.

## *Sig.* A. i

### SERMO FRATRIS HIERONYMI DE FERRARIA IN VIGILIA NATIUITATIS DOMINI CORAM FRATRIBUS SUIS RECITATUS

Bartholomeus Gallus Mutilianensis, Venerabilibus viris sacre theologiae professoribus Domino doctori Joh. yong Ecclesiae omnium sanctorum Honylane rectori, ac Domino Stephano Dowce sacri Whytyngton Collegii Magistro, S.P.D.

Nouit britania (ut de altero orbe sileam) Reverendi in Christo patres qua animi pietate qua charitate quo studio diu noctuque de Christi domini nostri ihesu pauperibus bene mereri certatim curetis: Vos enim duo lumina orbis huius in tenebris errantibus presto semper estis, ut in viam salutis aeterne redeant: vos afflictos consolamini, vos demum in omnibus opera facitis euangelistarum que pietatis opera ipse imprimis testari possum: nam ego homo exterus indoctus et peccator qui nullo meo beneficio beniuolentiam vestram promereri queo tot tamen sum a vobis meritis affectus ut maiora vix optare possem: et quia par pari referre non valui tanquam rusticus sterilis lapidosus ac incultus ager Immo sola ingratitudine tot tantisque beneficiis vestris hactenus respondi. Desiderastis enim iam diu cognoscere sermones Venerabilis Viri Fratris Hieronymi de Ferraria: & quia vernacula Italorum lingua conscripti sunt illius presertim loci ubi ego natus sum, quam vos minime noscitis ea de causa sepius admonuistis ut eos latinos facerem: quod (ut dixi) hucusque (me miserum atque ingratissimum) beneficiorum immemor: efficere distuli domesticis negociis impeditus: At vos assidua vestra religione et humanitate nihilominus indies magis magisque emolumentis ubertim cumulastis: Quare in presenti pudore victus non potui opus (etsi paruum) meis tamen humeris impar non aggredi: et quoniam nuper incepi longumque esset expectare finem et dimidium facti principium esse solet. Igitur sermonem hunc de Nativitate domini de verbo ad verbum suasu et consilio tuae Paternitatis Domine mi Stephane a me nuper in latinum versum vobis mittere decreui ut intelligatis me demum optatis vestris sanctissimis obtemperare non abnuisse penitus. Ergo optimi patres hylari vultu hoc munusculum accipitote aliud propediem accepturi sermonem videlicet de dominis curatis ac de eorum curae commissis super

quem inuigilare poterunt columbarum more super aquas residen-
tium: ut videant supervenientis accipitris umbram. Valete totius
Angliae aeternum decus. Ex Londonio viii Octobris, Anno Domini,
1509.

## Colophon

Bartholomeus Gallus Mutilianensis Erudito ac honesto viro Thome
Scrow, Domini doctoris Joh. yong clerico amicorum optimo S.D.P.

Non possum (edepol) non gaudere Amice quum intellexerim te
Oxonium breui petiturum studiendi gratia. Quam egregie illud
ouidianum decantare potes: dicite io pean et io bis dicite pean.
Incidit in casses preda petita meos. Quanto (bone deus) communi
patrono obnoxius sis qui tuo sponte annuit desiderio: tuipse (si
sapis) facile excogitare potes: aeterno enim (mihi crede) te deuinxit
beneficio pro quo diu noctuque geminas tendens ad sydera palmas
ut ei faueant superi tota mente rogabis. Rogabis? immo rogabimus
omnes: nonne vides? ut pauperum genus omne sub ipso sturnatim
congaudeat atque coturnatim confugiat omne genus. Cui si fata (ut
poetice loquar) meritam attribuissent gloriam tam diu in maximum
virum emersisse videres. Sed ut inquit poeta,

> Sponte malos homines et noxia gramina nutrit
>   At melius semen ferre recusat humus.
> Mitior est propriis alienaque pignora semper
>   Tractat inhumana dura nouerca manu.
> Vir bonus est caeli malus est telluris alumnus
>   Quos igitur caelum diligit odit humus.

Tu preterea quum voti compos fueris ad nos rescribas etiam atque
etiam oro: et si quid interea per me fieri possit, utere Gallo tibi
deditissimo: qui tuus est viuus mortuus idem erit. Vale, et ora pro
me. Ex Londonio viii Septembris, Anno Domini, 1509.

## LAUS DEO

# APPENDIX II

## The Recusant Traditions of Thomas More

THE mild conservatism and substantial integrity of the Catholic account of More under Mary invites comparison with the version produced after the second period of exile under Elizabeth had begun. Once again there is an important scholarly work, the edition of More's Latin *Opera*, by which we can measure recusant views. The new collection was intended to complement the *English Works*, and the claim of its title was comprehensive: *Omnia, quae hucusque ad manus nostras pervenerunt, Latina Opera*. It bridges the two eras of recusant activity, since the collection seems undoubtedly to come from the common archive which supplied the *English Works*. William Rastell, once more in exile, died while the work was at the printer's, and A. W. Reed suggested that the collection also was substantially his work.[1] It appeared at Louvain in 1565.

Between the appearance of the *English Works* in 1557 and the new collection there had occurred at least three momentous events likely to affect the second work. The first was the general condemnation of Erasmus's works by Paul IV in 1559, and the second was the accession of another Protestant sovereign in England. The third was the appearance of a distinctly Erasmian collection of More's Latin works in 1563 from Episcopius at Basle, entitled simply *Lucubrationes*. The Louvain *Opera* two years later claimed to represent all the Latin works known to its editors; the *Lucubrationes* was supposed to present such works as it included in their original integrity. The two books made a striking contrast.

Both editions printed the *Utopia* (with related correspondence), More's *Epigrams*, and the translations from Lucian. The *Opera Omnia* included in addition the Latin text of the History of Edward V and Richard III, More's reply to Luther under the name of Rossaeus, other controversial work against Luther, the *Expositio Passionis Domini*, and the two accompanying Latin works written

[1] Introduction to *The English Works of Sir Thomas More*, vol. i (1931), pp. 8 f.

in prison: the *Quod pro fide mors fugienda non est* and the *Precatio ex Psalmis collecta*, both (like the Richard III) appearing for the first time. The *Lucubrationes* contained none of this last material, but included sixteen important letters, mostly of More and Erasmus.

The purpose of the *Lucubrationes* is obvious: it is to present the Erasmian, humanistic More. Everything it prints is printed accurately, with standards befitting the heir to Erasmus's publishers. This is most immediately apparent in comparing the *Epigrammata* here with the version in the *Latina Opera* from Louvain. Apart from questions of editorial bias, the Basle version is simply more accurate and sophisticated. Combined with the *Utopia* and the Lucian translations, the *Epigrams* of More fully proclaim his early humanistic, reforming temper, and this is all of More that the reader of the *Lucubrationes* would have. To supplement this material and drive home the point, there are sixteen letters tracing the relations between More and Erasmus. They make amply clear their close agreement on matters of religious and political reform, their shared love for salutary satire of contemporary decadence, More's hearty approval of the now-deplored New Testament, their love of the Fathers: in general, their common aims. But above all, the collection includes the last two letters of More to Erasmus, which shatter the recusant version of their relationship in the years after Luther. Before dealing with this important problem we should give a general account of the Louvain *Opera*.

Here the hand of the censor can be discovered at work as it was in the *English Works*. The text of the *Utopia* was purged of a famous and very characteristic anecdote concerning an ignorant friar at the table of Cardinal Morton. The *Epigrams* were taken from the first and unrevised edition of 1518 and were also censored slightly. Although the recent editor of the epigrams concluded that the sponsors of the Louvain *Opera* were unaware of the 1520 edition, deletions cannot be explained simply on that supposition. From the 1518 text four 'sexually indelicate' epigrams were omitted, as were three poems praising Erasmus's edition of the New Testament.[1] However, it was by no means bowdlerized. The Louvain printing included the six complimentary poems addressed by More to Henry VIII at the time of his coronation, and retained trenchant material attacking superstitious religious devotion and ignorant, scandalous

[1] Bradner and Lynch, op. cit., pp. xvii–xviii.

clergy. Similarly, More's prefatory letter to the translations from Lucian, printed intact in both the Louvain and Basle editions, is a primary source for his approach to religious reform through sound scholarship and Lucianic satire. The Louvain *Opera*, then, if slightly pruned, is hardly the propaganda vehicle it has been represented to be.[1] The recusants, like the Basle editors, made their most telling points by discreet silence. For the former, it was silence about More's Erasmianism; for the latter, silence about his deep piety and vigorous defence of Catholic orthodoxy.

There remains the important recusant tradition that More reproved Erasmus for his earlier extravagance, and that their friendship cooled in their later years. This charge first appears in Harpsfield, and was actually published first by Stapleton in the *Tres Thomae*, where Stapleton adds that Erasmus destroyed the letter in question. What is the evidence for the relations of More and Erasmus in the years after 1520?

The surviving correspondence certainly suggests an extended interruption in their earlier intimacy in the years from 1520 to 1532. The earlier warm and often lengthy exchanges give way to perfunctory letters with long intervals of silence. Assuming that we have a reasonably accurate collection of their actual correspondence in this period, it is necessary to account for the change. In part it can no doubt be attributed to the preoccupations of both men, and more especially of More, burdened with the duties of his high office and of his controversial work. Perhaps there was also a real estrangement. But probably the most important explanation is that noticed by Professor de Vocht in the *Acta Thomae Mori*, that in a time of

---

[1] Notably by Mme Marie Delcourt, 'L'amitié d'Érasme et de More entre 1520 et 1535', *Bulletin de l'Association Guillaume Budé* (January 1936), and 'Recherches sur Thomas More: la tradition continentale et la tradition anglaise', *Humanisme et Renaissance*, vol. iii (1936). Mme Delcourt attacked the editors for excluding the correspondence of More, and wished to hold them responsible for fulfilling the claims of their title to the letter. She also asserted that in the Latin epitaph composed by More and used by the editors to open the volume she had evidence that they had deliberately suppressed the letter of June 1532. In this she seems to have been misled by the Leiden edition, which printed the epitaph incorrectly after that letter (Allen, x. 2659). In the later letter to which it belongs (Allen, x. 2831), More discussed his resignation and the epitaph, but says nothing to Erasmus about his reform work or reputation. Both letters appear in the *Lucubrationes* with customary accuracy.

dangerous controversy, when every letter was prey to pirated publication, More and Erasmus, like others in their circle, were exchanging the important news verbally by those messengers whose reliability and responsibility for verbal communication they so carefully noted to one another.

Whatever the explanation, it is clear that in 1532 and 1533 More suddenly returned to the easy and fulsome communication of the earlier and happier days. The letters (numbered 2659 and 2831 in volume x of Allen's *Epistolae*) were correctly printed in the Basle *Lucubrationes*. The first, dated 14 June 1532, announces his resignation from the Chancellorship, attributing it to fatigue and ill health, and asserts his desire to devote the rest of his life to God. More then moves to an admiring account of Erasmus's own incomparable industry in the face of ill health and advancing years, amid the distractions of critics inspired by spite and envy. With great tact, he then points out that even some good and learned men have been disturbed to find that Erasmus has, in their own view, handled some delicate matters rashly. More attaches little importance to this, since, as he says, these very men have often been guilty of the same fault, and since Erasmus admitted openly before the present outbreak of heresy that he had handled some points recklessly.[1] However, More continues, anyone objecting to Erasmus's vigorous spirit will also find it difficult to justify the holiest doctors of the early Church, who themselves (like the apostles and even our Saviour) have been misinterpreted and slandered during the present controversies. He concludes by congratulating Erasmus on his virtues, and advises him to ignore malicious detractors and to devote himself to his work in peace. After further comments on the dangers of current heresy, he almost pointedly concludes with the comment that Erasmus has been of great service to the true intellectual life.

The general tone and argument of this letter make it impossible to resist the conclusion that More was going out of his way to resume the connexion with his old comrade in arms. The gesture took the form of a virtual testimonial, intended to assist Erasmus in the midst of the attacks rained upon him from the conservative Catholic camp. The second letter, dated by Allen in June of 1533, contains conspicuous assurance that Erasmus should feel free to publish the earlier one, with its warm endorsement of his reforming

[1] See, for example, his letter to Wolsey, Allen, iii. 967, ll. 180 f.

activity. More further insists that, despite rumours to the contrary, his resignation from the office of Chancellor had been his own doing, that the King had been very reluctant to part with him, and that Erasmus should not be deterred from publishing the earlier letter by false rumours of an estrangement between the King and himself. He then includes a copy of the epitaph he had written for his own tomb in Chelsea, in which he had set forth the same explanation of his retirement.

It seems likely, then, that More's letter was intended at least in part to provide Erasmus with public vindication from a most distinguished friend, known throughout Europe as a champion of Catholic orthodoxy. If we are correct in this interpretation of More's gesture, his concern heightens the impression created by Erasmus's own restraint in protesting against More's execution. When the news of More's imprisonment reached him, Erasmus wrote his weary comment to Latomus, on 24 July 1535: 'Utinam periculoso negocio se numquam admiscuisset, et causam theologicam cessisset theologis.'[1] He evidently learned of More's death from Goclenius in a letter dated 10 August,[2] causing him to add a reference to the event to his preface to *Ecclesiastae libri IV*, published by Froben with the date of August 1535. Apart from that preface, his first reference to More's death is in a letter to Peter Tomiczki of 31 August:[3] 'In Anglia quid acciderit Episcopo Roffensi, ac Thomae Moro, quo hominum iugo numquam habuit Anglia quicquam sanctius aut melius, ex fragmento epistolae quod ad te mitto cognosces. In Moro mihi videor extinctus, adeo μία ψυχὴ iuxta Pythagoram duobus erat. Sed hi sunt rerum humanarum aestus.'

There were rumours in Paris in October that Erasmus was preparing a book denouncing Henry for More's death,[4] but no such work appeared. The *Carmen heroicum in mortem Thomae Mori* (Hagenau, 1536) included strong denunciation of Henry in verses falsely attributed to Erasmus,[5] but the *Ecclesiastae libri IV*, while eloquent on his sense of loss in the deaths of Fisher and More, dealt with Henry very gently. This mildness drew a strong rebuke from Christopher Stadion, to whom the work was dedicated. He found

---

[1] Allen, xi. 3048.                              [2] Ibid. 3037.
[3] Ibid. 3049, ll. 160–4.                        [4] *LP* xi. 521.
[5] Harpsfield, p. 255; on the true attribution of the *Carmen heroicum*, C. Reedijk, *The Poems of Desiderius Erasmus* (Leiden, 1956), App. III. 2.

Henry's action bestial, and plainly predicted the crown of martyrdom for More and Fisher.[1] Damião de Goes also protested in a
letter of 26 January 1536, in which he commented: 'Nonnulli
dicunt, mentionem, quam in prologo Ecclesiastis de eo [More]
atque Rofensi facis, dignam non esse tantis viris; quod prolixius
debebas, aiunt, in materiam tam dignam procedere. Tu scis qui[d]
sis facturus, ego tamquam amicus moneo.'[2]

Conceivably, disappointment at Erasmus's reaction to More's
fate may have contributed to the recusant belief that the two men
had been seriously estranged in their last years. A careful reading
even of More's controversial work, however, should have cast
doubt on this. In *The Confutacion of Tyndales Aunswere*, written
(like the first letter) in 1532, More is led by Tyndale's charges to
reflect on his attitude to Erasmus and to their common reforming
work of former years. Answering the charge that he had been
partial towards Erasmus, 'his derlyng', since he had attacked Tyndale
for substituting 'congregation' for 'church' in his translation of the
New Testament, whereas he had been content to let Erasmus change
*ecclesia* to *congregatio*, More replied that he found in Erasmus none
of Tyndale's 'shrewde entent and purpose'. On the contrary, More
asserted, Erasmus detested and abhorred 'the errours and heresies
that Tyndall playnly teacheth and abideth by'.

More then went on to consider the *Praise of Folly*. This, he
explained, was intended by Erasmus to reprove faults and follies of
people of every state, lay and spiritual. He denied that he, personally,
ever intended to hold saints' images and relics as such 'oute of
reuerence', and the *Praise of Folly* likewise jested only at abuses of
these salutary practices. There then follows a very significant remark:
More regretted that the growth of heresy had been such 'that
menne cannot almoste now speake of suche thynges in so muche as
a playe, but that suche euill hearers ware a great deale the worse'.[3]
He concluded that he would himself burn his *Utopia*, or such like
works by himself or by Erasmus, if there were any prospect of these
now being translated into English. Although the works were harmless
in themselves, the present confusions made it impossible even to
circulate the Scriptures in English, as the King and Council had
decided, and it would clearly be better to destroy such satirical

[1] Allen, xi. 3073 (27 Nov. 1535), ll. 10–20.
[2] Ibid. 3085, ll. 21–24.          [3] *Workes* (1557), 422F.

works, 'rather then folke should (though through theyr own faut) take any harme of them, seyng that I se them likely in these dayes so to doe'.[1]

The general spirit of this passage is clearly in harmony with the letter to Erasmus of the same year. More's reply to Tyndale adds valuable information about his attitude to his own work, and about the precise character of the dangers which he feared. There is perhaps nothing here or in the letter which is strictly incompatible with the recusant tradition that he had reproved Erasmus. On the other hand, there is no positive evidence for the tradition except the reputation of Harpsfield and Stapleton. Their presumptive common source would be John Harris, More's secretary, who might well have known if such a letter of rebuke had once existed. It is Stapleton, the last voice of the More circle, who gives the most detail.[2] He says that More urged Erasmus to follow the example of St. Augustine in his *Retractationes* and correct and explain his earlier views. When one thinks of the scale of effort required, it is not surprising that Erasmus ignored such advice, if it was ever given. Stapleton then goes on to say that Erasmus, who was as remote from the humility of St. Augustine as he was from his doctrine, would not permit the letter to survive.

For the present at least, the evidence ends here. Stapleton's account of More is, in general, an impressive achievement, and his candour and lack of bitterness suggest a temperament above partisan bias. However, he was not above suppressing unpleasant truth. In his account of More's trial, for example, he omitted More's admission that he placed the authority of a General Council over that of a Pope.[3] Similarly, Stapleton's handling of More's reply to Tyndale concerning the episode of 'Erasmus his derlyng' (which begins the above account of the estrangement of the two men) does not inspire confidence. Stapleton simplifies to the point of serious distortion, saying that where More could not excuse the fact of Erasmus's translation, he excused it because of its intent.

The truth is that by the time Stapleton was writing the atmosphere was much more dogmatic. Stapleton is remarkably moderate beside the young men who were the shock troops of Counter-

[1] Ibid. 423A.
[2] *Vita Thomae Mori*, Coloniae Agrippinae, M.DC.XII, p. 192.
[3] Rogers, letter 199, ll. 260–2, and note.

Reformation training. Toughened by the rigours of Elizabethan persecution and armed by Trent with dogmatic certainties of which More and his contemporaries had no inkling, they rode roughshod through the tentative opinions and honest confusions of an earlier generation, confident that More's final stand had made him a martyr of Trent by anticipation. Thus, according to Nicholas Sander, More found the Nun of Kent without 'any trace' of the fanaticism alleged against her.[1] Robert Parsons, S.J., berated Erasmus with a severity which made impossible any accurate appraisal of More's career before 1520: 'Whersoeuer Erasmus did but point with his fingar, Luther rushed upon yt, where Erasmus did but doubt, Luther affirmed. So as vpon Erasmus dubitations, Luther framed assertions and asseuerations; And not only Luther and Lutherans, but all the pestilent sect of new Arrians in our dayes, began vpon certayne doubtfull questions, and interpretations of Erasmus, whether such, or such places of scriptures vsed against them by the auncient Fathers, were well applyed, or no?'[2]

Parsons here proclaimed the standard post-Tridentine attitude to Erasmus, not heard before in England even under Mary. His colleague Edmund Campion aired similar views in his *Narratio Divortii Henrici VIII*. Here was the gravest failure in the Catholic tradition about Thomas More.

In summary, the recusant effort on behalf of More was a remarkable accomplishment. The men and women who undertook the task of preserving the memory and records of More's life were themselves a distinguished group. They mirrored the scholarship and devotion of their martyr hero and were recruited from the most accomplished members of England's humanist community. The most striking quality of their achievement is the distinction of the biographies, and the invaluable and even heroic service to later generations represented by the *English Works* and the Louvain *Opera Omnia*.

They had, of course, their characteristic preoccupations. They were concerned above all with More the martyr statesman, the great humanist who became the most widely respected Englishman of his day and died for the tie with Rome, as protomartyr of the English laity. In More the reformer they were less interested, and as

[1] *De origine ac progressu schismatis Anglicani* (Cologne, 1585), i, c. xv.
[2] *Three Conversions*, pt. iii (1604), pp. 307–8.

the tide of Tridentine reaction swelled, they were tempted to ignore his early evangelical commitments almost entirely.

The direct distortion of which they can be convicted is not ultimately very serious. They were most guilty in trying to preserve the fiction of the retrospective unity of the group, especially where the Nun of Kent was involved. The mild pruning of the Latin *Opera Omnia* likewise touched nothing of essential importance, and the general charge of editorial distortion is without foundation.

Their great failing was the common shortcoming of sectarian scholarship, *suppressio veri*. Their failure to include More's Latin correspondence in the *Opera Omnia*, although it certainly belied the strict claim of their title, is perhaps of secondary importance. No one interested could have failed to know of the contemporary collections of humanistic correspondence in which letters of More could be found. The biographers, however, did an unmistakable disservice in separating More from Erasmus. This separation is not complete, and one might disagree with the verdict that all More's biographers were 'radically anti-Erasmian'.[1] No final judgement can yet be made about their claim that More urged Erasmus to make public emendation of his earlier and more reckless writing. But it is amply clear that they deliberately ignored what they must have known: that More and Erasmus before Luther appeared were closely united in a common task of evangelical reform based on humanism and Lucianic satire, that More never in his life retracted this commitment, however much he may have regretted some of its unforeseen consequences, and that in the final years of his life he issued a striking endorsement of all that Erasmus had done. The whole of his reply to Tyndale on this subject is in effect an assertion that Erasmianism did not necessarily lead to heresy, and that in itself it was a highly salutary, if tragically unsuccessful, attempt to awaken the Church

---

[1] The charge of Mme Delcourt, in 'L'amitié d'Érasme et de More . . .' (as above, p. 287, n. 1). The best evidence that Harpsfield was not deeply anti-Erasmian sheds light on the recusant tradition itself. His *Historia Ecclesiastica Anglicana*, written in the 1570's but not published until half a century later, at Douay, was purged of an extended passage dealing with the friendship of Warham and Erasmus. In the course of a most complimentary account of Erasmus and his many English friends, Harpsfield mentioned by name such heroes of the recusant tradition as Reginald Pole, Cuthbert Tunstall, John Fisher, William Mountjoy, and Thomas More himself. See Chambers, *Harpsfield*, pp. cxcviii f., and MS. Arundel 73, fols. 96$^v$–97.

to urgent reform. Protestant commentators did no better. With their simple view that humanism led inevitably to Protestant reform, they were committed to the doctrine that More was either inconsistent or a fanatical hypocrite, or both. The Basle editors of the *Lucubrationes* stand as the only witnesses in that age of a truth about More and Erasmus as important as the Louvain assertion of More's indomitable orthodoxy. But this was a truth imperilled by the doctrinaire controversies of both Protestant and Catholic apologists.

# BIBLIOGRAPHY

A list of books and manuscripts cited. For early printed books see the List of Authors, pp. 309 ff.

## I. CONTEMPORARY SOURCES

A. MANUSCRIPT SOURCES

1. *Aberystwyth*

National Library of Wales: Peniarth MS. 119, fols. 504–735. Letterbook of Robert Joseph.

2. *Cambridge*

Cambridge University Library

MS. Nn. iv. 43. 'A Treatice ... of the benefitt that true christianes recevue by the dethe of Jesus Christe.'

MS. Dd. vii. 3. Gospels of S. Matthew and S. Mark.

*Cambridge (cont.)*
   *Corpus Christi College*
   MS. 355. Exposition on Romans.
   MS. 346. *Augustinus De civitate Dei*, Venice, 1475.
   *Emmanuel College*
   MS. 3.3.12. Treatise on 1 Corinthians.

3. *Hatfield House*
   Cecil Papers, vol. 314. Anonymous religious poem, French.
   Cecil Papers, vol. 332. Commonplace Book, Thos. Paynell.

4. *London*
   *British Museum*
   Additional Manuscripts:
      12060. Henry Parker, 'Miraculous examples . . . in support of the doctrine of Transubstantiation'.
      15673. Chrysostom, 1488.
      47675. Chrysostom, for Cardinal Morton.
   Arundel Manuscripts:
      8. Henry Parker, tr. Paolo Giovio, on the Turks.
      73, fols. 96ᵛ–97. Harpsfield's *Historia*.
   Cotton Manuscripts:
      Cleopatra E. VI, fol. 312. Council memorandum, 1533.
      Cleopatra E. VI, fols. 379 f. Starkey to Pole.
      Cleopatra F. II, fol. 238. 'A litle treatie . . .'.
      Galba B. X, fol. 2. Stephen Vaughan to Cromwell, 1532.
      Vespasian F. III, No. 35, fol. 37. Catherine Parr to Princess Mary.
   Harleian Manuscripts:
      1860. Eusebius.
      6561. Henry Parker, Epistles and Gospels.
      6989, fol. 45. Martin Tindall to Cromwell, 1533.
   Lansdowne Manuscripts:
      978, fol. 155. Bishop Kennett's Collections.
      1045, fol. 60. Inhibition on preaching, 25 Henry VIII.
   Royal Manuscripts:
      1 D. XI–XV. Epistles of S. Paul in Latin.
      1 E. III. Psalms in Latin.

*British Museum,* Royal Manuscripts (*cont.*)

   1 E. V. Gospels of S. Luke and S. John.

   7 D. IX. Catherine Parr's 'Prayers and Meditations'.

   7 D. X. Catherine Parr's 'Prayers and Meditations'.

   11 A. XVI. Richard Moryson, Treatise on Tenures.

   12 A. I–IV. Lady Mary Fitzalan, translations.

   12 C. VIII, pt. 2. Dialogues of Lucian.

   12 F. V. Simplicius on the *Physics.*

   13 B. X. Latin tr. of Greek Menology.

   16 C. VIII. Greek hexameter version of *Aeneid,* bk. i.

   16 E. XIV. Devotional works of Erasmus and Pico.

   16 E. XXIV and XXV. Translations from Pico.

   17 A. XXX. Henry Parker, tr. epistles of Seneca.

   17 A. XLVI. Henry Parker, tr. Erasmus's *Paean Virgini Matri.*

   17 A. XLIX. Lord Lumley, abstract of Erasmus's *Institutio principis Christiani.*

   17 B. XVIII. Homily of St. Basil of Caesarea.

   17 C. XII. Henry Parker, tr. St. Athanasius, preface to Psalms.

   17 C. XVI. Henry Parker, tr. from S. Thomas Aquinas and S. Anselm.

   17 D. II. Henry Parker, tr. from Plutarch.

   17 D. XI. Henry Parker, tr. from Plutarch.

   17 D. XIII. Henry Parker, exposition of Ecclesiastes.

   18 A. XV. Henry Parker, tr. John of Torquemada.

   18 A. L. Richard Moryson, scheme for Common Law code.

   18 A. LX. Henry Parker, tr. Cicero.

   18 A. LXII. Henry Parker, tr. Massucio of Salerno.

   18 B. XI. Nicholas Udall, 'Answer to the Commoners'.

*Guildhall Library*

   MS. 1353, fols. 13, 14, 17 et seq., transcript of Lambeth Palace Library MS. SR. 136.

*Lambeth Palace Library*

   MS. SR. 136. Register of Doctors' Commons.

*Public Record Office*

State Papers Henry VIII, Domestic and Foreign, General:

   SP 1/160, fols. 79–80. Leonard Cox to Cromwell.

   SP 1/69, fol. 82. Stephen Vaughan to Cromwell.

   SP 1/71, fol. 52. Richard Croke to Cromwell.

*Public Record Office*, State Papers Henry VIII (*cont.*)

    SP 1/73, fols. 143, 145. R. Taverner to Cromwell.

    SP 1/80, fol. 114. Stephen Vaughan to Cromwell.

    SP 1/83, fols. 57, 58. William Marshall to Cromwell.

    SP 1/84, fol. 24. Leonard Cox to John Toy.

    SP 1/85, fol. 94. Ralph Sadleyr to Cromwell.

    SP 1/85, fol. 132. John Rastell to Cromwell.

    SP 1/113, fol. 210. Richard Moryson to Cromwell.

    SP 1/160, fol. 79. Leonard Cox to Cromwell.

    SP 1/225, fol. 185. Dr. Coxe to Paget.

    SP 1/226, fol. 16. Dr. Coxe to Paget.

Theological Tracts:

    SP 6/12, fols. 14–35. Sir Anthony Cooke, tr. S. Cyprian on prayer.

Treasury of the Receipt:

    E. 36/193. Thomas Swinnerton, 'The Tropes and Figures of Scripture'.

Transcripts of Foreign Archives:

    MS. 31/3/10, f.v. 123. Baschet's transcripts, Paris.

5. *Oxford*

    *University Archives*

    Registrum F (reversed): Chancellor's Court register, 1506–1514.

    Registrum EEE (or 'B' reversed): Chancellor's Court register, 1527–1543. (Entries after *c.* 1535 are sparse.)

    Registrum G: Congregation register, 1505–1517.

    Registrum H: Congregation register, 1518–1535.

    *Bodleian Library*

    Bodley MS. 504 (S.C. 2168). Canones Horoptri.

    Corpus Christi Coll. MSS. XIII–XIV. Gospels and Acts of the Apostles.

    Douce MS. 110 (S.C. 21684). Canonical epistles and Ecclesiastes, &c.

    Laud MS. Misc. 684. Henry Parker, tr. Plutarch.

    University College MS. 40. Misc. collection of theological works, for Christopher Urswyke.

    *Christ Church*

    MS. 101. Lectionary.

*Magdalen College*
MS. 223. Lectionary.

*Merton College*
Registrum Annalium.

B. PRINTED SOURCES

1. *Record*

a. *Universities*

*Cambridge Grace Book B, 1488–1544*. In 2 parts. Ed. M. Bateson and others. Cambridge, 1903 and 1905.

*Cambridge Grace Book Γ, 1501–1542*. Ed. W. G. Searle, Cambridge, 1908.

*Register of the University of Oxford (1449–63; 1505–71)*. Ed. C. W. Boase. (O.H.S. i) 1884.

*Statutes of the Colleges of Oxford*. Printed by H.M. Commissioners. Oxford and London, 1853. 3 vols.

*Documents of . . . the University and Colleges of Cambridge*. H.M. Stationery Office, vol. iii, 1952.

*Early Statutes of the College of Saint John*. Ed. J. E. B. Mayor. Cambridge, 1859.

*Registrum Annalium Collegii Mertonensis, 1483–1521*. Ed. H. E. Salter. (O.H.S. lxxvi) 1923.

*Canterbury College, Oxford*. Ed. W. A. Pantin. Vol. I (O.H.S. New Series, vi), 1947 (for 1941).

*Collectanea, First Series*. Ed. C. R. L. Fletcher. (O.H.S. v) 1885.

*Collectanea, Second Series*. Ed. Montagu Burrows. (O.H.S. xvi) 1890.

F. J. Norton, 'The Library of Bryan Rowe, Vice-Provost of King's College (d. 1521)', *Transactions of the Cambridge Bibliographical Society*, vol. ii, pt. 5 (1958).

b. *Public and miscellaneous*

Bannister, A. T. *Diocesis Herefordensis, Registrum Ricardi Mayhew* (Cant. and York Soc., vol. xxvii, 1921).

Collier, J. Payne. *Trevelyan Papers* (Camden Soc., vol. lxvii, 1857).

Dasent, J. R. *Acts of the Privy Council of England*, New Ser. i, 1890.

Ellis, Sir Henry. *Original Letters, illustrative of English history . . .*, ser. 1, 1824, 3 vols.; ser. 2, 1827, 4 vols.; ser. 3, 1846, 4 vols.

Lyell, L., and Watney, F. D. *Acts of Court of the Mercers' Company, 1453–1527.* Cambridge, 1936.

Nicolas, N. H. *The Privy Purse Expenses of King Henry the Eighth,* from Nov. 1529 to Dec. 1532. 1827.

Pocock, N. *Records of the Reformation.* Oxford, 1870, 2 vols.

—— *Troubles connected with the Prayer Book of 1549* (Camden Soc., New Ser. xxxvii, 1884).

Pollard, A. W. *Records of the English Bible.* 1911.

2. *Narrative and Biographical*

Foxe, J. *The Acts and Monuments of John Foxe.* Preliminary dissertation, Rev. G. Townshend; edited by Rev. Stephen Reed Cattley. 1837–1841. 8 vols.

Hall, E. *The union of the two noble and illustre famelies York and Lancaster.* Ed. H. Ellis. 1809.

Harpsfield, N. *The Life and Death of Sr. Thomas Moore, knight.* Ed. R. W. Chambers and E. V. Hitchcock (E.E.T.S., Orig. Ser., no. 186), 1932 (for 1931).

Parsons, R. *A Treatise of three Conversions of England, from Paganisme to Christian Religion,* by N. D. [St. Omer], 1603–4. 3 vols.

Roper, W. *The Lyfe of Sir Thomas Moore, knighte.* Ed. E. V. Hitchcock (E.E.T.S., Orig. Ser., no. 197), 1935.

Sandar, N. *De origine ac progressu schismatis Anglicani.* Cologne, 1585.

Stapleton, T. *Vita Thomae Mori,* in *Tres Thomae,* Coloniae Agrippinae, M.DC.XII.

Stow, J. *Annales of England.* Ed. E. Howes. 1615.

—— *A Survey of London.* Ed. J. Strype. 1720. 2 vols.

Strype, J. *Ecclesiastical Memorials,* relating chiefly to religion . . . under King Henry VIII, King Edward VI, and Queen Mary I. . . . Oxford, 1822. 3 vols.

—— *The Life of the learned Sir John Cheke.* Oxford, 1821.

Verstegan, R. *A Declaration of the True Causes of the Great Troubles.* [Antwerp?] 1592.

Wood, A. *The History and Antiquities of the University of Oxford.* Ed. J. Gutch. Oxford, 1792–6. 2 vols.

Wriothesley, C. *A chronicle of England during the reigns of the Tudors, 1485–1559.* Ed. W. D. Hamilton (Camden Soc., New Ser., 11, 20), 1875 and 1877. 2 vols.

3. *Opera, correspondence, and editions of individual works*
a. *Erasmus and More*
   Erasmus, Desiderius:
   *Opera Omnia Desiderii Erasmi Roterodami.* Leyden, P. Vander Aa, 1703–6. 10 vols.
   *Opus Epistolarum Des. Erasmi Roterodami.* Ed. P. S. Allen, H. M. Allen, and H. W. Garrod. Oxford, 1906–58. 12 vols.
   *Erasmi opuscula.* Ed. W. K. Ferguson. The Hague, 1933.
   *The Poems of Desiderius Erasmus.* Ed. C. Reedijk. Leyden, 1956.
   *The Earliest English Translations of Erasmus' Colloquia, 1536–1566* (Humanistica Lovaniensia 2). Ed. H. de Vocht. Louvain, 1928.

   More, Thomas:

   *Thomae Mori . . . Omnia . . . Latina Opera.* Louvain, Bogard, 1565.
   *Thomae Mori . . . Lucubrationes.* Basle, Episcopius, 1563.
   *The Workes of Sir Thomas More Knyght.* (Ed. W. Rastell) R. Tottell, 1557.
   *The English Works of Sir Thomas More.* Ed. W. E. Campbell and A. W. Reed, 1927–31. 2 vols.
   *The Correspondence of Sir Thomas More.* Ed. E. F. Rogers. Princeton and London, 1947.
   *The Latin Epigrams of Thomas More.* Ed. L. Bradner and C. A. Lynch. Chicago, 1953.

b. *Others*
   Ascham, Roger:
   *The Whole Works of Roger Ascham.* Ed. Rev. Dr. Giles. 1864–5. 3 vols.

   Craneveldt, Francis:
   *Literae ad Franciscum Craneveldium* (Humanistica Lovaniensia 1). Ed. H. de Vocht. Louvain, 1928.

   Edward VI:
   *Literary Remains of King Edward VI.* (Roxburghe Club) Ed. J. G. Nichols, 1857. 2 vols.

   Elyot, Thomas:
   *The Boke named the Governour.* Ed. H. H. S. Croft. 1880. 2 vols.

Gardiner, Stephen:

*The Letters of Stephen Gardiner.* Ed. J. A. Müller. Cambridge, 1933.

Leland, John:

*Joannis Lelandi Antiquarii de Rebus Britannicis Collectanea.* Oxonii, 1715.

*Itinerary.* Ed. T. Hearne. vol. ii, 1711.

Lucian of Samosata:

*Luciani . . . Opuscula . . . ab Erasmo Roterodamo et Thoma Moro . . . traducta.* Ex off. Ascensiana ad Idus Septemb. MCVI.

Lupset, Thomas:

*The Life and Works of Thomas Lupset.* Ed. J. A. Gee. New Haven, U.S.A., 1928.

Starkey, Thomas:

*England in the Reign of Henry VIII*: Part 1, 'Starkey's Life and Letters', ed. J. S. Brewer; Part 2, 'England in the reign of King Henry the Eighth, a Dialogue . . .', ed. J. M. Cowper (E.E.T.S., Extra Ser., nos. xxxii and xii), 1878 and 1871.

Vives, Juan Luis:

*Opera.* Basle, Episcopius, 1555.

*Introductio ad Sapientiam: Satellitium sive Symbola.* Parisiis, apud Simonem Colinaeum. 1527.

## II. MODERN WORKS

### A. BIOGRAPHICAL DICTIONARIES, BIBLIOGRAPHIES, CALENDARS

Allison, A. F., and Rogers, D. M. *A catalogue of Catholic books in English printed abroad or secretly in England, 1558–1640.* Bognor Regis, 1956.

Brewer, J. S., and Gairdner, J. *Letters and Papers, Foreign and Domestic, of the reign of Henry VIII, 1509–47.* 1862–1910. 21 vols. in 33 parts.

Dibdin, T. F. *Typographical Antiquities . . .* begun by the late Joseph Ames, considerably augmented by William Herbert, and now greatly enlarged. 1810–19. 4 vols.

Emden, A. B. *A Biographical Register of the University of Oxford to A.D. 1500.* Oxford, 1957–9. 3 vols.

Foster, J. *Alumni Oxonienses: The Members of the University of Oxford, 1500–1714*. Oxford, 1891–2. 4 vols.

Gayangos, Pascual de. *Calendar of State Papers, Spanish*. Vols. III–VII (1525–55); and supplementary volume (1513–42), ed. G. Mattingly. 13 vols. and 2 supp., 1862–1954.

Ginori-Conti, P. *Bibliografia delle Opere del Savonarola*, a cura del principe P. Ginori-Conti. Vol. I, Cronologia e Bibliografia delle Prediche, con contributi storici e filologici di Roberto Ridolfi. Firenze, 1939.

Giovanozzi, L. *Bibliografia delle Opere del Savonarola*. Edizioni dei Secc. XV e XVI. Firenze, 1953.

Haeghen, F. vander. *Bibliotheca Erasmiana*. 3 Series. Gand, 1893.

Hain, L. *Repertorium Bibliographicum* . . . opera Lucovico Hain (Stuttgartiae, 1826–38), 2 vols.; with Supplement . . . in two parts by W. A. Copinger (London, 1895–1902) and Appendices, *ad Hainii-Coperingi* . . . edidit Dietericus Reichling (Monachii, 1905–8).

Kirby, T. F. *Winchester Scholars*. 1888.

Maitland, S. R. *A List of Early Printed Books in the Archiepiscopal Library at Lambeth*. 1843.

Newcourt, R. *Repertorium Ecclesiasticum Parochiale Londinense*. 1708–10. 2 vols.

Nijhoff, W., and Kronenberg, M. E. *Nederlandsche Bibliographie van 1500 tot 1540*, door Wouter Nijhoff met medewerking van M. E. Kronenberg. 's-Gravenhage, 1919– .

Pollard, A. W., and Redgrave, G. R. *A Short-Title Catalogue of Books Printed in England, Scotland and Ireland, and of English books printed abroad, 1475–1640*. (The Bibliographical Society, 1926.)

Proctor, R. *An Index to the Early Printed Books in the British Museum*. 1898– .

Stephen, Sir Leslie, and Lee, Sir Sidney. *Dictionary of National Biography*. Oxford and London, 1917– .

Sterry, Sir Wasey. *The Eton College Register (1441–1698)*. 1943.

Venn, J. and S. A. *Alumni Cantabrigienses*. Cambridge, 1922–7. 4 vols.

Wood, A. *Athenae Oxonienses*. A new edition with additions and a continuation by Philip Bliss. 1813–20. 4 vols.

B. MONOGRAPHS

Allen, P. S. *The Age of Erasmus*. Oxford, 1914.

Ames, R. *Citizen Thomas More and his Utopia*. Princeton, U.S.A., 1949.

Bailey, D. S. *Thomas Becon*. London and Edinburgh, 1952.

Bataillon, M. *Érasme et l'Espagne* (Bibliothèque de l'École des Hautes Études Hispaniques, Fasc. XXI). 1937.

—— *Études sur le Portugal au temps de l'humanisme*. Coimbra, 1952.

Baumer, F. Le Van. *The Early Tudor Theory of Kingship*. New Haven, U.S.A., 1940.

Bruce, F. F. *The English Bible*. 1961.

Butterworth, C. C. *The English Primers, 1529–1545*. Philadelphia, U.S.A., 1953.

Cantimori, D. *Eretici italiani del Cinquecento*. Firenze, 1939.

Caspari, F. *Humanism and the Social Order in Tudor England*. Chicago, 1954.

Churton, R. *The Life of Alexander Nowell*. Oxford, 1809.

—— *The Lives of William Smyth, Bishop of Lincoln, and Sir Richard Sutton, founders of Brasen Nose College*. Oxford, 1800.

Clarke, M. L. *Classical Education in Britain, 1500–1900*. Cambridge, 1959.

Cooper, C. H. *Annals of Cambridge*. Cambridge, 1842–1908. 5 vols.

—— *Memoir of Margaret, Countess of Richmond and Derby*. Ed. J. E. B. Mayor. Cambridge, 1874.

Coote, C. *English Civilians*. 1804.

Coppens, J. C. L. *Les Idées réformistes d'Érasme dans les préfaces aux Paraphrases du Nouveau Testament*. (Analecta Lovaniensia Biblica et Orientalia, Ser. III, Fasc. 27), Louvain, 1961.

Dolan, J. P. 'The Influence of Erasmus, Witzel and Cassander in the Church Ordinances and Reform Proposals of the United Duchees [*sic*] of Cleve during the Middle Decades of the 16th century', *Reformationsgeschichtliche Studien und Texte*, Heft 83. Münster, 1957.

Dugmore, C. W. *The Mass and the English Reformers*. 1958.

Emmison, F. G. *Tudor Secretary*. 1961.

Étienne, J. *Spiritualisme érasmien et théologiens louvanistes*. Louvain/Gembloux, 1956.

Exner, H. *Der Einfluß des Erasmus auf die englische Bildungsidee*. Berlin, 1939.

Feuillerat, A. *John Lyly*. Cambridge, 1910.

Fowler, T. *The History of Corpus Christi College*. (O.H.S. xxv), 1893.

Gairdner, J. *Lollardy and the Reformation*. 1908–13. 4 vols.

Hay, D. *Polydore Vergil*. Oxford, 1952.

Heaton, W. J. *The Bible of the Reformation*. 1910.

Herbst, H. *Das Benediktinerkloster Klus bei Gandersheim und die Bursfelder Reform*. Leipzig/Berlin, 1932.

Howell, W. S. *Logic and Rhetoric in England, 1500–1700*. Princeton, U.S.A., 1956.

Hunt, E. W. *Dean Colet and his Theology*. 1956.

Hyma, A. *The 'Devotio Moderna' or Christian Renaissance, 1380–1520*. Grand Rapids, U.S.A., [1925].

Janelle, P. *L'Angleterre catholique à la veille du schisme*. 1935.

Jayne, Sears. *John Colet and Marsilio Ficino*. Oxford, 1963.

Knight, S. *The Life of Dr. John Colet*. A new edition. Oxford, 1823.

—— *The Life of Erasmus*. Cambridge, 1726.

Knowles, D. M. *The Religious Orders in England*. Vol. iii. Cambridge, 1959.

Lecler, J. *Toleration and the Reformation* (tr. T. L. Westow), Vol. i. New York, 1960.

Lehmberg, S. E. *Sir Thomas Elyot, Tudor Humanist*. Austin, U.S.A., 1960.

London Topographical Society. *London Topographical Record*. Vol. xv (ed. W. H. Godfrey). Cambridge, 1931.

Lupton, J. H. *Life of Dean Colet*. 1887.

Mann, M. *Érasme et les débuts de la réforme française, 1517–1536*. 1933.

Mason, H. A. *Humanism and Poetry in the Early Tudor Period*. 1959.

Mestwerdt, P. *Die Anfänge des Erasmus, Humanismus und 'Devotio Moderna'*. Leipzig, 1917.

Miles, Leland. *John Colet and the Platonic Tradition*. Lasalle, U.S.A., 1961.

Mullinger, J. B. *The University of Cambridge from the earliest times to the royal injunctions of 1535*. Cambridge, 1873.

Ong, W. J. *Ramus, Method and the Decay of Dialogue*. Cambridge, U.S.A., 1958.

Pfeiffer, R. *Humanitas Erasmiana* (Studien der Bibliothek Warburg XXII). Leipzig/Berlin, 1931.

Pineau, J.-B. *Érasme et la papauté, étude critique du 'Julius Exclusus'*. 1924.

—— *Érasme, sa pensée religieuse*. 1924.

Pollard, A. F. *Henry VIII*. Revised edition. 1951.

Pope, H. *English Versions of the Bible.* 1952.

Porter, H. C. *Reformation and Reaction in Tudor Cambridge.* Cambridge, 1958.

Read, Conyers. *Mr. Secretary Cecil and Queen Elizabeth.* 1955.

Reed, A. W. *Early Tudor Drama.* 1926.

Renaudet, A. *Érasme et l'Italie.* Genève, 1954.

—— *Érasme, sa pensée religieuse et son action d'après sa correspondance, 1518–1521.* 1926.

—— *Études érasmiennes (1521–1529).* 1939.

—— *Préréforme et humanisme à Paris pendant les premières guerres d'Italie (1494–1517).* 1916.

Rupp, E. G. *Studies in the Making of the English Protestant Tradition.* Cambridge, 1947.

Rye, W. B. *England as seen by Foreigners.* 1865.

Seebohm, F. *The Oxford Reformers.* 3rd edition. 1887.

Senior, W. *Doctors' Commons and the Old Court of Admiralty.* 1922.

Smith, Lacey Baldwin. *Tudor Prelates and Politics.* Princeton, U.S.A., 1953.

Smith, Preserved. *A Key to the Colloquies of Erasmus.* Cambridge, U.S.A., 1927.

Stanier, R. S. *Magdalen College School.* 2nd edition. Oxford, 1958.

Surtees Society. *Publications of the Surtees Society of London.* Vol. lxxix. 1884.

Surtz, E. L. *The Praise of Pleasure.* Cambridge, U.S.A., 1957.

—— *The Praise of Wisdom.* Chicago, 1957.

Telle, E. V. *Érasme de Rotterdam et le septième sacrement.* Genève, 1954.

Thompson, C. R. *The Translations of Lucian by Erasmus and St. Thomas More.* Ithaca, U.S.A., 1940.

Vocht, H. de. *Acta Thomae Mori.* Louvain, 1947.

Watson, Foster. *Vives and the Renascence Education of Women.* 1912.

Weiss, R. *Humanism in England during the Fifteenth Century.* 2nd edition. Oxford, 1957.

White, H. C. *The Tudor Books of Private Devotion.* Madison, U.S.A., 1951.

Woodward, W. A. *Desiderius Erasmus Concerning the Aim and Method of Education.* 1904.

Zeeveld, W. G. *Foundations of Tudor Policy.* Cambridge, U.S.A., 1948.

C. ARTICLES

Allen, P. S. 'Dean Colet and Archbishop Warham', *English Historical Review*, xvii, 1902.

Axon, W. E. A. 'The Lady Margaret as a Lover of Literature', *The Library*, 2nd Ser., viii, 1907.

Baskervill, C. R. 'Taverner's Garden of Wisdom and the *Apophthegmata* of Erasmus', *Studies in Philology*, xxix, No. 2, Apr. 1932.

Bataillon, M. 'Sur la diffusion des œuvres de Savonarole en Espagne et en Portugal, 1500–1560', *Mélanges de philologie, d'histoire et de la littérature offerts à Joseph Vianey*, 1934.

Bouck, C. W. 'On the Identity of Papyrius Geminus Eleates', *Transactions of the Cambridge Bibliographical Society*, ii, pt. 5, 1958.

Brightman, F. E. 'The Litany under Henry VIII', *English Historical Review*, xxiv, 1909.

Church, C. M. 'Notes on the Buildings, Books and Benefactions of the Library of the Dean and Chapter of the Cathedral Church of Wells', *Archaeologia*, lvii, 1901.

Croce, B. 'Il "Beneficio di Giesu Cristo Crocifisso"', *La Critica,* Bari, xxxviii, 1940.

Delcourt, M. 'L'amitié d'Érasme et de More entre 1520 et 1535', *Bulletin de l'Association Guillaume Budé*, Jan. 1936.

—— 'Recherches sur Thomas More: la tradition continentale et la tradition anglaise', *Humanisme et Renaissance*, iii, 1936.

Devereux, E. J. 'Some Lost English Translations of Erasmus', *The Library*, 5th Ser., xvii, no. 3, 1962.

Dolan, J. P. 'Witzel et Érasme à propos des sacrements', *Revue d'histoire ecclésiastique*, liv, no. 1, 1959.

Elton, G. R. 'An Early Tudor Poor Law', *Economic History Review*, 2nd ser., vol. vi, no. 1 (1953).

Febvre, L. 'Une question mal posée: les origines de la réforme française', *Revue historique*, clxi, 1929.

Gee, J. A. 'Tindale and the 1533 *Enchiridion* of Erasmus', *Publications of the Modern Languages Association of America*, xlix, No. 2, 1934.

Hunt, R. W. 'The Manuscript Collection of University College, Oxford', *Bodleian Library Record*, iii, 1950–1.

Hutson, H. H., and Willoughby, H. R. 'The Ignored Taverner Bible of 1539', *The Crozier Quarterly*, xvi, 1939.

Hyma, A. 'Erasmus and the Oxford Reformers (1501–1519)', *Nederlands archief voor kerkgeschiedenis*, vol. xxxviii (1951).

Ker, N. R. 'Oxford College Libraries in the Sixteenth Century', *Bodleian Library Record*, vi, no. 3, 1959.

Lehmberg, S. E. 'Sir Thomas Elyot and the English Reformation', *Archiv für Reformationsgeschichte*, xlviii, 1957.

Manschreck, C. L. 'The Role of Melanchthon in the Adiaphora Controversy', *Archiv für Reformationsgeschichte*, xlviii, 1957.

Mozley, J. F. 'The English Enchiridion of Erasmus, 1533', *Review of English Studies*, xx, 1944.

Pächt, A. E. 'Holbein and Kratzer as collaborators', *The Burlington Magazine*, lxxxiv, 1944.

Ratcliff, E. C. 'The Liturgical Work of Archbishop Cranmer', *Journal of Ecclesiastical History*, vii, 1956.

Reed, A. W. 'The Regulation of the Book Trade before the Proclamation of 1538', *Transactions of the Bibliographical Society*, xv, 1920 (for 1919).

Sowards, J. K. 'Erasmus and the Apologetic Textbook: a study of the *De duplici copia verborum ac rerum*', *Studies in Philology*, lv, no. 1, 1958.

Thompson, W. D. J. Cargill. 'Notes on King's College Library, 1500–1750 . . .', *Transactions of the Cambridge Bibliographical Society*, vol. ii, pt. 1 (1954).

Tilley, A. 'Greek Studies in England in the Early Sixteenth Century', *English Historical Review*, liii, 1938.

Wind, E. 'Aenigma Termini: the Emblem of Erasmus', *Journal of the Warburg Institute*, i, 1937/38.

Wortham, J. 'Sir Thomas Elyot and the Translation of Prose', *Huntington Library Quarterly*, xi, 1948.

D. MODERN MANUSCRIPTS AND UNPUBLISHED DISSERTATIONS

Fletcher, J. M. 'The Teaching and Study of Arts at Oxford, c. 1400–c. 1520.' Oxford D.Phil. thesis, 1962.

Jackson, William A., editor, revised *Short-Title Catalogue*, the Houghton Library, Harvard University, Cambridge, Mass.

O'Kelly, Bernard. 'John Colet's *Enarratio in Primam S. Pauli Epistolam ad Corinthios*: a new edition of the text, with translation, notes and introduction.' Harvard Ph.D. thesis, 1960.

# LIST OF AUTHORS

An index of sixteenth-century books by English humanists (or in the translation of which English writers were involved) which are actually cited in the text. Other works, including those by Erasmus, are listed in the general index. In the present listing the *Short-Title Catalogue* number (or revised *Short-Title Catalogue* number) appears first, followed by the name of the author or subject as this is given in the *STC*. After a short title, the name of the publisher is listed only if the work is published in England. Dates are given as revised in this text. Books which do not appear in the *STC* are listed in appropriate alphabetical order.

20    A.B.C. The A.B.C. set forth by the Kynges majestie. W. Powell [1545?].
61    Abell, Thomas. Inuicta veritas. Luneberge, 1532.
193    Agapetus. The preceptes teachyng a prynce his duetie. Berthelet [bef. 1534].
201    Agrippa, H. Cornelius. The commendation of matrimony. Berthelet, 1540.
203    —— A treatise of the nobilitie and excellencye of woman kynde. Berthelet, 1542.
292    Alesius, Alexander. Of the auctorite of the word of God. . . . [Leipzig? 1537?].
837    Ascham, Roger. Toxophilus. Whitchurch, 1545.
862    Assault. The assaute and conquest of heuen. Berthelet, 1529.
908    Augsburg Confession. The confessyon of the fayth of the Germaynes in the councell. R. Redman, 1536.
923    Augustine, St. Twelve sermons. J. Cawood [no date].
—    Baynes, Ralph. Compendium Michlol. Paris, 1554.
1709    Becke, Edmund. A brefe confutacion. J. Day, 1550.
—    Becket, Saint Thomas. The Lyfe of the Blessed Martyr Saynte Thomas. R. Pynson [n.d.]. (Dibdin, ii, no. 673.)
1713    Becon, Thomas. A Christmas bankette. J. Mayler f. J. Gough, 1542.
1735    —— The new pollecye of warre. J. Mayler f. J. Gough, 1542.
1739    —— Newes out of heauen. J. Mayler f. J. Gough [1541?].
1756    —— The right pathwaye vnto prayer. J. Mayler f. J. Gough, 1543.
1801    Bekinsau, John. De supremo et absoluto regis imperio. Berthelet, 1546.
1908    Bernard, St. A compendius and a moche fruytefull treatyse of well liuynge. T. Petyt [1545?].
1911    —— Golden epistle. T. Godfray [1530?].
1966    Bernardinus, St., of Siena. The chirche of the euill men and women. [de Worde] 1511.
2067    Bible, Eng. The most sacred bible newly recognised by R. Taverner. J. Byddell f. T. Berthelet, 1539.
2726    —— Psalms. Certayne psalmes called the vii penitentiall psalmes. T. Raynold a. J. Harrington, 1549.

2748  Bible, Eng., Psalms. An epitome of the psalmes. [R. Bankes] 1539. Also 23710.

2854  ——, N.T. The first (second) tome or volume of the paraphrase of Erasmus upon the newe testamente. Whitchurch, 1548–9.

—  Bonaventure, St. Saint Bonaventure his lessons. de Worde, 1532 (Dibdin ii, no. 381).

3267  —— Vita Christi. de Worde, 1530.

3275  Bonde, Wm. A deuoute treatyse for them that ben tymorouse a. fearefull in conscience. [M. Fawkes, 1534?].

3278  —— A deuout treatyse called the Pylgrimage of perfection. de Worde, 1531.

4407  Calvin, Jean. An epistle both of godly consolacion and also of aduertisement. Whitchurch, 1550.

4602  Capgrave, John. Here begynneth the kalendre of the newe Legende of Englande. . . . R. Pynson, 1516.

4815  Catherine of Siena, St. The orchard of Syon. de Worde, 1519.

4818  Catherine (Parr). The Prayers stirryng the mynd vnto heauenlye medytacions. Berthelet, 1545.

4819  —— Prayers or medytacions. . . . Berthelet, 1545.

4827  —— The lamentacion of a sinner. Whitchurch, 1547.

4828  —— [anr. ed.] Whitchurch, 1548.

4843  Cato, Dionysius. Catonis disticha moralia. R. Taverner per R. Bankes, 1540.

4844  —— Catonis disticha moralia. Nicholas Hill, 1553.

4854  —— Preceptes of Cato. R. Grafton, 1553. Also 1545 (J. P. Morgan Library).

4891  Cebes. The Table of Cebes the philosopher. Berthelet [c. 1530].

4938  Chaloner, Sir Thos. De republica anglorum. T. Vautrollerius, 1579.

5016  Charles V. These ben the ordynaunces that the emperour caused to be red to the estates. R. Wyer [1532?].

5108  Cheke, Sir John. De obitu doctissimi doctoris M. Buceri. R. Wolf, 1551.

5109  —— The hurt of sedicion. J. Daye & W. Seres, 1549.

5160  Christian Faith. Declaracyon and power of the Chrysten fayth. R. Wyer [1530?].

5168  Christian Man. A necessary doctrine and erudition for any Christen man. Berthelet, 1543.

5313  Cicero, M. T. The Paradox of M. T. Cicero. J. Redman f. R. Redman, 1540.

5408  Clerk, John. Opusculum plane diuinum de mortuorum resurrectione. . . . J. Herforde, 1545.

5545  Colet, John. Oratio habita ad clerum in conuocatione, anno 1511. R. Pynson [1511–12].

5550  —— The sermon of Doctor Colete made to the conuocation at Paulis. Berthelet [1530?].

5641  Constantine, Emperor. A treatyse of the donation gyuen vnto Syluester, pope of Rhome. T. Godfray [1534].

5718   Cope, Sir Anthony. The historie of . . . Anniball and Scipio. Berthelet, 1544.
5879   Cousin, Gilbert. Of the office of seruauntes. Berthelet, 1534.
5946   Cox, Leonard. The arte or crafte of rhethoryke. R. Redman [1524].
—      Croke, Richard. Orationes Richardi Croci Duae. Paris, 1520.
6156   Cyprian, St. A sermon made on the Lordes Prayer. Berthelet, 1539.
6158   —— A swete and deuoute sermon of mortalitie of man. The rules of a christian lyfe by Picus . . . . Berthelet, 1539.
6159   —— A sermon touching mortalitie. [n.p. 1556].
6455   Declaration. A declaracion of the seremonies . . . of baptyme. [London?] 1537.
6895   Dionysius, Carthusianus. The mirrour of golde for the synfull soule. de Worde, 1522.
6896   —— [anr. ed.] J. Skot, 1522.
7377   Duwes, Giles. An introductorie for to lerne Frenche. T. Godfray [1534?].
7630   Elyot, Sir Thos. Bankette of sapience. Berthelet, 1539.
7635   —— The boke named The gouernour. Berthelet, 1531.
7643   —— The castel of helth. Berthelet, 1539.
7658   —— The defence of good women. Berthelet, 1545.
7659   —— The dictionary of syr T. Elyot. Berthelet, 1538.
7664   —— The image of gouernance. Berthelet, 1541.
7665   —— [anr. ed.] Berthelet, 1544.
7668   —— Of the knowledeg [sic] whiche maketh a wise man. Berthelet, 1533.
7671   —— Pasquil the playne. Berthelet, 1532.
7677   Emanuel, King of Portugal. Of the new landes and of the people founde by the messengers of the kynge of portyngale. [Antwerp] [1520?].
9177   England, Pub. Documents, Misc. Articles deuisid by the holle consent of the kynges counsayle. Berthelet, 1533.
10088  England, Church of. Iniunccions geuen by the moste excellente Prince Edwarde the vi. R. Grafton [1547].
—      Erasmus. De copia. de Worde, 1528 (Dibdin, ii, no. 330).
10437  —— Prouerbes or adagies. . . . R. Bankes, 1539.
10438  —— [anr. ed.] Whitchurch, 1545.
10443  —— Apophthegmes. R. Grafton, 1542.
10445  —— Flores aliquot sententiarum. R. Taverner, R. Bankes, 1540.
10449  —— Bellum Erasmi. Berthelet, 1533(-34).
10450  —— The Censure and iudgement of Erasmus: whyther dyuorsemente betwene man and wyfe stondeth with the lawe of God. Widow of J. Herforde f. R. Stoughton [1550?].
RSTC 10450. 2   —— Christiani hominis institutum in fide Jesu. de Worde, 1520?
RSTC 10450. 3   —— [anr. ed.] Pepwell, 1520.
RSTC 10450. 5   —— Colloquia. de Worde, 1519.
RSTC 10450. 7   —— [anr. ed.] de Worde, 1520.
RSTC 10453. 5   —— Funus. R. Copland for J. Byddell, 1534.

10454   Erasmus. A dialoge . . . of two persons. [J. Biddell? 1540?].
10459   —— Two dyaloges. J. Mychell (Canterbury) [1550].
10460   —— A very pleasaunt a. fruitful diologe called the epicure. R. Grafton, 1545.
RSTC 10465. 5  —— Comparation of a vyrgin and a martyr. Berthelet, 1537.
10467   —— A lytell booke of good maners for chyldren. de Worde, 1532.
10468   —— [anr. ed.] Byddell, 1540.
10471   —— De contemptu mundi. Berthelet, 1532.
10474   —— De immensa dei misericordia: a sermon. Berthelet [1526?].
10475   —— [anr. ed.] Berthelet, 1533.
10477   —— A Deuout treatise vpon the pater noster. Berthelet [1526?].
RSTC 10478. 7   —— Dicta sapientium. In the house of T. Berthelet [1527?] (Huntington Library).
10479   —— A booke called in latyn Enchiridion. de Worde f. J. Byddell, 1533.
10488   —— A shorte recapitulacion . . . of Erasmus Enchiridion. [Antwerp?] 1545.
10489   —— An Epystell unto Christofer . . . concernyng the forbedinge of eatynge of flesshe. T. Godfray [1530?].
10490   —— An Epistle concernynge the veryte of the Sacrament of Christes body and bloude. R. Wyer [1538?].
10491   —— The Epistle sente vnto Conrad Pelicanus. J. Cawood, 1554.
10492   —— Epystle in laude and prayse of matrymony. R. Redman [1531?].
10493   —— An exhortation to the diligent studye of scripture. (NB 2982.) 'Luft, Marburg' [Antwerp], 1529.
RSTC 10493. 5   —— An exhortacyon to the study of readynge the gospell. w. 'An exhortation . . . scripture', 2nd ed. R. Wyer, [1534?].
10494   —— [anr. ed.] R. Wyer [1534?].
RSTC 10494. 5   —— [anr. ed.] T. Ranalde a. W. Hyll [1548?].
10495   ——. An exposicyon of the .xv. psalme. J. Wayland, 1537.
10498   —— A lytle treatise of the maner and forme of confession. J. Byddell f. W. Marshall [1535?].
10500   —— The praise of folie. Berthelet, 1549.
10503   —— The Paraphrase . . . vpon the Epistle of Paule unto Titus. J. Byddell [1535?].
10504   —— A playne and godly exposytion of the commune crede and of the .x. commaundementes. R. Redman [1533].
10505   —— Preparation to deathe. Berthelet, 1538.
10506   —— [anr. ed.] Berthelet, 1543.
—   —— A seraphicall dirige, disclosing the 7. secret priuiledges graunted to St. Frauncis and all his progenie for euer. [n.p.d.] (Dibdin, iii, no. 1408.)
10508   —— A sermon [on the marriage at Cana]. R. Wyer [1533?].
10509   —— [A sermon of the chylde Jesus.] R. Redman [1540?].

10510 Erasmus. A Treatise perswadynge a man patientlye to suffre the deth of his frende. T. Berthelet [1532].
10555 Estienne, Robert. Dictionariolum puerorum tribus linguis. R. Wolfe, 1552.
10619 Exhortation. An exhortation vnto prayer. Berthelet [1543?].
10751 Felicius, C. Conspiracie of Lucius Catiline. Berthelet, 1541.
— Fisher, John. De causa matrimonii serenissimi Regis Angliae liber. Alcalá de Henares, 1530.
10902 —— This treatise concernynge the fruytfull saynges of Dauyd. . . . de Worde, 1508.
10909 —— . . . two fruytfull sermons. W. Rastell, 1532.
11218 Fox, Edward. Opus eximium. Berthelet, 1534.
11402 Frontinus, Sextus Julius. The stratagemes . . . of warre. Berthelet, 1539.
11470 Fullonius, Gulielmus. J. Palsgraui Londoniensis ecphrasis Anglica in comoediam Acolasti. Berthelet, 1540.
— Gararde, Brother. The Interpretacyon and sygnyfycacyon of the Masse. R. Wyer, 1532. (Dibdin, iii, no. 940.)
11584 Gardiner, Stephen. De vera obedientia oratio. Berthelet, 1535.
11594 Gardynare, Germen. A letter of a yonge gentylman. W. Rastell, 1534.
11719 Geminus, Papyrius. P. Gemini Eleatis Hermathena. (Cambridge) 1522.
11892 Gildas. Opus nouum: de calamitate, excidio et conquestu Britanniae. London, 1525.
11918 Glass. A glasse of the truthe. Berthelet [1530].
11919 —— [anr. ed.] Berthelet [1531].
11966 Goes, Damião de. The legacye or embassate of prester John vnto Emanuell, Kynge of Portyngale. W. Rastell, 1533.
12047 Goodwyn, Christopher. The maydens dreme. R. Wyer f. R. Bankes [1542?].
12102 Gosynhill, Edward. The prayse of all women. W. Myddylton [1542?].
12431 Guevara, Antonio. A dispraise of the life of a courtier. R. Grafton, 1548.
12436 —— The golden boke of Marcus Aurelius. Berthelet, 1535.
12510 Gulielmus, de Occam. Disputatio inter clericum et militem. Berthe-let [1531?].
12720a Halle, Edward. [The vnion of . . . York and Lancaster.] [Berthelet, 1542.]
12767 Hardyng, John. The chronicle of J. Hardyng. R. Grafton, 1543.
13080 Henry VIII. Henrici octaui ad Carolum Cesarem Augustum epistola. Berthelet, 1538.
13081 —— An epistle to the Emperours maiestie. Berthelet, 1538.
13082 —— Illusrissimi [sic]. . . regis, senatus populique angliae sententia de eo concilio quod Paulus episcopus Rom. Mantuae futurum simulauit. Berthelet, 1537.
13089a —— [A panegyric] [n.p.] 1536–7.
13090 —— A protestation that neyther his hyghenes nor his prelates is bound to come to Mantua. Berthelet, 1537.
13221 Herodian. The history of Herodian. W. Copland [1550?].

13604   Holt, John. Lac puerorum. de Worde [1510?].

—   Holy Ghost. The Abbaye of the Holy Ghost. [n.p.] 1531. (Dibdin, ii, nos. 379–80.)

13608   —— Deuout treatyse called the Tree and xii frutes of the holy goost. (i) R. Copland, 1534; (ii) R. Copland & M. Fawkes, 1535.

14042   Hylton, Walter. [Scala perfectionis] . . . boke whiche expowneth many notable doctrynes in contemplacyon. [de Worde] 1494.

14286   Italy and France. Gravissimae totius Italiae et Galliae Academiarum censurae. Berthelet, 1530.

14287   —— The determinations of the moste famous Universities of Italy and Fraunce. Berthelet, 1531.

14553   Jesus Christ. The myrrour or glasse of Christes passion. R. Redman, 1534.

14630   John Chrysostom, Saint. De providentia Dei ac Fato orationes sex. R. Wolfe, 1545.

14634   —— Τὸν ἐν ἁγίοις ᾿Ιωαννοῦ τοῦ Χρυσοστόμον ὁμιλίαι δύο. R. Wolfe, 1543.

14637   —— An homilie vpon that saying of S. Paul: . . . Berthelet, 1544.

14638   —— A sermon of pacience. N. Hill f. J. Shefelde, 1550.

14639   —— A sermon that no man is hurted but of hym selfe. Berthelet, 1542.

14642   —— A treatise concerning the restitucion of a synner. R. Calye, 1553.

14842   Julius II, Pope. The dyalogue bytwene Jullius the seconde, and saynt Peter. J. Byddell, 1535.

15118   Lactantius, L. C. L. Lactantii Firmiani carmen: ab Erasmo editum. [London? 1530?]

15185   Lamentation. A lamentation . . . of seditious rebellyon. Berthelet, 1536.

15286   Latimer, Hugh. Sermon . . . to the clergie. Berthelet, 1537.

15453   Le Maire, John. The abbreuyacyon of all generall councellys. J. Gough, 1539.

15602   Lily, William. De octo orationis partium constructione libellus. de Worde, 1533.

15604   —— [anr. ed.] Berthelet, 1540.

15605   —— An introduction of the eyght partes of speche. Berthelet, 1542–3.

15634   Linacre, Thomas. De emendata structura Latini sermonis. R. Pynson, 1524.

15635   —— Progymnasmata grammatices vulgaria. J. Rastell [1525?].

15988   Liturgies. A goodly prymer in englyshe. . . . J. Byddell f. W. Marshall, 1535.

15998   —— A goodly prymer in Englysshe. . . . [J. Byddell f. W. Marshall, 1537?]

16001   —— This prymer of Salysbury use. Paris, 1538.

16009   —— The manual of prayers . . . set forth by Ihon, Bysshoppe of Rochester at the comaundemente of Thomas Cromwell. J. Wayland, 1539.

16011 Liturgies. The primer in Englishe... for the educacyon of chyldren.... J. Wayland [1539?].

16034 —— The primer, set foorth by the Kynges maiestie. . . . R. Grafton, 1545.

16060 —— An vniforme and catholyke prymer. J. Wayland, 1555.

16795 Longland, John. A sermond spoken before the Kynge at Grenwiche. 1536. [T. Petyt? 1536?]

16820 Lord's Prayer. The pater noster ... in englysh. J. Byddell, 1537.

— Lucian of Samosata. Luciani ... opuscula ... ab Erasmo Roterodamo et Thoma Moro ... traducta. Paris, 1506.

16891 —— Complures Luciani dialogi a D. Erasmo in latinum conuersi. de Worde, 1528.

16892 —— Luciani dialogi aliquot. R. Redman, 1531.

16894 —— A dialogue betwene Lucian and Diogenes. Berthelet [n.d.]

16895 —— A dialog of the poet Lucyan. J. Rastell [1530?].

16896 —— Lepidissimum Luciani opusculum. Siberch (Cambridge), 1521.

16932 Lupset, Thomas. T. Lupsets workes. Berthelet, 1546.

16934 —— A compendious treatyse, teachynge the waye of dyenge well. Berthelet, 1534.

16936 —— An exhortation to yonge men. Berthelet, 1535.

16939 —— A treatise of charitie. Berthelet, 1533.

16962 Luther, Martin. A boke made by a certayne great clerke agaynst the newe idole, and olde deuyll. R. Wyer, 1534.

16963 —— The boke of the discrypcyon of the images of a verye chrysten bysshop.... [R. Wyer f.] W. Marshall [1536?].

16988 —— Here after ensueth a Propre treatyse of good workes. R. Wyer [1535?].

16999 —— A very excellent and swete exposition vpon the 22. psalme. J. Nicolson f. J. Gough, 1537.

17000 —— [anr. ed.] J. Nicolson, 1538.

17117 Lynne, Walter. A briefe and compendiouse table in a maner of a concordaunce. . . . f. Gwalter Lynne, 1550.

17300 Marbeck, John. A concordance, . . . a worke wherein by the ordre of the letters of the A.B.C. ye maie redely finde any worde conteigned in the whole Bible. R. Grafton, 1550.

17320 Margaret of Angoulême. A godly medytacyon of the christen sowle. [Wesel] 1548.

17326 Margaret, Saint. Here begynneth the lyfe of Saynte Margarete. R. Redman [1530?].

17500 Martin, Saint. The rule of an honest lyfe. [1538?]

17541 Mary, the Blessed Virgin. The myracles of oure blessyd Lady. de Worde, 1530.

17542 —— The Myrroure of oure Lady. R. Fawkes, 1530.

17817 Menandrinus, Marsilius. The defence of peace. R. Wyer f. W. Marshall, 1535.

— More, Sir Thomas. Omnia, quae hucusque ad manus nostras peruenerunt, Latina Opera. Louvain, 1565

—      More, Sir Thomas. Thomae Mori, . . . lucubrationes. Basle, 1563.

18076    —— The workes of Sir Thomas More Knyght, . . . in the Englysh tonge. J. Cawood, J. Waly, R. Tottell, 1557.

18077    —— The answere to . . . the poysened booke. W. Rastell, 1534.

18078    —— The apologye of syr T. More, knyght. W. Rastell, 1533.

—      —— Boke of the Fayre Gentilwoman. . . . R. Wyer, 1540 (Maitland, 522 b).

18079    —— The confutacyon of Tyndales answere. W. Rastell, 1532.

18080    —— The second parte of the confutacion of Tyndals answere. W. Rastell, 1533.

18081    —— The debellacyon of Salem and Bizance. W. Rastell, 1533.

18082    —— A dialoge of comfort against tribulacion. R. Tottel, 1553.

18083    —— Dialoge of comfort, now newly set foorth . . . . Antwerp, 1573.

18088    —— T. Mori epistola ad G. Brixium. R. Pynson, 1520.

18090    —— A letter impugnynge the erronyouse wrytyng of J. Fryth. W. Rastell, 1533.

18091    —— A mery geste how a sergeaunt wolde lerne to be a frere. J. Notary [1516?].

18094    —— A fruteful and pleasaunt worke . . . called Utopia. A. Vele, 1551.

18109    Morison, Sir Richard. Apomaxis calumniarum, confitiorumque. Berthelet, '1537' [1538].

18110    —— An exhortation to styr all Englyshe men to the defence of theyr countreye. Berthelet, 1539.

18111    —— An inuective ayenste . . . treason. Berthelet, 1539.

18414    Nausea, Frederick. A sermon of the sacrament of the aulter. W. Rastell, 1533.

18766    Ochino, Bernardino. Certayne sermons. J. Day [1550?].

18770    —— A tragoedie or dialoge. . . . [N. Hill] f. G. Lynne, 1549.

18846    Origen. Omelia origenis de beata maria magdalena. [W. Faques? 1504?]

18849    Original. The original and sprynge of all sectes and orders. J. Nicolson f. J. Gough, 1537.

19166    Palsgrave, John. Lesclarcissement de la langue francoyse. J. Hawkyns, 1530.

19211    Parker, Henry, Baron Morley. Exposition and declaration of the psalme Deus ultionum dominus. Berthelet, 1539.

19416    Parsons, Robert, S.J. A Treatise of three conversions of England. [St. Omer] 1603, 04. Allison and Rogers, No. 640.

19494    Paynell, Thomas. The piththy and moost notable sayinges of al Scripture. T. Gualtier at the costs of R. Toy, 1550.

20059†  Plutarch. Of the quyete of mynde. R. Pynson [1528?]. Huntington Library.

20060    —— Plutarchi de tuenda bona valetudine precepta, Erasmo Rotero-damo interprete. R. Pynson, 1513.

20061    —— The gouernaunce of good helthe. R. Wyer [1530?].

20116    Porcia, Jacopo di. Preceptes of warre. Whitchurch, 1544.

20140 Powell, Edward. Propugnaculum summi sacerdotii euangelici aduer. M. Lutherum. Pynson, 1523.

20176 Poynet, John. A defence for mariage of priestes. R. Wolff, 1549.

20373 Primer. A Prymmer, or boke of private prayer. W. Seres, 1553.

20413 Profits. The xii profytes of trybulacyon. de Worde, 1530.

20521 Pylbarough, John. A commemoration of the inestimable graces ... of God. Berthelet, 1540.

20719 Rastell, John. A new boke of Purgatory. J. Rastell, 1530.

20877 Remedy. A remedy for sedition. Berthelet, 1536.

21308 Rome, Church of. The sum of the actes a. decrees made by dyuerse bysshops of rome. T. Gybson [1539?].

21561 Saint German, Christopher. ... a dyaloge ... betwyxt a doctoure of dyuynyte and a student in the lawes of Englande. R. Wyer [1530].

21565 —— The secunde dyaloge ... bytwene a doctour of dyuynyte and a student. P. Treverys (Southwark), 1530.

21588 —— A treatyse concerninge the power of the clergye. ... T. Godfray [1535?].

21596 Salerno. Schola Salernitana. Regimen sanitatis Salerni. Berthelet, 1528.

21626 Sallust. ... the famous cronycle of the warre, wh. the romayns had agaynst Iugurth. R. Pynson [1520?].

21681 Sampson, Richard. R. Sampsonis oratio qua docet Anglos regiae dignitati ut obediant. Berthelet [1535?].

— Sander, Nicholas. De origine ac progressu schismatis Anglicani liber. Cologne, 1585.

21753 Sarcerius, Erasmus. Common places of scripture (STC 10465). J. Byddell, 1538.

21754 —— [anr. ed.] N. Hyll, 1553.

21790 Savonarola. An exposicyon upon the Lj psalme. [Paris] 1538.

21792 —— An exposicyon vpon the LI. Psalme. R. Redman, 1539.

21796 —— An exposicion after the maner of a contemplacyon, etc. (Psalm 51). T. Marsh f. M. Lobley [1558].

21798 —— Expositio ... in psalmum In te Domine speraui. de Worde [n.d.].

21799 —— A meditacyon vpon the psalme of In te domine speraui. J. Gough [1536?].

21800 —— Sermo in vigilia natiuitatis Domini. R. Pynson [1509].

22270 Seymour, Edward. The late expedicion in Scotlande. R. Wolfe, 1544.

22575 Singleton, Robert. A sermon preached at Poules Crosse, 1535. T. Godfray [1536].

22815 Smith, Richard. The assertion and defence of the sacramente of the aulter. J. Herford at costs of R. Toy, 1546.

22820 —— A defence of the blessed masse. J. Herford, 1546.

23207 Standish, John. A discourse ... whether the scripture should be in English. R. Caly, 1554.

23209 —— A lytle treatise agaist [sic] the protestacion of R. Barnes. R. Redman, 1540.

—        Stapleton, Thomas. 'Vita Thomae Mori', in Tres Thomae, Cologne,
         1612. First ed. Douai, 1588.

23236    Starkey, Thomas. An exhortation to the people instructynge theym
         to vnitie and obedience. Berthelet, 1536.

23407    Sturmius, Joannes. The epistle that J. Sturmius sent to the Cardynalles
         and prelates. Berthelet, 1538.

23552    Swinnerton, Thomas. A mustre of scismatyke bysshoppes of Rome.
         de Worde f. J. Byddell, 1534.

23709    Taverner, Richard. A catechisme ... of the Christen religion. 1539.

23711a   —— The garden of wysdom. in aed. R. Taverneri, 1539.

23916    Tertullian, Quintus. The seconde booke of Tertullian. R. Jugge,
         1550.

23955    Thomas à Kempis. A full deuout a. gostely treatyse. R. Pynson,
         1503, 04 (2 pts.).

23961    —— ... the folowynge of Cryste. R. Wyer [1531?].

23962    —— ... the fourth boke, of the folowyng of Chryste. R. Wyer
         [1532?].

23966    —— The folowinge of Chryste. J. Cawood, 1556.

24020    Thomas, William. Principal rules of the Italian grammer. In the
         house of T. Berthelet, 1550.

24023    —— The vanitee of this world. In the house of T. Berthelet, 1549.

24056    Thucydides. The hystory writtyne by Thucidides. London, 1550.

24236    Treatise. A treatyse concernynge diuers of the constitucyons prouyn-
         ciall and legantines. T. Godfray [1535?].

24237    —— A treatise concernynge generall counciles. Berthelet, 1538.

24238    —— A treatise ... that pyctures and other ymages ar in no wise to be
         suffred in churches. f. W. Marshall [1535].

24320    Tunstall, Cuthbert. C. Tonstalli in laudem matrimonii oratio. R.
         Pynson, 1518.

24322    —— A sermon ... vpon Palme Sondaye. Berthelet, 1539.

24465    Tyndale, William. The practyse of prelates. [Antwerp?] 1530.

24601    Vaughan, Robert. A dyalogue defensyue for women. . . . R. Wyer
         for R. Bankes, 1542.

24728    Villa Sancta, Alphonso de. De libero arbitrio aduersus Melanchtho-
         nem. R. Pynson, 1523.

24754    Vincent, St., of Lerins. The waie home to Christ. R. Caly, 1554.

24814    Virgilius Maro, Publius. Bucolica Virgilii cum commento. de Worde,
         1514.

—        Vives, Joannes Ludovicus. De institutione foeminae Christianae.
         Antwerp, 1524.

—        —— Introductio ad Sapientiam: Satellitium sive Symbola. Paris,
         1527.

24847    —— An introduction to wysedom. Berthelet, 1540.

24855    —— The office and duetie of an husband. J. Cawood [1553?].

24856    —— ... the instruction of a christen woman. Berthelet [1529?].

24943    Wakefield, Robert. Kotser codicis. Berthelet [1532?].

24944    —— Oratio de laudibus trium linguarum. de Worde [1524].

24946  Wakefield, Robert. R. Wakfeldi syntagma de hebreorum codicum incorruptione. [de Worde, 1530?].

25000  Walshe, Edward. The office and duety in fightyng for our countrey. J. Herford, at costs of R. Toy, 1545.

25127  Watt, J. von. A worke entytled of the olde god and the newe. J. Byddell, 1534.

25412  Whitford, Richard. Werke of preparacion vnto communion. (A werke for housholders). R. Redman, 1531.

25414  —— A dayly exercyse and experyence of dethe. J. Waylande, 1537.

25416  —— A dialoge . . . bytwene the curate and the parochaine. . . . The werke for housholders. J. Wayland, 1537.

25420  —— Dyuers holy instrucyons necessarye for the helth of mannes soule. W. Myddleton, 1541.

—      —— Pomander of Prayer. de Worde, 1532. (Dibdin, ii, no. 382.)

25421  —— The Pype, or Tonne, of the lyfe of perfection. R. Redman, 1532.

25422  —— A werke for housholders, newly corrected. de Worde, 1530.

25423  —— [anr. ed.] Newly corrected. de Worde, 1533.

25425  —— [anr. ed.] Newly corrected. R. Redman, 1537.

25799  Wilson, Sir Thomas. The arte of rhetorique. R. Grafton, 1553.

26063  Wyse, Richard. A consolacyon for chrysten people. J. Waylande, 1538.

26069  Xenophon. Xenophons treatise of householde. Berthelet, 1532.

26119  Ypres. The forme and maner of subuention for pore people practysed in Hypres. T. Godfray, 1535.

26136  Zwingli, Ulrich. Certeyne preceptes. Ipswich, 1548.

26137  —— [anr. ed.] W. Seres and R. Kele, 1550.

# INDEX

The A.B.C. set forth, 228 n., 233.
Abell, Thomas, Inuicta veritas, 128.
Abingdon, Benedictine abbey, 110.
Acciaiuoli, D., 153.
Advancement of True Religion, Act for the, 220, 232.
Aeginetus, P., 267.
Aesop, 64, 90.
Agapetus, Preceptes teachyng a prynce, 138, 140.
Agricola, R., 82, 92; De inventione dialectica, 268.
Agrippa, H. C., Commendation of matrimony, 190; Treatise of . . . Woman Kynde, 191, 203.
Alaygre, A., 255 n.
Alcalá, 5, 29, 54, 82, 125.
Aldridge, R., 59–60.
Aldus Manutius, 14, 44, 270.
Alesius, A., Of the auctorite of the word of god, 172.
Alexander IV, Pope, 153.
Alexander, Peter, 237.
Alger, De veritate corporis et sanguinis Dominici, 142, 176–7.
Alington, Alice, 276.
Allen, Edmund, 248.
— P. S., 288.
All Hallows, Honey Lane, 99, 100, 105, 219.
Ambrose, St., 20, 178; treatise of, 71.
Amerbach, B., 263 n.
Ammonius, Andrew, 6, 53, 100.
Amoenus, G., 57.
Andrewes, Lancelot, 281.
Angers, 86.
Annates, Statute of, 106, 139 n.
Anne of Cleves, Queen, 175.
Anselm, St., 90; translation by Henry Parker, 156–7.
Anwykyll, John, 50; Compendium totius gramaticae, 44.
Appeals, Statute of, 106, 139 n.
Apuleius, 262.
Aquinas, St. Thomas, 90; translation by Henry Parker, 156–7.

Arches, Court of, 52.
Argentine, Richard, translates Ochino, 217 n.; translates Zwingli, 250.
Arianism, 238.
Aristippus, 228.
Aristophanes, 82, 89.
Aristotle, 25, 42, 80, 86, 89, 91, 198, 209, 266.
Arthur, Prince, 134.
Articles deuisid by the holle consent of the Kynges counsayle, 128.
Ascham, R., 7, 202, 216, 217, 268, 270, 279; and Mountjoys, 60, 208–9; Toxophilus, 196, 203 n.; 206 sqq.; schooling of, 207; patrons of, 208 sqq.; and royal nursery school, 211–12, 217; on Machiavelli, 213; and adiaphorists, 237; and Queen Mary, 238; and Cecil, 260–1; on English learning, 262–3; and education of Princess Elizabeth, 263; and Margaret Roper, 265, 267; on Louvain exiles, 271.
Askew, Anne, see Kyme.
Assaute and conquest of heuen, 138.
Astley, Sir John, 212.
Athanasius, St., preface to Psalms, 155.
Atkinson, William, translation of Kempis, 55, 65, 123.
Audeley, Sir Thomas, 202.
Augsburg Confession, 136, 167, 170.
Augustine, St., 20, 47, 71, 83, 90, 100, 178, 262, 278; More's lectures on, 38; rule of, translated, 56; sermons of, translated, 139; Retractationes, 291.
Aurelius, M., The golden boke, 256.

Bacon, Lady Anne, see Cooke.
— Sir Francis, 217.
— Sir Nicholas, 217, 280.
Bakeham, John, 83.
Baldwin, William, Treatise of morall phylosophie, 258.
Bale, John, 143, 194, 237, 253; King John, 188; publishes Godly medytacyon, 254.
Barclay, A., translates Sallust and B. Mantuan, 59.

PRINTED IN GREAT BRITAIN
AT THE UNIVERSITY PRESS, OXFORD
BY VIVIAN RIDLER
PRINTER TO THE UNIVERSITY

# ENGLISH HUMANISTS
# AND REFORMATION
# POLITICS

*Oxford University Press, Amen House, London E.C.4*

GLASGOW NEW YORK TORONTO MELBOURNE WELLINGTON
BOMBAY CALCUTTA MADRAS KARACHI LAHORE DACCA
CAPE TOWN SALISBURY NAIROBI IBADAN
KUALA LUMPUR HONG KONG

# ENGLISH HUMANISTS AND REFORMATION POLITICS

UNDER HENRY VIII AND
EDWARD VI

BY

JAMES KELSEY McCONICA

OXFORD
AT THE CLARENDON PRESS
1965